Learning GNU Emacs

Learning GNU Emacs

Debra Cameron and Bill Rosenblatt

O'Reilly & Associates, Inc.
103 Morris Street, Suite A
Sebastopol, CA 95472

Learning GNU Emacs

by Debra Cameron and Bill Rosenblatt

Copyright © 1991 O'Reilly & Associates, Inc. All rights reserved.
Printed in the United States of America.

Editor: Mike Loukides

Printing History:

October 1991:	First Edition.
April 1992:	Minor corrections.

ISBN: 0-937175-84-6

[12/94]

Table of Contents

Figures

Tables

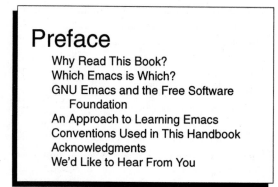

Preface

Emacs is the most powerful text editor in the UNIX world today. Unlike most other editors (in particular, unlike the standard UNIX editor, **vi**), Emacs is a complete working environment. No matter what you do, you can start Emacs in the morning, work all day and all night, and never leave it: you can use it to edit, rename, delete, and copy files; to compile programs; to do interactive work with the UNIX shell; and so on. Before window systems like X became popular, Emacs often served as a complete windowing system of its own. All you needed was an Ann Arbor terminal with a 64-line display, and you could live within Emacs forever. Emacs is also infinitely flexible; you can write your own commands, change the keys that are associated with commands, and (if you are willing to take the time) do just about anything you want.

Why Read This Book?

Because it does so much, Emacs has a reputation for being extremely complicated. To date, most of the Emacs manuals that have been published have been comprehensive reference manuals rather than how-to books designed for people who are new to Emacs. That's the reason for this book: to teach you how to learn Emacs from the ground up, covering first the basics and then some of the more advanced features.

In this book, we have tried to reach as broad an audience as possible: from the administrative assistant who only needs to use Emacs to write mail messages and office memos, to the professional writer who needs to write complex documents full of formatting codes, to the advanced programmer who would like to use Emacs to format source code. No matter what you do with Emacs, you will find that it's easy to learn; after one or two sessions, you'll know the basics of editing any file. After you learn the basics, you can go on to learn about more advanced topics, which provide the real benefits of using Emacs. These include:

- Using multiple windows and buffers so you can work on more files at once.

- Customizing your keyboard commands.

- Tailoring Emacs to fit your work style using variables.

- Making Emacs your work environment where you can do all your everyday tasks, such as reading mail, compiling programs, and issuing shell commands.

- Creating macros to streamline repetitive tasks.

- Using Emacs to support programming in many languages (including C, LISP, and FORTRAN).

- Formatting files for documentation environments such as TeX and **troff**.

- Using word abbreviations to avoid spelling out long phrases or to correct common misspellings.

Of course, many of the topics may not apply to you; some topics may be appropriate for a second reading, but not for the first. Towards the end of the preface, we'll sketch several different ways to approach the book, depending on your interests and experience.

We do make a few assumptions. We assume that you're basically familiar with UNIX (or, if not UNIX, whatever operating system you're using). In particular, you should know what files and directories are, how they are named, and the basic things that you can do with them (copy, delete, rename; under UNIX, these are done with the **cp**, **rm**, and **mv** commands). If you're completely new to UNIX, we recommend that you read the Nutshell Handbook, *Learning the UNIX Operating System*, by Grace Todino and John Strang.

Which Emacs is Which?

Many versions of Emacs are available, offering a wide range of features. For UNIX, the most important versions of Emacs are GNU Emacs, which we cover in this book; Unipress Emacs (also called Gosling Emacs, after its author); and CCA Emacs. Some versions (Freemacs, MicroEmacs, Epsilon) run on personal computers under MS-DOS. Some other versions offer a very limited set of features, but in return are relatively sparing of memory and CPU cycles; the "mainline" Emacs implementations tend to be hard on computers, particularly if many users share a central computer. Some Emacs-like editors (Epoch) are very closely integrated with the X Window System. Some versions are "free" (which may mean any of several different things), and some are rather expensive commercial products. Some other programs (like FrameMaker) are not Emacs implementations in any way but have a similar set of keyboard commands.

As you've probably gathered, Emacs isn't so much an "editor" as a family of editors. There are a lot of similarities; all of these editors allow to you to mix text and editor commands freely; most of these editors support work in multiple windows; they all provide some kind of support for working with special file types (like C programs, TeX files, etc.); and most of them are heavily customizable, usually by programming in some dialect of LISP.

Given all this confusing diversity, which version of Emacs have we described? This book covers GNU Emacs, Version 18.[1] Since its appearance, it has become by far the most popular Emacs implementation in the UNIX world, and there's no reason to believe that this will change. It is also the most powerful and the most flexible of these extremely powerful and flexible editors. If you know GNU Emacs, you will be able to adapt to any other Emacs implementation with no trouble; it's not so easy to go in the other direction. Given these facts, our only logical choice was to focus the book on GNU Emacs.

However, this book isn't limited to GNU Emacs users. Because of the "family relations" between different Emacs implementations, this book should help you get started with any Emacs editor. The basic keyboard commands change little from one editor to another—you'll find that **C-n** (CONTROL-n) almost always means "move to the next line." Emacs editors tend to differ in the more advanced commands and features—but if you are using these more advanced facilities, and you aren't using GNU Emacs, you should most certainly consider making the switch.

---

[1] Version 19 (with some significant extensions) wasn't available at this writing. The most significant addition to Version 19 is extended X Window System support.

GNU Emacs and the Free Software Foundation

You don't need to know history to use GNU Emacs, but its sources are an interesting part of recent computer history. The Free Software Foundation, which maintains and distributes GNU Emacs, has become an important part of computer culture.

A long time ago (1975), Richard Stallman at MIT wrote the first Emacs editor. According to the folklore, the original Emacs editor was a set of macros for TECO, an almost incomprehensible and now obsolete line editor. The name Emacs stands for "Editing Macros." Tradition also has it that Emacs is a pun on the name of a favorite ice cream store. Much has happened since 1975. TECO has slipped into deserved obscurity, and Emacs has been rewritten as an independent program. Several commercial versions of Emacs have appeared, of which "Unipress Emacs," also known as "Gosling Emacs," and "CCA Emacs" were the most important. For several years, these commercial implementations were the Emacs editors you were most likely to run across outside of the academic world.

Stallman's Emacs became prominent with the birth of the Free Software Foundation and the GNU Project. GNU stands for "GNU's Not UNIX" and refers to a complete UNIX-like operating system that Stallman and his associates are building. Stallman founded the Free Software Foundation to guarantee that some software would always remain "free." Free does not necessarily mean cheap (you may have to pay a fee to cover the cost of distribution); it most definitely means liberated from restrictions about how it can be used.

To understand what "free" means, we have to look at how software is typically distributed. Most commercial software comes with a highly restrictive license. You have to pay to use the program; you probably have to pay separately for each computer that runs the program; you may have to pay more money every year to continue using the program; in some cases, you even have to pay by the minute. You are most definitely *not* allowed to give the program to your friends, and you will probably *never* (unless you are very wealthy) see the program's source code. If a commercial program is broken or doesn't have some feature that you need, you are completely at the mercy of the company you bought it from. And they may well decide to ignore you.

GNU Emacs has none of these limitations. If you can find someone to give it to you (and you usually can), you can get it for free. It is available from many public archives, including UUNET and several "anonymous FTP" sites (we'll discuss this in Appendix A). It is always distributed with the source code, so if you're a programmer, you can add your own features and fix your own bugs.[2] You can give copies to your friends. You will never be asked to pay for the right to use it. About the only thing you cannot do is impose further restrictions on how Emacs is used: i.e., if you give a copy of Emacs away, or make some improvements to it, you cannot suddenly start charging licensing fees. GNU Emacs is free, and will remain free. Your rights and responsibilities as a user are described precisely in the "General Public License," which we have published in Appendix F.

The Free Software Foundation was created precisely to distribute programs under terms which encourage you to share software, rather than to "hoard" it. The General Public License is designed to prevent an unfortunately common practice: companies taking public-domain code, making a few modifications and bug fixes, and then copyrighting their modified version. Once this has happened, the program has essentially become "private property" and disappeared from the public domain. Stallman formed the Foundation because he finds this practice abhorrent. As he explains in the GNU Manifesto, "I cannot in good conscience sign a nondisclosure agreement or a software license agreement... So that I can continue to use computers without dishonor, I have decided to put together a sufficient body of free software so that I will be able to get along without any software that is not free." Elsewhere in the manifesto, Stallman calls sharing software the "fundamental act of friendship among programmers." Their software is free because it *can* be shared, and will *always* be shareable–without restriction.[3]

Since GNU Emacs was first released, many other pieces of the GNU operating system have fallen into place: C and C++ compilers (*gcc* and *g++*), a very powerful debugger (*gdb*), substitutes for **lex** and **yacc** (called *flex* and *bison*, respectively), a UNIX shell (*bash*, which stands for "Bourne-Again Shell"), and many other programs and libraries. Many pre-existing facilities, like the RCS source code control system, have been placed under the Free Software Foundation's protection. Among other things, the Foundation is currently developing a UNIX-like kernel. When this is finished, they will have a complete modern operating system. Given the quality of their software, the GNU kernel will certainly be competitive with, if not better than, any of the commercial UNIX implementations that are now available.

---

[2] Fortunately, there are very few bugs—indeed, the Free Software Foundation produces much better code than most for-profit companies, and they are very responsive to bug reports. But if you do find a bug, and can't wait for them to fix it, you can do it yourself.

[3] Free Software Foundation programs, like Emacs, are often distributed with commercial systems. Even in these cases, the General Public License guarantees your right to use and give away their programs without restriction. Of course, the license does not apply to other proprietary software with which GNU tools have been shipped.

An Approach to Learning Emacs

Just as there are many versions of Emacs, there are many types of Emacs users. This book is designed to get you started with Emacs as quickly as possible, whether you are an experienced computer user or a novice. The first two chapters give you the basics you need to know, and the rest of the book builds on these. After the first two chapters, you don't have to read the rest consecutively; you can skip to the topics that interest you. Additionally, the book is designed to give you just the level of "hand-holding" you want; you can either read the book in detail or skim it, looking for tables of commands and examples.

Here are some reading paths you could take:

If	Read
You are an administrative user	Preface, Chapters 1-3, 13.
You are a casual user	Preface, Chapters 1-3, 13.
You are a programmer	Preface, Chapters 1-4, 8-11.
You are a writer or production person	Preface, Chapters 1-4, 6-7, 13.
You want to customize Emacs	Chapter 9, possibly 11.
You want to use mail in Emacs	Chapter 5.
You use UNIX commands in Emacs	Chapter 5.

These reading paths are only offered as a guideline. Emacs is one gigantic, functionally rich editor. We've divided it up into digestible bites for you, so you don't have to be put off by its size and scope. The best way to learn Emacs is incrementally; learn a little now, then learn more features as you get curious about them or find you need to do something and don't know how to do it in Emacs. Emacs probably already does it; if it doesn't, you can learn how to write a LISP function to add it to Emacs (see Chapter 11 for details). The online help system in GNU Emacs is an excellent place to learn about new features on the fly; how to use online help is discussed in Chapter 1, and in more detail in Chapter 13.

Here's a list of some features you might want to learn about on a rainy day:

• Word abbreviation mode (Chapter 3).

• How to use macros (Chapter 8).

• How to map your function keys to Emacs commands (Chapter 9).

• How to issue (and edit) shell commands from Emacs (Chapter 5).

• How to use multiple windows (Chapter 4).

• How to make simple drawings in picture mode (Chapter 6).

Finally, if you insist on reading through the book from beginning to end, here's a quick summary of what's in each chapter:

Chapter 1, *Emacs Basics*, tells you how to start Emacs and how to work with files. It also provides a quick introduction to Emacs' online help system.

Chapter 2, *Editing Files*, explains editing with Emacs, including commands for moving around, copying and pasting text, and undoing changes.

Chapter 3, *Search and Replace Operations*, covers more editing features, including search and replace, word abbreviation mode, and checking spelling.

Chapter 4, *Using Buffers and Windows*, describes how to use multiple buffers and windows.

Chapter 5, *Emacs as a Work Environment*, talks about Emacs as a work environment, where you can do everything you can do at the shell prompt, including reading and writing mail, issuing shell commands, and working with directories.

Chapter 6, *Simple Text Formatting and Specialized Editing*, covers the basic text formatting (such as indentation and centering) that you can do in Emacs as well as some of the more rarified features like picture mode and outline mode.

Chapter 7, *Using Emacs with UNIX Text Formatters*, describes Emacs support for **troff** (and its relatives), TeX, LaTeX, and Scribe.

Chapter 8, *Writing Macros*, discusses using macros to eliminate repetitive tasks.

Chapter 9, *Customizing Emacs*, explains how to customize Emacs according to your preferences: setting up your terminal, customizing your keyboard commands, tailoring your editing environment, and loading Emacs packages for extra functionality.

Chapter 10, *Emacs for Programmers*, covers Emacs as a programming environment, including editing support for C, LISP, FORTRAN, and other languages, and Emacs' interface to compilers and the UNIX **make** utility.

Chapter 11, *Emacs LISP Programming*, describes the basics of Emacs LISP, the language you can use to customize Emacs even further than with the techniques discussed in Chapter 9.

Chapter 12, *Emacs for the X Window System*, discusses Emacs' interface to the X Window System, allowing you to use a mouse and pop-up menus if you use a graphics workstation.

Chapter 13, *Online Help*, describes Emacs' rich, comprehensive online help facilities.

Appendix A, *How to Get Emacs*, tells how you can get GNU Emacs as well as a few other versions of Emacs.

Appendix B, *Making Emacs Work the Way You Think It Should*, tells you how to ensure that your Emacs behaves as described in this book.

Appendix C, *Emacs Variables*, lists many important Emacs variables, including all the variables mentioned in this book.

Appendix D, *Emacs LISP Packages*, lists most of the LISP packages that are available as of this publication.

Appendix E, *Bugs and Bug Fixes*, tells you how (and when) to report bugs that you find in Emacs.

Appendix F, *Important Documents*, reprints the text of the General Public License, which gives the rules under which GNU Emacs is distributed.

Appendix G, *Give and It Shall Be Given*, tells you how you can support the Free Software Foundation in their efforts to create more quality software.

What We Haven't Included

GNU Emacs is an extremely large and powerful editor; in this book, we've only been able to give you a sample of what it does. Many features have been left out, and more features are added all the time.

However, there are some particular things that are missing:

- Compatibility modes: GNU Emacs provides compatibility modes for the UNIX **vi** editor, the VAX/VMS EDT editor, and the Gosling Emacs editor. We've left this out. In our experience "compatibility modes" tend to be poor emulations of the "real thing." If you really want to use **vi** or EDT, do so. You're better off getting to know Emacs on its own terms, rather than pretending it is something else.

- Many programming language modes: In this book, we discuss the editing modes for C, LISP, and FORTRAN. There are many modes for other languages; some work better than others, and new modes are added frequently. There's no way we could discuss everything.

- Advanced LISP programming: GNU Emacs incorporates a complete LISP interpreter. We give a very basic and brief introduction to Emacs LISP; Chapter 11 should be enough to get you started, but really only scratches the surface. The Free Software Foundation publishes a complete *Emacs LISP Reference Manual*; if there is sufficient demand, O'Reilly and Associates will consider publishing a book on advanced Emacs LISP programming.

- Porting, Debugging, and Installation: This book doesn't describe the problems that can arise while porting GNU Emacs to other systems. We believe that such a book is badly needed, but it's far beyond the scope of the present volume. Let us know if you'd find this useful, and we'll consider writing it.

- Games and Amusements: GNU Emacs includes an eclectic bunch of games and amusements, including the ability to pipe random quotations from Zippy the Pinhead into the famous "Eliza" pseudo-psychoanalyst. (Type **ESC-x psychoanalyze-pinhead RETURN** sometime and see what happens.) Alas, we had to draw the line somewhere.

Conventions Used in This Handbook

This section covers the conventions used in this book.

Emacs Commands

Emacs commands consist of a modifier, such as CTRL (CONTROL) or ESC (ESCAPE), followed by one or two characters. Commands shown in this book abbreviate CTRL to C:

C-G   Hold down the **CTRL** key and press **G**.

To complete a command you may need to press a carriage return:

RETURN   Press the **RETURN** key.
This key may be labelled **ENTER** on your keyboard.

Most Emacs manuals refer to the META key in addition to the CTRL key. Since most keyboards don't have a META key, this book refers to ESC instead of META:

ESC-x   Press **ESC**, *release it,*[4] then press **x**.

If your keyboard does have a META key, it works like the CTRL key described above, that is, you hold down the META key and press the desired key, such as G. Since you can continue to hold down the META key for repeated keystroke sequences, META keys do have an advantage. ESC tends to be less convenient for

---

[4] We emphasize this because pressing ESC twice (**ESC ESC**) or holding it down a second too long so that it repeats gives you an error message; see the Problem Checklist at the end of Chapter 2, *Editing Files,* for more information.

repeated keystroke sequences. In general, if you have a META key on your keyboard, you will probably prefer to use it instead of ESC.

A few mouse commands (used only with the X Window System, discussed in Chapter 12) use the SHIFT key as a modifier, often in combination with the CTRL key. This is abbreviated as:

S-right   Press the right mouse button in combination with the SHIFT key.

C-S-right   Press the right mouse button in combination with the SHIFT and CTRL keys.

All Emacs commands, even the simplest ones, have a "full name": for example, **forward-word** is equivalent to the keystrokes **ESC-f** and **forward-char** is equivalent to **C-f**. Many commands only have "full names"; there are no corresponding keystrokes.

When we're discussing a command, we'll give both its full name and the keystrokes (if any) that you can type to invoke it. We will assume that you are using the "default bindings" (the default assignment of keystrokes to Emacs commands).

Examples

Throughout the book, you'll find keystrokes to type, followed by an Emacs screen showing the results.

Type: **emacs** *myfile*

```
┌─────────────────────────────────────────────────────────────────┐
│ █                                                                 │
│                                                                   │
│                                                                   │
│                                                                   │
│                                                                   │
│ -----Emacs:  myfile             (Fundamental)--All------------- │
│ (New file)                                                        │
└─────────────────────────────────────────────────────────────────┘
```

Type **emacs** with a filename at the UNIX prompt to start an Emacs session.

As shown in the Keystrokes column, the word **emacs** is in bold constant width font, indicating that this is exactly what you type. *myfile* is shown in italics because you could substitute any filename you choose and need not type exactly what you see here. The cursor (the point at which you are currently editing) is shown in "reverse video," as is the Emacs "mode line" at the bottom of the screen.

Towards the end of the book, when we're discussing programming modes, customization, and LISP programming, showing a simulated Emacs screen becomes rather unwieldly. Therefore, we'll eventually stop using displays like the one above; instead, we'll only show one or two lines of text. If it's relevant, we'll show the cursor's position in reverse video:

```
/* This is a C comment */
```

Font Usage

This book uses the following font conventions:

- Emacs keystrokes, command names, and variables are shown in **boldface** type.

- Filenames are shown in *italic* type.

- LISP code, C code, and other excerpts from programs are shown in `constant width` type.

- Dummy parameters that you replace with an actual value are shown in *italic* type. (If they appear within a program, they are shown in `constant width italic` type.)

- Buffer names are shown in `constant width` type.

- UNIX commands are shown in **boldface** type.

To find a group of commands quickly, look for tables in each section that summarize commands. These tables are formatted like this:

Sample Command Table

Keystrokes	Command Name	Action
C-n	next-line	Move to the next line.
(none)	yow	Print wisdom from the Pinhead in the minibuffer.

The first column shows the default key binding for the command, the second shows the command's full name, and the third describes what the command does. Many commands aren't bound to particular keystrokes; for example, the **yow** command. In this case, we'll put "(none)" in the first column. This doesn't mean you can't use the command; just type **ESC-x**, followed by the command's full name, and type a **RETURN**. (Try **ESC-x yow** sometime.)

Acknowledgments

Debra Cameron: I'd like to thank Peter Mui for hatching the original concept of this book and keeping it alive, and Chris Genly, for lending a willing hand with his Emacs and LISP expertise in the early days of writing this book, Duffy Craven for infecting me with his boundless enthusiasm for Emacs and teaching me lots of helpful tricks, Ted Stefanik for giving us an idea of what programmers and other techies would like to see in this book, and all the people who supported me and helped me to get this book done in pretty outrageous circumstances: my wonderful husband Jim (and Meg and David, too), Barbra Gibson, Betty Avins, Barbara Burkhardt, Cary Rodgers, and Jeanie O'Hara.

Bill Rosenblatt: I would like to thank the following people: Professor Richard Martin (Princeton Classics Department), for planting the seed in me that eventually turned writing from a chore to a pleasure; Intermetrics, Inc., for giving me little enough to do that I could fritter away my workdays delving into GNU Emacs; Hal Stern, for getting me this gig; Sandy Wise, for his help with the X Window System chapter; Jessica Lustig, for her love and support; and most importantly, my grad-school housemates for putting up with a tied-up phone line at all hours of the day and night.

We'd also like to thank our technical reviewers who gave of their time and expertise: Andy Oram, Rick Farris (and his friend Rock Kent), Eileen Kramer, Linda Mui, and Chris Genly. In addition to their careful review on technical matters, Andy Oram gave us the perspective of an accomplished writer, Rick Farris kept us smiling, Chris Genly wisely read the last part first, and Linda Mui, Eileen Kramer, Bruce Barnett, and Judy Loukides gave us insight about how new users would view the book.

Most of all, we'd like to thank our editor, Mike Loukides, who—in addition to artful editing on every level—made sure that the book was as complete as possible, writing whole sections himself at times to make sure the job got done. And special thanks to Eileen Kramer and all the great folks at ORA who copyedited, produced, indexed, and made this book a reality.

We'd Like to Hear From You

To ask technical questions, report errors, or comment on the book, send email to:
bookquestions@ora.com (via the Internet)

To be put on the mailing list or request a catalog, send email to:
info@ora.com (via the Internet)
uunet!ora!info (via UUCP)

1

Emacs Basics

Some of you out there are probably dying to get your hands on the keyboard and start typing. We won't try to stop you; turn to the section called "Starting Emacs" and you can go ahead. But do read the beginning of this chapter later when you're ready for a break. Emacs is much easier to learn if you understand some of the basic concepts involved, and these are discussed in the introduction to this chapter.

Introducing Emacs!

GNU Emacs is one of the most commonly used text editors in the UNIX world today. Many users prefer GNU Emacs to **vi** (UNIX's standard editor) or to the editor that's built into most modern window systems (like Sun's **textedit**). Why is it so popular? It isn't the newest tool on the market, and it's certainly not the prettiest. But it may well be the most useful tool you'll ever learn. We want to present what you need to know about Emacs in order to do useful work, in a way that lets you use it effectively. This book is a guide for Emacs users; it tries to satisfy the needs of many readers, ranging from administrators and managers who write memos and reports, to advanced programmers who edit source code in several different languages.

Our approach therefore isn't to tell you absolutely everything that Emacs does. There are many features and commands that this book doesn't describe. We don't think that's a problem; Emacs has a comprehensive online help utility that will help you figure out what these are. We have focused our attention on describing how to use Emacs to get useful work done. After covering basic editing in the first three chapters, we describe how to use Emacs as a comprehensive working environment: how to send and receive mail, how to give UNIX commands without leaving the editor, how to take advantage of special editing modes, how to use Emacs for editing special types of files (source files for **troff**, TeX, and various programming languages), and so on. We cover the most important commands and the most important command modes. However, you should always keep one principle in mind: Emacs does many things well, but it isn't important for that reason. Emacs is important because of the integration between different things you like to do.

What does integration mean? A simple example will help. Assume that someone sends you a mail message describing a special command for accessing a new printer. You can use Emacs to read the mail message. Then you can try the command by starting a UNIX shell within Emacs, copying the command, and executing it directly. If it works, you can edit your *.cshrc* file to create an alias (or abbreviation) for the command. You can do all this without leaving the editor, and without having to retype the command once. That's why Emacs is so powerful. It's more than just an editor; it's a complete environment that can change the way you work.

An initial word of advice, too. Many people think that Emacs is an extremely difficult editor to learn. We don't see why. Admittedly, there are a lot of features; you probably will never use all of them. But any editor, no matter how simple or how complex, has the same basic functions. If you can learn one, you can learn any of them. We'll give you the standard mnemonic devices that will help you to remember commands (like **C-p** means "previous line"), but we really don't even think these are necessary. They get you over an initial hump in the learning process, but don't make much difference in the long run. Learning to use an editor (whether it is Wordstar, **vi**, Emacs, FrameMaker, or any other) is basically a matter of learning finger habits: learning where to put your fingers to move to the previous line. If you experiment with Emacs and try typing a few of our examples, you'll quickly acquire these finger habits. And once you've acquired these habits, you'll never forget, any more than you'll forget how to ride a bicycle. After using Emacs for a day or two, we never had to think, "**C-p** means previous." Our fingers just knew where to go. Once you're at this point, you're home. Once you're at this point, you can become creative with Emacs. You can start thinking about how to put the special features to work for you.

The "finger habits" approach also implies a different way of reading this book. Intellectually, it's possible to absorb a lot from one reading; but you can only form a few new habits each day. (Unless, of course, they're bad habits.) Chapter 2, *Editing Files*, covers most of the basic editing techniques that you'll use. You may need to read it several times, with a slightly different focus each time. For example, Emacs gives you many different ways to move forward: you can move forward one character, one word, one line, one sentence, one paragraph, one page, etc. All of these are covered in Chapter 2 but you shouldn't feel obligated to learn them all at once. Start by learning how to move forward and backward; then gradually add more complex commands. Similarly, Emacs provides more different ways to search through a file than any editor we've seen. These are covered in Chapter 3, *Search and Replace Operations*. Don't feel obliged to learn them all at once; pick something, practice it, and move on to the next topic. No one will complain if you have to work through the first three chapters of our book several times before you're comfortable. Time spent developing good habits and reflexes is time well spent.

Understanding Files and Buffers

Editors don't edit an actual file. Rather, they put the contents of the file into a temporary buffer and edit that. The actual file on the disk doesn't change until the editor saves your buffer. Remember: a buffer seems a lot like a file, but it's really only a temporary workspace that may contain a copy of a file.

Like files, buffers have names. The name of a buffer is usually the same as the name of the file that you're editing. There are a few exceptions. For example, you can have a buffer that doesn't have a file associated with it and that is assigned a name (like `*scratch*`). And the "Help" facility displays help messages in a buffer named `*Help*`, which also isn't connected to a file. But you don't have to worry about these now. For the moment, just remember that when you start editing a file, Emacs copies the file into the buffer. As you edit the file, you are modifying the buffer, not the file itself. When you're satisfied with your changes, you can save them. Your file is only modified when you deliberately choose to save your changes. If you decide you don't like your changes, you can quit Emacs without saving the file, and no harm will be done. More on saving files in a while.

A Word about Modes

Emacs achieves some of its famed versatility by having various editing modes in which it behaves slightly differently. The word "mode" may sound technical or complicated, but what it really means is that Emacs becomes sensitive to the task at hand. When you're writing, you often want features like word wrap so that you don't have to press RETURN at the end of every line. When you're programming, the code must be formatted correctly depending on the language. For writing, there's text mode; for programming, there are modes for different languages, including C mode. Modes, then, allow Emacs to be the kind of editor you want for different tasks.

Text mode and C mode are *major modes*. A buffer can be in only one major mode at a time; to exit a major mode, you have to enter another one. Table 1-1 lists some of the major modes, what they do, and where they're covered in this book.

Table 1-1. Important Major Modes

Mode	Function
Fundamental mode	The default mode; no special behavior.
Text mode	For writing text (Chapter 2).
Indented text mode	Indents all the text you type (Chapter 6).
Picture mode	For creating simple line drawings (Chapter 6).
C mode	For writing C programs (Chapter 10).
FORTRAN mode	For writing FORTRAN programs (Chapter 10).
Emacs LISP mode	For writing Emacs LISP functions (Chapter 10).
LISP mode	For writing LISP programs (Chapter 10).
LISP interaction mode	For writing and evaluating LISP expressions (Chapter 10).
nroff mode	For formatting files for nroff (Chapter 7).
TeX mode	For formatting files for TeX (Chapter 7).
LaTeX mode	For formatting files for LaTeX (Chapter 7).
Scribe mode	For formatting files with Scribe (Chapter 7).
Outline mode	For writing outlines (Chapter 6).
View mode	For viewing files but not editing (Chapter 5).

Whenever you edit a file, Emacs attempts to put you into the correct major mode for what you're going to edit. If you edit a file that ends in *.c*, it puts you into C mode. If you edit a file that ends in *.el*, it puts you in LISP mode. Sometimes it

looks at the contents of the file rather than just its name. If you edit a file formatted for TeX, Emacs puts you in TeX mode. If it cannot tell what mode you should
be in, it puts you in fundamental mode, the most general of all.

In addition to major modes there are also minor modes. These define a particular
aspect of Emacs behavior and can be turned on and off within a major mode. For
example, fill mode means that Emacs should do word wrap; when you type a long
line, it should automatically make a line break that is appropriate. Table 1-2 lists
some minor modes, what they do, and where they're covered in this book.

Table 1-2. Important Minor Modes

Mode	Function
Abbrev mode	Allows you to use word abbreviations (Chapter 3).
Fill mode	Enables word wrap (Chapter 2).
Overwrite mode	Replaces characters as you type instead of insert-ing them (Chapter 2).
Auto-save mode	Saves your file automatically every so often (Chapter 2).

There are many other modes that we won't discuss, including modes for some
obscure but interesting programming languages (like Muddle and Scheme). And
there are some other modes that Emacs uses itself, like dired mode for the directory editing feature (described in Chapter 5, *Emacs as a Work Environment*).

You can set up your *.emacs* file so that your favorite modes turn on automatically
every time you start Emacs. More about this later in the chapter and in Chapter 9,
Customizing Emacs.

In addition, if you're particularly brave and good at LISP programming, you can
add your own modes. Emacs is almost infinitely extensible.

Starting Emacs

To start Emacs, simply type **emacs** followed by the name of the file you want to edit.[1] If you use a filename that doesn't exist, Emacs creates a new file. You'll most likely see something like this:

% **emacs** *myfile*

```
█



-----Emacs:  myfile          (Fundamental)--All---------------
(New file)
```

Type **emacs** with a filename at the UNIX prompt to start an Emacs session.

Of course, if the file you request already exists, Emacs reads the file and displays it on the screen:

% **emacs** *dickens*

```
█t was the best of times, it was the worst of times, it
was the age of wisdom, it was the age of foolishness,
it was the epoch of belief, it was the epoch
of incredulity, it was the season of Light, it was
the season of Darkness, it was the spring of hope, it
was the winter of despair, we had everything before us, we
had nothing before us, we were all going direct to
Heaven, we were all going direct the other way--in
short, the period was so far like the present period,
that some of its noisiest authorities insisted on its
being received, for good or for evil, in the
superlative degree of comparison only.

-----Emacs:  dickens          (Fundamental)--All---------------
```

If the file already exists, Emacs displays it on the screen.

---

[1] The command name may vary somewhat from site to site. GNU Emacs is sometimes called *gmacs*, particularly at sites with many editors installed. It may also be necessary for you to modify your UNIX search path. If typing *emacs* or *gmacs* gives you a "Command not found" error message, ask your system administrator for help.

You can omit the filename, if you want. If you just type **emacs**, you'll see a short message describing the version of Emacs that you're running, how to start the help system, and a few other trivia. This message disappears as soon as you type the first character. Emacs then puts you in an empty buffer called `*scratch*`, which is an ideal place for you to experiment.

About the Emacs Screen

When you enter Emacs, you can see that you have a large workspace at the top of the screen (usually 20 or more lines) where you do your editing. (See Figure 1-1.) A *cursor* marks your position in the file. The cursor is also called "point" or "dot," particularly among people who are more familiar with Emacs and in the online help system; therefore, it's useful to remember these terms.

You don't have to do anything special before you start typing: just start typing at your keyboard and, as long as you type alphanumeric characters and punctuation, Emacs inserts them into your text. The cursor shows where Emacs will insert the new characters; it will move as you type. Unlike many editors (particularly **vi**), Emacs does not have separate modes for inserting text and giving commands. Try typing something right now, and you'll begin to see how easy Emacs is to use.

Just above the bottom of your screen (on the second-to-the-last line), Emacs prints a lot of information about what it's doing. This line is called the "mode line." At the left edge of the mode line, you may see two asterisks (**). If the asterisks are there, this means that whatever you're editing has been modified since the last time you saved it. If you haven't made any changes, the asterisks won't be there. Next, Emacs prints "Emacs:" followed by the name of the buffer you are editing (myfile). In parentheses following this is the editing mode you are in. (Modes are discussed in the introduction to this chapter.) Following this, Emacs shows where you are in the file. If you're still at the beginning of the file, Emacs prints the word **Top**; if you're at the end, it prints **Bot**; if you're in the middle, it shows you a percentage (for example, 50% means you're looking at the midpoint of the file); and if the entire file is visible on the screen, Emacs prints the word **All**.

When you're an advanced Emacs user, you will often work with several buffers simultaneously. In this case, each buffer has its own mode line. Don't worry about this for now; just remember that every buffer always has a mode line to describe it.

At the bottom of your screen below the mode line is the *minibuffer*. This is the area where Emacs echoes the commands you enter and where you specify filenames for Emacs to find, values for search and replace, and so on.

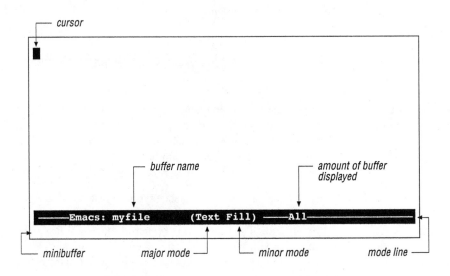

Figure 1-1. Understanding the Emacs Screen

Emacs Commands

You're about to start learning some Emacs commands, so let's discuss them a bit first. Emacs has hundreds, if not thousands, of commands. Don't worry, you don't have to learn or use them all. How do you give commands? Each command has a formal name, which (if you're fastidious) is the name of a LISP routine inside of Emacs. These names are very long; you usually wouldn't want to type the whole thing. So we need some way to abbreviate commands.

Instead of typing out command names (which you could do), Emacs ties each command name to a short sequence of keystrokes starting with CTRL or ESC. This tying of commands to keystrokes is known as "binding."

The authors of Emacs tried to "bind" the most frequently used commands to the key sequences that are the easiest to reach. Here are the varieties of key sequences you'll encounter:

- The most commonly used commands (such as cursor movement commands) are bound to **C**-*x* (where *x* is any character). This means "press and hold the **CTRL** key and type **x**, then release both keys."

- Slightly less commonly used commands are bound to **ESC**-*x*, where *x* is any character. This means "press the **ESC** key, release it, then type **x**."[2]

- Other commonly used commands are bound to **C**-**x** *something* (**C**-**x** followed by something else—a single character or another control sequence). Among other types, file manipulation commands, like the ones you are about to learn, are generally bound to **C**-**x** *something*.

- Some specialized commands are bound to **C**-**c** *something*. These commands often relate to one of Emacs' more specialized modes, such as picture mode or mail mode. You won't encounter them until much later in this book.

- This still doesn't take care of all the possibilities. You can get at the remaining commands by typing **ESC**-**x** **long-command-name RETURN**. (This works for any command really, but the keystrokes are usually easier to learn.)

Emacs also lets you define your own special keystrokes. This is particularly convenient if you find yourself using the "long form" of a command all the time. You'll learn more about this in Chapter 9, *Customizing Emacs*.

Enough talk; now let's learn some commands so you can get down to work.

Reading a File

You can read a file into a buffer in one of two ways: by specifying the filename when you start Emacs (as we did earlier) or by typing **C**-**x** **C**-**f** (the long command

---

[2] The Emacs documentation and online help facility refer to the META key, which they abbreviate as M. The META key is, for all practical purposes, equivalent to the ESC key. It doesn't exist (or it's hidden) on most keyboards, so we're going to talk about the ESC key instead. If you can find the META key, it does differ from ESC in one important way. If you're issuing a chain of ESC commands, you have to type ESC before every command. If you have a META key, you can hold META down while you issue the chain of commands. In this sense, the META key is similar to the CTRL key. On a Sun workstation, the keys labelled RIGHT and LEFT are META keys. On other workstations or terminals, you'll have to find it yourself, if it exists.

name for this is **find-file**). **C-x C-f** creates a new buffer which has the same name as the file.

Type: **C-x C-f**

```
It was the best of times, it was the worst of times, it
was the age of wisdom, it was the age of foolishness,
it was the epoch of belief, it was the epoch
of incredulity, it was the season of Light, it was
the season of Darkness, it was the spring of hope, it
was the winter of despair, we had everything before us, we
had nothing before us, we were all going direct to
Heaven, we were all going direct the other way--in
short, the period was so far like the present period,
that some of its noisiest authorities insisted on its
being received, for good or for evil, in the
superlative degree of comparison only.

-----Emacs: dickens          (Fundamental)--All--------------
Find file:  ~/█
```

Emacs prompts you for a file; respond by typing the file you want, followed by a RETURN.

Type: *myfile* **RETURN**

```
█




-----Emacs: myfile          (Fundamental)--All--------------
(New file)
```

Emacs starts another buffer with the new file in it.

To type **C-x C-f**, hold down **CTRL**, press **x** and then press **f**. Now release **CTRL**. This may sound complicated, but after you try it a couple of times it's easy.

After you type **C-x C-f**, Emacs uses the minibuffer to ask you for the filename. Remember that whenever Emacs wants information from you, it automatically puts the cursor in the minibuffer. When you're done typing in the minibuffer, you need to press **RETURN** to enter the command. You don't need a RETURN after normal editing commands (i.e., commands that use the control or escape keys).

What if you try to read the same file twice? Instead of creating a new buffer, Emacs just moves you to the buffer the file is in.

This is a good time to try typing if you haven't already. You may find yourself wanting to learn more about cursor movement and editing; that's fine. Feel free to skim the rest of this chapter and go on to Chapter 2. We recommend that you read the sections on saving files and exiting Emacs. There's also a table of commands at the end of this chapter for future reference. If you'd like to learn more about working with files as well as some shortcuts that will help you, stay with us through the rest of the chapter.

If You Read the Wrong File

If you happen to read the wrong file (perhaps because you were in the wrong directory or because of a typo), an easy way to get the right file is by typing **C-x C-v** (for **find-alternate-file**). This command means "Read a different file instead of the one I just read." After typing **C-x C-v**, you type the correct filename and press **RETURN**. Emacs replaces the buffer's contents with the alternate file.

Letting Emacs Fill in the Blanks

Emacs has a very helpful feature known as *completion*. If you're asking for a file that already exists, you need only type the first few letters of the name, enough to make a unique filename. Press **TAB**, and Emacs completes the filename for you. For example, suppose you are trying to find an existing file called *dickens*.

Type: **C-x C-f di**

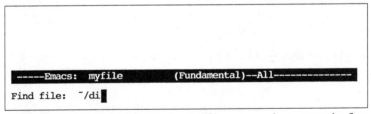

```
-----Emacs:  myfile          (Fundamental)--All--------------
Find file:  ~/di█
```

After **C-x C-f**, Emacs prompts for the filename, and you type the first few letters.

Press: **TAB**

```
-----Emacs:  myfile           (Fundamental)--All--------------
Find file:  ~/dickens█
```

When you press **TAB**, Emacs fills in the rest of the filename.

Press: **RETURN**

```
It was the best of times, it was the worst of times, it
was the age of wisdom, it was the age of foolishness,
it was the epoch of belief, it was the epoch
of incredulity, it was the season of Light, it was
the season of Darkness, it was the spring of hope, it
was the winter of despair, we had everything before us, we

-----Emacs:  dickens          (Fundamental)--All--------------
```

Emacs reads the file *dickens*; you can start editing it.

If more than one file starts with *di*, Emacs displays a window that shows you the various files that start with that string, and you choose one.

Completion is a wonderful Emacs feature that can save you time; it inspired the developers of korn shell and tcsh, for example. To read more about completion, see Chapter 13, *Online Help*.

You should also know that Emacs doesn't allow you to use the UNIX wildcards (*, ?, etc.). You can use the tilde (~) as an abbreviation for your home directory.

Inserting and Appending Files

If you want to insert one file within another, you simply move to the point in the file where you want to insert and type **C-x i**. (Yes, we know: we haven't told you how to move around in a file yet. That's in the next chapter.) To append a file, move to the end of the file (**ESC->**)[3] and type **C-x i**. As with **C-x C-f**, Emacs prompts you for the file's name in the minibuffer.

---

[3] To type **ESC->**, press **ESC** and release it, then press **>**.

How Emacs Chooses a Default Directory

When you use any command that asks for a filename (such as **C-x C-f**), Emacs displays a default directory in the minibuffer and asks you to type the rest of the filename. How does Emacs choose the default directory? The default directory is taken from the buffer that the cursor is currently in. If you are editing a file in your home directory when you type **C-x C-f**, Emacs assumes you want to edit another file in your home directory. If you are editing the file */sources/macros/troff.txt*, then Emacs makes the default directory */sources/macros*. If you want to find a file in another directory, just use normal editing commands (which we'll discuss in the next chapter) to edit the default directory that Emacs has supplied.[4]

Saving Files

To save the file you are editing, you type **C-x C-s**. Emacs writes the file. To let you know that the file was saved correctly, it puts the message "Wrote *filename*" in the minibuffer. If you haven't made any changes to the file, Emacs puts the message "(No changes need to be saved)" in the minibuffer.

If you type **C-x C-s** and your terminal "freezes" (nothing you type is accepted), your terminal probably uses **C-s** and **C-q** as flow control characters. To your terminal, **C-s** means "stop receiving input." Type **C-q** to restart the terminal. To understand more about flow control problems, see Chapter 9, *Customizing Emacs*.

If you have problems with **C-s** (or even if you don't), you may want to use the **write-file** command (**C-x C-w**) to save your files. The **write-file** command is slightly different from **save-buffer**. **Save-buffer** assumes that you don't want to change the file's name. **Write-file** assumes that you do; it asks you to type a new name in the minibuffer. However, if you just type a **RETURN** instead of a new filename, **write-file** saves the file with its old name—just like **C-x C-s** would have done.

The **write-file** command is also useful for editing files that you do not have permission to change. Use the **find-file** command to get the file you want into a buffer, and then before you make any changes, use **write-file** to create your own

---

[4] Now let's ask a trick question. What if you're editing a buffer that isn't connected to a file? For example, what if you're editing the `*scratch*` buffer that Emacs displays if you start it without a filename? Well, there are rules, but the answer is: you really don't care. Just type **C-x C-f**; look at the directory that Emacs provides in the minibuffer; and edit it if it's incorrect. Emacs is reasonably good at guessing which directory you want.

"private" version, with a different name and possibly a different pathname as well. This essentially copies the file to one that you own (by giving it a new name); you can then make changes. Of course, this doesn't affect the original file.

Leaving Emacs

To end a session in Emacs, type **C-x C-c**. If you have made changes to files that you have not saved, Emacs asks you if you want to save the changes. If you type **y**, Emacs writes the file, then exits. If you type **n**, Emacs asks you to confirm that you really want to leave and abandon the changes you made to this file by typing **yes** or **no** in full.[5] If you say no, your normal Emacs session continues just like you never typed **C-x C-c**. If you say yes, you exit Emacs and the changes you made during this session do not become permanent. This is often useful if you make changes you didn't intend to make. When you have answered all of the questions satisfactorily, Emacs returns you to your UNIX prompt (usually % or $).

Temporarily Suspending Emacs

In most cases, you can stop Emacs temporarily by typing **C-z**. You arrive at the UNIX prompt. To get back into Emacs, type either **fg** (if the shell has job control) or **exit** (if your shell uses a subshell to simulate job control). If you're not sure about the capabilities of the shell you're using, or if you're a new user and don't yet understand what "job control" means, it won't hurt to try both of these commands. One will work; the other will give you a harmless error message.

When you return to Emacs, you'll see that everything is exactly as you left it. The same files are displayed on the screen, in exactly the same states. You don't even have to save your files before suspending Emacs; you can wait until after you return. Having said this, we heartily recommend that you *do* save your files first. No one knows what will happen while you're gone: you may forget and go to lunch, the computer may crash in the meantime, and you'll lose a lot of work.

It's extremely useful to be able to suspend Emacs and do something else for a while, especially if you're on an old-fashioned terminal rather than a modern graphics workstation. However, one word of warning: it's very easy to forget that you have a "paused" emacs and start another Emacs session to edit the same

---

[5] Emacs is picky about whether you type **y** or **yes**. Sometimes it wants one, sometimes the other. If it asks for a **y**, you can sometimes get away with typing **yes** but not vice versa. If it beeps and displays, "Please answer yes or no," that means you didn't enter the whole word and it wants you to.

file. This can lead to massive confusion, particularly if you're lazy about saving files. You can have several different versions of Emacs running, each with a slightly different version of the same file. The UNIX **ps** command, which has moderately confusing output, will show you if you have old Emacs sessions lying around. The display below shows that two sessions of Emacs are running:

```
% ps
  PID TT STAT   TIME COMMAND
  129 co IW    0:01 sunview
  131 co IW    0:01 selection_svc
  134 co IW    2:39 clock -Wp 497 32 -Ws 210 47 -WP 704 0 -Wi
  135 co IW    1:01 mailtool -Wp 492 71 -Ws 670 770 -WP 908 0 -Wi
  137 co IW    0:00 Mail -N -B -f /tmp/MTda00135
 3474 p2 S    1:16 emacs ch01.2.mS
 3585 p2 T    0:01 emacs others
 3484 p3 S    0:00 -bin/csh -i (csh)
 3586 p3 R    0:00 ps
```

If the shell you're using supports the **jobs** command (**csh** and **ksh**), you'll get much clearer output:

```
% jobs
[1]  + Stopped              emacs ch01.2.mS
[2]  - Stopped              emacs others
```

If you don't know which shell you are using, or if you don't know what a shell is, there's no harm in trying the **jobs** command. If it doesn't work, you'll get a harmless "Command not found" error message.

Note that the **ps** and **jobs** commands only tell you how you started your Emacs session; they can't tell you what you're currently doing. The files listed by these commands, *ch01.2.mS* and *others*, are the ones you used when *starting* Emacs. Because Emacs lets you switch between many different files while you're editing, you may not be editing either of these files right now.

And a final word to the wise: there is almost never, ever, any reason to leave Emacs. If the Free Software Foundation got rid of the **C-z** command tomorrow, you shouldn't miss it. We won't tell you why right now—but remember these words when you read Chapter 5.

Customizing Emacs and its Pitfalls

Now that you can start Emacs and use a few very basic commands, it's a good time to become aware of an important aspect of Emacs' behavior—customization. By default, Emacs works in a certain way. But you can change almost anything about the way it behaves; Emacs is extremely flexible. You can create your own commands, change the definition of any keystrokes you wish, and generally fool around with anything you want. For the advanced user, customization is a blessing. But if you're new to Emacs, it's a curse. What's the problem? If you're a new user and sit down at someone else's terminal, you may find that he or she has redefined all of the basic commands, and that the editor is completely unfamiliar to you. Even worse, a system administrator may have defined some system-wide customization, or may have given you an Emacs initialization file that contains a set of "standard" or allegedly "useful" customizations.

In short, this means that you might invoke Emacs and end up with an editor that's substantially different from what we're describing here. What to do? First, be aware that this is a possibility. And there's a cure. If you start seeing discrepancies between this book and your editor, take these steps:

- Quit Emacs by typing **C-x C-c**. (Of course, even this may be redefined—although redefining the "quit" command is in very bad taste. If this doesn't work, type **ESC-x save-buffers-kill-emacs RETURN**.)

- When you see the UNIX prompt again, look and see if there is a file called *.emacs* in your home directory. This is your personal customization file. Your system administrator may have given it to you when setting up your account. If you see a *.emacs* file, rename it:

```
% cd
% ls .emacs
.emacs          The ls command says that a .emacs file exists.
% mv .emacs .emacs.ORIG
                Rename the .emacs file so it won't hurt you.
```

When you're more familiar with Emacs, you may want to return to this file and see what it tries to do.

- Then, using any editor you want to, create a new *.emacs* file. This file should contain the following line:

```
(setq inhibit-default-init t) ; no global initialization
```

This line tells Emacs to ignore any global initialization file, if there is one.[6] You may be able to skip this step. However, it's a useful precaution, and can't hurt.

---

[6] If you are completely new to UNIX, the following commands will work:

```
% cd
% cat > .emacs
(setq inhibit-default-init t) ; no global initialization
C-d
%
```

where **C-d** means "type the letter d while holding down the CTRL key."

- If you have logged in under someone else's name, start Emacs by giving the command **emacs -u** *yourname*. For example, if your user name is "thomas," start Emacs by giving the command **emacs -u thomas**. This forces Emacs to read *your* initialization file.

- Finally: don't bother to memorize these commands. Just remember: if Emacs behaves strangely, you read something in Chapter 1 that just might fix the problem.

We won't debate the wisdom of any individual customization. Most people who have used Emacs for a long time have tuned it to fit their preferences, and many of these "adjustments" are really useful, once you know what they do. We've devoted Chapter 9 to customization, and we'll often tell you about commands (or variations of commands) that you might want to stick into your *.emacs* file. We strongly encourage you to look at other users' *.emacs* files and experiment. However, we *will* debate the wisdom of exposing a new user to an Emacs that has been tweaked so that it doesn't match any known documentation. System administrators who set up new accounts like this are only asking for trouble.

Getting Help

GNU Emacs has extensive online help, which is discussed further in Chapter 13. To enter help, either type **emacs** with no filename at the UNIX prompt or, from within Emacs, press **C-h**.

Pressing **C-h** gives a you a list of options. Pressing **t** after **C-h** starts a tutorial that is an excellent introduction to Emacs. Pressing **k** asks Emacs to give you documentation on whatever keystroke you type next. For example, if you type **C-h k C-x i**, Emacs displays a description of the **insert-file** command. Pressing **f** after **C-h** asks Emacs to describe a function (really just a command's full name, such as **find-file**). Essentially, **C-h k** and **C-h f** give you the same information; the difference is that with **C-h k** you press a key and ask what it does, whereas with **C-h f** you type a command name and ask what it does.

Assume you want to find out about what **C-x i** does. First, type **C-h k** as shown in Figure 1-2.

```
█t was the best of times, it was the worst of times, it
was the age of wisdom, it was the age of foolishness,
it was the epoch of belief, it was the the epoch
of incredulity, it was the season of Light, it was
the season of Darkness, it was the spring of hope, it
was the winter of dispair, we had everything before us, we
had nothing before us, we were all going direct to
Heaven, we were all going direct the other way--in
short, the period was so far like the present period,
that some of its noisiest authorities insisted on ots
being received, for good or for evil, in the
superlative degree of comparison only.

——*∗—Emacs: myfile        (Fundamental) ———All——
Describe key:
```

You've now asked for help
about a keyboard command.

Figure 1-2. Asking for Help about a Keyboard Command

You've now asked for help about a keyboard command. Type **C-x i** to get help
information about **insert-file** (as shown in Figure 1-3).

```
█t was the best of times, it was the worst of times, it
was the age of wisdom, it was the age of foolishness,
it was the epoch of belief, it was the the epoch
of incredulity, it was the season of Light, it was
the season of Darkness, it was the spring of hope, it

——*∗—Emacs: myfile        (Fundamental) ———All——
Insert-file:
Insert contents of file FILENAME into buffer after point.
Set mark after the inserted text.


——*∗—Emacs: *Help*        (Fundamental) ———All——

```

Emacs displays help
information about **insert-file**

Figure 1-3. Emacs Help Screen

A few things to notice: The screen is now split into two parts because you're looking at two separate buffers. Each buffer has its own mode line. The lower buffer is the "help" buffer; it contains the information about the **insert-file** command that you wanted to look up. Emacs keeps the cursor in the "dickens" buffer because it knows there's no good reason for you to edit the "help" buffer. To make the "help" buffer disappear from the screen, type the command **C-x 1**; to remember this, think "return to 1 buffer."[7] The other "help" commands have more-or-less the same behavior.

You might also notice that in the text describing this command, Emacs calls the cursor "point." This is true in all GNU Emacs documentation, both online and in your GNU Emacs manual.

In this section, we've given a very brief introduction to three of the paths you can take in the help system. There are many more help facilities; they are described thoroughly in Chapter 13, *Online Help*. The "help" features we've described here should be enough to get you started; if you want to learn more, jump ahead to Chapter 13.

Summary

Now you know the basic commands for starting and stopping Emacs and for working with files. Chapter 2 builds on these commands to give you the skills you need for editing with Emacs. Table 1-3 summarizes the commands that we covered in this chapter.

Table 1-3. File-handling Commands

Keystrokes	Command Name	Action
C-x C-f	find-file	Find file and read it.
C-x C-v	find-alternate-file	Read an alternate file, replacing the one read with C-x C-f.
C-x i	insert-file	Insert file at cursor position.
C-x C-s	save-buffer	Save file (and may hang terminal; use C-q to restart).
C-x C-w	write-file	Write buffer contents to file.
C-x C-c	save-buffers-kill-emacs	Exit Emacs.

---

[7] This is really jumping ahead to Chapter 4, *Using Buffers and Windows*, but it's not fair to leave you with a "help" buffer taking up half your screen.

Table 1-3. File-handling Commands (continued)

Keystrokes	Command Name	Action
C-z	suspend-emacs	Suspend Emacs (use exit or fg to restart).
C-h	help-command	Enter the online help system.
C-h f	describe-function	Gives online help for a given command name.
C-h k	describe-key	Gives online help for a given keystroke sequence.

Problem Checklist

√ **Accidentally ending up in help.** You pressed **C-h** (or a key mapped to **C-h**), which is the ASCII sequence for backspacing but which is the GNU Emacs method for getting into help. Press **C-g** to get out again. Instead of **C-h**, use **C-b** to backspace. You can remap help to another key if you want to use **C-h** to backspace as well as **C-b**. First, you need to find or create a file in your home directory called *.emacs*. If you insert these lines in your *.emacs* file, you can use **C-h** to backspace and **C-x ?** to access help:

```
(define-key global-map "\C-x?" 'help-for-help)
(define-key global-map "\C-h" 'backward-char)
```

After inserting these lines in your *.emacs* file, save the file and restart Emacs to have the new settings take effect.

√ **Terminal freezes.** You probably pressed **C-s,** which is the flow control character that stops data flow to a terminal. Even if your terminal usually allows **C-s,** this can happen if you are using Emacs through an rlogin or a modem. Press **C-q** to restart. If this is a persistent problem, you may want to consider remapping key sequences that use **C-s.** See Chapter 9 for more information on flow control problems and remapping keys.

√ **Emacs doesn't do what this book says**. Make sure that you have GNU Emacs running (as opposed to some other Emacs version). If you do have GNU, look for a *.emacs* file in your home directory. If it exists, rename it. Create a new *.emacs* that says:

```
(setq inhibit-default-init t) ; no global initialization
```

√ **Gibberish appears on the screen when you start Emacs or find a file.** It's likely the file you're editing is a "binary file." This is most likely to happen if you've misspelled a filename. Try again to find the right file by typing **C-x C-v** *filename* **RETURN**. If nothing's right—you can't even tell if there's a buffer, a mode line, or a minibuffer, your terminal settings are wrong for Emacs. You need help from a system administrator or a guru.

√ **You get a message that says, "This terminal is not powerful enough to run Emacs."** You have problems with your terminal setting—or (just possibly) you may be using an ancient terminal that really can't run Emacs. However, this is *very* unlikely. This message usually means that the **TERM** environment variable is not set correctly. If you don't understand what this means, ask your system administrator for help.

2

Editing Files

Text Mode and Fill Mode
Moving the Cursor
Deleting Text
Marking Text to Delete, Move, or Copy
Reformatting Paragraphs
Stopping and Undoing Commands
Editing Tricks and Shortcuts

Now that you know how to enter and exit Emacs as well as the basics of working with files, it's time to learn how to move around in and edit files. Emacs offers lots of ways to move around in files. At first, you might find it confusing that there are so many ways to do the same thing. Be patient—as you learn, the confusion will wear off, and you'll begin to see why there are so many commands. The more ways you learn, the fewer keystrokes you'll need to get to the part of the file you want to edit.

If you want to practice commands while you're reading—which will help you learn faster—start by typing in a page or two from any book you happen to have handy. That will give you some text to work with as you learn editing skills in this chapter. Don't worry if you make mistakes; just keep on typing. You can correct any mistakes once you learn the basic editing skills outlined here. Learning any editor is primarily a matter of forming certain "finger habits," rather than memorizing what the book says. You will only learn the right "finger habits" if you start typing.

Text Mode and Fill Mode

Before you start typing, look at the mode line at the bottom of the screen. If the word `Fill` appears, you are in fill mode. In fill mode, when you type past the end of a line, Emacs automatically starts a new line, formatting paragraphs. This feature is what many word processors call "word wrap." If fill mode is not on, you can turn it on for this session by typing **ESC-x auto-fill-mode RETURN**. If you decide that you don't like fill mode, type **ESC-x auto-fill-mode RETURN** again. This command is like a light switch: it "toggles" fill mode on and off.

When you've become more proficient, you may decide that you want to enter fill mode automatically whenever you edit. If you do, edit your *.emacs* file and add the following lines:

```
(setq default-major-mode 'text-mode)
(setq text-mode-hook 'turn-on-auto-fill)
```

After adding these lines to the *.emacs* file, exit Emacs, then re-enter. The lines above not only turn on fill mode, but set up text mode as the default major mode. This means that whenever you start Emacs, it assumes that you want to use the "text mode" (for editing regular text files) with the "fill mode" feature enabled.

What Happens Without Fill Mode

If Emacs isn't in fill mode, you have to type a carriage return at the end of every line. When you are typing text, this is an inconvenience (which is why fill mode and text mode often go together), but when you are typing programs, it is preferable.

If you type a long line and don't type a carriage return, Emacs waits until you reach the end of the screen. Then it puts a backslash (\) at the end of the line, and moves to the next line. For example, the following represents one long line:

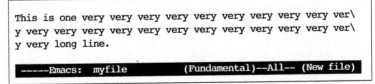

Emacs uses a backslash to show you when a line is too long.

The backslashes aren't part of the line; they are just markers to remind you that the next line on your screen really belongs to the same line.[1]

In fill mode, Emacs behaves differently. It waits until you get close to the end of the line, then waits until you type a space, and finally it moves the previous word (in some cases, several words) to the next line.

Moving the Cursor

To move the cursor forward one space, type **C-f** ("f" for forward). As you might guess, **C-b** moves the cursor backward. To move up, type **C-p (previous-line)**, and to move down, type **C-n (next-line)**. It's easier to memorize commands if you remember what the letters stand for. Figure 2-1 illustrates how to move up, down, left, and right.

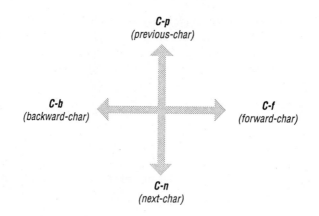

Figure 2-1. Basic Cursor Motion

Often, the arrow keys on your terminal are also mapped to these commands. Try them and see if they indeed move the cursor up, down, left, and right. Even if

---

[1] In some situations (which we will discuss much later), Emacs puts a dollar sign ($) at the right edge of the screen and does not show you the rest of the line. If you prefer this behavior, add the following line to your *.emacs* file:

```
(setq default-truncate-lines t)
```

If you're a beginner, we recommend that you leave this untouched.

they do, it's still a good idea to learn the commands so that no matter what terminal you use, you'll be able to move around easily.

If you're at the end of a line, **C-f** moves to the first character on the next line. Likewise, if you're at the beginning of a line, **C-b** moves to the last character of the previous line. If there's no place to go, Emacs beeps and displays the message "Beginning of buffer" or "End of buffer." There's one important exception to this rule. If you are at the end of a buffer, typing **C-n** *will* move to the next line, adding a new line to the buffer. In this situation (and only in this situation) **C-n** is identical to a **RETURN**.

Repeating Commands

In order to do anything efficiently, you have to move more than one character or line at a time. Emacs lets you repeat any command as many times as you want to. First, you can repeat a command any number of times by pressing **ESC-***n* before the command, where *n* is the number of times you want to repeat it.[2] This is called the **digit-argument** command. For example, let's say you want to move forward 5 characters. You would type **ESC-5 C-f**; the number **5** is called an *argument*.

Initial state:

```
 It was the best of times, it was the worst of times, it
was the age of wisdom, it was the age of foolishness,
it was the epoch of belief, it was the epoch
of incredulity, it was the season of Light, it was
the season of Darkness, it was the spring of hope, it
was the winter of despair, we had everything before us,
we had nothing before us, we were all going direct to
Heaven, we were all going direct the other way--in short,
the period was so far like the present period, that some
of its noisiest authorities insisted on its being
received, for good or for evil, in the superlative
degree of comparison only.

-------Emacs: dickens          (Fundamental)--All----------
```

Cursor in upper-left corner.

---

[2] When you use commands that start with ESC, it's easy to type ESC ESC by mistake. The Problem Checklist at the end of this chapter shows how to disable ESC ESC and preserve your sanity.

Type: **ESC-5 C-f**

```
It wa█ the best of times, it was the worst of times, it
was the age of wisdom, it was the age of foolishness,
it was the epoch of belief, it was the epoch
of incredulity, it was the season of Light, it was
the season of Darkness, it was the spring of hope, it
was the winter of despair, we had everything before us,
we had nothing before us, we were all going direct to
Heaven, we were all going direct the other way--in short,
the period was so far like the present period, that some
of its noisiest authorities insisted on its being
received, for good or for evil, in the superlative
degree of comparison only.

-----Emacs: dickens          (Fundamental)--All----------
```

The cursor moves forward five characters.

Type: **ESC-4 C-n**

```
It was the best of times, it was the worst of times, it
was the age of wisdom, it was the age of foolishness,
it was the epoch of belief, it was the epoch
of incredulity, it was the season of Light, it was
the s█ason of Darkness, it was the spring of hope, it
was the winter of despair, we had everything before us,
we had nothing before us, we were all going direct to
Heaven, we were all going direct the other way--in short,
the period was so far like the present period, that some
of its noisiest authorities insisted on its being
received, for good or for evil, in the superlative
degree of comparison only.

-----Emacs: dickens          (Fundamental)--All----------
```

The cursor moves down four lines.

You can give **ESC-n** a large argument if you want it to repeat the command many times. For example, let's say you are editing a large file of 1000 lines. If you typed **ESC-500 C-n**, the cursor would move down 500 lines, to the halfway point in a file. This is often the fastest way to move around in a very large file. If you give **ESC-n** a larger argument than it can execute, it repeats the command as many times as possible and then stops.

There's another multiplier command you can use, too: **C-u** (the **universal-argument** command). You can give **C-u** an argument just like you do ESC-*n*. Typing either **ESC-5** and **C-u 5** repeats the command that follows 5 times. But unlike **ESC-n**, **C-u** doesn't need an argument to repeat commands. With no argument, **C-u** multiplies the next command by 4. If you type **C-u C-u**, it multiplies the command by 16. In this way, you can "stack up" **C-u**'s to get multipliers of 16, 64, 256, and so on.[3]

Other Ways to Move the Cursor

In Emacs you can also move to the beginning or end of the line. **C-a** moves you to the beginning of the line (just like a is the beginning of the alphabet). **C-e** moves you to the *end* of the line. Other ways to move include forward and backward by word: **ESC-f** moves *forward* a word; **ESC-b** moves *backward* a word. You can move backward one sentence by typing **ESC-a**; to move forward one sentence, type **ESC-e**. And to move forward a whole paragraph at a time, type **ESC-]**; to move backward a paragraph, type **ESC-[**. If you're in the middle of a sentence or paragraph, moving back a sentence or paragraph means moving to the beginning of the current sentence or paragraph.

Figure 2-2 uses a few paragraphs of Victor Hugo's *Les Miserables* to show how you can move the cursor more than one character at a time.

---

[3] Most often, you'll use **C-u** as we've described here. However, it doesn't always work as a multiplier; sometimes **C-u** modifies the command's function. Later in this chapter, you'll see one case in which **C-u** modifies a command's function. However, if you're doing something where "multiplier" makes sense, **C-u** is almost certain to work.

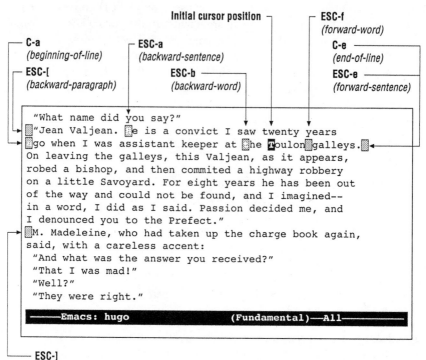

Initial cursor position ⌐

⌐ ESC-f
  (forward-word)

⌐ **C-a**
  (beginning-of-line)

⌐ **ESC-a**
  (backward-sentence)

C-e
(end-of-line)

⌐ **ESC-[**
  (backward-paragraph)

ESC-b
(backward-word)

ESC-e
(forward-sentence)

```
   "What name did you say?"
   "Jean Valjean. He is a convict I saw twenty years
   go when I was assistant keeper at the Toulon galleys.
   On leaving the galleys, this Valjean, as it appears,
   robed a bishop, and then commited a highway robbery
   on a little Savoyard. For eight years he has been out
   of the way and could not be found, and I imagined--
   in a word, I did as I said. Passion decided me, and
   I denounced you to the Prefect."
   M. Madeleine, who had taken up the charge book again,
   said, with a careless accent:
   "And what was the answer you received?"
   "That I was mad!"
   "Well?"
   "They were right."
 ─────Emacs: hugo              (Fundamental)──All─────
```

⌐ **ESC-]**
  (forward-paragraph)

Figure 2-2. Moving the Cursor More Than One Character at a Time

Here's an important hint for memorizing basic editing commands. Notice the difference between commands starting with CTRL and those starting with ESC. CTRL commands generally move in smaller units than their associated ESC commands. For example, **C-b** moves the cursor backward one character, while **ESC-b** moves the cursor back one word. Likewise, **C-a** moves to the beginning of the line, while **ESC-a** moves to the beginning of a sentence.

Emacs defines a sentence pretty strictly. You need *two* spaces after the final punctuation mark, unless you're at the end of the line. If there's only one space, Emacs won't recognize it. This definition of a sentence conforms with all standard descriptions of English manuscript style. However, should you need to change it, you can modify the variable **sentence-end**. For more information, see Chapter 9, which discusses customization.

Similarly, moving backward and forward by paragraph involves Emacs' understanding of what a paragraph is. Paragraphs are either indented with a tab or at least one space or have blank lines between them (block style). While this definition is appropriate for plain text, you may want to customize it for special purposes—for example, some text processing systems may require a special command between paragraphs. This definition is controlled by the variable **paragraph-end**; if you need to change it, see Chapter 9, *Customizing Emacs*.

Moving a Screen (or More) at a Time

If you want to "page" through a file one screen a time, use the command **C-v**. Emacs displays the next full screen from your file. It leaves a couple of lines from the previous screen at the top to give you a sense of context. Likewise, **ESC-v** shows you the previous full screen. Together, **ESC-v** and **C-v** provide a convenient way to "scroll" through a file quickly.

Scrolling also happens automatically if you type any motion command that takes you beyond the limits of the text currently displayed. For example, if you are on the last line of the screen and press **C-n**, Emacs scrolls forward. Similarly, if you are at the top of the screen and press **C-p**, Emacs scrolls backward. (This automatic scrolling only happens if there's text to scroll backward or forward to.)

You often want to move all the way to the beginning or the end of a file. To go to the end, type **ESC->**. To go to the beginning, type **ESC-<**. It may help you to remember that **>** "points to" the end of the file, while **<** "points to" the beginning.

There are two more ways that may come in handy. **ESC-x goto-line** *n* **RETURN** moves the cursor to beginning of line *n* of the file. Of course, Emacs starts counting lines from the beginning of the file. Likewise, **ESC-x goto-char** *n* **RETURN** goes to the *n*th character of the file, counting from the beginning. In both cases, *n* is a number.

For programmers, these commands are useful because many programs give error messages like "Incorrect input data on line 356." By using these commands, you can move exactly to the location of your error. There are some more complicated ways to link Emacs with error reports from compilers and other programs. In addition, there are several other cursor motion commands that are only applicable within programs. But we'll discuss these later, in Chapter 10, *Emacs for Programmers*.

Redisplaying the Screen

The command **C-l** (that's "l" as in the letter "L") serves two functions:

- It redraws the entire Emacs display.

- It puts the line that has the cursor in the center of the screen. (More precisely, we should say "the center of the window," but we haven't discussed windows yet; see Chapter 4.)

There are many situations in which you need this command. First, from time to time other processes may send messages to your terminal and mess up Emacs' display. For example, you may get messages telling you that electronic mail has arrived, or that someone wants to communicate with you using **talk**, or that a disk is full, and so on. These messages don't confuse Emacs, but they might confuse you: there is text on the screen that isn't in your file, the cursor's true position isn't where it seems to be, and so on. To fix these problems, just type **C-l**, and Emacs redraws the screen correctly.

Emacs also takes the line on which the cursor appears and places it in the center of the screen. This is very useful if you're typing at the bottom or the top of the screen. Typing **C-l** quickly moves the material that you care about to the middle of the screen, where it is more visible.

Table 2-1 is a list of Emacs cursor movement commands. In the list, if the command is mnemonic, the word to remember is given in *italics*.

Table 2-1. Cursor Movement Commands

Keystrokes	Command Name	Action
C-f	forward-char	Move *forward* one character (right).
C-b	backward-char	Move *backward* one character (left).
C-p	previous-line	Move to *previous* line (up).
C-n	next-line	Move to *next* line (down).
ESC-f	forward-word	Move one word *forward*.
ESC-b	backward-word	Move one word *backward*.
C-a	beginning-of-line	Move to beginning of line.
C-e	end-of-line	Move to *end* of line.
ESC-a	backward-sentence	Move backward one sentence.
ESC-e	forward-sentence	Move forward one sentence.
ESC-[	backward-paragraph	Move backward one paragraph.
ESC-]	forward-paragraph	Move forward one paragraph.
C-v	scroll-up	Move forward one screen.
ESC-v	scroll-down	Move backward one screen.

Table 2-1. Cursor Movement Commands (continued)

Keystrokes	Command Name	Action
C-x [	backward-page	Move backward one page.[5]
C-x]	forward-page	Move forward one page.
ESC->	end-of-buffer	Move to end of file.
ESC-<	beginning-of-buffer	Move to beginning of file.
(none)	goto-line	Go to line n of file.
(none)	goto-char	Go to character n of file.
C-l	recenter	Redraw screen with current line in the center.
ESC-n	digit-argument	Repeat the next command n times.
C-u n	universal-argument	Repeat the next command n times.

Deleting Text

As you start practicing deletion commands, you might want to know the undo command, which is discussed fully later in this chapter. Typing **C-x u** will undo your last edit.

Emacs provides many ways to delete text. The simplest way to delete text is to press the DEL key; this deletes the character immediately to the left of the cursor. (The full name of the command bound to the DEL key is **backward-delete-char**.) Unfortunately, since keyboards aren't standard, your DEL key may not be labeled DEL or DELETE, so you may have some trouble finding it. It's easier to find by what it does: it deletes the previous character. If you're typing and you decide to erase the last character you typed, what key on your keyboard do you reach for? For Emacs' purposes, that key is the DEL key.

Emacs provides a number of other deletion commands—perhaps too many for your taste, although if you're patient, you'll eventually use most of them. For example, **C-d** (for **delete-character**) deletes the character under the cursor. The command for deleting the next word, **ESC-d** (for **kill-word**), deletes some or all

---

[5] If the file does not contain page breaks (which are formfeed characters that tell the printer to move to the next page before continuing to print), Emacs moves to the beginning or end of the file. If you want to insert page breaks in your file, type **C-q C-l**. **C-q** is the "quote" command we mentioned briefly earlier. It tells Emacs to put a **C-l** character in your file, rather than interpreting **C-l** as the "recenter" command.

of a word depending on where the cursor is. Once again, note how the ESC key augments the command: **C-d** operates on a character, while **ESC-d** operates on a word. For example:

If the cursor is here:	ESC-d makes this edit:
It was the w█rst of times	It was the w█of times
It was the █orst of times	It was the █of times
It was the wors█ of times	It was the wors█of times

Similarly, if you are in the middle of a word and ask Emacs to delete the previous word (**ESC-DEL**, for **backward-kill-word**), it deletes from the cursor position back to the space following the previous word.

If you want to delete an entire line, or a part a line, use the command **C-k** (for **kill-line**). This deletes everything from the cursor to the end of the line. Typing **C-k** on a blank line deletes the line itself. As a result, it usually takes two **C-k**s to delete a line: one to delete the text, and one to delete the resulting blank line. If you want to delete everything from the beginning of the line up to the cursor, try the more complex incantation **ESC- – C-k** (i.e., press ESC, followed by a dash, and then CTRL-k).

NOTE

You often want to precede **C-k** with **C-u** to delete a group of lines. The description of **C-k** that we just gave implies that **C-u C-k** should delete two lines: we said it normally takes two **C-k**'s to delete a line, so four **C-k**'s should delete two lines. However, **C-u C-k** deletes *four* lines. Likewise, **ESC-***n* **C-k** will delete *n* lines. Don't let this confuse you.

Recovering What You've Deleted

When you use **C-k**, the material that you delete doesn't just disappear. Emacs hides it away in a special place called the "kill ring." You can get back what you've typed by typing **C-y** (for **yank**)[6]. Conveniently, if you kill several lines in succession, Emacs "collects" then into a single item and places the whole unit into the kill ring; a single **C-y** command will bring everything back. In the

---

[6] A quick warning to **vi** users who are learning Emacs: **vi** also uses the term "yank," but its meaning is almost the exact opposite. Don't get confused.

following example, we'll use **C-k** four times to delete the first two lines of "A Tale of Two Cities" (remember: the first **C-k** deletes the text; the second **C-k** deletes the remaining blank line). Then we'll use a single **C-y** to bring everything back.

Initial state:

```
It was the best of times, it was the worst of times, it
was the age of wisdom, it was the age of foolishness,
it was the epoch of belief, it was the epoch
of incredulity, it was the season of Light, it was
the season of Darkness, it was the spring of hope, it
was the winter of despair, we had everything before us,
we had nothing before us, we were all going direct to
-----Emacs:  dickens              (Fundamental)--All----------
```

Cursor is in upper-left corner.

Type: **C-k C-k C-k C-k**

```
It was the epoch of belief, it was the epoch
of incredulity, it was the season of Light, it was
the season of Darkness, it was the spring of hope, it
was the winter of despair, we had everything before us,
we had nothing before us, we were all going direct to
Heaven, we were all going direct the other way--in short,
the period was so far like the present period, that some
-----Emacs:  dickens              (Fundamental)--All----------
```

Deleted the first two lines with **C-k**.

Type: **C-y**

```
It was the best of times, it was the worst of times, it
was the age of wisdom, it was the age of foolishness,
it was the epoch of belief, it was the epoch
of incredulity, it was the season of Light, it was
the season of Darkness, it was the spring of hope, it
was the winter of despair, we had everything before us,
we had nothing before us, we were all going direct to
-----Emacs:  dickens              (Fundamental)--All----------
```

Got everything back with a single operation.

What exactly goes into the kill ring? Everything you delete with **C-k**, in addition to everything you delete with **C-w** and everything you copy with **ESC-w** (two commands that you'll learn shortly). Words, sentences, and paragraphs that you delete with **ESC-d**, **ESC-DEL**, and their relatives also go into the kill ring. In addition, text that you delete with **C-u** followed by either **DEL** or **C-d** goes into the kill ring. About the only things that Emacs *doesn't* save in the kill ring are single characters, deleted with **DEL** or **C-d**.

Emacs is clever about what you put into the kill ring: when it is assembling a big block of text from a group of deletions, it always assembles the text correctly. For example, you can type a few **ESC-d**'s, followed by some **ESC-DEL**'s, with some **C-k**'s thrown in. When you type **C-y**, Emacs "yanks" all the text that you've deleted in the proper order.

However, there's one thing you have to watch out for. Emacs stops assembling these blocks of text as soon as you give any operation that *isn't* a kill operation. For example, if you type **C-k**, then delete a single character with **C-d**, then another **C-k**, you've broken the chain. In this case, you haven't made a single chain of deletions; you've made two separate deletions. Later, we'll see how to get the older deletions back.

Table 2-2 summarizes the commands for deleting, killing, and yanking text.

Table 2-2. Deletion Commands

Keystrokes	Command Name	Action
DEL	backward-delete-char	Delete previous character.
C-d	delete-char	Delete character under cursor.
ESC-DEL	backward-kill-word	Delete previous word.
ESC-d	kill-word	Delete the word the cursor is on.
C-k	kill-line	Delete from cursor to end of line.
ESC-k	kill-sentence	Delete sentence the cursor is on.
C-x DEL	backward-kill-sentence	Delete previous sentence.
C-y	yank	Restore what you've deleted.
C-w	kill-region	Delete a marked region (see next section).
(none)	backward-kill-paragraph	Delete previous paragraph.
(none)	kill-paragraph	Delete from the cursor to the end of the paragraph.

Marking Text to Delete, Move, or Copy

What if the text you want to delete is just a phrase? Or half a paragraph? Or several paragraphs? You could use the various delete commands in combination to delete just the part you want to, but Emacs offers an easier way: defining the area you want to delete by marking text. The marked area is called a *region*. To define a region, you use a secondary pointer called a *mark*. Some versions of Emacs display the mark on the screen; unfortunately, in GNU Emacs, the mark is invisible. You set the mark at one end of the region by pressing **C-@** or **C-SPACE** (the latter may or may not work depending on your terminal),[7] then move the cursor to the other end of the region. The cursor is referred to as the *point*. Figure 2-3 illustrates point, mark, and region.

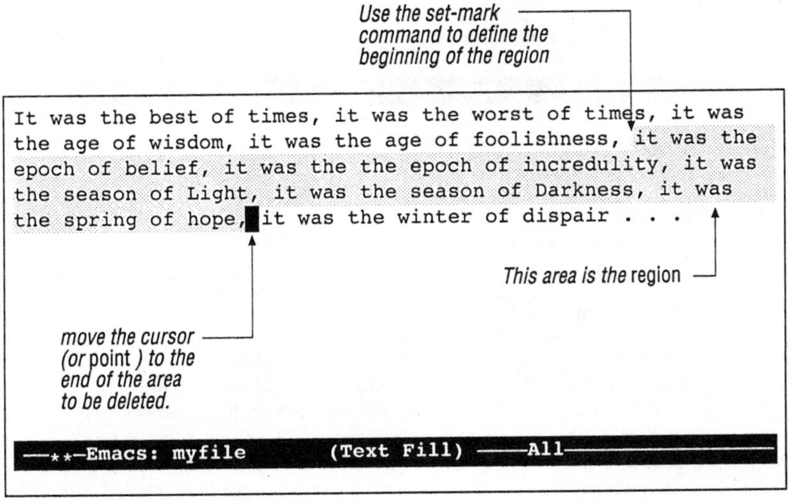

Use the set-mark
command to define the
beginning of the region

```
It was the best of times, it was the worst of times, it was
the age of wisdom, it was the age of foolishness, it was the
epoch of belief, it was the the epoch of incredulity, it was
the season of Light, it was the season of Darkness, it was
the spring of hope, it was the winter of dispair . . .
```

This area is the region

move the cursor
(or point) to the
end of the area
to be deleted.

```
—*—Emacs: myfile      (Text Fill) ——All—
```

Figure 2-3. Point, Mark, Region

---

[7] Since **C-SPACE** doesn't work on some keyboards and **C-@** is awkward (requiring you to hold down CTRL, press and hold down SHIFT, then press 2 to type @), you may want to map **set-mark** to another key sequence such as **ESC-.**. If you want to try **ESC-.** for one session, type: **ESC-x global-set-key RETURN ESC-. set-mark RETURN**. If you want to use this sequence regularly, add this line to your *.emacs* file:

```
(define-key global-map "\M-." 'set-mark-command)
```

Let's mark a sample region. In this example, we want to remove the phrase "it was the worst of times" from the first line of the paragraph. First, we'll find the beginning of the phrase. Then we will set the mark, move forward six words, and then delete. We'll use shading (which you won't see on your screen) to indicate the region that is selected.

Move to the beginning of "it" and type **C-@**

```
It was the best of times, █t was the worst of times, it
was the age of wisdom, it was the age of foolishness,
it was the epoch of belief, it was the epoch
of incredulity, it was the season of Light, it was
the season of Darkness, it was the spring of hope, it
was the winter of despair, we had everything before us,
we had nothing before us, we were all going direct to
Heaven, we were all going direct the other way--in short,
the period was so far like the present period, that some
of its noisiest authorities insisted on its being
received, for good or for evil, in the superlative
degree of comparison only.


-----Emacs:  dickens          (Fundamental)--All----------
Mark set
```

Set the mark; "mark set" appears in the minibuffer.

Move to the end of the phrase:

```
It was the best of times, it was the worst of times, █t
was the age of wisdom, it was the age of foolishness,
it was the epoch of belief, it was the epoch
of incredulity, it was the season of Light, it was
the season of Darkness, it was the spring of hope, it
was the winter of despair, we had everything before us,
we had nothing before us, we were all going direct to
Heaven, we were all going direct the other way--in short,
the period was so far like the present period, that some
of its noisiest authorities insisted on its being
received, for good or for evil, in the superlative
degree of comparison only.


-----Emacs:  dickens          (Fundamental)--All----------
```

Move the cursor to the end of the phrase to be deleted. We move forward six words (to the end of "times"), plus two characters.

Now the region is marked. You may want to make sure it is marked correctly before giving the delete command. To do this, type **C-x C-x** (for **exchange-point-and-mark**); this swaps the locations of the mark and the cursor. If the cursor moves to where you thought the mark was, the region is marked correctly. You can type **C-x C-x** again to switch the point and mark back to where they were. Especially because you can't see the mark, it's a good habit to check its location using **C-x C-x** before deleting the region. People who have used Emacs for years still forget to set the mark and then make a deletion without knowing what they've just deleted. (If you make this mistake, just type **C-y**.)

Now we'll delete the region using **C-w**.

Type: **C-w**

```
It was the best of times, █t
was the age of wisdom, it was the age of foolishness,
it was the epoch of belief, it was the epoch
of incredulity, it was the season of Light, it was
the season of Darkness, it was the spring of hope, it
was the winter of despair, we had everything before us,
we had nothing before us, we were all going direct to
Heaven, we were all going direct the other way--in short,
the period was so far like the present period, that some
of its noisiest authorities insisted on its being
received, for good or for evil, in the superlative
degree of comparison only.

-----Emacs:  dickens          (Fundamental)--All----------
```

C-w deletes the region.

As we've already mentioned, Emacs saves everything that you delete with **C-w**. So you can retrieve whatever you've deleted with **C-y**. This is really convenient if you delete the wrong text by mistake: just type **C-y** before doing anything else. It also gives you an easy way to move text from one part of the file to another. To move text: mark it, press **C-w** to delete the region, then move to the place you want to insert the text. Press **C-y** to insert the text. If you yank the text back into the wrong location, just type **C-w** again. "Yanked" text is always marked as a region, so a **C-w** will always undo a **C-y**.

When you're defining a region, you normally set the mark at one end and then move the cursor to the other end of the region. There are a few shorthands that are helpful in some of the most common situations. Assume that you want to mark a paragraph. You could put the mark at one end and then move to the other end. However, there's an easier way: type **ESC-h** (for **mark-paragraph**). This sets the mark at the end of the paragraph and places the cursor at the beginning automatically. Similarly, **C-x h** (for **mark-whole-buffer**) marks the entire buffer; the cursor goes to the beginning, and the mark is placed at the end. Finally, **C-x C-p** marks the current page, where "pages" are defined by the **C-l** character.[8]

---

[8] **C-l** is a special character (called "formfeed") that is recognized by most printers and many utilities; it is typically used to make page boundaries.

Of course, marking a paragraph, page, or buffer is usually only the prelude to some other operation, like "killing" (**C-w**).

Copying Text

To copy text: mark it, then press **ESC-w** (for **copy-region-as-kill**) to copy the region into the kill ring. Move to the place where you want to copy the text and press **C-y**. Copying text is exactly the same as "killing" it, except that Emacs doesn't delete anything. The text you have copied is placed in the kill ring, so you can use **C-y** to access it as often as you like. Again, if you yank the text back in the wrong place, just type **C-w** to delete it.

One advantage to **ESC-w** is that it works on files or buffers that are read-only. For example, if you wanted to create a special file with Emacs hints, you could use **ESC-w** to copy some text from Emacs' online help into one of your buffers.

Here are the steps for some common deletion tasks.

To mark a region and delete it:

1. Move the cursor to the beginning of the area you want to delete.

2. Press **C-@** or **C-SPACE**. Emacs displays the message "Mark set".

3. Move the cursor to the end of the region you want to delete.

4. If desired, press **C-x C-x** to exchange point and mark, ensuring that the region is marked correctly.

5. Press **C-w** to delete the region.

6. Emacs deletes the region.

To move text from one part of a file to another:

1. Delete the text you want to move using the procedure for marking and deleting text.

2. Move the cursor to the point where you want to insert the text.

3. Press **C-y**.

4. Emacs inserts the text you deleted.

To copy text:

1. Move the cursor to the beginning of the area you want to copy.

2. Press **C-@** or **C-SPACE**. Emacs displays the message "Mark set".

3. Move the cursor to the end of the region you want to copy.

4. Press **ESC-w** to copy the text.

5. Move the cursor to the place where you want to insert the copied text and press **C-y**.

6. Emacs inserts the text you copied.

Table 2-3 summarizes the different commands for defining regions.

Table 2-3. Commands for Working with Regions

Keystrokes	Command Name	Action
C-@ or C-SPACE	set-mark-command	Mark the beginning (or end) of a region.
C-x C-x	exchange-point-and-mark	Exchange location of cursor and mark.
ESC-h	mark-paragraph	Mark paragraph.
C-x C-p	mark-page	Mark page.
C-x h	mark-whole-buffer	Mark buffer.

More about the Kill Ring

Earlier we mentioned the "kill ring," a temporary storage area in which Emacs saves the stuff you delete. So far, we've assumed that you're interested in resurrecting what you've most recently killed. However, the kill ring does a lot more. It actually stores your last 30 deletions. We've seen that **C-y** restores the text that you deleted most recently. Typing **ESC-y** deletes the text that you just yanked and gets the next-most-recent text from the kill ring.

Here's how it works. In the text below, assume that you've just killed the words "most recent." Then **C-y** will retrieve these words from the kill ring. When you type **ESC-y**, Emacs gets rid of "most recent" and gets the next entry from the kill ring ("second-last"):

Keystrokes	Action
C-y	This was the most recent█deletion.
ESC-y	This was the second-last█deletion.
ESC-y	This was the third-last█deletion.
ESC-y	This was the fourth-last█deletion.

You can keep on typing **ESC-y**, retrieving successively more ancient deletions, until you reach the end of the kill ring.

If saving the last 30 deletions isn't enough, you can change the size of the kill ring. There's really no reason to do this, unless you have strange requirements or almost infinite patience. However, if you want to experiment, give the command: **ESC-x set-variable RETURN kill-ring-max RETURN** *new-value* **RETURN** (where *new-value* is a number).

Reformatting Paragraphs

If you're in fill mode, Emacs tries to make your lines as neat as possible by inserting line breaks so that each line is roughly the same length. Of course, this only helps when you're first writing the file. As you edit, you'll make some lines longer and some shorter. Soon, you'll no longer have a neatly formatted file. Depending on the editing you've done, some lines may be short and some may be so long that they no longer fit on your terminal's screen.

Emacs won't reformat your text of its own accord. If you want to restore your file to its original beauty, you need to give a "fill" command. The simplest way to reformat your text is to give the **fill-paragraph** command by typing **ESC-q**. Emacs reformats the paragraph, then positions the cursor at the end of the paragraph.

There's one important pitfall here. In text mode, a paragraph is any text that is indented or has a blank line before and after it. If you have a file with no blank lines, Emacs thinks it is all one long paragraph. Typing **ESC-q** by mistake takes all the text, ignoring line breaks, and makes it one long paragraph. This is a particular problem if you use the **nroff**, **troff**, or TeX text formatting systems. One of the authors of this book learned this the hard way after having to untangle a few long files. If you use **troff** or TeX, or if (for any other reason) you regularly create files with no blank lines, here are some suggestions:

• For **nroff** or **troff**, use nroff mode, described in Chapter 7, *Using Emacs with UNIX Text Formatters*. You can reformat paragraphs with **ESC-q** and the formatting commands remain intact. For TeX users, use TeX mode, also described in Chapter 7. These special modes redefine what a paragraph means so that the **fill-paragraph** command works correctly. Otherwise, these modes are very similar to text mode.

• Instead of filling a paragraph, fill a region. Define the region you want to fill and press **ESC-g** (the **fill-region** command). This command takes a region and formats each individual paragraph within it.

One last note: if you type **C-u** (or **ESC- –**) before **ESC-q**, Emacs changes the definition of "fill" slightly. The normal fill command leaves the right margin ragged. With either prefix, the fill commands justify the right margin by inserting extra spaces into each line. Frankly, however, right-justification with fixed-width spacing makes your document much less readable.

Table 2-4 summarizes the commands for reformatting paragraphs.

Table 2-4. Paragraph Reformatting Commands

Keystrokes	Command Name	Action
ESC-q	fill-paragraph	Reformat paragraph.
ESC-g	fill-region	Reformats individual paragraphs within a region.

Stopping and Undoing Commands

Sometimes you start a command by accident or change your mind about it. No worry—with Emacs, you can quit in the middle or undo it.

Stopping Commands

When you want to stop any command that's in progress, press **C-g**. The phrase "Quit" or "Aborted" appears in the command area. If you come from a PC software background, you may need to retrain your fingers to press **C-g** instead of the familiar **ESC**.

Undoing Changes

What happens if you make a mistake while you're editing? You can slowly restore a buffer to its original state by pressing **C-x u (undo)** to undo your changes. By typing **C-x u** repeatedly, you can gradually work your way back to a point before your mistake. This is convenient if you've made a mistake four or five commands back. It is marginally useful if you've made a mistake twenty or thirty characters back. And it is completely useless if your mistake is ancient history.

NOTE

We have seen situations that the "undo" command can't handle. Therefore, it is always a good idea to save your file frequently. We usually save a file whenever we stop typing—even if only for a few seconds. It is also a good idea to keep "backup" copies (perhaps using RCS or some other source control system) so you can restore older versions.

If the undo command isn't useful, there's another way to restore a file to an earlier state. If you want to get the file back to the state that is stored on disk, type **ESC-x revert-buffer RETURN**. The **revert-buffer** command has a few complications. Every few hundred keystrokes, Emacs creates an auto-save file.[9] The auto-save file minimizes the amount of work that you lose if the computer crashes and you haven't saved your file recently. The name of an auto-save file is the same as the name of the file you are editing, with a sharp (**#**) added to the beginning and the end. For example, if you are editing the file *text*, its auto-save file is

---

[9] You can change the frequency with which Emacs creates auto-save files by changing the variable **auto-save-interval**. By default, Emacs creates an auto-save file every 300 keystrokes. For more information on changing variable values, see Chapter 9, *Customizing Emacs*.

#text#. If the auto-save file was created since the last time you saved your file, Emacs asks the following question:

```
Buffer has been auto-saved recently.  Revert from auto-save file? (y or n)
```

If you type **y**, Emacs prepares to restore your file from the auto-save file. To verify your intentions, it then asks:

```
Revert buffer from file filename? (yes or no)
```

The filename is the name of the auto-save file or the name of your original file. Type **yes** if you want to restore the file, **no** if you've changed your mind.

If you saved your file *after* the last auto-save file was created, Emacs won't bother asking you about the auto-save file. However, it always asks you to verify your intentions before reverting the file.

While this command is called **revert-buffer**, note that it cannot revert a temporary buffer that is not connected with a file. Table 2-5 summarizes the commands for stopping commands and undoing changes.

Table 2-5. Stopping and Undoing Commands

Keystrokes	Command Name	Action
C-g	keyboard-quit	Abort current command.
C-x u	advertised-undo	Undo last edit (can be done repeatedly).
(none)	revert-buffer	Restore buffer to the state it was in when the file was last saved (or auto-saved).

Backup Files

The first time you save a file, Emacs creates a "backup file." If something disastrous happens and the other techniques for undoing changes won't help you, you can always return to the backup file. The name of the backup file is the same as the name of the file you're editing, with a tilde (˜) added. For example, if you are editing the file *text*, the backup file is *text˜*.

Emacs doesn't provide any special commands for restoring a buffer from the backup copy. The easiest way to do this is to exit Emacs and then use the UNIX

mv command. For example, the **mv** command below restores the original version of the file *text*:

```
% mv text˜ text      restore backup version
% emacs text         continue editing
```

GNU Emacs also has a "numbered backup" facility. If you enable numbered backups, Emacs creates a backup file (with the suffix ˜*n*˜) *every time you save your file*. *n* is a number that increases by one with each successive "save." This facility resembles VAX/VMS version numbering. If you are very nervous about deleting old versions, it might be worth having: you can keep all of your old versions forever, if you want to. However, numbered backups can also waste a lot of disk space. The variables that control numbered backups are described in Appendix C, *Emacs Variables*.

Editing Tricks and Shortcuts

Now that you've learned the basics of editing—moving the cursor to the right position, deleting, copying, and moving text—you can learn some tricks that make editing easier.

Fixing Transpositions

The most common typo involves the transposition of two letters, and most typos are noticed immediately after you make them. Pressing **C-t** transposes two letters:

Transposing Letters

Before C-t	After C-t
the best of tims█, it	the best of times█ it

To transpose two letters, put the cursor on the space following the two letters to be transposed (if the typo is at the end of a line) or on the second of the two letters to be transposed (if the typo is in the middle of a line). Press **C-t**. If you often transpose letters, you may want to think about using word abbreviation mode, discussed in Chapter 3, to clean up typos for you automatically.

You can also transpose two words, lines, paragraphs, or sentences. To transpose two words, put the cursor between the two words and press **ESC-t**. After Emacs has finished, the cursor follows the second of the two (transposed) words:

Transposing Words

Before ESC-t	After ESC-t
one three█two	one two three█

To transpose two lines, put the cursor anywhere on the second of the two and press **C-x C-t**. Emacs moves the first before the second:

Transposing Lines

Before C-x C-t	After C-x C-t
second line █irst line third line	first line second line █hird line

Table 2-6 shows a quick summary of the different transposition commands.

Table 2-6. Transposition Commands

Keystrokes	Command Name	Action
C-t	transpose-chars	Transpose two letters.
ESC-t	transpose-words	Transpose two words.
C-x C-t	transpose-lines	Transpose two lines.
(none)	transpose-sentences	Transpose two sentences.
(none)	transpose-paragraphs	Transpose two paragraphs.

Capitalization

Mistakes in capitalization are also common and annoying typing errors. Emacs has some special commands for fixing capitalization. To capitalize the first letter of any word, put the cursor on the first letter and press **ESC-c**. To put a word in lowercase, press **ESC-l**. To put a word in uppercase, press **ESC-u**. Note that if the cursor isn't on the first letter in the word, Emacs takes action only from the character under the cursor on. You can easily use **ESC-u** to put the the last half of a word in uppercase, and so on.

If you notice that the previous word is incorrect, you can use these commands prefaced by **ESC- –** (press **ESC** followed by a dash). This corrects the previous word without moving the cursor. If the cursor is positioned in the middle of a word, using **ESC- -** before a command causes it to work on the first part of the word (the part preceding the cursor), rather than the part following the cursor.

For example, if you start with: `abcd`█`fhij`

And press	You'll get
ESC-u	`abcdEFGHIJ`█
ESC- – ESC-u	`ABCD`█`fghij`
ESC-c	`abcdEfghij`█
ESC- – ESC-c	`Abcd`█`fghij`

ESC- – makes almost any command operate on the preceding item rather than the current item. Similarly, you can use **C-u** with a negative argument to repeat commands backward as well as forward.

Emacs also has commands that allow you to uppercase, lowercase, or capitalize regions—remember that a region is the area between the point (or cursor) and the mark (set by **C-@**). Since they aren't commonly used, we won't discuss these commands here; you can experiment with them on your own. Table 2-7 summarizes the capitalization commands.

Table 2-7. Capitalization Commands

Keystrokes	Command Name	Action
ESC-c	capitalize-word	Capitalize first letter of word.
ESC-u	upcase-word	Uppercase word.
ESC-l	downcase-word	Lowercase word.
ESC- – ESC-c	negative-argument; capitalize-word	Capitalize previous word.
ESC- – ESC-u	negative-argument; upcase-word	Uppercase previous word.
ESC- – ESC-l	negative-argument; downcase-word	Lowercase previous word.
(none)	capitalize-region	Capitalize region.
C-x C-u	upcase-region	Uppercase region
C-x C-l	downcase-region	Lowercase region.

Typing over Old Text with Overwrite Mode

Particularly if you come from a PC background, and even if you don't, you may be used to pressing a certain key, then being able to simply type over old text rather than having to bother deleting it. There is a certain satisfaction in destroying some really bad text in this way. You can do this in Emacs, too, by entering a minor mode called overwrite mode. When you're in overwrite mode, any new text you type wipes out the text that's underneath. When you're not in overwrite mode (i.e., in normal Emacs), any new text you type is inserted at the cursor position and any existing text is pushed to the right. (On other systems this may be referred to as insert mode; since it is normally the way GNU Emacs behaves, it doesn't have a name here.)

To enter overwrite mode, type **ESC-x overwrite-mode RETURN**. "Ovwrt" appears on the mode line. You can turn off overwrite mode by typing **ESC-x overwrite-mode RETURN** again. Using Emacs' command completion, you can simply type **ESC-x ov** and then press **RETURN**. This is enough of a unique string to tell Emacs you want to toggle overwrite mode. Completion, one of the best shortcuts in Emacs, is discussed further in Chapter 13, *Online Help*.

Now you've learned enough commands for most of the editing you'll do with Emacs. The next chapter covers topics such as searches, query-replace, spell checking, and word abbreviation mode. If you want to learn these features, go on to the next chapter. From this point on, you do not need to read chapters sequentially but can skip around according to your areas of interest.

Problem Checklist

√ **Accidentally pressing ESC ESC.** One common and annoying mistake is pressing **ESC** twice instead of once. On many terminals, this key will even repeat if you hold it down too long. When this happens, you get dumped into the **eval-expression** command, which is useful only to LISP programmers. By default, this command is disabled, and Emacs shows a window that asks you if you want to re-enable it. If you type **ESC ESC** accidentally all the time, this can drive you crazy. You can set **ESC ESC** to mean nothing to Emacs; this is called "unbinding" the key sequence. (This is described in more detail in Chapter 9, *Customizing Emacs*.) To disable **ESC ESC**, add this line to your *.emacs* file:

```
(global-unset-key "\e\e")
```

Even if you do this, you can still use the **eval-expression** command by typing **ESC-x eval-expression RETURN**.

√ **Error messages that say "auto-save error" or "cannot create backup file."** These error messages are pretty arcane; what they really mean is that you are editing in a directory you don't have write permission in and as a result Emacs can't write an auto-save file or backup file. This error can also appear if the directory doesn't exist. Emacs allows you to create buffer names like *foo/bar*, even if the directory *foo* doesn't exist. This works fine until Emacs tries to auto-save. Either copy the file you are editing to another directory or change the permissions on the directory you're in.

√ **The screen doesn't look right when you move around, insert, or delete.** For instance, patches are in reverse video or the ends of lines disappear. You have terminal setting problems. For a temporary workaround, try **C-l** to clear the screen. Then ask your system administrator for help in getting your terminal settings right.

3

Search and Replace Operations

Different Kinds of Searches
Search and Replace
Checking Spelling
Word Abbreviation Mode

The commands we discussed in the first two chapters are enough to get you started. But they're certainly not enough to do any serious editing. If you're using Emacs for anything longer than a few paragraphs, you'll want the support for serious document preparation this chapter describes. In this chapter, we cover the various ways that Emacs lets you search for text and replace it. Emacs provides the traditional *search* and *search and replace* facilities that you would expect in any editor: it also provides several important variants, including incremental searches, regular expression searches, and query-replacement. We also cover the spelling checker, because it is integrated into the search and replace facility. Finally, we cover word abbreviation mode; this is a kind of automatic replacement that can be a real time-saver.

Different Kinds of Searches

While you're editing, you frequently want to find something you've already typed. Rather than hunt through the file trying to find what you're looking for, virtually all editors provide some kind of search feature that lets you look for a particular text string. Emacs is no exception to the rule. It supplies a search command—in fact, it provides a dizzying array of search commands. Here's a quick summary of the different kinds of searches that are available:

Simple search

You give Emacs a text string (called a *search string*), and it finds the next occurrence. You will find this search on almost any editor.

Incremental search

An incremental search starts to search the file as soon as you type the first character of a search string. It continues to search as you type in more characters.

Word search

A word search is like a simple search, except that it only searches for full words and phrases. For example, if you are searching for the word "hat," you don't have to worry about finding the word "that." A word search is also useful when you need to find something that is spread across two lines.

Regular expression search

To search for patterns that may vary slightly, you can use a regular expression search. For example, if you wanted to find all instances of **B1** and **B2**, you could search for them using the regular expression **B[12]**. However, regular expressions can be extremely complex. We'll give a brief introduction here; they are discussed more fully in Chapter 11, *Emacs LISP Programming*.

Incremental regular expression search

A combination of an incremental search and a regular expression search.

You can either search forward or backward. Searches can be either case-sensitive, meaning that Emacs will consider uppercase and lowercase letters to be different (i.e., "This" and "this" are different); or case-insensitive, which doesn't differentiate between upper- and lowercase (i.e., "This" and "this" are the same). By default, searches are case-insensitive; upper- and lowercase letters are considered to be the same.

Replacement operations are closely related to searches. Again, Emacs offers you several different flavors:

Simple search and replace

Replace all occurrences of one string with another.

Query-replace

Conditionally replace a string throughout a file. Whenever Emacs finds the string you're interested in, it stops and asks you whether or not to perform the replacement. This is useful if you need to change some but not all instances of a word or phrase throughout a file.

Regular expression replacement

Regular expression replacement uses "regular expressions" to find the replacement string. This is only for the truly brave.

So now you know what you'll be looking at. Don't be intimidated by the wealth of different searches that are available. In practice, you'll probably settle on one search command and one replace command and use these for 99 percent of your work. For example, we use incremental search and query-replace most of the time. If you're a writer, you may use word search all the time; if you're a programmer, you might want a regular expression search. If you're just beginning, you may want to learn incremental search and read the rest of this chapter later. However, if you know what's available, you'll be able to make use of the other search commands when they become useful.

Incremental Search

Incremental searches start to work from the moment you type the first character of the search string. For the beginner, they aren't the easiest kind of search to use, but they have lots of advantages. Many users like the efficiency of incremental searches, but if you're inclined to make typos, you may find incremental search rather frustrating and want to use a simple search instead. However, we'll start with incremental search because Emacs clearly *wants* you to use it and offers some perks for doing so.

To start an incremental search, type **C-s** and then type the text you want to find.[1] Notice how this search works: it searches for each character as soon as you type it. For example, if you are searching for the word "meter," an incremental search finds the next "m" as soon as you type the **m**; it finds the next "me" as soon as you type the **e**; it finds the "met" as soon as you type the **t**; and so on. Sooner or later, you either find what you want, or Emacs is unable to find anything. If you find what you want type **ESC**; this tells Emacs to stop searching at the current

---

[1] If **C-s** causes your terminal or workstation to freeze, that means it is being used as a flow control character. You can remap incremental search to another key (such as **ESC-s**) by inserting the following line in your *.emacs* file:

```
(define-key global-map "\M-s" 'isearch-forward)
```

As a reminder, you will also have to remap **C-x C-s** (**save-buffer**), or use a variation like **C-x C-w** (**write-file**). More information on flow control problems and remapping keys is found in Chapter 9, *Customizing Emacs*.

place in the file. If Emacs can't find anything that matches your search string, it prints the message "Search failed" at the bottom of your screen and then it beeps.

Here's what happens when we search for the word "meter"; the numbers show how the cursor moves with each new letter in the search string.

Type: **C-s meter ESC**

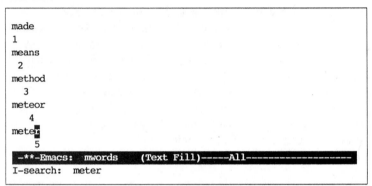

In this incremental search, Emacs moves the cursor from position 1 to 2 to 3, and so on, as you type the search string "meter."

What happens if you find the string you're looking for, but not the right occurrence of the string? Let's say you're searching for the word "eschatology," which appears several times in the file. What do you do when you find the word you want, but you're still not in the right place? Simply press **C-s** again. This finds the next occurrence of the current search string. Emacs uses the same search string; you don't have to retype it.

Always remember to type **ESC** when you've found the text you want. Forgetting to type ESC is a very common mistake: you type a few things, and suddenly Emacs is off looking at some completely different part of the file. What has happened? Emacs thinks you're still searching, and has just added the characters you've typed to the search string.

Pressing any control sequence also gets you out of an incremental search. Most users prefer this behavior. Since the next command that you type is usually C-something, having Emacs exit the search and execute the command is usually what you want to happen. If you need to search for control characters in a weird file, you don't want control sequences to stop an incremental search. In this case, use the **set-variable** command to set **search-exit-option** to **nil**.[2] When

---

[2] If you want this behavior whenever you start Emacs, add the following line to your *.emacs* file:

```
(setq search-exit-option nil)
```

search-exit-option is set to "nil," ESC is the only way to exit an incremental search.

Much of the frustration with incremental search comes from typing your search string incorrectly. If you type a letter in your search string incorrectly, press DEL.[3] Emacs eventually deletes the incorrect character and lets you continue searching. If Emacs is in the process of searching, you may have to wait until it finishes working through the file and attempts to read the next character of the search string. It then deletes the incorrect character and search again.

To cancel a search (that is, to give up searching), type **C-g**. This brings you back to the place where the search began.

NOTE

When Emacs is actually *in the process* of searching, the meaning of **C-g** changes slightly. This is important if you need to cancel a search before Emacs finds what it is looking for. A single **C-g** brings you back to the last character that Emacs found successfully, letting it continue the search. Typing **C-g** twice cancels the search completely, bringing you back to the point where you started.

To search backwards through a file, use **C-r**, which works exactly like **C-s** except that it searches in the opposite direction. It puts the cursor at the beginning of the text you found.

As you will see in Table 3-1, once you're in an incremental search, certain keys (such as **ESC** and **DEL**) have different functions than they normally do. This sounds confusing but it's actually fairly easy to get used to. Table 3-1 shows a summary of special key functions during incremental search.

Table 3-1. Incremental Search Commands

Keystrokes	Command Name	Action
C-s	isearch-forward	Start incremental search forward; follow by search string. Also, find next occurrence (forward) of search string.

---

[3] As we've pointed out elsewhere, terminals don't label the DEL key consistently. Your best approach is to identify the likely candidates (including backspace, delete, and keys with funny arrows on them) and trying them until you find the one with the right behavior.

Table 3-1. Incremental Search Commands (continued)

Keystrokes	Command Name	Action
C-r	isearch-backward	Start incremental search backward; follow by search string. Also, find next occurrence (backward) of search string.
ESC	(none)	Exit a successful search.
C-g	keyboard-quit	Cancel incremental search, and return to starting point.
DEL	(none)	Delete incorrect character of search string.

Simple Searches

Incremental searches are very efficient if you always type the search string correctly. If you sometimes make errors and have to wait for the incremental search to stop, delete the incorrect characters, and then go on, you may become frustrated with incremental search. Emacs also offers a simple or nonincremental search. To use a more straightforward search, type **C-s ESC**, followed by the search string. Press **RETURN** and Emacs begins the search. Press **C-s** again to repeat the search. (You need only press **ESC** when specifying the search string.) Press **C-r ESC** *searchstring* **RETURN** to start a nonincremental search backwards through the file. Table 3-2 shows a quick summary of the simple search commands.

Table 3-2. Simple Search Commands

Keystrokes	Action
C-s ESC *searchstring* RETURN	Start nonincremental search forward.
C-s	Repeat nonincremental search forward.
C-r ESC *searchstring* RETURN	Start nonincremental search backwards.
C-r	Repeat nonincremental search backward.

Word Search

Sometimes you might want to find a phrase that appears in your document but covers two lines or has punctuation in the middle of it. Word search is a nonincremental search that ignores line breaks, spaces, and punctuation. It also requires that your search string match entire words in the file.

To do a word search, type **C-s ESC C-w** (**word-search-forward**). The prompt "Word search" appears in the minibuffer. (Don't be put off by the earlier prompts: you'll see an "I-search" prompt after typing **C-s**, and a "search" prompt after typing the **ESC**. Ignore these.) Then type the search string and press **RETURN**. Emacs searches for the given string. To do a word search backwards, **type C-r ESC C-w** instead. For example, assume that you have the following text:

```
He said "all good elephants are wise, aren't they?"
She answered "some are smarter than others, but we
think this is socially conditioned."
```

The command **C-s ESC C-w they she RETURN** positions the cursor after the word "She." It looks horrible, but it's nothing more than a word-search (**C-s ESC C-w**) for the word "they," followed by the word "she." It ignores the punctuation (?") and the new line between "they" and "she."

The most useful feature of a word search is that it only finds entire words. Assume that you're looking for the word "the." You don't want to bother with "thence," "there," "theater," "thesis," or any other word that happens to contain the letters "the." In this situation, neither an incremental search nor a simple search is very useful—you need a word search. If you're writing a paper, word search is often exactly what you need. It is the *only* one of the three basic search commands that can find what you want even if it is split between two lines.

Now that you've seen the three most commonly used searches, you might want to experiment and see which you find most useful.

Search and Replace

You often want to combine a search operation with a replacement operation. For example, if you spell poorly, you may want to replace every occurrence of "recieve" with "receive." The hard way to do it is to search for "recieve" and, whenever you find it, make your change by hand. Emacs provides a search and replace operation that lets you make changes like this very quickly. By using a search and replace operation, a single command can fix every occurrence of the word "recieve."

Simple Search and Replace Operations

First, let's assume you're in the situation we described above. You want to replace every occurrence of one string with another. There is no conceivable way that "recieve" could be correct, and absolutely no ambiguity about how you want to replace it. When you want to replace every instance of a given string, you can use a simple command that tells Emacs to do just that. Type **ESC-x replace-string RETURN**, then type the search string and press **RETURN**. Now type the replacement string and press **RETURN** again. Emacs replaces all occurrences in the file from the cursor position onward. If you want to search and replace throughout the file, go to the beginning of the file before typing this command.

Here's a quick example of using **replace-string**.

Initial state:

```
We were very anxious to recieve your order and were
pleased when it came in today.

Now that we've recieved it, we'll begin work
on filling the order.  You should recieve the
merchandise in about six weeks, provided that we can
get materials from the factory quickly to do the
necessary customization.
-**-Emacs:   ordermemo      (Text Fill)-----All-------------
```

"Receive" is misspelled "recieve" three times on this screen, but the cursor is positioned after the first instance.

Now we'll fix them.

Type: **ESC-x replace-string RETURN recieve RETURN receive RETURN**

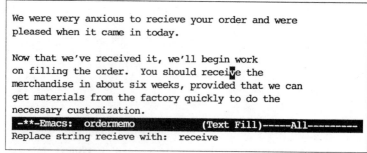

```
We were very anxious to recieve your order and were
pleased when it came in today.

Now that we've received it, we'll begin work
on filling the order.  You should receive the
merchandise in about six weeks, provided that we can
get materials from the factory quickly to do the
necessary customization.
-**-Emacs:   ordermemo              (Text Fill)-----All---------
Replace string recieve with:   receive
```

The misspelling was corrected only from the cursor position onward; the word "recieve" in the first sentence is still incorrect.

What if you're not sure about capitalization? The word "recieve" might begin a sentence, in which case it is capitalized. Do you need two separate searches? No. We'll describe what actually happens a little later—but for now, let's just say that Emacs does its best to match capitalization when doing a replacement.

Query-replace

Often you're not sure that you want to replace every appearance of your search string. If you want to decide whether to replace the string on a case-by-case basis, you need to use a *query-replace*. Query-replace allows you to change a string conditionally throughout a file. After Emacs finds an occurrence of the search string, it asks whether it should replace it and you respond accordingly.

To use query-replace, type **ESC-%**. The prompt "Query replace:" appears in the minibuffer. Type your search string and press **RETURN**. Now "Query replace *searchstring* with:" appears. Type the replacement string and press **RETURN**. So far, this is almost identical to a "replace-string" operation: only the prompts are different.

Emacs now searches for the first occurrence of the search string. When it finds one, a new prompt appears: "Query replacing *searchstring* with *newstring*." Before performing the replacement, Emacs waits for a response to tell it what to do. Table 3-3 lists the possible responses and their results.

Table 3-3. Responses During Query-replace

Keystrokes	Action
SPACE	Replace searchstring with newstring and go on to the next instance of the string.
y	Replace searchstring with newstring and go on to the next instance of the string.[4]
DEL	Don't replace; move on to next instance.
n	Don't replace; move on to next instance.
.	Replace the current instance and quit.
,	Replace but don't move on.
!	Replace all the rest and don't ask.
^	Back up to the previous instance.
ESC	Exit query-replace.
C-r	Enter recursive edit (discussed in detail below).
ESC-C-c	Exit recursive edit and resume query-replace.
C-]	Exit recursive edit and exit query-replace.

This seems like a lot of keys to remember, but you can get away with knowing two or three. Most of the time, you'll respond to the prompt by pressing **SPACE**,

---

[4] Query-replace only accepts lowercase **y** and **n**; uppercase **Y** and **N** won't work.

telling Emacs to go ahead and perform the replacement in this location. After performing the first few replacements, you may realize that there's no need to inspect every change individually. Typing an exclamation mark (!) tells Emacs to go ahead and finish the job without bothering you anymore. And typing **n** tells Emacs not to make the substitution, but to move on. If you remember these three, you're all set.

How does this work in practice? Let's revisit our previous example.

Type: **ESC-% recieve RETURN receive RETURN**

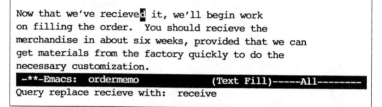

```
Now that we've recieve█ it, we'll begin work
on filling the order.  You should recieve the
merchandise in about six weeks, provided that we can
get materials from the factory quickly to do the
necessary customization.
-**-Emacs:  ordermemo                (Text Fill)-----All--------
Query replace recieve with:  receive
```

Ready to replace the first word; type a **SPACE** to go on.

Press: **SPACE**

```
Now that we've received it, we'll begin work
on filling the order.  You should recieve█the
merchandise in about six weeks, provided that we can
get materials from the factory quickly to do the
necessary customization.
-**-Emacs:  ordermemo                (Text Fill)-----All--------
Query replace recieve with:  receive
```

Pressing a **SPACE** replaces the first word; query-replace moves to the second.

And so on, until you reach the end of the file. As we've said, typing ! fixes the rest of the file.

In Table 3-3 of query-replace responses, you might have noticed that several keys, such as SPACE, have specialized meanings while the replacement is in progress. In practice, using these keys for a different function is not confusing, though it might sound bad on paper. You might want to try a query-replace on a practice file to get the hang of using different responses.

Recursive Editing

It's almost inevitable that when you do a query-replace, you see something else you want to change in the file. Try it a few times—you'll see what we mean! Your first reaction will be to remember your error until you're done; your second reaction will be anger and frustration when you've finished the replacement and realize that you've forgotten what was wrong.

Fortunately, Emacs provides an easier way. It allows you to start a "recursive edit" while you're in the middle of a query-replace. By starting a recursive edit, you effectively put query-replace on hold while you make any normal editing changes you want to. When you exit the recursive edit, the query-replace resumes from where you left off.

To start a recursive edit while in query-replace, press **C-r**. (Note that like many other keystrokes, **C-r** has a different meaning in query-replace than in standard Emacs.) When you start a recursive edit, square brackets ([ ]) appear on the mode line. Let's go back, one more time, to our order memo. You've used query-replace to find the first "recieve," and you are about to type a **SPACE** to fix it, when you notice that you left out the apostrophe in "we've." A quick recursive edit saves the day.

Type: **C-r**

```
Now that weve recieve█ it, we'll begin work
on filling the order.  You should receive the
merchandise in about six weeks, provided that we can
get materials from the factory quickly to do the
necessary customization.
-**-Emacs:  ordermemo          [(Text Fill)]------All--------
```

Entering a recursive edit.

Now do any editing you want to; you are in an editing mode just like standard Emacs. Move back a few characters and fix "we've." When you want to resume the query-replace, press **ESC-C-c**. This tells Emacs to leave the recursive edit and reactivate the query-replace. Emacs moves back to the point where you left off. You can then continue making replacements, just as if nothing had happened.

Type: **ESC-C-c**

```
Now that we've recieve█ it, we'll begin work
on filling the order.  You should receive the
merchandise in about six weeks, provided that we can
get materials from the factory quickly to do the
necessary customization.
-**-Emacs:  ordermemo              (Text Fill)-----All--------
Replace string recieve with:  receive
```

Done with the recursive edit; back to query-replace. Type a **SPACE** to fix "recieve."

If you decide to exit the recursive edit and cancel the query-replace in one fell swoop, you can type **C-]** (**abort-recursive-edit**) or **ESC-x top-level RETURN** rather than **ESC-C-c**.

More advanced users: Note that you can start a recursive edit at any time, not just when you're in a query-replace. The command **ESC-x recursive-edit RETURN** puts you into a recursive edit; **ESC-C-c** takes you out of the recursive edit and moves you back to what you were doing before. You can even have recursive edits within recursive edits, although the possibility for confusion increases with each new level.

Are Emacs Searches Case-sensitive?

By default, Emacs is set up to search regardless of case. If you search for the word "random," the search finds random, Random, and RANDOM, as well as oddities like RanDoM and rANdOM. When doing replacements, Emacs pays attention to the form of the word being replaced and replaces it with the same case. If you replaced random with tandem, Random would be replaced with Tandem, and RANDOM would be replaced with TANDEM.

Therefore, the default search and replacement operations usually do what you want: they find a search string regardless of its case, and adjust the replacement appropriately for its context. However, there are times when you need finer control. The variable **case-fold-search** determines whether or not searches are case insensitive. It applies to all searches: incremental searches, word searches, searches within search-and-replace operations, and so on. By default, **case-fold-search** is set to **t**, which means "ignore case." If you need case-specific searches, set **case-fold-search** to **nil** by giving the command **ESC-x set-variable RETURN**. Emacs prompts you for a variable name; type **case-fold-search RETURN**. Emacs then asks you for the new value; type **nil RETURN**.

Likewise, if you don't want Emacs to adjust the case of your replacement strings, you can set the variable **case-replace**. Again, its value is **true** by default, which means "adjust the case of a replacement string to match the original text"—i.e., capitalize the replacement if the original word was capitalized, and so on. Setting this variable to **nil** means "never adjust the case of the replacement string; always put it in exactly as you typed it." To change the value of **case-replace**, use the **set-variable** command we described above. We feel that turning case replacement "on" is very useful, particularly if you use case-insensitive searches; but you should spend some time experimenting with it, just so you're sure you understand what it does.

The **set-variable** command only changes the behavior of Emacs temporarily. If you start a new editing session, or even if you edit another file within the same Emacs session, you'll be back to the default behavior. This is probably what you want: it's very inconvenient to search separately for capitalized and non-capitalized words. However, you can set these variables permanently by adding the following lines to your *.emacs* file:

```
(setq-default case-fold-search nil)  ; require exact matches
(setq-default case-replace nil)      ; never modify case when replacing
```

To get these lines to take effect, save the *.emacs* file and restart Emacs.

Regular Expressions for Search and Replacement Operations

Sometimes none of the more simple searches described in this chapter are adequate. Regular expressions are a standard UNIX feature that has been incorporated into Emacs. Often used by programmers and UNIX hackers, regular expressions allow you to build searches with strings that contain various wildcards. While regular expressions in general are discussed in more detail in Chapter 11, *Emacs LISP Programming*, this section outlines the basics of using regular expression search, teaching you most of what you need to know to build and use regular expressions for searching. For even more information about regular expressions, see the Nutshell Handbook, *Sed and Awk*, by Dale Dougherty.

Table 3-4 shows some of the characters that you can use in creating a regular expression.

Table 3-4. Characters for Creating Regular Expressions

Character	Match
^	Matches the beginning of a line.
$	Matches the end of a line.
.	Matches any single character (like ? in filenames).
.*	Matches any group of zero or more characters (i.e., it's a "real" wildcard, like * in filenames).
\<	Matches the beginning of a word.
\>	Matches the end of a word.

If you do a regular expression search for `^word$`, you would find instances of "word" on a line by itself. The `^` says that the **w** must be the first character on the line, the `$` says that the **d** must be the last character.

If you wanted to find all words starting with **beg** and ending with the letter **s**, you would use `beg[a-z]*s` as your regular expression. This would find the words: begins, begets, and begonias, in addition to mutants like: shibegrees and altbegaslia. If you don't want these mutants—that is, if you really want words that begin with **beg** and end with **s**, use `\<beg[a-z]*s\>`. The `\<` is a special sequence that matches the beginning of a word; `\>` matches the end of a word. If you wanted to find the words: beg, big, and bag; but not begonias, and certainly not any strange words with **beg** on the inside, you would use `\<b[a-z]g\>` as the regular expression.

To search for a `^`, `$`, `.`, `*`, `[`, `]`, or any number of other special things, you obviously can't use the character itself. Put a backslash (\) first—i.e., to search for a period, search for \. For example, to search for the electronic mail address:

```
howie@mcds.com
```

the regular expression would be:

```
howie@mcds\.com
```

Regular expressions can be used in incremental searches and in query-replace. Table 3-5 lists the commands you use for regular expression searches. Except for initiating these searches with slightly different commands, the searches are the same as those described earlier in this chapter.

Table 3-5. Regular Expression Search Commands

Keystrokes	Action
ESC-x re-search-forward	Simple regular expression search forward.
ESC-x re-search-backward	Simple regular expression search forward.
ESC-x isearch-forward-regexp	Search incrementally forward for a regular expression.
ESC-x isearch-backward-regexp	Search incrementally backward for a regular expression.
ESC-x query-replace-regexp	Query-replace a regular expression.
ESC-x replace-regexp	Replace a regular expression uncondition-ally.[5]

Many of these complicated searches can be invoked with "short" keyboard sequences. We didn't bother to put these in Table 3-5 because they're incredibly awkward. The horrible key bindings are reasonable enough; these are advanced and specialized search techniques and shouldn't be bound to keyboard sequences that you're likely to type by accident. If you think you'll be using regular expression searches often, read Chapter 9 on customization and create your own key bindings for them.

Checking Spelling

Emacs has a built-in spelling checker that lets you check for spelling errors. You can check a word, a buffer, a region, or a string. Emacs looks up the words in an English dictionary supplied by UNIX.

The command **ESC-$** checks the word the cursor is on (or the word behind the cursor if you are betweeen words). It begins by printing the message "Checking spelling of *word*" in the minibuffer; this tells you that the search is going on, and that you shouldn't do any editing. If the word is spelled correctly, Emacs tells you so.[6] If Emacs doesn't think the word is spelled correctly, it displays the

---

[5] Unconditional search and replace of regular expressions is not for the faint of heart. Unless you have considerable experience with regular expressions, you may not be certain of all the combinations Emacs may find in the file and may get more replacements than you really want.

[6] "Correct" and "incorrect" really mean "in the dictionary" or "not in the dictionary." The UNIX spelling checker can account for a reasonable amount of grammatical variation—but it's far from perfect. It accepts some words that are incorrectly spelled, and rejects many correct (or alternate) spellings. A spell checking program is no substitute for real proofreading.

message: *"word is not recognized; edit a replacement: word."* If the word is correct but not in the dictionary (for example, a proper name), press **RETURN**. If a word is incorrect, use the standard Emacs editing commands to correct it. Emacs then starts a "query-replace" and shows you the word in context. You use query-replace responses in telling Emacs whether or not to replace the word—that is, type **SPACE** to correct the spelling, **C-g** to quit and do nothing, or **n** to do nothing and go on to the next occurrence of the misspelled word. See the section, "Using Query-replace," earlier in this chapter for a complete list of responses.

For example, here's how to correct our memo by using the spelling checker.

Type: **ESC $**

```
We were very anxious to rec█eve your order and were
pleased when it came in today.

Now that we've recieved it, we'll begin work
on filling the order.  You should recieve the
merchandise in about six weeks, provided that we can
get materials from the factory quickly to do the
necessary customization.
-**-Emacs:  ordermemo      (Text Fill)-----All-----------------
Checking spelling of recieve...
```

ESC $ invokes the spelling checker on the word "recieve."

The spelling checker tells you that "recieve" is incorrect:

```
We were very anxious to recieve your order and were
pleased when it came in today.

Now that we've recieved it, we'll begin work
on filling the order.  You should recieve the
merchandise in about six weeks, provided that we can
get materials from the factory quickly to do the
necessary customization.
-**-Emacs:  ordermemo      (Text Fill)-----All---------------
'recieve' not recognized; edit a replacement:  recieve█
```

Now correct the spelling of "recieve" in the minibuffer. When you're finished, type a **RETURN**, and the query-replace starts.

Correct spelling and press **RETURN**.

```
We were very anxious to recieve your order and were
pleased when it came in today.

Now that we've recieved it, we'll begin work
on filling the order.  You should recieve the
merchandise in about six weeks, provided that we can
get materials from the factory quickly to do the
necessary customization.
-**-Emacs:  ordermemo        (Text Fill)-----All---------------
Query replacing \recieve\ with receive:
```

Type **SPACE** to make the replacement and go on to the next misspelling of "receive."

Press: **SPACE**

```
We were very anxious to receive your order and were
pleased when it came in today.

Now that we've recieved it, we'll begin work
on filling the order.  You should recieve the
merchandise in about six weeks, provided that we can
get materials from the factory quickly to do the
necessary customization.
-**-Emacs:  ordermemo        (Text Fill)-----All---------------
Query replacing \recieve\ with receive:
```

And so on, until you've finished the entire buffer.

The spelling facility has two features that might confuse you:

- The **spell-word** command checks the entire buffer for misspellings of the
  word you give it. It starts at the beginning and works to the end. Therefore,
  when it begins the query-replace, it moves the cursor to first occurrence of
  your word (in this case, "recieve") in the buffer—not necessarily the word
  that you're on.

- The **spell-word** command *only* checks for misspellings of the word you give
  it. In our example, it fixes "recieve," but not "recieved." However, if you
  notice that "recieved" is misspelled, there's no reason you can't use a recursive edit to fix it.

Now on to some other spell check commands. To check a string, give the command **ESC-x spell-string RETURN**. Emacs then asks you for the string. Type the
word or words you want to check; Emacs tells you which (if any) are incorrect.

Type: **ESC-x spell-string RETURN**

```
-**-Emacs:   *scratch*       (Text Fill)-----All-----------------
Spell string: █
```

Emacs is ready for you to type a word or phrase.

Type: **In teh beginning RETURN**

```
█


-**-Emacs:   *scratch*       (Text Fill)-----All-----------------
teh incorrect
```

Emacs tells you that "teh" is incorrect.

To check the spelling of an entire buffer, give the command **ESC-x spell-buffer RETURN**. Emacs then starts searching for incorrect words at the beginning of the buffer. Whenever it finds an incorrect word, it prints the message "*word* is not recognized; edit a replacement: *word*." If the word is really spelled correctly, type **RETURN** (just as you would with **ESC-$**), and Emacs goes on to the next misspelled word. If the word is incorrect, use standard editing commands to fix it. Emacs then enters a query-replace (as with **ESC-$**), giving you an opportunity to fix the word whenever it appears in the buffer. When the query-replace is finished, Emacs continues with the next misspelled word.

You can also check the spelling of a selected region of text. Put a mark at one end of the region; then move the cursor to the other end; and finally, give the command **ESC-x spell-region RETURN**. The behavior of **spell-region** is identical to **spell-buffer**.

NOTE

If you confirm the spelling of a word (by pressing **RETURN**), Emacs won't ask you about it again during this session. However, this "memory" only applies to **spell-buffer** and **spell-region**; it does not apply to **ESC-$**.

Some versions of Emacs allow you to save any "special" spellings (for example, personal names) in a *.spell* file.[7] To take advantage of this, you change the value of the variable **spell-command**, which gives the UNIX command that Emacs uses

---

[7] For the purists: Version 18.55 and following (released August, 1989). If you don't have this version, ask your system administrator to get it for you.

to check spelling. By default, the value of this variable is **spell**. Change the value of **spell-command** to `spell +.spell`. You can make this change by using the **set-variable** command (a temporary change, for experimentation), or by adding the line:

```
(setq spell-command "spell +.spell")
```

Then put your personal spellings into a file called *.spell*. This file must be sorted alphabetically, and may contain only one word per line. Note that this command requires a different *.spell* file in every directory. That's appropriate for most applications: each project you work on may have a separate list of "private" spellings (names, technical words, and so on).

Table 3-6 summarizes the commands for checking spelling.

Table 3-6. Spell Checking Commands

Keystrokes	Command Name	Action
ESC-$	spell-word	Checks spelling of the word the cursor is on or in front of.
(none)	spell-string	Checks spelling of the string you type in minibuffer.
(none)	spell-buffer	Checks spelling of the current buffer.
(none)	spell-region	Checks spelling of the current region.

Word Abbreviation Mode

Word abbreviation mode lets you define abbreviations for special words and phrases. There are many ways to use it. Traditionally, abbreviation mode is used so that you don't have to type long words or phrases in their entirety. For example, let's say you are writing a contract which repeatedly references the National Institute of Standards and Technology and you are not allowed to use an acronym. Rather than typing the full name, you can define the abbreviation "nist." Once you have made this definition, Emacs inserts the full name whenever you type the abbreviation "nist," followed by a space or punctuation mark. Emacs watches for you to type an abbreviation, then expands it automatically as soon as you press **SPACE** or a punctuation mark (such as any of these: . , ! ? ; :).

Before showing you how to get into word abbreviation mode and define your abbreviation list, we'll start with an example. Our favorite nontraditional use for word abbreviation mode is to correct misspellings as you type.[8] Almost everyone has a dozen or so words that they habitually type incorrectly, due to some worn neural pathways. You can simply tell Emacs that these misspellings are "abbreviations" for the correct versions, and Emacs fixes the misspellings every time you type them; you may not even notice that you typed the word wrong before Emacs fixes it. So assume that you've entered abbreviation mode, and that you've defined "receive" as an abbreviation for "recieve." Now, as you're typing, you make an innocent mistake.

Type: **You will recieve**

```
You will recieve█



-**-Emacs:  letterb        (Text Abbrev Fill) ---(All)-------
```

You type the offending word but haven't yet pressed **SPACE**, which cues Emacs to correct it.

Type: **SPACEthe materials you requested shortly.**

```
You will receive the materials you requested shortly.█



-**-Emacs:  letterb        (Text Abbrev Fill) ---(All)-------
```

Emacs corrects the word automatically after you press **SPACE**; you need not stop typing or even be aware that a mistake has been made and corrected.

Besides the convenience of being able to invent abbreviations for phrases that you frequently type, you can see that setting up a short list of abbreviations for common misspellings could reduce the time that it takes to proofread files and reduce the number of common typing errors.

When you define abbreviations, never use abbreviations that are words in their own right, or Emacs expands the word when you don't want it to, since expansion takes place without asking. For example, if you frequently write about the World Association for Replicant Technology, don't define an abbreviation of "wart" or

---

[8] Some versions of Emacs, such as CCA Emacs, come with abbreviations predefined for common typos, such as "teh" and "adn" for "the" and "and."

you won't be able to write about the difficulties of handling toads. (If you use the word "wart" so infrequently that you think the convenience of the acronym warrants it, you can use **ESC-x unexpand-abbrev RETURN** to have Emacs undo the abbreviation when you really want to type "wart.")

You also have to realize that Emacs only knows the abbreviations exactly as you define them. If you define "recieve" as an abbreviation for "receive," you must also define "recieves", "recieving", and "recieved" as abbreviations to cover all the forms of the word you might misspell.

Before you go ahead and define some abbreviations, there's one more basic fact you should know. Emacs classifies abbreviations as either "local" or "global," and you use different commands depending on whether you want global or local abbreviations. A global abbreviation works all the time, regardless of the major mode that you are in. A local abbreviation only works when you're in the current major mode. (See Chapter 1, *Emacs Basics*, for a discussion of modes.) For example, if you want abbreviations to work only in text mode and not in C mode, define them as *local* while you are in text mode. If you want abbreviations to work in any mode, you define them as *global*. Remember: abbreviations are local to modes, not to files or buffers.

Trying Word Abbreviations for One Session

Usually, if you go to the trouble of defining a word abbreviation, you will use it in more than one Emacs session. But if you'd like to try out abbreviation mode to see if you want to make it part of your startup, you can use the following procedure.

To define word abbreviations for this session:

1. Enter word abbreviation mode by typing **ESC-x abbrev-mode RETURN**. "Abbrev" appears on the mode line.

2. For a global abbreviation, type the abbreviation you want to use and type **C-x -**. (For a local abbreviation, type **C-x C-h** instead.) Emacs then asks you for the expansion.

3. Type the definition for the abbreviation and press **RETURN**. Emacs then expands the abbreviation and will do so each time you type it followed by a space or punctuation mark. The abbreviations you've defined will work only during this Emacs session.

If you find that you like using word abbreviation mode, you may want to make it part of your startup, as described in the following section.

Making Word Abbreviations Part of Your Startup

Once you become hooked on using abbreviation mode, it's easiest to make it part of your *.emacs* file so that you don't have to remember to follow the steps listed above every time. This procedure also creates a permanent file of your word abbreviations which is loaded every time you start Emacs. You can later delete some abbreviations from this file, as we'll talk about later in this chapter.

To define word abbreviations and make them part of your startup:

1. Add these lines to your *.emacs* file:

    ```
    (setq-default abbrev-mode t)
    (read-abbrev-file "~/.abbrev_defs")
    (setq save-abbrevs t)
    ```

2. Save the *.emacs* file and re-enter Emacs. "Abbrev" appears on the mode line.

3. Type an abbreviation you want to use and type **C-x -** following the abbreviation. **C-x -** creates a global abbreviation; if you want to create a local abbreviation instead, type **C-x C-h**. Emacs asks you for the expansion.

4. Type the definition for the abbreviation and press **RETURN**. Emacs expands the abbreviation and will do so each time you type it followed by a space or punctuation mark. You can define as many abbreviations as you want to by repeating steps 3 and 4.

5. Give the command **ESC-x write-abbrev-file RETURN** to write your abbreviation file. Emacs asks for the filename.

6. Type ~**/.abbrev_defs RETURN**. Emacs then writes the file.

You need only take steps 5 and 6 the first time you define abbreviations using this procedure. After this file exists, the lines in your *.emacs* file load the abbreviations file automatically.

When you define word abbreviations in subsequent sessions, Emacs asks whether you want to save the abbreviations file. Respond with a **y** to save the new abbreviations you've defined and have them take effect automatically.

Deleting a Word Abbreviation

If you use word abbreviations frequently, you may define an abbreviation and later change your mind. You can edit the word abbreviation list by typing **ESC-x edit-abbrevs RETURN**. You can see (but not edit) the list by typing **ESC-x list-abbrevs RETURN**.

Once the list is displayed, use **C-k** (or any other editing commands) to delete the abbreviations you don't want to use. Because Emacs itself formats this list, don't try to edit lines or add new lines; deleting is about the only operation that's safe. Here's how the abbreviations look when you edit word abbreviations. The file is divided into different sections based on whether the abbreviations are global or local to a particular mode:

"iwthout"	1	"without"
"prhase"	1	"phrase"
"teh"	1	"the"
"fo"	1	"of"
"eamcs"	2	"Emacs"
"wrok"	1	"work"
"aslo"	1	"also"
"sotred"	1	"stored"
"inforamtion"	1	"information"
"esc"	6	"ESC"
"taht"	1	"that"
"chatper"	1	"chapter"
"adn"	1	"and"
"iwth"	1	"with"
"chpater"	1	"chapter"
"tex"	36	"TeX"
"loaction"	1	"location"

The first column is the abbreviation; in this case, the abbreviations are actually misspellings. The second column is part of Emacs' internal record-keeping; you don't care about it. The third column is the *value* of the abbreviation, the *word* that Emacs substitutes whenever it sees the abbreviation.

To delete any abbreviation, use your normal editing commands to move to the line on which it is described. Then kill the entire line with **C-k** and save the file by typing **C-x C-s** (for **save-buffer**). You can move back to the buffer you were editing before by typing **C-x b**. (This is a command for working with multiple buffers, discussed in Chapter 4, *Using Buffers and Windows*.)

Disabling Word Abbreviations

You can get rid of word abbreviations completely in one of two ways. First, you can type **ESC-x kill-all-abbrevs RETURN**. This disables word abbreviations for the current session.

Second, you can delete the file the abbreviations are in. If you made word abbreviations part of your startup, delete the **read-abbrev-file** line out of your *.emacs* file.

Abbreviations and Capitalization

Usually, you'll find that the way Emacs capitalizes abbreviations is exactly what you want it to do. If you run into special situations with abbreviations and capitalization, however, it's helpful to know what's going on behind the scenes. Here are the rules:

- If the abbreviation's definition contains any uppercase letters, Emacs always inserts the definition without changing anything. For example, if you define "ora" to be an abbreviation for "O'Reilly and Associates," then "O'Reilly and Associates" will always be capitalized exactly as given.

- If the abbreviation's definition is all lowercase, Emacs capitalizes according to the following rules:
  - If you type all of the letters of the abbreviation in lowercase, Emacs inserts the definition in lowercase.
  - If you type any of the letters of the abbreviation in uppercase, Emacs capitalizes first letter of the first word.
  - If you type all of the letters of the abbreviation in uppercase, Emacs capitalizes the first letter of every word, unless the variable **abbrev-all-caps** is set; in this case, it capitalizes all letters.

Here are some examples:

Abbrev	Definition	You Type	Expands To	Because
lc	lamb chop	lc	lamb chop	"lc" lowercase, so "lamb chop" lowercase.
lc	lamb chop	Lc	Lamb chop	One capital in "Lc," so "Lamb" capitalized.
lc	lamb chop	lC	Lamb chop	One capital in "Lc," so "Lamb" capitalized.
lc	lamb chop	LC	Lamb Chop	All capitals in "LC," so both words capitalized.
lc	Lamb Chop	lc	Lamb Chop	Capitals in definition are always unchanged.
lc	Lamb Chop	LC	Lamb Chop	Capitals in definition are always unchanged.

As we said, the rules are a lot to memorize. Fortunately, you don't need to remember the rules. Emacs will usually capitalize properly on its own. And with a little experimentation, you'll become comfortable with Emacs' behavior.

Now that we're finished with abbreviation mode, Table 3-7 provides a quick summary of its commands.

Table 3-7. Word Abbreviation Commands

Keystrokes	Command Name	Action
(none)	abbrev-mode	Enter (or exit) word abbreviation mode.
C-x -	inverse-add-global-abbrev	After typing the global abbreviation, type the definition.
C-x C-h	inverse-add-local-abbrev	After typing the local abbreviation, type the definition.
(none)	unexpand-abbrev	Undo the last word abbreviation.
(none)	write-abbrev-file	Write the word abbreviation file.
(none)	edit-abbrevs	Edit the word abbreviations.
(none)	list-abbrevs	View the word abbreviations.
(none)	kill-all-abbrevs	Kill abbreviations for this session.

4

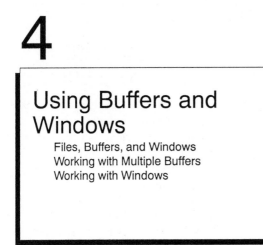

Using Buffers and Windows

Files, Buffers, and Windows
Working with Multiple Buffers
Working with Windows

One of the most universally useful features of Emacs is the ability to edit multiple buffers at once and to display more than one buffer on the same screen using windows. The commands for doing this are simple; you learn only a few commands and yet experience a tremendous boost in productivity. The more you use multiple buffers and windows, the more uses you'll think of for them.

Files, Buffers, and Windows

All the editing you do in Emacs occurs in *buffers*. A buffer is usually a working copy of a file, although they have many other uses. When you are editing a buffer that contains a copy of a file and you save your changes, Emacs takes the contents of the buffer and copies it into the file. In practice, this means that you can cavalierly change a buffer and then not save the changes. On the other hand, you can save your changes from buffer to file as many times as you want to in a given session, a good practice if you are making changes you intend to keep.

In addition to buffers that are working copies of files, you can have buffers that are work areas with no relationship to files. This is especially good for practice or scratchpad usage. At any time, you can save your practice buffers to a file using the **write-file** command, **C-x C-w**, or the **save-buffer** command, **C-x C-s**. (If you try to save a practice buffer that isn't associated with a file, **C-x C-s** first asks you for a filename by displaying the prompt "File to save in:", followed by a default directory, in the minibuffer.)

There's really no limit to the number of buffers you can have. Most of the time, only one or two buffers will be displayed—but even if you can't see them, all the buffers you create in an Emacs session are still active. You can think of them as a stack of pages, with the one being displayed as the top page. At any time, you can turn to another page, another buffer. Or create a new page.

You can create buffers and so can Emacs itself. The names for buffers that Emacs creates generally have the format `*buffer name*`. `*Help*`, `*Mail*`, and `*Buffer List*` are just a few of the buffers that Emacs creates. Chapter 5, *Emacs as a Work Environment*, describes how you would use some of the Emacs buffers like `*Mail*` and `*Dired*`.

Each buffer has a major mode attached to it. This determines much about how Emacs behaves in that buffer. For example, text mode, designed for writing English text, behaves differently from LISP mode, which is designed for writing LISP code.

Now, what about windows? A window is just an area on the screen in which a buffer is displayed. Each window has a mode line associated with it. Within reason, you can have as many different windows on the screen as you want. This lets you edit several files at the same time (by "bouncing" from one window to another), compare files, copy from one file to another, and do all sorts of useful things.

It is very easy to confuse windows and buffers, but the difference between the two is really very simple. As we've said, a buffer is Emacs' working copy of a file. A window is a display on your terminal. You can have several windows on the screen displaying the same buffer—for example, you might want to look at two different parts of one file, or copy something from one part to another. More often, you have several windows representing different files on the screen, or one window that displays a file and another that displays one of Emacs' working buffers—a topic we'll begin to explore later in this chapter.

As you work through this chapter, the distinction between files, buffers, and windows will become more intuitive. We'll start by discussing how to work with different buffers. When we're through with buffers, we'll discuss how to put several windows on your screen and work with them simultaneously. Finally, we'll discuss some shortcuts for displaying buffers in windows.

Working with Multiple Buffers

You already know how to get into Emacs by typing **emacs** *filename*. If you want to create a second buffer that contains a file, simply type **C-x C-f** to find the file. Emacs automatically creates a second buffer and moves you there. If you already have a copy of the file in a buffer, **C-x C-f** just moves you to the existing buffer. This is very sensible and probably really what you want anyhow; if **C-x C-f** read the file from disk every time, you could end up with many versions of the same file that were each slightly different. If the filename you give **C-x C-f** doesn't exist, Emacs assumes you want to create a new file by that name and moves you to a blank buffer.

C-x C-f is always followed by a filename. The command for moving between buffers, **C-x b**, is followed by a buffer name. Did you realize that the mode line doesn't display filenames but only buffer names? Some versions of Emacs show both, but GNU shows only the buffer name. The buffer name and the filename, if any, are the same unless you change them (see the section, "Renaming Buffers," later in this chapter).

You can do the following with **C-x b**:

If you type C-x b followed by	Emacs
A new buffer name	Creates a new buffer that isn't connected with a file and moves there.
The name of an existing buffer	Moves you to the buffer (it doesn't matter whether the buffer is connected with a file or not).

To move between the buffers, type **C-x b**. Emacs shows you a default buffer name. Press **RETURN** if that's the buffer you want, or type the first few characters of the correct buffer name and press **TAB**. Emacs fills in the rest of the name. Now press **RETURN** to move to the buffer.

If you want to create a second (or third or fourth, etc.) buffer that is empty, type **C-x b**. Emacs asks for a buffer name. You can use any name, for example, `practice`, and press **RETURN**. Emacs creates the buffer and moves you there. For example, assume you've been working on your tried-and-true Dickens buffer. But you'd like something new, so you start a new buffer to play with some prose from James Joyce.

Initial state; you're editing `dickens`.

Type: **C-x b**

```
It was the best of times, it was the worst of times, it
was the age of wisdom, it was the age of foolishness,
it was the epoch of belief, it was the epoch
of incredulity, it was the season of Light, it was
the season of Darkness, it was the spring of hope, it
was the winter of despair, we had everything before us,
we had nothing before us, we were all going direct to
Heaven, we were all going direct the other way--in short,
the period was so far like the present period, that some
of its noisiest authorities insisted on its being
received, for good or for evil, in the superlative
degree of comparison only.



-----Emacs:  dickens          (Fundamental)--All-------------
Switch to buffer:  (default *scratch*) ▐
```

Ready to type a new buffer name.

Type: **joyce RETURN**

```
▐




-----Emacs:  joyce            (Fundamental)--All-------------
```

Now you have a new buffer named `joyce` to type in.

This isn't all that different from using **C-x C-f** (**find-file**); about the only differ-ence is that the new buffer, `joyce`, isn't yet associated with a file. Therefore, if you quit Emacs, the editor won't ask you whether or not you want to save it.

C-x b is especially useful if you don't know the name of the file you are working with. Assume you're working with some obscure file with a weird name like */tmp/80b16.12344*.[1] Now assume that you accidentally do something that makes this buffer disappear from your screen (you don't know what this might be yet, but we'll introduce these commands later in the chapter). How do you get */tmp/80b16.12344* back onto the screen? Do you need to remember the entire name, or even a part of it? No—before doing anything else, just type **C-x b**. The

---

[1] This isn't as weird as it sounds. Many programs create temporary files with names like this. Just imagine you're debugging one of these programs.

"default" buffer is the buffer that most recently disappeared; type **RETURN** and you'll see it again.

Saving Multiple Buffers

You know about saving buffers individually by typing **C-x C-s**. Once you're using multiple buffers, you should also know that you can save them all at once by typing **C-x s** (**save-some-buffers**). Emacs asks you if you want to save each buffer, and you type **y** or **n** as it displays each buffer name.

Deleting Buffers

It's easy to create buffers, and just as easy to delete them when you want to. You may want to delete buffers if you feel your Emacs session is getting cluttered with too many buffers. Perhaps you started out working on a set of five buffers and now want to do something with another five. Getting rid of the first set of buffers makes it a bit easier to keep things straight. Deleting a buffer can also be a useful "emergency escape." For example, some replacement operation may have had disastrous results. You can delete the buffer and choose not to save the changes, then read the file again.

Deleting a buffer doesn't delete the underlying file. Nor is it the same as not displaying a buffer; buffers that are not displayed are still active whereas deleted buffers are no longer part of your Emacs session. Using the analogy of a stack of pages, deleting a buffer is like taking a page out of the current "stack" of buffers you are editing and filing it away.

Deleting buffers doesn't put you at risk of losing changes, either. If you've changed the buffer (and if the buffer represents a file), Emacs asks if you want to save your changes before the buffer is deleted. You will lose changes to any scratch buffers, because they aren't connected to files. But you probably don't care about these.

To delete the buffer you're currently editing, type **C-x k**. Emacs shows the name of the buffer currently displayed; press **RETURN** to delete it or type another buffer name if the one being displayed is not the one you want to delete, then press **RETURN**. If you've made changes that you haven't yet saved, Emacs displays a message that says "Buffer *buffer name* modified. Kill anyway? (yes or no)." To ditch your changes, type **yes** and Emacs kills the buffer. To stop the buffer deletion process and save your changes, type **no**. You can then type **C-x C-s** to save the buffer, followed by **C-x k** to kill it.

You can also have Emacs ask you about deleting each buffer and you can decide whether to kill each one individually. Type **ESC-x kill-some-buffers** to weed out unneeded buffers this way. Emacs opens another window, then displays each buffer as it asks whether you want to kill it. (It also tells you whether you've changed the buffer and gives you an opportunity to go back and save your changes.) Unfortunately, Emacs leaves this window on the screen when it's done killing buffers. To get rid of the extra window, type **C-x 1**. (This window command and others are described later in this chapter.)

Renaming Buffers

If you are editing a file, buffers always take on the name of the file. If you have long filenames, you may find it convenient to rename buffers to shorter names (this doesn't affect the filename, just the buffer name). This feature is mostly useful on versions of Emacs that don't offer good completion capabilities; in GNU, whenever you have to type a buffer name, you just type the first few unique letters and press **TAB** to have Emacs complete the name for you. Still, there are times when you may want to rename buffers.

To rename a buffer type **ESC-x rename-buffer**. Emacs asks for the new name; type it and press **RETURN**. The new name is displayed on the mode line.

As mentioned earlier, in GNU Emacs, only the buffer name is displayed on the mode line, rather than the buffer name and the filename. Even if you rename a buffer that contains a file, Emacs remembers the connection between buffer and file, which you can see if you save the file (**C-x C-s**) or display the buffer list (described next).

What if you have two buffers with the same name? Let's say you are editing a file called *memo* from your home directory and another file called *memo* from one of your subdirectories. Both buffers are called **memo**, but Emacs differentiates them by appending **<2>** to the name of the second buffer. Here's a case where renaming buffers can be useful. If you want to remember which file comes from which directory, you might rename the buffers with names that include their directories, such as **home:memo** and **staff:memo**.

One word of advice: If you have a lot of buffers with names like **memo**, **memo<2>**, and **memo<3>** around, you're probably forgetting to edit the directory when you ask for a file. If you try to find a file but get the directory wrong, Emacs assumes that you want to start a new file. For example, let's say that you want to edit the file `~/work/memo`, but instead you ask for the file `~/novel/memo`. Since `~/work/memo` doesn't exist, Emacs creates a new, empty buffer named **memo**. If you correct your mistake (**C-x C-f `~/work/memo`**), Emacs renames your buffers accordingly: your empty buffer **memo** is associated with the `~/novel/memo`; the buffer you want is named **memo<2>**.

Here's a hint for dealing with the very common mistake of finding the wrong file. If you notice that you've found the wrong file with **C-x C-f**, use **C-x C-v** to replace it with the one you want. **C-x C-v** finds a file, but instead of making a new buffer, it replaces the file in the current buffer. It means "get me the file I really meant to find instead of this one." Using this command circumvents the problem of having unnecessary numbered buffers (i.e., memo, memo<2>, and so on) lying around.

Read-only Buffers

While you're working, you may need to read some file that you don't want to change: you just want to browse through it and look at its contents. Of course, it is very easy to touch the keyboard accidentally and make spurious modifications. We've discussed several ways to restore the original file, but it would be better to prevent this from happening at all. How?

You can make any buffer read-only by pressing **C-x C-q**. Try this on a practice buffer and you'll notice that the two asterisks that normally appear on the left side of the mode line beside the word Emacs change to percent signs (%). The percent signs indicate that the buffer is read-only. If you try to type in a read-only buffer, Emacs just beeps at you and puts an error message ("Buffer is read-only") in the minibuffer. Now, what happens when you change your mind and want to start editing the read-only buffer again? Just type **C-x C-q** again. This command "toggles" the buffer's read-only status: that is, typing **C-x C-q** repeatedly makes the buffer alternate between read-only and read-write.

Of course, toggling read-only status doesn't change the permissions on a UNIX file. If you are editing a buffer containing someone else's file, **C-x C-q** does not change the read-only status. The only way to edit someone else's file is to write it (essentially making a copy of your own) using the **write-file** command, then make changes. Let's say you want to change the phone list document, owned by someone else. Read the file, write the file as one you own using **C-x C-w**, then change it from read-only to writable status by pressing **C-x C-q**. None of this, of course, modifies the original phone list; it just gives you a copy you can muck around with.

Getting a List of Buffers

With the ability to create an unlimited number of buffers in an Emacs session, it's possible to have so many buffers going that you can't remember all of them. At any point, you can get a list of your buffers. This list tells you important things like whether you've changed the buffer since you last saved it.

If you press **C-x C-b**, Emacs lists your buffers. It creates a new window on the screen (more about windows later) with the name `*Buffer List*` on the mode line. This shows you all the buffers.

Type: **C-x C-b**

```
It was the best of times, it was the worst of times, it
was the age of wisdom, it was the age of foolishness,
it was the epoch of belief, it was the epoch
of incredulity, it was the season of Light, it was
the season of Darkness, it was the spring of hope, it


-----Emacs:  dickens              (Fundamental)--Top------------

MR Buffer          Size  Mode              File
-- ------          ----  ----              ----
.*  dickens        2904  Text              /us/deb/dickens
 *  *Buffer List*  0     Buffer Menu
*%  RMAIL          92228 RMAIL             /home/deb/RMAIL
    outline        4211  Text              /us/deb/outline
    *scratch*      0     LISP Interaction
    *mail*         316   Mail

-%%-Emacs:  *Buffer List*      (Buffer Menu)----All----------
```

Emacs displays a list of buffers.

This screen always lists at least two buffers you didn't overtly create. The `*Buffer List*` is created when you press **C-x C-b** to ask for a list; the `*scratch*` buffer is a blank buffer created by Emacs in every session. You can use this list as an informational display ("these are my buffers") or you can actually work with buffers from this list, as covered in the next section.

Figure 4-1 shows what each of the symbols in the buffer list means.

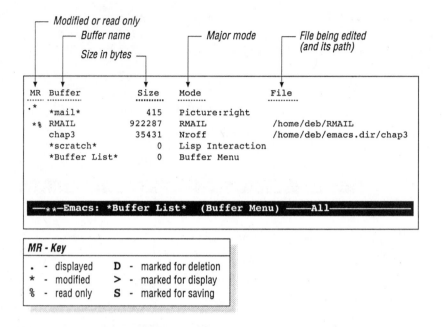

Figure 4-1. Understanding the Buffer List

Working with the Buffer List

The buffer list is more than a display. From the buffer list, you can display, delete, and save buffers.

To move to the buffer list window, type **C-x o** (this is one of the window commands we'll talk about later in this chapter). Emacs puts the cursor in the first column. To move to the line for a particular buffer, press **C-n** to move down a line or **C-p** to move up a line. You can also press **SPACE** to move down to the next line. In this situation (and in similar situations, like directory editing, which we'll discuss in Chapter 5), **SPACE** and **C-n** are equivalent.

You use a set of one-character commands to work with the buffers that are listed. To delete a buffer, go to the line for the buffer you want to delete and type **d** or **k**. **D** appears in the first column. You can mark as many buffers for deletion as you want to. The buffers aren't deleted immediately; when you're finished deciding what you want to delete, press **x** (which stands for "eXecute") to delete them. If any of the buffers you want to delete are connected with files, Emacs asks if you want to save the changes before doing anything. (Note that it does not ask you about practice buffers that aren't connected with files, so be sure to save any that you want before deleting them.)

If you change your mind about deleting a buffer before typing **x**, you can "unmark" the buffer by going to the appropriate line and typing **u**. As a convenience, the DEL key also unmarks the previous buffer in the list. Why would you do this? Simple; **d** automatically moves you down one line. If you mark a file for deletion and immediately change your mind, you can type a single DEL rather than typing **C-p u** (move to the previous line, followed by "unmark").

To save a buffer, go to the line for the buffer you want to save and press **s**. The letter S appears in the first column. Press **x** when you really want to save the buffer. Therefore, you can look at the buffer list, choose which buffers you want to delete and which you want to save, and then type **x** to do everything at once. Again, you can use the **u** and DEL keys to "cancel" saves if you change your mind.

One command that affects a buffer immediately when you type it is tilde (~). Typing ~ marks a buffer as unmodified. In effect, this tells Emacs not to save changes automatically (since the buffer is "unmodified," there is no reason for Emacs to save changes). Of course, if you have made changes, the changes are still in the buffer; it's just that you're in essence "lying" to Emacs to say that no changes have been made. Also, if you change the buffer again after marking it unmodified, Emacs once again knows it has been modified and saves it automatically in a backup file, which (not coincidentally) has the format *filename~*.

There are quite a few commands that deal with displaying buffers from the buffer list and since many of them have to do with windows, we'll discuss them at the end of this chapter.

To get rid of the `*Buffer List*` window, type **C-x 0** if you are in the buffer list window or **C-x 1** (the number one, not the letter L) if you are in the window for one of your buffers. These window commands are described in the next section.

Table 4-1 shows a summary of buffer manipulation commands.

Table 4-1. Buffer Manipulation Commands

Keystrokes	Command Name	Action
C-x b	switch-to-buffer	Moves to the buffer specified.
C-x C-b	list-buffers	Displays the buffer list.
C-x k	kill-buffer	Deletes the buffer specified.
(none)	kill-some-buffers	Asks about deleting each buffer.

Table 4-1. Buffer Manipulation Commands (continued)

Keystrokes	Command Name	Action
(none)	rename-buffer	Changes the buffer's name to the name specified.
C-x s	save-some-buffers	Asks whether you want to save each modified buffer.

Table 4-2 summarizes the commands for working with the buffer list.

Table 4-2. Buffer List Commands

Keystrokes	Action	Occurs
C-n	Move to the next buffer in the list (i.e., down one line).	Immediately.
C-p	Move to the previous buffer in the list (i.e., up one line).	Immediately.
SPACE	Move to the next buffer in the list.	Immediately
d	Marks buffer for deletion.	When you press x.
k	Marks buffer for deletion.	When you press x.
s	Saves buffer.	When you press x.
u	Unmarks buffer.	Immediately.
x	Executes other one-letter commands on all marked buffers.	Immediately.
DEL	Unmarks the previous buffer in the list.	Immediately.
~	Marks buffer as unmodified.	Immediately.
C-x C-q	Toggles read-only status of buffer.	Immediately.
1	Displays buffer in a full screen.	Immediately.
2	Displays this buffer and the next one in horizontal windows.	Immediately.
f	Replaces buffer list with this buffer.	Immediately.
o	Replaces other window with this buffer.	Immediately.
m	Marks buffers to be displayed in windows.	When you press q.
q	Displays buffers marked with m; Emacs makes as many windows as needed.	Immediately.

Working with Windows

Until the introduction of X Windows, many people happily used Emacs as their sole windowing system. Now Emacs and X have been integrated (see Chapter 12 for more information on running Emacs under X Windows), but in spite of this many people still use Emacs' windowing capabilities alone, even on X terminals. If you have a plain ASCII terminal, or even if you don't, you should know about Emacs' windowing capabilities. Especially after you learn about all the things you can do in Emacs in Chapter 5—such as issuing shell commands and reading mail—you may find that having multiple windows on your screen gives you much of the functionality of X Windows, if not the beauty of one of the graphic user interfaces layered on top of X Windows.

Earlier, we said that windows are areas on the screen in which Emacs displays the buffers that you are editing. You can have many windows on the screen at one time, each displaying a different buffer. Granted, the more windows you have, the smaller each one is; unlike X Windows, Emacs windows can't "overlap," so as you add more windows, the older ones tend to shrink. You can place windows either side-by-side or horizontally, and you can mix side-by-side and horizontal windows almost arbitrarily. Each window has its own mode line that identifies the buffer name, the modes you're running, and your position in the buffer. To make it clear where one window begins and another ends, mode lines are usually in reverse video (provided that your terminal allows it).

As we've said, windows are not buffers. In fact, you can have more than one window on the same buffer. For example, it's often helpful to do this if you want to look at different parts of a large file simultaneously. You can even have the same part of the buffer displayed in two windows, and any change you make in one window is reflected in the other. (The entertainment value of this is probably greater than its practical value, however, and it certainly won't give you good feelings about your system's response time.)

The difference between buffers and windows becomes important when you think about marking, cutting, and pasting text. Marks are associated with buffers, not with windows, and each buffer can have only one mark. If you go to another window on the same buffer and set the mark, Emacs just remembers the place you set it last.

As for cursors, you can have only one cursor on the screen at a time, so you are really in just one window at a time. However, although there is only one cursor at a time, each window does keep track of your current editing location separately. That is, you can move the cursor from one window to another, do some editing, jump back to the first window, and be in the same place. A window's notion of your current position (whether or not the cursor is in the window) is called the *point*. Each window has its own point. It's easy to use the terms "point" and "cursor" interchangeably —but we'll try to be specific.

The distinction between buffers and windows may sound confusing, but in practice it's very intuitive; we've been using multiple windows on the same buffer for years without giving these niceties a second thought.

Creating Horizontal Windows

To create two windows (one on top of another), type **C-x 2**. If you are already in a window, typing **C-x 2** splits the current window into two more horizontal windows.

Initial state:

```
It was the best of times, it was the worst of times, it
was the age of wisdom, it was the age of foolishness,
it was the epoch of belief, it was the epoch
of incredulity, it was the season of Light, it was
the season of Darkness, it was the spring of hope, it
was the winter of despair, we had everything before us,
we had nothing before us, we were all going direct to
Heaven, we were all going direct the other way--in short,
the period was so far like the present period, that some
of its noisiest authorities insisted on its being
received, for good or for evil, in the superlative
degree of comparison only.

-----Emacs:  dickens           (Fundamental)--All-------------
```

Before splitting the window.

Type: **C-x 2**

```
It was the best of times, it was the worst of times, it
was the age of wisdom, it was the age of foolishness,
it was the epoch of belief, it was the epoch
of incredulity, it was the season of Light, it was
the season of Darkness, it was the spring of hope, it
-----Emacs:  dickens              (Fundamental)--Top-----------
It was the best of times, it was the worst of times, it
was the age of wisdom, it was the age of foolishness,
it was the epoch of belief, it was the epoch
of incredulity, it was the season of Light, it was
the season of Darkness, it was the spring of hope, it
-----Emacs:  dickens              (Fundamental)--Top-----------
```

The screen is divided into two horizontal windows; the mode line demarcates each window.

Creating Vertical or Side-by-side Windows

It's also possible to split the screen vertically into two windows that are side-by-side: to split the screen vertically into two windows, type **C-x 5**. If you are already in a window, Emacs splits the current window into two side-by-side windows.

Type: **C-x 5**

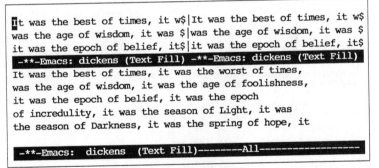

Dividing a window into two vertical windows.

Since vertical windows don't usually show full lines of text (a dollar sign ($) at the end of a line tells you the line is continued), you need to know how to scroll text to the left and right.

To push the text currently being displayed to the left (so you can see what's on the right), type **C-x <**. To push the text being displayed to the right (so you can see what's on the left), type **C-x >**. You can use these commands whenever one of your lines is too wide for your screen, which can happen with or without windows (especially if you have fill mode turned off).

Most terminals are fairly narrow. 80 characters is standard, although you'll occasionally see 128- or 132-character terminals. If you insist on a tolerably large "screen font," most graphics workstations can't do too much better. Consequently, when you split windows vertically, Emacs usually doesn't have enough room to display a full line of text across the screen. And it is a real pain to be scrolling left and right; it's much harder to get used to than scrolling up and down. Therefore, most Emacs users limit themselves to "horizontal" windows (i.e., windows stacked one on top of the other). But vertical windows do have their place, and you should know how to use them.

Moving Between Windows

To move from one window to another, type **C-x o** (o stands for "other" in this command). Emacs moves from one window to another, as shown in Figure 4-2. If you have more than two windows displayed, Emacs moves to the next window clockwise. There's no way to specify which window to move to, so you may have to press this a few times to get to the one you want if you have more than two windows displayed. Alternately, using **ESC-*n* C-x o** (where *n* is a number) will move you forward *n* windows, in clockwise order.

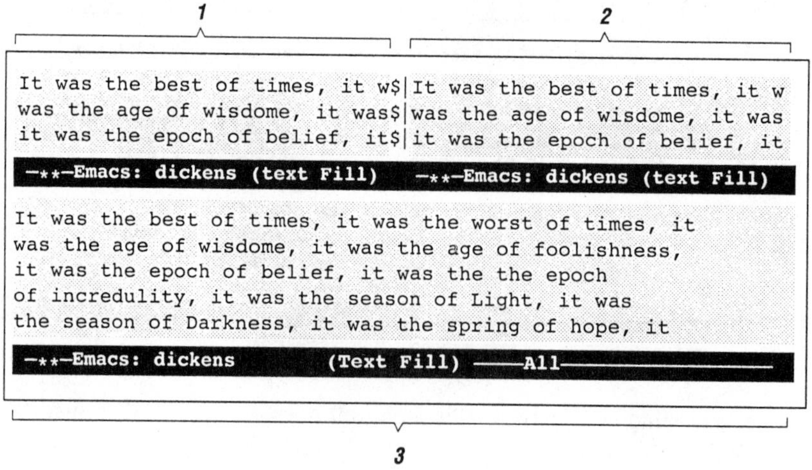

Figure 4-2. Moving Between Windows Clockwise

Now that you can create two windows and can move between them, what else can you do? Practically anything. First, let's look at two Dickens windows, one on top of the other. Initially, both of these windows are looking at the same file.

Type: **C-x 2**

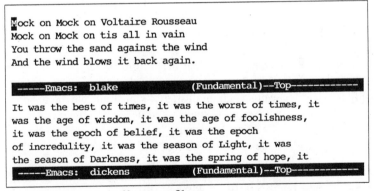

```
It was the best of times, it was the worst of times, it
was the age of wisdom, it was the age of foolishness,
it was the epoch of belief, it was the epoch
of incredulity, it was the season of Light, it was
the season of Darkness, it was the spring of hope, it
-----Emacs:  dickens          (Fundamental)--Top------------
It was the best of times, it was the worst of times, it
was the age of wisdom, it was the age of foolishness,
it was the epoch of belief, it was the epoch
of incredulity, it was the season of Light, it was
the season of Darkness, it was the spring of hope, it
-----Emacs:  dickens          (Fundamental)--Top------------
```

Two windows open to *dickens*.

Within either window, we can give any editing commands we want. We can move back and forth in one window without affecting the other, and so on. Let's see what happens if we want to edit another file.

Type: **C-x C-f blake**

```
Mock on Mock on Voltaire Rousseau
Mock on Mock on tis all in vain
You throw the sand against the wind
And the wind blows it back again.

-----Emacs:  blake          (Fundamental)--Top------------
It was the best of times, it was the worst of times, it
was the age of wisdom, it was the age of foolishness,
it was the epoch of belief, it was the epoch
of incredulity, it was the season of Light, it was
the season of Darkness, it was the spring of hope, it
-----Emacs:  dickens          (Fundamental)--Top------------
```

Two windows, two buffers, two files.

By using **C-x C-o**, we can edit one file, then the other. We can "kill" text from one buffer and "yank" it back in another. For example, let's move the first line of Blake's poem to the top of the Dickens buffer.

Type: **C-k C-x C-o ESC-< C-y**

```
Mock on Mock on tis all in vain
You throw the sand against the wind
And the wind blows it back again.

-----Emacs:  blake          (Fundamental)--Top------------
Mock on Mock on Voltaire Rousseau
It was the best of times, it was the worst of times, it
was the age of wisdom, it was the age of foolishness,
it was the epoch of belief, it was the epoch
of incredulity, it was the season of Light, it was
-----Emacs:  dickens        (Fundamental)--Top------------
```

Multi-buffer editing.

Editing with multiple buffers is particularly useful if you want to copy material from one file to another; if you want to read a file containing reference material while editing another; and so on. For programmers, it is often important to be able to look at several different files at the same time: for example, a header file and a "code" file, or a function call site and the routine that's being called. Once you get used to the commands for moving between different windows, you may spend most of your time with two, three, or even four windows on your screen.

Getting Rid of Windows

Deleting a window only means that it isn't displayed anymore; it doesn't delete any of the information or any of your unsaved changes. The underlying buffer is still there and you can switch to it using **C-x b**. To delete the window you're currently in, type **C-x 0** (zero). If you want to delete all windows but the one you're working on, type **C-x 1** (one), meaning "make this my one and only window." As you'd expect, the remaining window "grows" to fill up the rest of the space.

You can also delete all windows on a certain buffer by typing: **ESC-x delete-windows-on RETURN buffer name RETURN.**

Growing Windows and Shrinking Them

Emacs always splits windows into two equal parts. This is often good enough, but sometimes it's not, particularly if you become a window maniac. When you have four or five or six windows on your screen at once, it becomes important to control each window's size. Otherwise, the windows you are most interested in will eventually become too small, and useful editing is almost impossible when you can see only five or six lines from a file. If you want to make the window you're working on taller, type **C-x ^**. Emacs lengthens the current window and makes the others smaller accordingly. To make the current window wider, type **C-x }**. Emacs makes this window wider, again at the expense of the other ones.

To make windows smaller, you can shrink them. To shrink a window vertically, type **ESC-x shrink-window**.[2] Emacs shrinks the current window by one line and the other windows on the screen grow accordingly. To shrink a window horizontally, type **C-x {**. This makes the window one column narrower than it was and grows the other windows on the screen horizontally.

Usually you want to work in larger increments than one line or one column at a time, however. Type **C-u** preceding any of these commands; this makes the command work in increments of four lines or columns at a time. For example, let's use **C-u C-x ^** to "grow" the `dickens` window from our earlier example.

Type: **C-u C-x ^**

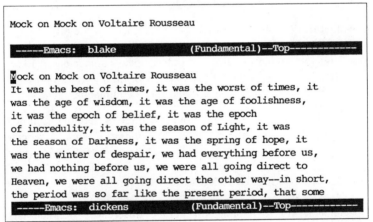

Enlarging the window onto `dickens`.

As you would expect, when you make the window larger, it's automatically filled with more text from the buffer.

---

[2] If you need to do this a lot, consider binding it to a key, like **C-x v**. See Chapter 9, *Customizing Emacs*, for information about how to do this.

Limits on Window Size

Windows in Emacs can be as big as your screen. There's a limit to how small windows can be, however, and this is specified by the variables **window-min-height** (whose default is 4 lines) and **window-min-width** (whose default is 10 characters). If you grow other windows to the point that their counterparts become less than 10 characters wide or 4 lines high, Emacs deletes the smaller windows. You can set these variables to other values if you want to; more information on setting variables is found in Chapter 9, *Customizing Emacs*.

Shortcut Commands for Working with Other Windows

Emacs offers a number of commands that allow you to operate on another window without moving to it. For example, one of the most frequent operations is to scroll the other window. To scroll the next window (speaking of the next window in clockwise sequence), type **ESC-C-v**.

A number of the "other window" commands are just the ordinary command with a 4 inserted in it. For example, to find a file in another window, type **C-x 4 f**. (If there's only one window currently, Emacs opens another one.) To select a different buffer in another window, type **C-x 4 b**. Many users find these commands preferable to the "normal" **C-x C-f** and **C-x b** commands.

You can also send mail and run Dired (the directory editor) from other windows; these features are described in Chapter 5, *Emacs as a Work Environment*.

Comparing Files Between Windows

Especially if you're looking for minute differences between large files, the **compare-windows** command comes in handy. For example, suppose that you want to see the difference between the auto-save file and the version you're currently working with. First find the files, then use **compare-windows** to find the first difference between them.

To use **compare-windows**, you must first have the buffers you want to compare in two windows, either side-by-side or horizontal.[3] For best results, go to the beginning of each buffer, then type **ESC-x compare-windows**. Emacs scrolls each buffer to the place where the discrepancy is. (If you don't have them at the beginning, Emacs only scrolls one buffer to show the difference, and you have to manually move the other one to that place if you want to do detailed comparisons.) It places the "point" in each buffer at the place of the discrepancy, so using **C-x o** to move the cursor between buffers will show you exactly where the files differ.

---

[3] You can have more than two windows on the screen, but only two are compared: the one the cursor is in and the "next" window in a clockwise direction.

Of course, this only finds the first difference between the two buffers. Finding the second, third, etc., is a bit tricky. The **compare-windows** command only works if "point" in both buffers is in exactly the same place. Therefore, you need to move past the discrepancy in both buffers before you can type **ESC-x compare-windows** again. The UNIX **diff** command provides a more comprehensive (although somewhat ugly) way to find the differences between two files.

Now that we've worked through the important window commands, Table 4-3 shows a summary of them.

Table 4-3. Window Commands

Keystrokes	Command Name	Action
C-x 2	split-window-horizontally	Divides the current window horizontally into two.
C-x 5	split-window-vertically	Divides the current window vertically into two.
C-x >	scroll-right	Scrolls the window right.
C-x <	scroll-left	Scrolls the window left.
C-x o	other-window	Moves to the other window; if there are several, moves to the next window in clockwise order.
C-x 0	delete-window	Deletes the current window.
C-x 1	delete-other-windows	Deletes all windows but this one.
(none)	delete-windows-on	Deletes all windows on a given buffer.
C-x ^	enlarge-window	Makes window taller.
(none)	shrink-window	Makes window shorter.
C-x }	enlarge-window-horizontally	Makes window wider.
C-x {	shrink-window-horizontally	Makes window narrower.
ESC-C-v	scroll-other-window	Scrolls other window.
C-x 4 f	find-file-other-window	Finds a file in the other window.
C-x 4 b	switch-to-buffer-other-window	Selects a buffer in the other window.
(none)	compare-windows	Compares two buffers and shows the first instance where they are different.

Displaying Buffers from the Buffer List

Now that you've learned how to create different kinds of windows, you can use the buffer list (which you display by pressing **C-x C-b**) to display multiple buffers in windows.

To display one of the buffers in a full screen, move the cursor into the buffer list's window; use **C-n** and **C-p** to move to the buffer that you want; and press **1**. Emacs displays the buffer in a full-screen window.

If you want to display one of the buffers in place of the buffer list, you can press **f**. To put a buffer in place of the other window (i.e., the one not occupied by the buffer list), type **o**. Emacs displays the buffer in the other window.

There is one final buffer display command. You can ask Emacs to display as many as four buffers and have Emacs create windows for them dynamically. To select buffers to be displayed in windows, press **m** (for mark) next to the buffers you want. Emacs displays a > next to the buffers you mark with **m**. To tell Emacs to display the buffers you've marked, press **q**. Emacs makes horizontal windows to display the buffers you've chosen.

Now that you know how to work with multiple buffers and windows, why not read the next chapter to discover some of the things you can do with them? Some, like sending mail and using the UNIX shell from within Emacs, have been alluded to in this chapter. Between using multiple buffers and windows and the features described in the next chapter, you will find that it's hardly ever necessary to leave Emacs.

5

Emacs as a Work Environment

Working with Mail
Executing UNIX Commands in Shell
  Windows
Working with Directories
Printing from Emacs
Reading Man Pages from Emacs
Using Your Emacs Work Environment

Many of the everyday things you do from your UNIX shell can be done from within Emacs. You can read and write mail messages, mail files you've written in Emacs, execute UNIX commands, work with directories, and print files—all without leaving Emacs. Changing tasks is as simple as jumping between buffers or windows. If you have room for several windows on your screen, you can move between tasks by typing **C-x o**.

What's important about this? Of course, it's nice to be able to move between tasks easily. What's even more important is that you have the same editing environment no matter what you're doing: you can use all of Emacs' editing commands to work on a file, then write a mail message, then give shell commands, and so on. It is trivial to move text from one window to another. You can execute a UNIX command, and then use Emacs commands to cut the result and paste it into a file or a mail message. Despite the many advantages of modern window systems, Emacs often provides the best way to integrate the many kinds of work you do daily.

Working with Mail

Emacs offers facilities for reading and writing mail. RMAIL is for reading mail; sendmail is for writing and sending mail messages.[1] You may already be using a mail agent on your system that you are very familiar and happy with. If this is the case, there's really no reason for you to learn sendmail or RMAIL (although sendmail is very convenient for sending quick messages from within Emacs). If you haven't fully exploited the capabilities of your mail system and want to do most of your work from within Emacs, you will probably want to learn sendmail and RMAIL. Even if you use another mail system, keep in mind that you can still read your mail from within Emacs using a shell buffer (discussed later in this chapter).

Using sendmail is a little easier than RMAIL (though neither is very hard), so we'll discuss sending mail first. In the following sections, we'll talk about sending mail to people, but remember that you have to type in real e-mail addresses in order to have the mail delivered to the right person. If you regularly send e-mail to people who have complicated e-mail addresses, read the section, "Using Aliases," later in this chapter, for a way to make your life easier.

Sending Mail from within Emacs

Sending mail from inside Emacs is very easy. To send a message, type **C-x m**, which brings you into an Emacs-created buffer called `*mail*`.

Type: **C-x m**

```
To: ▌
Subject:
--text follows this line--



--Emacs: *mail*                    (Mail)---All-------------
```

You're ready to type a mail message.

Type the e-mail address of the person you're sending mail to in the `To:` field, then the subject, if you want to, on the next line. You can send a single message to several recipients by putting many addresses on the `To:` line. Make sure you

---

[1] Emacs' sendmail facility is not to be confused with the **sendmail** program which is the unseen program at the heart of most UNIX mail systems.

put a comma between each address. If you have more than one line of recipients, leave a blank space on the second and subsequent lines and keep typing (this works for all the fields you can put e-mail addresses in, such as CC: and BCC: fields which we'll discuss shortly).

When you're ready to write the body of the message, move the cursor below the "--text follows this line--" message and write your message as you would any Emacs file. Don't erase or modify the marker "--text follows this line--"; sendmail needs it to divide the header from the body of the message and breaks if you erase it. This message won't be sent with your mail; it only shows you where the mail's header (the recipients, the subject, etc.) ends and the text begins.

While you're writing the message, you can use any of Emacs' features, including the spelling checker, abbreviation mode, and so on. When you're finished, you can send the message by typing **C-c C-c**. You can do much fancier things with sendmail, as we'll see shortly, but that is the basic way you send a message. Any mail you send will say it's from you and include the date and time sent, even though these fields aren't displayed in the *mail* buffer.

Normal editing to create the message:

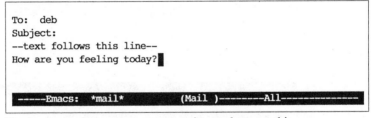

You've created a message; now you're ready to send it.

Type: **C-c C-c**

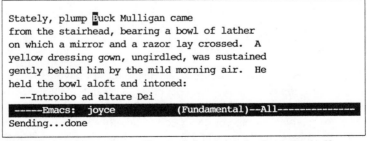

You've sent the message; Emacs brings you back to the buffer you were editing.

When you send the message, Emacs takes your mail buffer from the screen and returns you to the buffer you were previously editing—in this case, a buffer called `joyce`.

One thing to watch out for: it's unfortunately easy (and embarrassing) to send a half-completed message by mistake by typing a stray **C-c C-c** or **C-c C-s** (a command that sends mail but leaves you in the mail buffer), since both these sequences have common uses outside of sendmail. If you find this is a problem, you could write your messages in a separate buffer, then copy them into the `*mail*` buffer when you're ready to send them.

Sending Mail from a Window

It is usually more convenient to put the mail buffer in another window, rather than in the window you're currently editing; this makes it easier to copy from one buffer to another. To send a mail message in another window, type **C-x 4 m**. Emacs puts a new window on your screen. Fill in the **To:** and **Subject:** fields, then move down and type your message.

Type: **C-x 4 m**

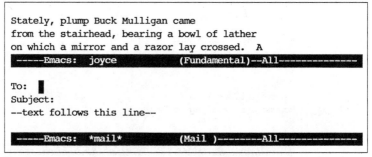

Ready to type a new message in another window.

To send the message (and exit mail), press **C-c C-c**. As it did before, Emacs takes your mail message from the screen. However, it leaves an extra window on the screen. To get rid of this extra window, type **C-x 0**.

Sending Copies to Other Recipients

You'll notice that the ordinary mail template doesn't have a **cc:** line where you can send carbon copy messages to people who are not on the **To:** list.[2] However, you can either type **C-c C-f C-c** to have Emacs create a **cc:** field or type your own **cc:** field. To type your own **cc:** field, after you type the recipients in the **To:** field, press **RETURN** to create a blank line. Type **CC:** followed by every-

---

[2] CC, FCC, BCC, and the other fields in the mail header really aren't part of Emacs itself. Emacs just makes it a lot easier to use these fields, but they are really defined by the underlying mail system. You can therefore use these fields in any mail you send, whether or not the recipient is using Emacs.

one who should receive a copy of the message. Remember to put a comma between each address. If there are too many addresses for one line, press **RETURN** again and type **CC:** again followed by more recipients. (Sometimes it's easier to type it yourself rather than remembering the command to have Emacs put it in for you.)

Sending Blind Copies

If you want to send a copy to someone but don't want their name to appear on the header as receiving a copy (called sending a "blind" copy), type **BCC:** in the header followed by the names of those who should receive the message. You can also type **C-c C-f C-b** and Emacs adds the BCC: field for you.

There are any number of reasons (some good, some bad) for using blind copies—you're the only judge of when it's appropriate and when it isn't. However, blind copies provide a neat solution to one perpetual mail problem. It's easy to forget to keep a copy of your outgoing mail. Days or weeks later, you'll want to refer to the message you originally sent, and you just won't have it. Configuring Emacs to send you a "blind" copy of the mail automatically goes a long way towards solving this problem.

If you want to use this blind copy feature to send yourself copies of all your mail, set the **mail-self-blind** variable to **t**. Then Emacs will include a BCC: with your user name in every mail message header. If you don't want to receive a copy of any particular message, you can delete the BCC: field by hand. To set **mail-self-blind** permanently, add the following line to your *.emacs* file:

```
(setq mail-self-blind t)
```

Save the file and restart Emacs to have this line take effect.

Once you have done this, whenever you send a mail message Emacs will automatically add the line:

```
BCC: yourname
```

to the header of every message you send, where *yourname* is your user name.

Sending a Copy to a File

You can receive copies of your mail automatically using the BCC: feature. But you can also have Emacs send a copy to a certain file by typing **FCC:** in the header followed by a filename for the message to be appended to (along with the file's complete path). This way, your mailbox will not be cluttered with messages you have sent to yourself and you will still have a record of mail that you send.

As with the BCC: field, you can ask Emacs to send copies of your mail to a file by default. To do so, set the variable **mail-archive-file-name**. For example, to keep copies of all your outgoing messages in a file called *outbox.txt* in your home directory, put the following line in your *.emacs* file:

```
(setq mail-archive-file-name "outbox.txt")
```

Then exit Emacs and restart. The next time you send a mail message, you'll see the line:

```
FCC:  outbox.txt
```

If you send a lot of mail, your "outbox" file will eventually become very large. If you are short on disk space, this may lead to problems. Check your outgoing mail file periodically to make sure that it doesn't grow too large.

Mailing an Emacs File

You can mail a file by typing **C-x i** followed by the filename. Emacs inserts the file; you can edit it if necessary, then mail it by typing **C-c C-c**.

Signing Your Mail Messages

If you have a standard signature that you like to put on your mail messages, put it in a file in your home directory called *.signature*. Type **C-c C-w** to insert this file into your mail messages. (Note that your site may be set up to include the *.signature* file automatically; in that case, typing **C-c C-w** puts in a second signature.) Many people like to create interesting pictures to use as their signature. For information on drawing pictures in Emacs, see the section on picture mode in Chapter 6, *Simple Text Formatting and Specialized Editing*. Other people like to use a text signature, which may be formatted like this:

```
-----------------------------------------------------------
Your name.                        A brief quotation.
Your work address.
Your e-mail address.              Your phone number.
-----------------------------------------------------------
```

The "brief quotation" is often some kind of disclaimer, stating that the author's opinions aren't the views of his or her employer. These are often worded very cleverly: perhaps something like, "If anyone speaks for Btsfphbl Grommets, Inc., it's certainly not me."

The following example shows how it works.

Type: **C-c C-w**

```
To:  david
Subject: grommets
--text follows this line--
Your ideas about grommets are completely losing.

Sincerely,
Joe
-----------------------------------------------------------
Joe Btsfphbl                     "It's not my fault-
Btsfphbl Grommets, Inc.   I was born obnoxious"
e-mail:  joe@grom.com                  phone:  (777)666-4444
-----------------------------------------------------------
-----Emacs: *mail*          (Mail )--------All--------------
```

C-c C-w added the signature to the end.

Of course, **C-c C-w** won't work if you don't create the *.signature* file in advance.

Using Aliases

Using aliases has nothing to do with Emacs per se, but they can make your life easier if you send mail to people with long addresses. For example, let's say you mail to a friend named Fred whose e-mail address is:

    fred@plan9fromouterspace.galaxy.universe.COM

What a pain to type this every time you send mail to Fred! You don't have to. Mail aliases let you define abbreviations for common names, or groups of names; the latter are often called "mailing lists", and are useful for work groups, or simply lists of friends. To define aliases, use the command **ESC-x define-mail-alias RETURN**. Emacs puts the prompt "Define mail alias" into the minibuffer; type the name of your alias (**fred**), followed by **RETURN**. Emacs then prompts you with "Define fred as mail alias for:"; then type Fred's full address (fred@plan9fromouterspace.galaxy.universe.COM). To define a mailing list, just type a list of names (separated by spaces).

Aliases defined in this way only last for your current Emacs session. It is much more useful to define aliases permanently. To do so, put the alias commands in your *.emacs* file like this:

    (define-mail-alias "fred" "fred@plan9fromouterspace.galaxy.universe.COM")
    (define-mail-alias "club" "kathy ray allen fred nadine esther charles")

Mail aliases are surprisingly confusing, given that they are essentially a simple concept. The problem is that aliases are defined in many places: in your local

.*emacs* file, in customization files for other mail tools (for example, .*mailrc*), and in system-wide files (often called */etc/aliases*, but there are other names).

To help understand how aliases work, it's very helpful to define one or two aliases, use them to send messages, and look at the header fields they generate. If you send *club*, include yourself as one of the members. Then when you send a message to *club*, look at how it arrives. The `To:` field won't say *club* at all; it will just contain the aliases. Aliases may be expanded several times: you may list *nadine* as a club member, and some other alias may convert *nadine* into *nadine_fuller*, and yet another may convert *nadine_fuller* into *nxf@orbis.com*.

Using the Reply-to Field

Mail messages can use a `Reply-to:` field to guarantee that replies will be sent to the correct place. Normally, you can ignore this; mailers can usually generate the address for a reply correctly on their own. However, there are times when setting the `Reply-to:` field explicitly might be helpful. For example, let's say that replies to your mail tend to go astray because of problems in your system's mail configuration. Yes, that should be fixed, but fooling with the guts of the mail system is difficult. If you know that you will always receive mail that's sent to the address *george@futons.com*, you can do a lot to solve your problem by putting the address in the `Reply-to:` field of your outgoing mail.

The `Reply-to:` field is also useful if you're temporarily using someone else's account (or someone else's computer) to send mail, but want any replies to be directed back to you. For example, you might use a friend's computer when yours is broken. However, when you send mail from that system, it's often better for replies to go back to your own system: receiving mail on two different systems is inconvenient, and your own probably won't be broken for that long.

The Emacs mail facility lets you set the `Reply-to:` field automatically by setting the variable **mail-default-reply-to**. For example, to set the `Reply-to:` field to *george@futons.com* in all outgoing mail, put the following line in your .*emacs* file:

```
(setq mail-default-reply-to "george@futons.com")
```

You can also use the **set-variable** command if you only want to use the `Reply-to:` line for a single session: **ESC-x set-variable RETURN mail-default-reply-to RETURN george@futons.com RETURN**.

Outgoing Mail Summary

Table 5-1 shows a list of the commands you can use in sendmail. There are a few commands in this table not discussed above, so you may want to take a look at it.

Table 5-1. Sendmail Commands

Keystrokes	Command Name	Action
C-x m	mail	Open the *mail* buffer, complete with template.
C-x 4 m	mail-other-window	Open the *mail* buffer in a window.
C-c C-f C-t	mail-to	Move to the To: field.
C-c C-f C-c	mail-cc	Move to the CC: field (create one if there is none).
C-c C-f C-b	mail-bcc	Move to the BCC: field (create one if there is none).
C-c C-f C-s	mail-subject	Move to the subject field.
C-c C-w	mail-signature	Insert the contents of the .signature file.
C-c C-c	mail-send-and-exit	Send the mail message and exit the *mail* buffer.
C-c C-s	mail-send	Send the mail message and stay in the *mail* buffer.
(none)	define-mail-alias	Define an abbreviation for a name or a mailing list.

Table 5-2 shows the fields you can put in mail headers. By default, one **To:** and one **Subject:** field appears.

Table 5-2. Sendmail Header Fields

Header	Function
To:	Who the message should be sent to.
CC:	People who should receive a copy of the message.
FCC:	File to which a copy of the message should be appended.
BCC:	People who should receive a copy of this message but whose names should not appear in the header.
Subject:	The subject of the mail message.
From:	Who the message is from (if different from your user id); this is used when you are sending messages from someone else's account.
Reply-to:	Address to which a reply should be sent.

Reading Mail from within Emacs

Sending electronic mail wouldn't be too useful if you couldn't also receive mail. Emacs has a built-in mode for reading your incoming mail. To read your mail from within Emacs, type **ESC-x rmail RETURN**. Emacs reads your inboxes[3] and the file that your old mail messages are stored in (*~/RMAIL* by default)[4]. In case you ever need it, the RMAIL file is backed up in *~/RMAIL~*.

If you're a new user, you may not have any mail at all, and RMAIL displays a message that says so. If you do have some mail, after reading your inboxes, Emacs displays your mail on a screen that looks like Figure 5-1.

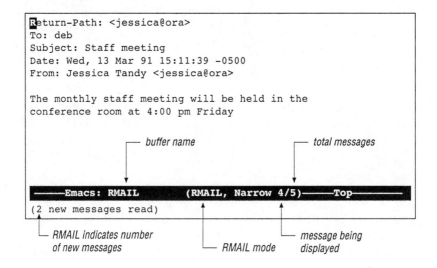

Figure 5-1. After Reading Your Mail with RMAIL

---

[3] An "inbox" is just a place where the system stores your incoming mail. Normally, you don't have to worry about it. Emacs reads mail from *~/mbox, /usr/spool/mail/username* or */usr/mail/username*. If none of these files exist, it means that your e-mail system is set up a little bit differently from the standard, and you will have to see your system administrator to find out where your inbox is. Once you find out, use the variable **rmail-primary-inbox-list** to specify the complete pathname for your incoming mail.

[4] If you want to use some file other than *~/RMAIL* to store your mail messages, set the variable **rmail-file-name** to the name of the file. For example, to save your mail messages in the file *~/mail/inbox.rmail*, add the following line to your *.emacs* file:

```
(setq rmail-file-name "~/mail/inbox.rmail")
```

The mode line shows that the current buffer is called **RMAIL**, and that you are in the RMAIL mode. This is a special mode for reading your mail. The **4/5** means that, in this case, you are looking at the fourth of five messages. These numbers vary depending on how much mail you currently have. The line at the bottom tells you that two new messages have arrived since the last time you read your mail. One of these messages is displayed on the screen.

If there is no new mail for you, Emacs displays the mail message you've most recently received. It puts a message saying "(No new mail has arrived)" into the minibuffer.

If you receive a lot of mail, you may find out that there are 10 or 20 (or more) new messages when you start RMAIL. In that case, you often want to see a summary list that describes each message briefly. For more information, see the section, "Working with a List of Mail Messages," later in this chapter.

Aside from the fact that it is read-only, the **RMAIL** buffer is not very different from any other Emacs buffer. You can switch to another buffer and back by typing **C-x b** *buffername*. You can leave RMAIL entirely by pressing **q** to quit or by exiting Emacs as you usually do (**C-x C-c**).

Moving Around in RMAIL

Many standard Emacs movement commands work in RMAIL mode, but if you use RMAIL frequently, you may want to learn a set of simple one-character commands that do mail-oriented tasks. For example, you could scroll through a mail message by typing **C-v** as in any Emacs file, but in RMAIL you could also press **SPACE**.

By default, RMAIL keeps all your mail in one file, with a path of ⁓*/RMAIL*. When you look at the file through RMAIL, Emacs considers each message a separate entity within the file. For example, if you run RMAIL in a full screen, each message appears on a separate screen, even if the message is only one line long, and header information always appears at the top of the screen. This makes it easier to concentrate on each individual message.

Table 5-3 shows a list of one-letter commands for moving around in RMAIL and what they do.

Table 5-3. RMAIL Commands

Keystroke	Function
SPC	Scrolls to the next screen of this message.
DEL	Scrolls to the previous screen of this message.
.	Moves to the beginning of this message.
n	Moves to the next message.
p	Moves to the previous message.
>	Moves to the last message.
j	Jumps to the first message in the file.
n	Repeat the command typed next *n* times.

Getting New Mail

In RMAIL, you can check to see if you have new mail anytime by typing **g**. Emacs checks your inboxes, and if there is new mail, displays it after saving the *RMAIL* file.

Deleting Unwanted Mail

Just as there are one-letter commands for moving between RMAIL messages, there are also simple commands like this for deleting mail.

Deleting mail is a two-step process. First, you mark a message for deletion using the command **d** or **C-d** (**d** moves you to the next message whereas **C-d** moves you to the previous message). However, the mail messages aren't gone permanently. You can change your mind about deleting the message and use the command **u** to "undelete" the message (pressing **u** moves you backward to the last message marked for deletion). When you're sure that you want to destroy the messages that you've marked, you tell Emacs to go ahead and delete all the marked messages in one operation. You can do this in several ways:

- Type the command **e**.

- Type the command **x**.

- Type **s** to save the *RMAIL* file.

- Type **q** to quit RMAIL.

Once you've done any of these things, the message is deleted and you can't retrieve it with the undelete command. Table 5-4 summarizes the commands for deleting mail.

Table 5-4. Mail Deletion Commands

Keystroke	Action
d	Marks this message for deletion and moves forward.
C-d	Marks this message for deletion and moves backward.
ESC-n	Moves to the next message, even if it was marked for deletion.
ESC-p	Moves to the previous message even if it was marked for deletion.
u	Undeletes a message that has been marked for deletion.
x	Deletes all messages marked for deletion.
e	Deletes all messages marked for deletion.

Replying to Mail Messages

Mail is often a substitute for telephone calls, letters, or meetings. You often want to reply to the mail you receive.

To reply to the message currently displayed, press **r**. Emacs opens a `*mail*` window and puts in all the correct header information to send your reply; you can modify it to add or delete more recipients if you want to.

By default, RMAIL doesn't include the message in your reply. You can do this easily by typing **C-c C-y**. Emacs inserts the message you're replying to and indents it. (The indentation makes it easy to see what was part of the original message versus what is part of your reply.) Since this may make some lines too long, you can fill the paragraphs using **C-c C-q**, which preserves the indentation. If you prefer, you can insert the entire original message, header and all, without indentation by typing **C-u C-c C-y**.

For example, assume we've just received mail about a staff meeting, and want to send a reply. Just type **r** after you've read the message. Emacs creates a new window for your reply as shown in Figure 5-2.

original message

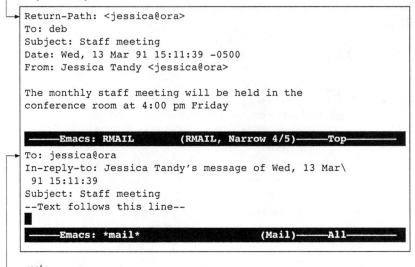

```
Return-Path: <jessica@ora>
To: deb
Subject: Staff meeting
Date: Wed, 13 Mar 91 15:11:39 -0500
From: Jessica Tandy <jessica@ora>

The monthly staff meeting will be held in the
conference room at 4:00 pm Friday

———Emacs: RMAIL          (RMAIL, Narrow 4/5)———Top———
To: jessica@ora
In-reply-to: Jessica Tandy's message of Wed, 13 Mar\
 91 15:11:39
Subject: Staff meeting
--Text follows this line--
█

———Emacs: *mail*               (Mail)———All———
```

reply

Figure 5-2. Starting a Reply Window

Typing C-c C-y inserts the original message as shown in Figure 5-3.

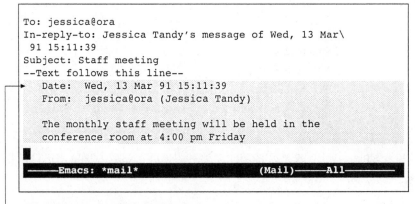

```
To: jessica@ora
In-reply-to: Jessica Tandy's message of Wed, 13 Mar\
 91 15:11:39
Subject: Staff meeting
--Text follows this line--
   Date:  Wed, 13 Mar 91 15:11:39
   From:  jessica@ora (Jessica Tandy)

   The monthly staff meeting will be held in the
   conference room at 4:00 pm Friday
█

———Emacs: *mail*               (Mail)———All———
```

*The original message is inserted in the
reply and indented. You can now respond
to the message in context.*

Figure 5-3. Original Message Inserted

When you insert the original message, Emacs deletes the **RMAIL** window. There's really no need to have two copies of the message on the screen at once.

After inserting the original message, you can type your reply, edit the original, and do anything necessary to compose the new message. It's a good idea to trim unnecessary parts of the original message so that the reply isn't overly long; if the original sender makes five points, but you only want to respond to two, delete the three points that you won't comment on. If you are replying to a reply to a reply (and so on), you'll see more than enough indentation levels to confuse your reader. It's often useful to annotate your reply to make it clear who wrote what.

When you're done, send the message just like you would send any other message: by pressing **C-c C-c**. Emacs returns you to RMAIL with the message you've just replied to displayed. Now "answered" appears on the mode line to indicate you've sent a reply.

Forwarding Mail Messages

Sometimes you get mail that you want to send along to another person. To forward a mail message, type **f**. Emacs displays a mail buffer that includes the current message and puts the cursor in the **To:** field so you can fill in who should receive the forwarded copies. You can put any comments you want into the message (to indicate why you're forwarding it, for example), then send it by typing **C-c C-c**. Emacs moves you back to the **RMAIL** buffer with "forwarded" on the mode line for this message.

Saving Messages in a File

As you're reading your mail, you may find that you want to save some messages for later reference. You can do this easily from within RMAIL, although you have a decision to make before you start: whether you want to save your mail in Emacs RMAIL format or in ASCII format. You shouldn't mix these two formats in the same file.

If you use Emacs and only Emacs for reading your mail, RMAIL format is fine. It's designed to let you use RMAIL on mail you've stored. For example, you can save your mail in a file, then decide later you want to write a reply. RMAIL format gives you a "live" file. ASCII format, on the other hand, is better for people who move their mail between various mailers or computers. These other mailers will get severe indigestion over the RMAIL format, but they should be able to read the ASCII format without trouble.

If you decide to use Emacs for mail handling, always use the RMAIL format to save your mail. Use the ASCII format only when you need to generate a mail file that some other mailer can read. Never mix RMAIL and ASCII formats in the same file.

To save in RMAIL format, type **o**. Emacs prompts you for a filename; type the filename, followed by **RETURN**. If you omit the filename, Emacs puts the message into a file called *XMAIL* in your home directory.

Type: **o**

```
Return-Path:  <jessica@ora>
To:  deb
Subject:  Staff meeting
Date:  Wed, 13 Mar 91 15:11:39 -0500
From:  Jessica Tandy <jessica@ora>

The monthly staff meeting will be held in the
conference room at 4:00 pm Friday.



----Emacs:  RMAIL              (RMAIL Narrow 4/4)-----Top--------
Output message to Rmail file:  (default XMAIL) ~/█
```

Ready to type the output filename.

To save it in plain ASCII format with no special control characters, type **C-o**. Again, Emacs prompts you for a filename. Type your filename, followed by a **RETURN**. If you omit the filename, Emacs saves ASCII mail in the file *xmail* in your home directory.

If you output mail to an existing file, Emacs appends this message onto the end of the file. You have to know that this works; RMAIL gives you no reassuring message that it appends the message and doesn't overwrite the current file contents. Emacs does tell you if it can't save the message for some reason (for example, if the disk is full).

Any message that you save in a file remains in RMAIL as well. If you want messages that you've saved in a file to be automatically deleted when you exit RMAIL, set the value of variable **rmail-delete-after-output** to **t**.

Many UNIX users keep a special directory (often called *Mail*) for all their saved mail messages. You may find this convention helpful; or you may find it more helpful to mix your mail files with other files, according to whatever directory organization scheme you use.

Reading Mail Files

If you saved your mail in RMAIL format using the **o** command, put Emacs into the RMAIL mode (**ESC-x rmail**) and type **i**. Emacs prompts you "Run rmail on RMAIL file:" in the minibuffer. Then type the name of the file you want to read. After reading the file, Emacs displays the last message. You can then use commands like **n** and **p** to move forward and backward, **r** to reply to old messages, **f** to move forward, and so on.

Reading Mail Files Saved in ASCII Format

To read ASCII mail and leave it in ASCII format, you can read it like any other file with Emacs itself by typing **C-x C-f** (**find-file**). Alternatively, you can use the UNIX **more** command. Never read an ASCII file with RMAIL; Emacs converts such files to RMAIL format, defeating the purpose of saving it in ASCII and making it impossible for other tools to read the file.

Table 5-5 summarizes the commands for working with mail files.

Table 5-5. Commands for Mail Files

Keystrokes	Action
o *filename* RETURN	Save message in RMAIL file format.
C-o *filename* RETURN	Save message in Unix mail file format (a standard ASCII text file).
i *filename* RETURN	Read messages from saved file and convert the file to RMAIL format.

Using Searches in RMAIL

Because mail messages are nothing more than Emacs buffers, you can use the normal search commands when you're reading them. As you might expect, **C-s** works normally: it's the incremental search command that we introduced in Chapter 3, *Search and Replace Operations*. It searches through the current mail message, but no more.

The RMAIL facility introduces a special search command for searching through an entire mail file. This is often useful: for example, you may have 120 messages in your mail file (if you do, you should consider splitting it into many smaller files, but that's another issue). You want to find the message about "widgets," but you don't know which one it is. You get a list of mail headers (we'll describe how to do this shortly), but it doesn't help: none of your correspondence mentions widgets as its subject. The only solution is to search the entire file.

To do so, type **ESC-s**. Emacs then prompts you for a "regular expression." Chapter 3 has a brief introduction to regular expressions, but if you've ignored it or forgotten it, don't worry. For the time being, any standard phrase will do. Type your search string, and Emacs finds the mail message that has it.

Type: **ESC-s**

```
Return-Path:  <jessica@ora>
To:  deb
Subject:  Staff meeting
Date:  Wed, 13 Mar 91 15:11:39 -0500
From:  Jessica Tandy <jessica@ora>

The monthly staff meeting will be held in the
conference room at 4:00 pm Friday.



----Emacs:  RMAIL        (RMAIL Narrow 4/5)-----Top--------
Rmail search (regexp):
```

Ready to type the search string.

Type: **grommets RETURN**

```
Return-Path:  <george@grom.com>
To:  deb
Subject:  your recent order
Date:  Wed, 13 Mar 91 15:11:39 -0500
From:  george@grom.com

We received your order for grommets.
When shall we ship them?

----Emacs:  RMAIL        (RMAIL Narrow 5/5)-----Top--------
Rmail search for grommets...done
```

You've found the message with "grommets."

If you type **ESC-s** again, Emacs remembers your search string, and prompts you with "Rmail search (regexp): (default grommets)." To search for the string "grommets" again, just type a **RETURN**. If you want to search for some other text, type the new string and then type **RETURN**.

It's often useful to use the **j** command (jump to the first message) before searching to make sure that you are searching through all your mail. However, this isn't strictly necessary because RMAIL also includes a reverse-search. The command **C-u - ESC-s** searches from the current message back to the beginning of the file.

There's one big pitfall with this search facility. It cannot search the current message, either in forward or reverse. This can be confusing at times: you can be staring right at your search string, and wondering why **ESC-s** won't find it. It's not your fault; **ESC-s** always starts at the end of the current message, and works to the end of the file; **C-u - ESC-s** always starts before the beginning of the current message, and works back to the beginning of the file.

More information on incremental search and regular expression search can be found in Chapter 3, *Search and Replace Operations*, and Chapter 11, *Emacs LISP Programming*.

Working with a List of Mail Messages

Like many other mail systems, RMAIL lets you work with a list of your mail messages. To see a list, just type **h**. Emacs opens a window called **RMAIL-summary**, like the one shown in Figure 5-4.

```
Return-Path: <jessica@ora>
To: deb
Subject: Staff meeting
Date: Wed, 13 Mar 91 15:11:39 -0500
From: Jessica Tandy <jessica@ora>

The monthly staff meeting will be held in the
conference room at 4:00 pm Friday

——————Emacs: RMAIL        (RMAIL, Narrow 4/5)————Top————
    1    3-Mar              land photo wanted
    2    7-Mar              mark PO number
   3D   11-Mar              sue  Corporate policy
   4    13-Mar              jessica Staff meeting
    5   26-Mar              george your recent order
—%%—Emacs: RMAIL-summary      (RMAIL, Summary: All)——All——
```

Figure 5-4. RMAIL Summary List

From this list, you can display mail messages, delete and undelete them, and scroll through mail using one letter commands. (If you learned the commands for working with the buffer list in Chapter 4, *Using Buffers and Windows*, these may look familiar to you.) For example, if you type **n** to move to the next message, Emacs moves the cursor to the next line of the summary and, in the **RMAIL** window, displays the message selected. Similarly, **p** moves up one line in the summary, and automatically displays the message you've selected. Finally, to exit the summary and remove the window, type **x**. To exit both the summary *and* the RMAIL facility, type **q**.

Typing a **d** marks a message for deletion; a "D" in the summary line (as in message 3, above) shows that you've marked the message. The message isn't deleted until later; you can type **u** to undelete the message. Unlike the buffer list, giving the **x** command in the summary window does *not* perform the deletion. You must go back into RMAIL and type the **x** command to delete the messages. However, typing the **q** command in the summary window **does** delete the "marked" messages. What's the difference? The **x** command quits the summary mode, and returns you to RMAIL. The **q** command quits both the summary mode and RMAIL; when RMAIL quits, it deletes the marked mail.

It's inconvenient to jump back and forth between the summary list and the mail message. Therefore, Emacs lets you read mail messages without leaving the summary list. If you type a space in the summary list, Emacs scrolls to the next page of the mail message that's displayed in the RMAIL window. If you press **DEL**, Emacs scrolls to the previous page of the mail message. Remember: these commands don't have any effect on the summary window at all. By using **n** and **p** to move between messages, and **SPACE** and **DEL** to move back and forth within messages, the summary list has everything you need to read your mail.

Table 5-6 is a list of commands that you can use in the summary window.

Table 5-6. Mail Summary List Commands

Keystrokes	Action
SPACE	Scroll the mail message in the RMAIL window forward.
DEL	Scroll the mail message in the RMAIL window backward.
d	Mark the message for deletion (D appears next to the message number).
u	Undelete the current message.
n	Move to the next message and display it in the RMAIL window.
p	Move to the previous message and display it in the RMAIL window.
x	Exit the summary window and delete it.
q	Exit RMAIL.

Labeling Mail

If you have a lot of mail, it may be helpful to categorize it using labels. To label a mail message, type:

    a label RETURN

You can delete a label by typing:

    k label RETURN

For example, let's add the label "meetings" to the mail message about our staff meetings.

Type: **a**

```
 ┌─────────────────────────────────────────────────────────────┐
 │   Return-Path:  <jessica@ora>                                 │
 │   To:  deb                                                    │
 │   Subject:  Staff meeting                                     │
 │   Date:  Wed, 13 Mar 91 15:11:39 -0500                        │
 │   From:  Jessica Tandy <jessica@ora>                          │
 │                                                               │
 │   The monthly staff meeting will be held in the               │
 │   conference room at 4:00 pm Friday.                          │
 │                                                               │
 │                                                               │
 │  ────Emacs:  RMAIL        (RMAIL Narrow 4/5)─────Top────────  │
 │   Add label: █                                                │
 └─────────────────────────────────────────────────────────────┘
```

Ready to add a label.

Type a label in response to the prompt in the minibuffer. If you've already used the **a** command, Emacs remembers the previous label and asks if you want to use it by default; this makes it easy to label a group of messages in succession.

Once you've added the label, Emacs displays it on the mode line.

Type: **meetings RETURN**

```
Return-Path:  <jessica@ora>
To:  deb
Subject:  Staff meeting
Date:  Wed, 13 Mar 91 15:11:39 -0500
From:  Jessica Tandy <jessica@ora>

The monthly staff meeting will be held in the
conference room at 4:00 pm Friday.



----Emacs:  RMAIL              (RMAIL Narrow 4/5;meetings)-Top-
```

Label "meetings" added to this message.

Now, if we look at the header listing, we'll see the label.

Type: **h**

```
Return-Path:  <jessica@ora>
To:  deb
Subject:  Staff meeting
Date:  Wed, 13 Mar 91 15:11:39 -0500
From:  Jessica Tandy <jessica@ora>

The monthly staff meeting will be held in the
conference room at 4:00 pm Friday.

----Emacs:  RMAIL              (RMAIL Narrow 4/5)-----Top--------
   1    3-Mar               land   photo wanted
   2    7-Mar               mark   PO number
  3D  11-Mar                sue    Corporate policy
  4   13-Mar                jessica { meetings } Staff
   5   26-Mar               george your recent order
-%%-Emacs:  RMAIL-summary     (RMAIL Summary:  All)--All---
```

The summary list now includes the label "meetings" on message 4.

We can also create a special summary list that only includes messages with a specific label or labels. The command for this is **ESC-C-l**, followed by the label (or labels) that you want to include.

Type: **ESC-C-l**

```
Return-Path:  <jessica@ora>
To:  deb
Subject:  Staff meeting
Date:  Wed, 13 Mar 91 15:11:39 -0500
From:  Jessica Tandy <jessica@ora>


The monthly staff meeting will be held in the
conference room at 4:00 pm Friday.


 -%%-Emacs:  RMAIL-summary        (RMAIL Summary:  All)--All---

Labels to summarize by: █
```

Creating a header list, keyed on a particular label.

Type: **meetings RETURN**

```
Return-Path:  <jessica@ora>
To:  deb
Subject:  Staff meeting
Date:  Wed, 13 Mar 91 15:11:39 -0500
From:  Jessica Tandy <jessica@ora>


The monthly staff meeting will be held in the
conference room at 4:00 pm Friday.
 ----Emacs:  RMAIL            (RMAIL Narrow 4/15)-----Top---------

█4   13-Mar        jessica { meetings } Staff
10   27-Mar        george { meetings } Can't make it
15   30-Mar        deb    { meetings } You lazy bum
 -%%-Emacs:  RMAIL-summary        (RMAIL Summary:  labels meetings
```

Summary list of messages with the label "meetings."

This list is no different from any other summary list: you can move up and down within the list, delete messages, and so on. You don't see, and don't have to worry about, messages that aren't in the list. Therefore, the "label" facility gives you a convenient way to group messages, and to work with these message groups. You can review all of your messages about meetings and decide which you want to keep without being distracted by the other material in your mailbox.

You can assign as many labels to a message as you like. At some point, it becomes impossible to fit them all onto the mode line, but Emacs won't prevent you from using more if you want to.

If you want to remove the label from any message, give the command **k**. For example, to remove the label "meeting" from a message, use RMAIL to display the message and type the command **k meeting RETURN**.

There are a few built-in labels that Emacs manages automatically. These are shown in Table 5-7.

Table 5-7. Built-in Labels for Mail Messages

Label	Meaning
Filed	The message has been saved in a mail file.
Unseen	You have not read the message yet.
Answered	You have sent a reply (using **r**) to the mail message.
Forwarded	You have forwarded the message to someone else.
Deleted	You have marked the message for deletion.

You have probably noticed these labels on the mode line, although they don't show up in the header summary. They really aren't different from any other labels, except that you never have to assign or delete them. Emacs assigns them automatically, based on what you have done (or not done) to the message: for example, incoming messages are automatically labeled "unseen" until you read them, at which point Emacs deletes the "unseen" label. Messages are automatically marked "filed" when you save them in a file. It's interesting to notice that removing the label "deleted" is the same as unmarking a message that has been marked for deletion. The **d** and **u** commands aren't doing anything more mysterious than adding and removing labels. (You can try this if you're not convinced.) Likewise, labeling a message "unseen" tells Emacs to pretend that you haven't yet read the mail; and so on.

Once you're familiar with mail, the next step is USENET news: depending on your perspective, either a wealth of information or a tremendous waste of time and disk space, or both. Emacs has an excellent news reader. It is called GNUS. GNUS isn't part of the standard distribution, and won't be discussed here; but you should be aware that it exists, and may be available at your site. GNUS is vastly superior to any of the other news readers that are available.

Executing UNIX Commands in Shell Windows

One of Emacs' most important features is its ability to run a UNIX shell within a window. Once you have started a shell window, you can do all of your normal UNIX work within Emacs. What does this buy you?

• You don't have to leave Emacs to get a UNIX prompt. If you want to print or compile a file that you're editing, you can do that immediately.

- You can use all of Emacs' editing features to write your commands. This is much simpler than using the primitive command-line editing that UNIX shells provide.

- You can use Emacs' editing features to "back up" through your command list, copy an old command, modify it, and re-execute it. This is much simpler than using the UNIX **history** command.

- You can save your shell buffer, keeping a transcript of your editing session—which automatically includes the output from every command that you ran.

- You can copy output from commands into other windows (other files, mail messages, etc.).

And so on. As you get used to working within Emacs, you will undoubtedly discover more and more ways to put it to use. We have even written macros (macros are discussed in Chapter 8) that execute UNIX commands: after all, why not?

Emacs also provides several features that give you access to UNIX without using the shell. We've already discussed the built-in mail facility, which eliminates the need for the UNIX **mail** command. Emacs also has a facility for working with directories (listing and deleting files), which is arguably more convenient than **ls** and **rm** and, in any case, lets you do without them if you so choose. It also has built-in commands for compiling files (i.e., running **make**) and printing files.

In this section, we'll discuss Emacs' shell mode. Later in this chapter, we'll discuss directory editing and printing. Right now, we'll start with a simple variation on shell mode: a feature that lets you execute UNIX commands one at a time. To run a UNIX command while you're in an Emacs session, type **ESC-!** Emacs asks for the command you want to run. Type the command and press **RETURN**. Emacs then opens a window called `*Shell Command Output*` where it displays the results of your command. Press **C-x 1** to get rid of this window.

Type: **ESC-!**

```
Stately, plump Buck Mulligan came
from the stairhead, bearing a bowl of lather
on which a mirror and a razor lay crossed.  A
yellow dressing gown, ungirdled, was sustained
gently behind him by the mild morning air.  He
held the bowl aloft and intoned:
  --Introibo ad altare Dei
-----Emacs:  joyce               (Fundamental)--All----------
Shell command: █
```

Emacs prompts you for a command to execute.

Type: **diff joyce joyce2**

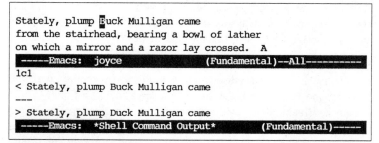

```
Stately, plump Buck Mulligan came
from the stairhead, bearing a bowl of lather
on which a mirror and a razor lay crossed.  A
-----Emacs:  joyce               (Fundamental)--All----------
1c1
< Stately, plump Buck Mulligan came
---
> Stately, plump Duck Mulligan came
-----Emacs:  *Shell Command Output*      (Fundamental)-----
```

Emacs executes the **diff** command and puts the output into a "shell command" buffer.

Because the output from the **diff** command is in a buffer, you can edit it, save it, or do anything you would like.

An interesting twist to the shell command facility is that you can use a region of a buffer as input to the command rather than a traditional file. For example, let's say that we want to sort a phone list. First, we put the cursor somewhere in the list (say, on the first character of "Mike"); then we give the **mark-paragraph** command (**ESC-h**). This defines the phone list as a region, excluding the header line: the cursor is at the beginning of the paragraph, and the mark is at the end. In the following example, the shaded lines show the extent of the region that we want to sort. Of course, these lines won't be shaded on your screen. After selecting a region, we press **ESC-|** (for **shell-command-on-region**), and Emacs prompts for the shell command to run.

Type: **ESC-h ESC-|**

```
Name     Number

  Mike    444-5555
  John    843-9876
  Debra   909-1234
  Susan   606-1234

-----Emacs:  phones              (Text)------All-----------
Shell command on region:█
```

Emacs prompts you for a command to execute.

Now we give the command **sort** without specifying any input file.[5] Emacs is taking care of the input for us.

Type: **sort RETURN**

```
  Mike    444-5555
  John    843-9876
  Debra   909-1234
  Susan   606-123█

-----Emacs:  phones              (Text)------All-----------
  Debra   909-1234
  John    843-9876
  Mike    444-5555
  Susan   606-1234
-----Emacs:  *Shell Command Output*            (Text)-----
```

Emacs runs "sort" on the region.

Emacs has sorted the phone list (i.e., everything within the region).

A useful variation for **ESC-!** is that you can put the output directly into the current buffer, rather than into a "command output" buffer. To do so, precede the command with **C-u**: for example, **C-u ESC-!** runs a shell command, sticking the output in the current buffer.

---

[5] In reality, **ESC-x sort-lines** would be faster, but bear with us for the sake of a simple example.

Type: **C-u ESC-! ls RETURN**

```
Here's a list of the files in my current
directory:

ORIG
V2
bash.help
broken.ps
-----Emacs:  message              (Text)------All----------
```

Emacs runs **ls** and inserts the result at your current location.

If you try **C-u ESC-|**, you get something even more interesting (and undocumented). Emacs deletes the region that you've selected and inserts the output of your command in its place. This command is really the ideal solution to our "sort the phone list" example. There's one pitfall, which may be why the Free Software Foundation left this feature undocumented. If the command generates an error, Emacs deletes the original region and inserts the error message in its place. The "undo" command (**C-x u**) gives you your original text back, but a simple "yank" won't; the deleted text isn't put in the kill ring.

Normally, Emacs uses your default shell to execute any commands. If you normally use the C shell (**csh**), it will use the C shell; if you normally use the Bourne shell (**sh**), Emacs will use the Bourne shell to execute any commands; and so on. You can set the variable **shell-file-name** to request a different shell. Its value must be the complete path for the shell executable. For example, to request the GNU project's "Bourne-Again Shell" (**bash**)[6] to execute commands, add a line like the following to your *.emacs* file:

```
(setq shell-file-name "pathname for bash")
```

Using Shell Mode

Now we're ready to discuss Emacs' shell mode, the interactive facility for running UNIX commands. To start a shell window, give the command **ESC-x shell**. This creates a buffer named `*shell*`. You see the prompt for your UNIX shell within this buffer.

---

[6] The location of **bash** varies from system to system. It may not even be available on your system.

Type: **ESC-x shell**

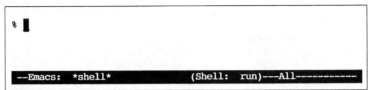

```
  %
```
`--Emacs: *shell*              (Shell: run)---All-----------`

You're ready to type shell commands.

For the most part, this is exactly like the normal UNIX command interface, except you can use Emacs to edit the commands as you type them. You can copy commands from one place to another, copy the results into a file, and so on.

A few tricks are worth knowing, though. For example, you normally terminate a job by typing **C-c**. If you type **C-c** to terminate a program in shell mode, Emacs thinks that the **C-c** is part of a command meant for it. Therefore, you have to type **C-c C-c** to terminate the current job. Likewise, you type **C-c C-z** to stop a job, instead of **C-z**; and **C-c C-d** instead of **C-d**; etc. Table 5-8 shows a list of special shell characters and their Emacs replacements.

Table 5-8. Special Shell Characters

Shell Character	Emacs Keystrokes	Command Name	Function
C-c	C-c C-c	interrupt-shell-subjob	Terminate the current job.
C-d	C-c C-d	shell-send-eof	End of file character.
C-u	C-c C-u	kill-shell-input	Erase current line.
C-w	C-c C-w	backward-kill-word	Erase the previous word.
C-z	C-c C-z	stop-shell-subjob	Suspend the current job.

Shell mode also provides a few other convenient shorthands. The command **C-c C-y** retrieves the last shell command you typed, no matter how far back in the buffer it is.

Type: **C-c C-y**

```
bronx.txt       fossa.ms      whales.txt
coatimundi.txt  lemurs.c      zooanimals.txt
detroit.ms      ocelot.txt    zygotes.c
fish.not        quetzal.c     zymurgy.ms
% ls zoostuff█
```

--Emacs: *shell*   (Shell: run)---All------------

C-c C-y retrieves the last command, even if it isn't on the screen.

In the example above, the previous command was **ls zoostuff**. It's no longer on the screen; its output (a long list of files) has pushed it off the top. The command **C-c C-y** retrieves the **ls** command, but doesn't execute it; you can edit the command line before typing a **RETURN**.

Another useful feature is the ability to delete the output from your last command. To do this, type **C-c C-o** (**kill-output-from-shell**).

Type: **C-c C-o**

```
% ls zoostuff
*** output flushed ***
% █
```

--Emacs: *shell*   (Shell: run)---All------------

C-c C-o automatically deletes the output from the last command.

The previous command (**ls zoostuff**) remains on the screen, but its output, a long list of files, is deleted. **C-c C-o** can only delete output from the most recent command; it can't delete output from your previous commands. **C-c C-o** is very useful if you give a command that you immediately regret, or if you give a command that produces voluminous output that you don't really care about. **C-c C-o** also provides a convenient way to copy the result from a UNIX command into another buffer. Simply move to the other buffer and use **C-y** (**yank**) to bring the output back.

Another useful command for shell mode is **C-c C-r** (**show-output-from-shell**). This is useful if a command produces a lot of output, scrolling the first few lines of output off the screen. **C-c C-r** repositions the window so the first line of output from your last command is at the top of the window.

One big advantage of the shell mode is that you can start a command and then continue editing some other buffer while the command is running. The shell buffer doesn't even need to be on the screen; just type **ESC-x shell** to get the buffer back again. (In contrast, **ESC-!** and **ESC-|** force you to wait until the UNIX command finishes before you can continue editing.) If you don't have "job control," the ability to continue editing while your command is running is a blessing. And even if you do have job control, Emacs' shell mode is still more convenient than running commands in the background while you continue working. With Emacs, you don't have to worry about output from your background job obscuring what you're currently doing; its output is saved neatly in the shell buffer.

The Current Directory

In the beginning of this book, we discussed Emacs' default directory. As a rule, if the cursor is in a file, Emacs' default directory is the directory that the file is in. When you start a shell, Emacs automatically puts you in its default directory: that is, your initial working directory is the directory of the file you last visited.

Here's where things get tricky. Emacs watches for **cd**, **popd**, and **pushd** commands (the C shell commands for changing directories), and uses them to change its notion of the default directory. Provided that you don't confuse it, Emacs' default directory for finding a file is always the same as your current directory. For example, assume that you give the shell command **cd /home/src/emacs/lisp** and then try to edit a file with **C-x C-f**. The default directory for finding a file will be */home/src/emacs/lisp*.

There are a few problems with this feature:

- Emacs can only detect **cd**, **popd**, and **pushd** commands if they are the first thing you type on the line.

- Emacs does not understand aliases or any other programs that might change directories. You can fix this by modifying the variables **shell-cd-regexp**, **shell-pushd-regexp**, and **shell-popd-regexp**. The values of these variables are "regular expressions" that match the commands you use for **cd**, **pushd**, and **popd**. Regular expressions are discussed thoroughly in Chapter 11, *Emacs LISP Programming*.

- Finally, some users (like us) think this feature gets in the way, rather than doing anything useful. We don't like having our default directory change "underneath" us. If you don't like it, add the following three lines to your *.emacs* file:

```
(setq-default shell-cd-regexp nil)
(setq-default shell-pushd-regexp nil)
(setq-default shell-popd-regexp nil)
```

Shell Initialization

How does Emacs know which shell to start? First, it looks at the variable **explicit-shell-file-name**. It then looks for a UNIX environment variable named ESHELL. It finally looks for an environment variable named SHELL. Therefore, if you want to run another particular shell (for example, the Bourne shell) when you're within Emacs, you can give the UNIX command **setenv ESHELL /bin/sh** before you start the editor, or you can add the following command to your *.emacs* file:

```
(setq explicit-shell-file-name "/bin/sh")
```

When Emacs starts an interactive shell, it runs an additional initialization file after your shell's normal startup files. The name of this file is *.emacs_shell-name*, where *shell-name* is the name of the shell you're using. It must be located in your home directory. For example, if you use the C shell, you can add Emacs-only startup commands by placing them in the file *.emacs_csh*. Let's say when you're in Emacs, you want to change the prompt to "emacs:%", and that you want an environment variable called **WITHIN_EDITOR** to be set to **T**. Here's the contents of your *.emacs_csh* file:

```
set prompt="emacs:% "
setenv WITHIN_EDITOR T
```

Within a shell window, Emacs also sets the environment variable EMACS to **t**, and sets your terminal type (the **TERM** variable) to **emacs**.

Problems with Remote Shells

If you're on a network, you might want to run Emacs, start a shell window, and then run **rlogin** in the window to access another system. This usually creates a minor problem with terminal handling. You will probably see your UNIX commands echoed twice, and you will probably see ^M printed at the end of most lines. Otherwise, everything will work normally.

Initial state:

```
% rlogin remhost
remhost % pwd
pwd^M
/home/remhost/deb^M
remhost % ls
ls^M
file1 file2 file3^M
remhost% ▮
--Emacs:  *shell*              (Shell:  run)---All-----------
```

Extra copies of each command and spurious ^M's.

There's an easy fix for this. Within the shell window on the remote system, give the UNIX command **stty -echo nl**.

Type: **stty -echo nl**

```
% rlogin remhost
remhost% stty -echo nl
stty -echo nl^M
remhost% pwd
/home/remhost/deb
remhost% ▮
--Emacs:  *shell*              (Shell:  run)---All-----------
```

Output from remote system fixed by **stty**.

Ideally, you would like to issue the **stty** command automatically. This can be done by modifying the *.cshrc* (for C shell users) or your *.profile* (for Korn or Bourne shell users) on all remote systems that you're likely to use. Here's what to do:

For csh:
if ($TERM == emacs) stty -echo nl

For ksh or sh:
if [$TERM = "emacs"]
then
    stty -echo nl
fi

For the **ksh/sh** example, be sure to surround each bracket with spaces. Leaving out the spaces is a common error.

Working with Directories

The directory editing mode is one of Emacs' most interesting features—and, for a new user, perhaps one of the scariest. It provides a way of editing a directory. You can look at all of the files in a directory, delete them, rename them, copy them, and perform almost all basic file operations. Once you have gotten used to Dired, you never need the UNIX **cp**, **rm**, or **mv** commands.

Getting into Dired

There are two ways to start directory editing. If you're not in Emacs, invoke Emacs with a directory name as an argument, for example:

```
% emacs ARCHIVE
```

Emacs will start up editing the directory *ARCHIVE*: you'll see a single window, which will contain a listing of the *ARCHIVE* directory. You can also start the directory editor by using **C-x C-f** (or any other command for visiting a file) and naming a directory, rather than a plain file. For example, **C-x C-f ARCHIVE** will get you ready to edit the *ARCHIVE* directory. No matter how you start the editor, the result will be the same.

Type: **C-x C-f ARCHIVE RETURN**

```
total 1100
drwxrwxr-x  9 deb   ora 1536 Apr  9 19:59 .
drwxr-xr-x 66 root  ora 1072 Mar 27 10:58 ..
-rw-rw-r--  1 deb   ora  717 Apr  9 10:44 files.c
-rwxrwxr-x  1 deb   ora  269 Apr  9 08:44 files.c~
-rw-rw-r--  1 deb   ora  140 Apr  9 09:45 format.h
-rw-r--r--  1 deb   ora  230 Apr  8 12:41 format.h~
-rw-rw-r--  1 deb   ora  345 Feb 13 09:40 iostuff.c
-rw-rw-r--  1 deb   ora 2526 Mar  7 14:52 math.h
-rw-rw-r--  1 deb   ora   88 Feb 13 12:55 mathlib.c
--%%-Dired:  deb          (Dired)----------Top-----------------
```

Basic directory editor display.

As you can see, this is similar to what you see when you type **ls -l** at the UNIX prompt. The permissions associated with the file, the owner, the system name, the size of the file, and its date last modified all precede the filename. All files and directories are listed, including those whose names start with a dot.

If you remember how to edit the mail header list (earlier in this chapter) or the buffer list (Chapter 4, *Using Buffers and Windows*), you will find that the directory editor is almost identical. You can do many additional things, but the basic commands are the same. Remember, though: in the directory editor, you are working directly with files, not with buffers. When you delete a file, it's gone permanently.

You should be aware that all the file operations you do in Dired, like deleting, renaming, and so on, appear on the screen as you execute them and these changes affect your files on disk. If you make changes to the directory outside of Dired (for example, through shell mode, pausing Emacs and going to the Unix shell, or through outputting mail to files in the directory), these changes are not reflected in the Dired buffer but of course are reflected on disk. To see these kind of changes in the Dired buffer, type **C-x C-f** followed by the directory name to restart Dired; Emacs reads the directory from disk again and your changes appear.

There are several ways to move around in Dired. The commands **SPACE, C-n**, and **n** all move you to the next file in the list. **DEL, C-p**, and **p** all move you to the previous file. You can also use any of the search commands (incremental search, word search, and so on) to find a particular file. When looking at a directory listing, it's nice to be able to get a quick look at the files. Dired's **v** command does just this; put the cursor on the file you want to view and press **v**. Emacs displays the file in a buffer marked `View`. This is a read-only buffer, so you can't modify the file.

Emacs uses a recursive edit (remember this?) to display the file that you're viewing. Therefore, to return to the directory list, you can type **ESC-C-c**. You can also return by typing **C-c** or **q**—whichever is more convenient. While you're viewing the file, you can use **s** to start an incremental search, **RETURN** to scroll the display down one line. Typing **=** tells you what line the cursor is currently on. There are a number of shorthands for other Emacs commands (like marking text), but frankly, most of the long versions work correctly. There's no reason to remember a special set of commands when the ones you already know work.

If you want to edit a file from the Dired window, type the letter **e** or **f**. Emacs puts the file you want into a window and allows you to edit it. This is a completely normal editing buffer: you can make any changes you want, save them, visit other files, and so on. It is not a recursive edit, so there's no simple way to get back to the directory editor. However, typing **C-x b** followed by the name of the directory you were editing moves you back to the Dired buffer. Or you can use the buffer menu (**C-x C-b**) to find and display the Dired buffer.

Deleting Files with Dired

Of course, you're all waiting for the interesting stuff: how to delete files. Viewing and editing files is nice, but you already know how to do that—right?

As we've said, file deletion is almost identical to buffer deletion with the buffer list or, for that matter, deleting mail messages from the header summary. If you read either of these sections, you know the basics of deleting files with Dired. First, you mark a file for deletion by moving to the file's name and typing **d**. Doing this places a D on the left margin and moves the cursor to the next file in the list. You can mark as many files as you want. You can change your mind at this point and type **u** to undelete the file. At some later time, you type **x** to delete the files (more on this in a minute). The following screen shows what the Dired window looks like when you delete a few files.

Type: **d**

```
total 1100
drwxrwxr-x  9 deb  ora 1536 Apr  9 19:59 .
drwxr-xr-x 66 root ora 1072 Mar 27 10:58 ..
-rw-rw-r--  1 deb  ora  717 Apr  9 10:44 files.c
D -rwxrwxr-x  1 deb  ora  269 Apr  9 08:44 files.c~
-rw-rw-r--  1 deb  ora  140 Apr  9 09:45 format.h
-rw-r--r--  1 deb  ora  230 Apr  8 12:41 format.h~
-rw-rw-r--  1 deb  ora  345 Feb 13 09:40 iostuff.c
D -rw-rw-r--  1 deb  ora 2526 Mar  7 14:52 math.h
-rw-rw-r--  1 deb  ora   88 Feb 13 12:55 mathlib.c
--%%-Dired:  deb                (Dired)----------Top----------
```

Two files marked for deletion.

To help in streamlining backup files, Emacs offers some special commands for deleting them. Typing **#** marks all the auto-save files (files whose names start and end with #) for deletion. Typing **˜** marks all the backup files (whose names end with ˜) for deletion.

If you use numbered backup files Emacs offers another deletion command. To mark extra backup files for deletion, preserving the oldest few and the newest few copies, type a dot (.). This command is only useful if you have Emacs set to keep multiple backup copies. By default, you don't get enough backup copies to make this command work. This isn't a feature that most UNIX users use; a brief discussion of the variables that control it appears in Appendix C, *Emacs Variables*.

As we mentioned, you can type **u** at any time to undelete the files. This moves you to the next file in the list. You can also use **DEL** to undelete files. This undeletes the *previous* file in the list, and then moves up one line (to the file it has just undeleted).

After you have marked a file for deletion, you can still view it by typing **v**; this is an easy way to check files before deleting them. For that matter, you can type **e** to edit a file that you've marked for deletion. However, editing a file implicitly undeletes it because Emacs assumes that you don't want to lose your changes. Anything you're willing to edit you must want to keep.

When you really want the files to be deleted from disk, type **x**. Emacs displays the names of all the files that are marked for deletion and asks you if you want to delete them.

Type: **x**

```
 ┌─────────────────────────────────────────────────────────────────┐
 │  files.c~      math.h                                             │
 │                                                                   │
 │                                                                   │
 │                                                                   │
 │                                                                   │
 │ ──%%─Dired:   deb             (Dired)──────────Top──────────      │
 │ Delete these files (yes or no) ▐                                  │
 └─────────────────────────────────────────────────────────────────┘
```

x deletes the files; typing **yes** says "go ahead."

Type **yes** to delete them all or type **no** to return to the Dired buffer so you can undelete those you don't really want to delete by typing **u** next to them.

To make Dired's deletion capabilities even more useful, it would be nice if there were some other ways to delete files as well, such as by date or using wildcards to specify filenames for deletion. We've seen a few more advanced Direds floating around the net, but they aren't currently part of the regular Emacs distribution.

Copying and Renaming Files with Dired

To copy a file with Dired, type **c** next to it. Emacs asks for the name of the file you want to copy to. Type the name and press **RETURN**. The new filename is reflected in the directory listing, but not put in alphabetical order.

To rename a file with Dired (similar to the UNIX command **mv**), type **r** next to the filename. Emacs asks you what the new name should be. Type it and press **RETURN**. The directory listing reflects the new name.

As you can see, much of your file maintenance and cleanup can be done easily from within Dired. Table 5-9 summarizes Dired commands.

Table 5-9. Dired Commands

Keystrokes	Action	Similar to UNIX command
r	Rename file.	mv
e	Edit file.	emacs
c	Copy file.	cp
d	Mark for deletion.	rm
~	Mark all files ending with ~ for deletion.	rm *~
#	Mark all auto-save files for deletion.	rm #*#
.	Mark all "extra" backups for deletion.[7]	(none)
u	Undelete.	(none)
x	Delete files that are marked.	rm and rmdir
v	View files.	more
SPACE	Move forward by filename.	(none)
DEL	Move backward by filename.	(none)
M	Change file permissions.	chmod
n	Move forward by filename.	(none)
p	Move backward by filename.	(none)

There are two commands that give you a buffer with simple directory listings. **C-u C-x C-d** gives a verbose directory listing, similar to **ls -l**. The command **C-x C-d** gives a simple directory listing, like what you see with **ls -F**: directories are followed by a slash, executables are followed by a star, and symbolic links are followed by an at sign.

Unlike the Dired listing that we have just discussed, these listings are just temporary buffers that can be edited like any other Emacs buffer. The changes you make on the screen do not affect the underlying file structure. This feature is useful if you want to print your directories so you can make notes about what the files are or decide what you want to delete.

---

[7] Only important if you're saving multiple numbered backup files.

Printing from Emacs

Emacs offers several commands for printing buffers and regions. To print a buffer using the UNIX print command (which prints page numbers and headers with the filename) type **ESC-x print-buffer RETURN**. This command takes the entire buffer and sends it to **pr** (a program that does simple formatting for listings), followed by **lpr** (which sends the listing to the printer).[8] If you want to print the file directly, without the headers and page numbers that **pr** provides, give the command **ESC-x lpr-buffer RETURN**. You can also use these commands to print a selected portion of a file. First define a region by setting a mark at one end, and moving the cursor to the other. Then give the command **ESC-x print-region RETURN** (or **ESC-x lpr-region RETURN**).

The **lpr-buffer** and **lpr-region** commands always check the variable **lpr-switches** to determine if there are any options that should be passed to the UNIX **lpr** command. These options are used to request a particular printer, and for many other purposes—see the UNIX reference manual's discussion of **lpr** for more information. For example, if you want to use the printer named "lpt1" whenever you print from Emacs, you would want to set **lpr-switches** to "-Plpt1." To do so, add the following line to your *.emacs* file:

```
(setq lpr-switches '("-Plpt1"))
```

Note the single quote preceding, and the parentheses surrounding, the string "-Plpt1". This is just weird-but-necessary LISP syntax; see Chapter 11, *Emacs LISP Programming*, for more details.

Emacs' print commands are most generally useful if you are primarily interested in printing straight ASCII text on a dot matrix or daisywheel printer. They're not too good if you need to print **troff** or TeX files, or if your ASCII files need to be converted to PostScript for printing on a laser printer. In these cases, it's conceivable that you could set up your system so that you could use **lpr-buffer** and its relatives, but it's probably a lot of effort. (This would require setting up a number of "print filters," and we have yet to see a site where these were installed correctly.) It's more common for systems to have completely separate commands for processing **troff** or TeX documents. For example, your system might use a command like **psprint** to list an ASCII file on a laser printer. In this case, there is still a relatively convenient way to print your output directly from Emacs—*provided* your print command accepts a standard input in lieu of a filename: just use the

---

[8] The equivalent UNIX commands are slightly different for System V UNIX implementations.

ESC-! (for **shell-command**) command described earlier in this chapter and type your print command at the prompt.[9]

Table 5-10 provides a summary of commands for printing.

Table 5-10. Printing Commands

Keystrokes	Action
ESC-x print-buffer	Prints the buffer (similar to UNIX pr | lpr).
ESC-x print-region	Prints the region (similar to UNIX pr | lpr).
ESC-x lpr-buffer	Prints buffer with no page numbers (similar to UNIX lpr).
ESC-x lpr-region	Prints region with no page numbers (similar to UNIX lpr).

Reading Man Pages from Emacs

You can read UNIX online documentation (called "man pages") from within Emacs using the **manual-entry** command. This command creates a buffer with a formatted man page in it, which you can scroll through (or copy from) using Emacs commands. Simply type: **ESC-x manual-entry RETURN unix-command-name RETURN**.

For the UNIX command name, you can use either a simple name, like **ls**, or a man page section name like **ttytab(5)**.

The advantage of using the **manual-entry** command is that you can scroll through the man page much easier than you can under many versions of UNIX. Also, if you try to view man pages in shell mode, they come out garbled, whereas **manual-entry** gives you clean text. The only disadvantage to using this command is that you lose control over Emacs while the man page is processing; you can't abort it using **C-g**, for example.

---

[9] TeX mode provides some special commands for formatting and printing files. See Chapter 7, *Using Emacs with UNIX Text Formatters*, for details. Alas, these commands probably aren't useful either, unless you're willing to do some hacking—the way TeX is configured varies a lot from system to system. But they're there, and can be made to work.

Using Your Emacs Work Environment

Now you've learned many of the things that you can do without ever leaving Emacs. The next two chapters discuss text formatting, but if you're not interested in that, you might want to go on to Chapter 8, *Writing Macros*, so you can learn how to create macros and streamline your work in Emacs even further.

6

Simple Text Formatting and Specialized Editing

Indenting Text
Centering Text
Inserting Page Breaks
Rectangle Editing
Making Simple Drawings
Using Outline Mode

Emacs is fundamentally a file editor, rather than a word processor. It is a tool that creates files containing exactly what you see on the screen, rather than a tool that can make text files look beautiful when printed. However, Emacs does give you the capability to:

- Indent text in a variety of ways.

- Center words, lines, and paragraphs of text.

- Create simple diagrams, rough sketches, and pictures to insert in papers or in mail messages (something most word processors and graphics packages can't do at all).

- Edit by column rather than by line (especially helpful when you create or change tables), referred to in Emacs as rectangle editing.

- Hide and show portions of a document using outline mode, which gives you a feel for the document's overall structure. Outline mode can make it easier to go from rough outline, to detailed outline, to rough draft, to the final product.

Emacs also has special modes for use with the **troff**, TeX, and Scribe formatting programs. These are described in the next chapter.

Indenting Text

In writing outlines, papers, specs, or almost anything, you may find you want to indent some text. Emacs offers several ways to do this. First we'll talk about using tabs, the simplest way to indent text. Next we'll discuss fill prefixes, which can be used to indent text but also for other things like prefacing each line with a string of characters (good for special notes in informal documents or comments in programs). The most elaborate Emacs tool for indenting text is indented text mode, which you'll want to use if you write documents with various indentation levels.

Using Tabs

Under Emacs, the TAB key works pretty much the way you would expect. It moves the cursor to the next tab stop. The text that's before the cursor moves forward, opening up some clear space on the line—even if you're in overwrite mode.[1] For example, to indent the first line of a paragraph, you can type a regular "block" paragraph, move to the first line, and press **TAB**.

Press: **TAB**

```
    It was the best of times, it was the worst
of times, it was the age of wisdom, it was the age of
foolishness, it was the epoch of belief, it was the
epoch of incredulity, it was the season of Light, it
was the season of Darkness, it was the spring of hope,
it was the winter of despair, we had everything before
------Emacs:  dickens        (Fundamental)--All--------------
```

Tab indents the first line, moving the rest of the text with it.

If you want to indent the entire paragraph by hand, you can certainly do so: type a **TAB** at the beginning of each line. There are some ways to automate the process, which we'll discuss shortly. For now, we'll assume that you do your tab formatting by hand.

---

[1] We stress this because we've seen editors on which a tab worked exactly as it works on a typewriter: pressing TAB moves the cursor forward but doesn't change the text.

Formatting Indented Paragraphs

Using tabs makes lines longer, and some lines may overflow the right margin, as shown in the following screen.

Press **TAB** at the beginning of each line:

```
            It was the best of times, it was the worst
            of times, it was the age of wisdom, it was the age \
of
            foolishness, it was the epoch of belief, it was the
            epoch of incredulity, it was the season of Light, it
            was the season of Darkness, it was the spring of ho\
pe,
            ▮t was the winter of despair, we had everything bef\
ore
------Emacs:  dickens          (Fundamental)--All--------------
```

Tabs make some lines overflow the right margin.

How can you fix this? If you've only indented the first line of a paragraph, you can type **ESC-q** (for **fill-paragraph**). We introduced this command back in Chapter 2; it rearranges your text so that there's an acceptable margin on the right side. It won't touch your initial tab, and it won't touch the preceding paragraph; the whitespace at the beginning of the line tells Emacs that a new paragraph has begun.

However, if you've indented the entire paragraph, you can't use **ESC-q**. In this case, it will treat every line as a separate paragraph, because every line begins with some whitespace. In this case, define the paragraph as a region, then type **ESC-x fill-individual-paragraphs RETURN**. The **fill-individual-paragraphs** command works on a region, rather than a single paragraph. It divides the region into paragraphs according to indentation; every change of indentation constitutes a new paragraph. It then reformats each paragraph with a reasonable right margin, preserving that paragraph's indentation. For example, consider the text in the following screen.

Initial state:

```
My second correspondent, also a woman, sends me the
following statement:
     Life seemed difficult to me at one time.  I
     was always breaking down, and had several
     attacks of what is called nervous prostration,
     with terrible insomnia...
Here is another case, more concrete, also that of
a woman.  I read you these cases without comment--
they express so many varieties of the state of mind
we are studying.
```
```
-----Emacs:  hjames              (Fundamental)--All--------------
```

Indented paragraphs.

This consists of three paragraphs, because there are three areas in which the indentation is different. If you need to reformat this kind of text, set the mark at one end (with **C-@**), move to the other end, and type **ESC-x fill-individual-paragraphs RETURN**.

Setting Tab Stops

By default, tabs are set every 8 characters. Emacs allows you to change the positions of the tab stops. To change the tab stops, type **ESC-x edit-tab-stops**. A `*Tab Stops*` buffer appears.

Type: **ESC-x edit-tab-stops**

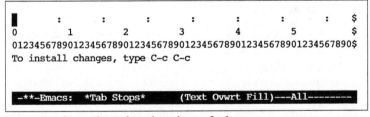

```
█         :         :         :         :         :         :         :       $
0         1         2         3         4         5                           $
01234567890123456789012345678901234567890123456789012345678901234567890$
To install changes, type C-c C-c
```
```
-**-Emacs:  *Tab Stops*        (Text Ovwrt Fill)---All--------
```

Tab stop ruler; colons show locations of tab stops

The colons in the first line of the display show you where tab stops are currently located. The next two lines form a ruler that shows each character position on the line. To insert a tab, use **C-f** to move to the desired column, and then type a colon (**:**). To delete a tab, move to the desired tab, and type **SPACE**. The `*Tab Stops*` buffer is in "overwrite" mode, so these changes won't change the position of other tabs. Make sure that you do all your editing in the first line of the display. Changes made to the other lines won't have any effect.

When you're satisfied with the tab stops, press **C-c C-c** to install them. If you don't make any changes, press **C-c C-c** to exit the buffer. If you make some changes and then decide you don't want them after all, kill the buffer by using the buffer editor—or, for that matter, just ignore the tab stop buffer and continue editing. (Typing **C-x 0** removes the buffer from your screen.) The default tab stops remain in effect.

The tab stops you set are in effect for this Emacs session only, and the new tab settings affect all buffers that you create.

Changing Tabs to Spaces

If your response to the section title, "Changing Tabs to Spaces," is "Why?", you may not need to know about it and can feel free to skip this section. This topic is most relevant to people who are moving files from one system or software package to another and to people who are having printing problems.

Tabs provide an easy way to do some simple formatting. However, they have one big problem: they're not "portable." There's no agreement on standard tab settings. A tab is usually represented by a particular character (ASCII 9 or **C-i**, if you're curious). When a terminal, an editor, a printer, or anything else sees this character, it means "move to the next tab stop"—just like it does on a typewriter. As we've just seen, Emacs lets you put tab stops wherever you want—but it's not so easy to reset the tab stops on your printer. Your file may look perfect on the screen, but it will be a disaster if the printer's tab stops differ from Emacs'. Tabs are particularly problematic with **troff** and TeX documents. Many users have spent their time wondering why Emacs shows one thing and the printer something else—all because of a few hidden tabs.

The authors of GNU Emacs wisely provided a way to banish tabs from your files, without losing their advantages: simple and easy formatting. This means that you can use them for editing, and then convert all of your tabs to the appropriate number of spaces, so that the appearance of your file doesn't change. Unlike tabs, a "space" is almost always well defined. The command for eliminating tabs is **ESC-x untabify**. There's a corresponding command to convert spaces into tabs: **tabify**. However, we trust that you'll take our advice and forget about it.

The **untabify** command works on a region. Therefore, to use it, you must put the mark somewhere in the buffer (preferably the beginning); move to some other place in the buffer (preferably the end); and type **ESC-x untabify RETURN**. The command **C-x h** (for **mark-whole-buffer**) automatically puts the cursor at the beginning of the buffer and the mark at the end. It makes "untabification" a bit easier, since you can do it all at once with the simple sequence **C-x h ESC-x untabify RETURN**.

Having said this, there is one kind of file you must not untabify: a *makefile*. Tabs mean something special within *makefiles*, and changing them to spaces will cause errors. (This is an unfortunate problem in the design of one of UNIX's most useful programs.) If you don't know what a *makefile* is, don't worry; just don't untabify any file whose name is either *makefile* or *Makefile*.

You can also tell Emacs that it should never use the tab character. If you're writing a new file, this is a great way to ensure that you won't corrupt it with unwanted tabs. The variable **indent-tabs-mode** controls whether or not Emacs is allowed to use the tab character. If you set this variable to **nil**, Emacs will always insert spaces instead of tab characters. You can still type **TAB** and tab stops will work as you expect, and the indentation modes that we'll discuss later will work correctly; but Emacs will only insert spaces into your file. If you need to have the tab character in your file, and nothing else will do (as in the *makefiles* we mentioned above), you have to give the command **C-q C-i**.[2] Note that **indent-tabs-mode** is a variable, not a mode as the name implies; you can use it in any mode.

You can turn tabs off permanently by putting the following line in your *.emacs* file:

```
(setq-default indent-tabs-mode nil)
```

Table 6-1 summarizes the tab commands.

Table 6-1. Summary of Tab Commands

Keystrokes	Command Name	Action
(none)	edit-tab-stops	Opens a buffer called *Tab Stops* where you can change the tab settings.
(none)	tabify	Changes groups of three or more spaces to tabs where possible without affecting text placement.
(none)	untabify	Changes all tabs into the equivalent number of spaces.
(none)	fill-individual-paragraphs	Reformats paragraphs, following indentation.

---

[2] **C-q** is the "quote" command; it means "insert the next thing I type literally, even if it is a control character."

Using Fill Prefixes

Now let's talk about putting whitespace in front of paragraphs automatically. There are several ways of doing this. One way is to use a "fill prefix." A fill prefix is simply a string of text that Emacs automatically puts at the beginning of every line you type. The term fill prefix comes from the fact that Emacs calls word wrap "auto-fill mode"; in other words, a fill prefix is a string that Emacs should insert at the beginning of, or "prefix" each line with, when doing word wrap.

To use fill prefixes, it's best to be in auto-fill mode. If your mode line says "Fill" on it, you're already in auto-fill mode. If it doesn't, type **ESC-x auto-fill-mode RETURN**.

Now let's assume that you want to indent a memo. For the first line of the memo, type your indentation by hand—say, 8 spaces, to indent one inch. Then type **C-x . (set-fill-prefix)**. Emacs displays the message: "fill prefix "   "" in the minibuffer. Then start typing normally. Whenever you type past the right margin and Emacs breaks a line for you, it automatically inserts your 8-space indentation at the beginning of the line.

Here's a slightly more exciting example. There's no reason that fill prefixes have to be spaces; they can be anything you choose. Assume that you're sending an electronic mail message to your colleagues, and that you want an eye-catching fill prefix.

Type: **ELEPHANT RIDING PARTY!!! C-x .**

```
 ELEPHANT RIDING PARTY!!!█




 -**-Emacs:  elephant              (Text Fill)------75%---------
 fill prefix:  "ELEPHANT RIDING PARTY!!!"
```

Type the prefix, and the **C-x .** to set it.

Once you've set the prefix, you can type your message normally.

Type: **The time ... the zoo.**

```
ELEPHANT RIDING PARTY!!!The time for the annual
ELEPHANT RIDING PARTY!!!elephant riding party is
ELEPHANT RIDING PARTY!!!nearly upon us.  Plan to
ELEPHANT RIDING PARTY!!!be at the San Diego Zoo
ELEPHANT RIDING PARTY!!!at 3:30 on Saturday,
ELEPHANT RIDING PARTY!!!June 10.  You can give a
ELEPHANT RIDING PARTY!!!$5.00 donation per elephant
ELEPHANT RIDING PARTY!!!ride to benefit the zoo.█
-**-Emacs:  elephant             (Text Fill)------75%---------
```

Emacs inserts the fill prefix at the beginning of each line of the message.

You only had to type "ELEPHANT RIDING PARTY!!!" the first time; Emacs inserted the rest automatically. Here are some things you might want to know about fill prefixes:

- Emacs never applies the fill prefix to the first line of a paragraph. You obviously can't apply it to the first line of the first paragraph (you have to type it somewhere). But Emacs can't apply it to the first line of *any* paragraph. In other words, if the "elephant riding" memo had two paragraphs, you'd have to type (or yank) the words "elephant riding party" at the beginning of the second paragraph.

  However, you don't need to set the fill prefix again. Emacs supplies your prefix for all lines but the first in subsequent paragraphs. It just gets confused about the initial line of any paragraph.

- Once you've started using the fill prefix, how do you turn it off? There's no special command. All you do is put the cursor at the left margin and type **C-x .** to define a new fill prefix. This time, the fill prefix happens to be the "null string," or nothing.

- Finally, if you need to reformat your paragraphs later, after you've cancelled the fill prefix, define it again, then type **ESC-q**. This simple command is all you need: commands like **fill-individual-paragraphs** don't work with fill prefixes.

Indented Text Mode

If you use indentation heavily, you should consider using indented text mode. This is a special editing mode that provides some extra support for managing indentation. It's very helpful if you're writing outlines (although you should also consider outline mode, discussed later in this chapter). It's also useful if you're writing a paper that includes long quotations; indented text mode can help you to set the quotations off from the rest of the text.

To enter indented text mode, type **ESC-x indented-text-mode RETURN**. "Indented" appears on the mode line. Also, if "Fill" is not on your mode line, type **ESC-x auto-fill-mode RETURN**. Indented text mode won't work without auto-fill mode turned on.

Now that you've gotten indented text mode turned on, let's see how to use it. Starting on the left edge of the screen, use the TAB key or type spaces until you've established as much indentation as you want. Now just type. Whenever you reach the end of a line, Emacs automatically indents the new line to match the previous line. The following is an example of using indented text mode to set off a quotation.

Type: **ESC-x indented-text-mode RETURN**

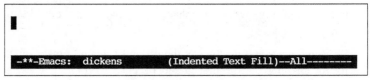

"Indented" appears on the mode line.

Press **TAB**, followed by your text:

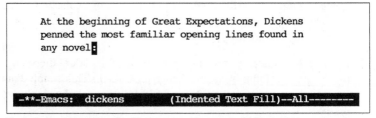

In indented text mode, Emacs continues to indent text as you type. You only type **TAB** at the beginning of the paragraph.

Press **RETURN TAB TAB** followed by the quote:

```
    At the beginning of Great Expectations, Dickens
    penned the most familiar opening lines found in
    any novel:
        It was the best of times, it was the worst
        of times, it was the age of wisdom, it was
        the age of foolishness, it was the epoch of
        belief, it was the epoch of incredulity, it
-**-Emacs:  dickens            (Indented Text Fill)--All--------
```

Once the first line is indented properly, Emacs indents the quotation automatically.

Emacs assumes that you want to indent all your paragraphs the same amount. To start a new paragraph, press **RETURN** twice (to leave a blank line) then press **TAB** once (to set the indentation level for this paragraph). After you've initially set the indentation level, you only have to type one TAB to get the same indentation as the previous paragraph. One TAB automatically brings you to a point directly under the first column of text, regardless of where your tab stops are or how far you have indented.

If you want less indentation, press **DEL** to erase as much as you want to (even all of it). If you want more indentation, press **TAB** again.

Now that you can write text in indented text mode, what about editing it? As you edit, it will become messy; soon, you will need to reformat it into neat paragraphs again. Mark the beginning and end of the region you want to fill, and type **ESC-x fill-individual-paragraphs**, which we discussed earlier.

To get out of indented text mode, enter another major mode, such as text mode. For example, to enter text mode, type **ESC-x text-mode**; "Text" appears on the mode line instead of "Indented Text."

Tab Settings in Indented Text Mode

In indented text mode, Emacs ignores the predefined tab stops. How do tab stops work, then? First, Emacs looks for the previous non-blank line. The first tab takes you to a point directly under the first non-blank character on the line; the second takes you to the beginning of the next word; and so on. After the line ends, the regular tab stops "take over" for the rest of the line. Figure 6-1 shows how Emacs defines tab stops.

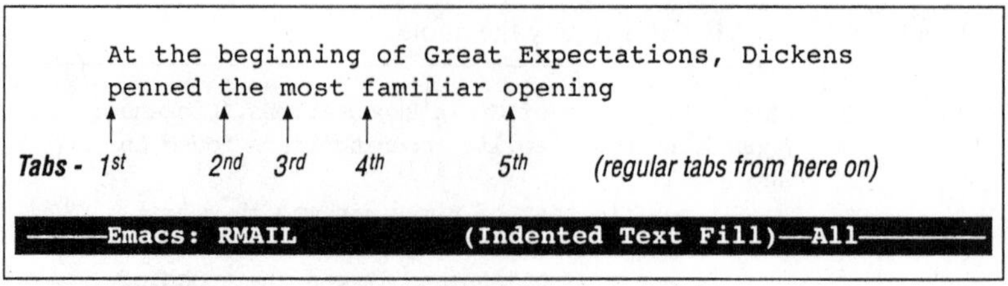

```
        At the beginning of Great Expectations, Dickens
        penned the most familiar opening
         ↑      ↑   ↑    ↑        ↑
Tabs - 1st     2nd 3rd  4th      5th      (regular tabs from here on)

  ────Emacs: RMAIL            (Indented Text Fill)──All────
```

Figure 6-1. Defining Tab Stops

One tab brings you to the column under "p"; the second gets you to the column under "t"; and so on. Watch out—this can be an inconvenience. If you're writing an outline in indented text mode, remember that typing two (or more) tabs does *not* always bring you to the same point on the line. But tabs aren't your only option: you can type spaces to set the indentation level anywhere you want it.

Indenting Regions

What if you have already typed your text without indentation, and want to indent it later? Take these steps:

1. Enter indented text mode (**ESC-x indented-text-mode RETURN**).

2. Move to the end of the region you want to indent, and set the mark.

3. Move to the beginning of the region you want to indent, and type the desired indentation, using either spaces or tabs.

4. Then type **ESC-C-**. Emacs indents the entire region to match the first line.

If the area you want to indent has several levels of indentation, define each block of text with a different indentation level as a separate region when following these steps.

Some Other Tricks

Whenever you are using indentation (and whether or not you're in indented text mode), you can use **ESC-m** to move to the first non-blank character on a line. On a line that's not indented, this command simply moves you to the beginning of the line. In other words, **ESC-m** brings you to the "logical" beginning of the line: it's what you usually mean when you type **C-a**.

Another indentation command is **ESC-C-o** (for **split-line**). You can use this command to create a stairstep effect. You don't have to be in indented text mode to use it. Move the cursor to the text that you want to put on the next line and press **ESC-C-o**.

Initial state:

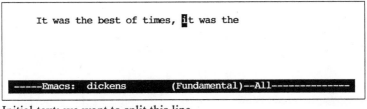

Initial text; we want to split this line.

Type: **ESC-C-o**

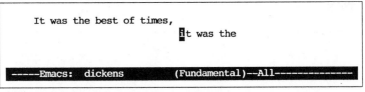

ESC-C-o splits a line at the cursor position.

While this command produces an interesting effect in text mode and might be helpful in writing certain types of poetry, it is more useful in picture mode, described later in this chapter.

Table 6-2 shows a list of the commands for controlling indentation that we've discussed.

Table 6-2. Indentation Commands

Keystrokes	Command Name	Action
C-x .	set-fill-prefix	Uses the information up to the cursor column as a prefix to each line of the paragraph; typing this command in column 1 cancels the fill prefix.
(none)	indented-text-mode	Enters a major mode in which pressing tab defines a new indentation level for subsequent lines of a paragraph.

Table 6-2. Indentation Commands (continued)

Keystrokes	Command Name	Action
(none)	text-mode	Exits indented text mode and returns the buffer to text mode (entering any other major mode also works fine).
ESC-C-\	indent-region	Indents a region to match the first line in the region.
ESC-m	back-to-indentation	Moves the cursor to the first character on a line.
ESC-C-o	split-line	Splits the line at the cursor position and indents it to the column of the cursor position.
(none)	fill-individual-paragraphs	Reformats indented paragraphs, preserving indentation.

Centering Text

Another common formatting task is simply centering some text. For example, you might want to center the title of a document or individual headings within a document. Emacs provides commands to center lines, paragraphs, and regions.

First make sure you're in text mode. Look at the mode line and if the word "Text" is displayed, you are in text mode. If not, type **ESC-x text mode RETURN** to enter text mode. Now you can center a line by simply typing the line you want to center (or moving anywhere on an existing line), then pressing **ESC-s**.

Type: **Annual Report**

```
 Annual Report█




-**-Emacs:  annreport         (Text Fill)------All------------
```

Before centering.

Type: **ESC-s**

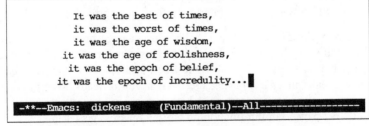

```
                    Annual Report█



 _**_Emacs:  annreport          (Text Fill)-----All------------
```

Emacs centers the line.

You can also center paragraphs and regions. In both cases, Emacs does line-by-line centering rather than block centering. To center a paragraph, use the command **ESC-x center-paragraph**; to center a region, use **ESC-x center-region**. For example, let's say you wanted to center the following quotation.

Initial state:

```
 It was the best of times,
 it was the worst of times,
 it was the age of wisdom,
 it was the age of foolishness,
 it was the epoch of belief,
 it was the epoch of incredulity..█

 _**_Emacs:  dickens         (Fundamental)--All------------
```

Quotation to be centered.

Type: **ESC-x center-paragraph RETURN**

```
            It was the best of times,
            it was the worst of times,
            it was the age of wisdom,
          it was the age of foolishness,
           it was the epoch of belief,
         it was the epoch of incredulity...█

 _**_Emacs:  dickens         (Fundamental)--All------------
```

After centering.

In this case, line-by-line centering looks rather artistic. But there are many times when you might wish Emacs did block centering. You can replicate this effect by using the **indent-region** command, discussed earlier in this chapter. You just have to play with the indentation to see how far the block of text should be indented to look centered.

Table 6-3 is a summary of the commands used to center text.

Table 6-3. Centering Commands

Keystrokes	Command Name	Action
ESC-s	center-line	Centers the line the cursor is on.
(none)	center-paragraph	Centers the paragraph the cursor is on.
(none)	center-region	Centers the currently defined region.

Inserting Page Breaks

Although Emacs doesn't provide any pagination features, you can insert page breaks in your file. First, type the quote command (**C-q**), which tells Emacs to insert the following character into the text, whatever it is (rather than interpreting the character as a command). Then type **C-l** in the first column of the line. On your screen this will look like `^L`. Even though this appears to be two characters, it's really one; try erasing it and you'll see what we mean.

C-l is a special character called a *formfeed*. Many printers (particularly line printers, daisywheel printers, and dot matrix printers) and some UNIX utilities (for example, **more**) interpret a formfeed as a page break. **C-l** is meaningless (or worse, may cause problems) to formatting programs like **troff** and TeX, and to many laser printers (although many laser printers have a "line printer emulation" mode, which will probably interpret a formfeed correctly).

The only disadvantage to using this type of page break is that it's a *hard* page break. If you edit your text and a page grows or shrinks, you'll have to put in new page breaks to make it look right when printed. One approach is to never put page breaks in your working file. When you're ready to print the file, copy it, then use a macro to insert page breaks every *n* lines, where *n* is the number of lines per page. For information on writing macros, see Chapter 8.

Rectangle Editing

When you mark regions to move or delete, they always cover the full width of the screen. Editing by region is fine for most of the work that you do in Emacs. But what if you wanted to edit a table? What if you want interchange the second and fourth columns? Since regions cover the full width of the screen, they can't handle this case. Emacs offers another way to define areas to delete, copy, and move around: using *rectangles*. Rectangles are just what they sound like: rectangular areas that you define and manipulate using special rectangle editing commands. Editing with rectangles is useful whenever you want to move or delete vertical columns of information, as in moving a column of a table, creating multi-column text for a newsletter, or simply commenting or uncommenting some code.

For example, let's say you wanted to edit the following table, moving the "Working Hours" column to the right side. There's no way to do this using regions, but it's easy if you learn some rectangle editing commands.

Initial state:

```
                  Flex-time Schedule


   Name      █orking Hours  E-mail Address   Home Phone

   Fred      7:30-4:30     fred             (814)722-3940
   Olivia    9:00-6:00     liv              (814)827-3344
   Nicole    10:00-7:00    ncm              (412)734-0492
   Alvin     6:00-3:00     al               (814)437-9320

   -----Emacs:  flextime        (Fundamental)--All------------
```

Original table.

You define a rectangle the same way you define a region; it's the commands that you use after marking the area that tell Emacs whether it's a region or a rectangle you want to work with.

To define a rectangle, move the cursor to the upper-left corner and set the mark by pressing **C-@** or **C-SPACE**, then move the cursor to the lower-right corner of the rectangle. After you're at the lower-right corner of the rectangle, move *one character further*. Why move one character further? Remember that when you define a region, the character that the cursor is on *isn't* part of the region. (The character that the mark is on *is* part of the region.) Rectangles work the same way, but in two dimensions. Let's define a rectangle that covers the second column of our table.

Type: **C-@**

```
                       Flex-time Schedule

      Name    Working Hours   E-mail Address   Home Phone


      Fred    7:30-4:30       fred             (814)722-3940
      Olivia  9:00-6:00       liv              (814)827-3344
      Nicole  10:00-7:00      ncm              (412)734-0492
      Alvin   6:00-3:00       al               (814)437-9320


      -----Emacs:  flextime            (Fundamental)--All------------
      Mark set
```

The mark is set at the upper-left corner of the rectangle to be moved.

Move the cursor to the space following bottom-right corner of the rectangle, the "a" in "al."

```
                       Flex-time Schedule

      Name    Working Hours  E-mail Address   Home Phone

      Fred    7:30-4:30      fred             (814)722-3940
      Olivia  9:00-6:00      liv              (814)827-3344
      Nicole  10:00-7:00     ncm              (412)734-0492
      Alvin   6:00-3:00      al               (814)437-9320


      -----Emacs:  flextime            (Fundamental)--All------------
```

The cursor follows the bottom-right corner of the rectangle. (The shading is added so you can see the rectangle that we've marked.)

Type: **ESC-x kill-rectangle**

```
                       Flex-time Schedule

      Name    E-mail Address   Home Phone

      Fred    fred             (814)722-3940
      Olivia  liv              (814)827-3344
      Nicole  ncm              (412)734-0492
      Alvin   al               (814)437-9320


      -----Emacs:  flextime            (Fundamental)--All------------
```

The rectangle is deleted; it's in a special rectangle kill buffer.

Once again, when you mark a rectangle, you put the cursor on the upper-left corner and set the mark, then you move to the lower-right corner of the rectangle and *over one more space*. Emacs expects rectangles to be rectangles. If necessary, it will pad an area with spaces to make up the straight line on the right side.

You can move anywhere on the screen and reinsert the rectangle last killed with the **yank-rectangle** command. To put the "Working Hours" column on the right side of the table, we move to some place after "Home Phone."

Move the cursor following "Home Phone" and press **TAB**:

```
                       Flex-time Schedule

    Name      E-mail Address   Home Phone    █

    Fred      fred             (814)722-3940
    Olivia    liv              (814)827-3344
    Nicole    ncm              (412)734-0492
    Alvin     al               (814)437-9320

 ------Emacs: flextime          (Fundamental)--All-----------
```

Move to where we want to re-insert the rectangle.

Type: **ESC-x yank-rectangle RETURN**

```
                       Flex-time Schedule

    Name      E-mail Address   Home Phone    Working Hours

    Fred      fred             (814)722-3940  7:30-4:30
    Olivia    liv              (814)827-3344  9:00-6:00
    Nicole    ncm              (412)734-0492  10:00-7:00
    Alvin     al               (814)437-9320  6:00-3:00   █

 ------Emacs: flextime          (Fundamental)--All-----------
```

Emacs inserts the rectangle we killed earlier.

Emacs inserts the rectangle exactly where you tell it to. We moved past "Home Phone," and then pressed TAB to put some space between "Home Phone" and "Working Hours." Otherwise, Emacs would have blithely inserted the working hours into the middle of the phone number column. Note that there's no equivalent of the "kill ring" for rectangles, except in picture mode. You can only yank the most recent rectangle.

Killing and yanking rectangles requires a little bit of practice. Once you get the hang of it, it is an easy way to edit tables and other column-dependent material.

There are a few other commands for creating blank rectangles on the screen. For example, let's say we wanted to put two more spaces between the Name and E-mail Address columns. To do this, we use a command called **open-rectangle**, which inserts a blank rectangle anywhere on the screen and pushes the remaining text over to the right. First, we define the rectangle, then use the **open-rectangle** command to insert some blank space between the first two columns.

Move the cursor to the "E" in E-mail and type **C-@**

```
                       Flex-time Schedule                        ·

        Name      E-mail Address      Home Phone       Working Hours


        Fred      fred                (814)722-3940    7:30-4:30
        Olivia    liv                 (814)827-3344    9:00-6:00
        Nicole    ncm                 (412)734-0492    10:00-7:00
        Alvin     al                  (814)437-9320    6:00-3:00


     -----Emacs:  flextime          (Fundamental)--All-------------
     Mark set
```

Emacs sets the mark at the upper-left corner of the rectangle.

Now we need to define the amount of space we want to insert. Move down to the bottom of the region (the "Alvin" line), and then move over two spaces. Finally, type **ESC-x open-rectangle** to add the new space to the drawing.

Move the cursor following "al" and type **ESC-x open-rectangle**

```
                       Flex-time Schedule

        Name      E-mail Address      Home Phone       Working Hours

        Fred      fred                (814)722-3940    7:30-4:30
        Olivia    liv                 (814)827-3344    9:00-6:00
        Nicole    ncm                 (412)734-0492    10:00-7:00
        Alvin     al█                 (814)437-9320    6:00-3:00


     -----Emacs:  flextime          (Fundamental)--All-------------
     Mark set
```

Emacs inserts a blank rectangle that is two spaces wide. It moves the rest of the table to the right.

The **clear-rectangle** command wipes out text, leaving a blank rectangle in its place. It's just like you erased the column on a blackboard. And, like the blackboard column, the text that is wiped out is gone, not stored in the rectangle kill buffer. To continue with our example, let's say that after reviewing the Flex-time

Schedule, everyone agreed that they'd rather not have their home phone numbers listed.

Move the cursor to the "H" in Home and type **C-@**

```
                     Flex-time Schedule

     Name       E-mail Address    ▊ome phone      Working Hours

     Fred       fred              (814)722-3940   7:30-4:30
     Olivia     liv               (814)827-3344   9:00-6:00
     Nicole     ncm               (412)734-0492   10:00-7:00
     Alvin      al                (814)437-9320   6:00-3:00

    -----Emacs:  flextime            (Fundamental)--All-------------
    Mark set
```

The upper-left corner of the rectangle to be cleared is marked.

Move to the end of the last phone number and type **ESC-x clear-rectangle**

```
                     Flex-time Schedule

     Name       E-mail Address                     Working Hours

     Fred       fred                               7:30-4:30
     Olivia     liv                                9:00-6:00
     Nicole     ncm                                10:00-7:00
     Alvin      al                  ▊              6:00-3:00

    -----Emacs:  flextime            (Fundamental)--All-------------
```

The **clear-rectangle** command removes the Home Phone column and leaves blank space in its place.

As you can see, the spacing of our table still isn't perfect; you'd probably want to use the **delete-rectangle** command to delete the extra space between the second and the third columns. Unlike **kill-rectangle**, **delete-rectangle** doesn't store what you delete. To do this, start by moving the cursor to the space following "E-mail Address" and press **C-@** to set the mark. Then move to the opposite corner of the box you want to delete and type **ESC-x delete-rectangle RETURN**.

Move to the end of "E-mail Address" and type **C-@**

```
                Flex-time Schedule


   Name      E-mail Address█            Working Hours

   Fred      fred                       7:30-4:30
   Olivia    liv                        9:00-6:00
   Nicole    ncm                        10:00-7:00
   Alvin     al                         6:00-3:00


  -----Emacs:  flextime        (Fundamental)--All-----------
  Mark set
```

The upper-left corner of the rectangle to be deleted is marked.

Move a few spaces before 6:00 on the last line and type **ESC-x delete-rectangle**

```
                Flex-time Schedule

   Name      E-mail Address   Working Hours

   Fred      fred             7:30-4:30
   Olivia    liv              9:00-6:00
   Nicole    ncm              10:00-7:00
   Alvin     al         █     6:00-3:00

  -----Emacs:  flextime        (Fundamental)--All-----------
```

The **delete-rectangle** command deletes the blank space.

If you're doing some really fancy table editing, it's helpful to be able to store several rectangles. That way, you could have every column as a rectangle, as well as a rectangle for the exact amount of blank space that should go between each column. You can store an unlimited amount of rectangles if you use the rectangle commands while in picture mode, described in the next section of this chapter.

Table 6-4 shows a summary of the rectangle commands.

Table 6-4. Rectangle Commands

Keystrokes	Command Name	Action
(none)	kill-rectangle	Deletes a rectangle and stores it.
(none)	delete-rectangle	Deletes a rectangle and does not store it.
(none)	yank-rectangle	Inserts the last rectangle killed.
(none)	clear-rectangle	Blanks out the area marked as a rectangle and doesn't store it.
(none)	open-rectangle	Inserts a blank rectangle in the area marked.

Making Simple Drawings

Emacs is not a graphics package by any means, but it does provide some limited drawing capabilities. Emacs includes a "picture mode," which allows you to draw very simple pictures using keyboard characters. It's great for inserting a quick drawing or diagram in a mail message, something that most graphics packages can't do. It's also good for making block diagrams, timing diagrams (for electrical engineers), timelines, and other simple drawings.

Don't overlook this simple facility! We have seen many papers that were carefully formatted with **troff** or TeX, with a simple "star and bar" diagram dropped in the middle. Sure, you can use some picture processor to create a much nicer drawing; but in the real world, using **pic** or any of its TeX equivalents can be time-consuming and painful. "Star and bar" diagrams aren't pretty, but they are easy.

Picture mode turns the area being edited into a kind of drawing board consisting of columns and rows. In picture mode, you can create simple pictures (such as the one in Figure 6-2) using keyboard characters without having them "rearranged" by the word wrap capabilities of auto-fill mode, for example.

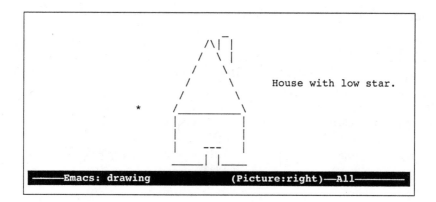

Figure 6-2. Drawing in Picture Mode

To enter picture mode, type **ESC-x edit-picture**. The word "Picture" appears on the mode line, followed by the default drawing direction (more on that shortly). Typing **C-c C-c** exits picture mode and returns you to whatever major mode you were in before.

Drawing in Picture Mode

In picture mode, you can "draw" with any character in any of eight directions. Although you can draw in eight directions, only one direction is available at a time; this is referred to as the *default direction*. When you first enter picture mode, the default direction is right, meaning that if you press the dash key four times, you would draw a line to the right, as follows: ----. The default direction is displayed on the mode line, like this:

    (Picture:right)

By typing special commands that change the default direction, you can draw in seven other directions as well. For example, **C-c ** makes the default direction "southeast"; the mode line would then read **(Picture: se)**. If you typed four hyphens in this direction, they would look like stairsteps:

        -.
          -
            -
              -

Figure 6-3 illustrates the commands for setting various directions as the default in picture mode.

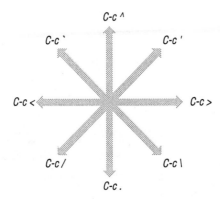

Figure 6-3. Moving Around in Picture Mode

Picture mode tries to make these commands easy to remember, and it doesn't do too badly: for example, **C-c** ^ points upward, **C-c** ` arguably points to the northwest, and so on. If you can come up with a good mnemonic device for **C-c .** let us know! Maybe you can think of it as "dot for down."

After you set a default direction, pressing any character draws a line of characters in that direction. Give it a try in a scratch buffer, using the commands in the figure to change the default direction. Try drawing a box, using a different direction for each side.

Type: **ESC-x edit-picture**

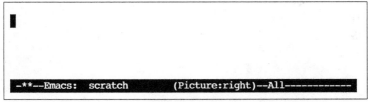

Putting the buffer into picture mode, default direction "right."

Type: **TAB ESC-20 -**

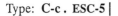

```
    ┌─────────────────────■
```

```
    -**--Emacs:  scratch        (Picture:right)--All-----------
```

Emacs draws a line to the right. Next, we'll change the default direc-
tion to down, and use | for the right side of the square.

Type: **C-c . ESC-5 |**

```
    ┌─────────────────────┐
                          │
                          │
                          │
                          ■
    -**--Emacs:  scratch        (Picture:down)--All------------
```

Emacs draws a line down. Now we'll set the default direction to
"left," then draw the bottom of the square.

Type: **C-c < ESC-20 -**

```
    ┌─────────────────────┐
                          │
                          │
                          │
    ■─────────────────────┘
    -**--Emacs:  scratch        (Picture:left)--All------------
```

Emacs draws a line to the left. Next, use **C-c ^** to set the default direction to "up," and then draw vertical bars back to the starting point.

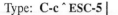

Type: **C-c ˆ ESC-5 |**

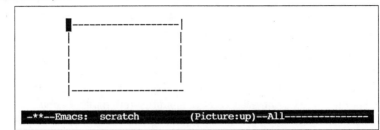

Emacs draws a line up that completes the box.

Editing in Picture Mode

By now, you should have a basic understanding of what picture mode can do for you. It's one of the more complicated minor modes because it redefines what many of the major editing keys do—and with good reason. The editing techniques that you use for most ASCII files just won't work well for pictures. You don't really want to insert characters; the standard "insert mode" would prevent you from editing effectively, since any character you type distorts the rest of the line. Therefore, picture mode implicitly changes to "overwrite" mode. Many other features are redefined—some in insignificant ways, others in more substantial ways.

Therefore, to do justice to picture mode, we have to revisit most of the basic editing concepts. Please bear with us, or skip this section if you aren't interested in pictures. Let's start at the beginning: basic cursor motion.

Moving the Cursor in Picture Mode

Picture mode makes some small but important changes in the basic cursor commands. There's an easy way to summarize these changes: in picture mode the concept of "direction" is absolute and two-dimensional, rather than relative to the file. For example, consider what **C-f** does in most other modes: it moves forward through the file, one character at a time. Typing **C-f** repeatedly moves you across the screen, then at the end of the screen, it jumps to the first character on the next line. Eventually, you reach the end of the file. In picture mode, **C-f** means "move to the right." When you reach the end of the screen in picture mode, **C-f** won't "wrap" to the next line; it continues adding characters to the current line. This also means that once you're past the end of a line, typing **C-f** is the same as typing a **SPACE**.

There are similar changes for **C-b**. In other modes, **C-b** means to move back towards the beginning of the file. In picture mode, it means move backwards one column. When you get to the beginning of a line, it stops and won't go any further.

C-p and **C-n** become "up" and "down" commands, respectively. Try editing some sample text, moving to the end of a line, and typing **C-p**. Normally, as you type **C-p**, the cursor stays at the end of the line; if the previous line is short, the cursor moves to the left when it goes up. In picture mode, **C-p** and **C-n** are absolute: they always move precisely up (or down) in a straight line.

You can get to every place you need to go with **C-f**, **C-b**, **C-p**, and **C-n**. But you may want to know the cursor movement commands for moving in the default direction, too, so you can also go sideways when it's faster. **C-c C-f** moves you forward in the default direction (so "forward" here could mean to the left, up, right, or down, as well as all directions in between). **C-c C-b** moves you backwards in the default direction. (Moving "up" and "down" relative to the default direction aren't defined.)

For example, let's say you had drawn the house shown in Figure 6-2 and you wanted to move the cursor down the left side of the roof. You would set the default direction to southwest by typing **C-c /**. If the cursor was on the top shingle on the left side of the roof, typing **C-c C-f** would move you down the left side of the roof while typing **C-f** would move you to the top right shingle, as shown in Figure 6-4.

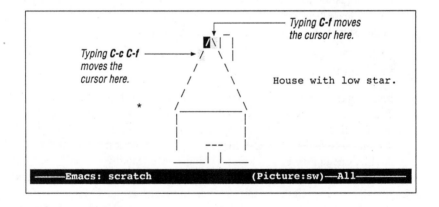

Figure 6-4. Using the Default Direction

Inserting and Repeating Lines

As you continue to work in picture mode, you'll find a few more surprises. Typing **RETURN** in picture mode moves you to the beginning of the next line, without inserting a blank line—on the assumption that you probably don't want to change the relationship between lines. If you want to insert a new line, type **C-o**; this inserts an empty line beneath the current line and does not move the cursor. For example, the cursor is initially on the 0 in the first line. We want to open another line between the two; to do so, type **C-o**.

Initial state:

```
abcdefghijklmnopqrstuvwxyz0123456789ABCDEFGHIJKLMNOP
abcdefghijklmnopqrstuvwxyz0123456789ABCDEFGHIJKLMNOP



-**--Emacs:  scratch          (Picture:se)--All---------------
```

Initial text; cursor on zero in the first line.

Type: **C-o**

```
abcdefghijklmnopqrstuvwxyz0123456789ABCDEFGHIJKLMNOP

abcdefghijklmnopqrstuvwxyz0123456789ABCDEFGHIJKLMNOP

-**--Emacs:  scratch          (Picture:se)--All---------------
```

C-o opens a new line but doesn't move the cursor.

If you want to repeat a line on the next line, press **C-j** (or the LINEFEED key if you have one). Let's say you had drawn a box and wanted to make it taller.

Initial state:

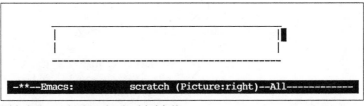

This is how the box looked initially.

Now, let's make the box taller. There's an easy way to do this. Press **C-j** three times to duplicate the second line, which makes up the "sides."

Type: **C-j C-j C-j**

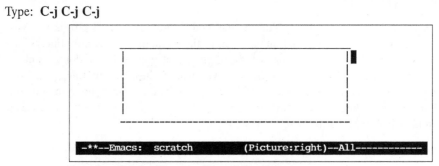

Pressing **C-j** duplicates a line of the picture.

One of the more difficult things to do in picture mode is to type a standard "carriage return" that breaks a line in the middle. You can move to a point in the middle of a line; type **C-k** to kill the right-hand portion; type **C-o** to insert a blank line; type **RETURN** to move to the beginning of this blank line; and type **C-y** to yank the right-hand part of the line back. Or use the split-line command (**ESC-C-o**), then delete the blank space at the beginning of the new line.

Deletion also isn't quite the same. **C-c C-d** is the "delete character" command that you're used to: it deletes the character under the cursor, and moves the rest of the line to the right. An unadorned **C-d** deletes the character under the cursor, replacing it with a space. And **DEL** deletes the character to the left of the cursor, replacing it with a space.

Table 6-5 summarizes the picture mode commands.

Table 6-5. Picture Mode Editing Commands

Keystrokes	In Text Mode	In Picture Mode	Picture Mode Alternative
RETURN	Inserts blank line.	Moves cursor down.	C-o inserts blank lines.
C-d	Deletes character and moves text to left.	Replaces character with SPACE and doesn't move remaining text.	C-c C-d is like C-d in text mode.

Table 6-5. Picture Mode Editing Commands (continued)

Keystrokes	In Text Mode	In Picture Mode	Picture Mode Alternative
SPACE	Moves text to the right and inserts a space.	Moves the cursor to the right and deletes any character you space over.	None; go back to text mode to insert blank spaces.[3]
C-k	Erases text on current line; pressing C-k twice deletes a line.	Erases text on current line, but doesn't delete the line.	To delete a line, go back to text mode.
TAB	Inserts TABs and moves remaining text to right.	Moves the cursor across the screen but doesn't affect underlying text.	To insert a tab's worth of space, go back to text mode.
C-n	Moves to the next line.	Moves down, staying in the same column.	(none)
C-p	Moves to the previous line.	Moves up, staying in the same column.	(none)
C-f	Moves one character forward in the file.	Moves one character to the right.	(none)
C-b	Moves one character backward in the file; adds spaces after end of line.	Moves one character to the left; stops at beginning of line.	(none)

To do some things, it's easier to switch back to the mode you're used to temporarily. **C-c C-c** moves you back to the previous mode you were in if you find you need to do some of the editing functions not available in picture mode. Then re-enter picture mode by typing **ESC-x edit-picture**.

---

[3] If you want to insert a block of blank space, you can use a rectangle command such as open-rectangle. See the discussion of this command earlier in this chapter for more information. Also, if you want to insert blank space at the end of a line, you can use **C-f**.

If you want to move something you've drawn, the easiest way is to use rectangles in picture mode, as described in the next section.

Using Rectangle Commands in Picture Mode

Rectangle editing and picture mode work together very well. It's often convenient to use a rectangle command to cut out a portion of a picture and move it somewhere else. You can use all the rectangle editing commands described earlier in this chapter plus a few more that work only in picture mode.

For example, instead of only being able to save one rectangle, you can save many in *registers*. Registers are storage spaces that Emacs sets up; they remain in memory only for the current Emacs session. The ability to save more than one rectangle is especially helpful if you're doing a complex editing job like rearranging columns of a five-column table. To delete a rectangle and save it in a register, type **C-c C-w** *r*, where *r* is the one-character "name" of the register you're saving it to, such as 1. Any character works as a value for *r*, numbers as well as letters, uppercase letters as well as lowercase letters, so you can store as many rectangles as your keyboard has unique characters! (Don't try to use special-function keys, though. These often send sequences of characters, which will confuse Emacs.) To insert a stored rectangle, type **C-c C-x** *r*, where *r* is the one-character name of the register you put the rectangle in.

Another special rectangle editing command for picture mode is **C-c C-k** (**picture-clear-rectangle**). Clearing a rectangle with **C-c C-k** "blanks out" the current text, leaving whitespace in its place. With **C-c C-y** you can put back the rectangle you blanked out with **C-c C-k**. **C-c C-k** only lets you save one rectangle at a time, and, as you may remember, **C-c C-y** only lets you yank the most recently killed rectangle.

Table 6-6 summarizes the commands for editing in picture mode.

Table 6-6. Picture Mode Commands

Keystrokes	Command Name	Action
(none)	edit-picture	Enters picture mode.
C-c C-c	picture-mode-exit	Exits picture mode and returns you to the previous mode.
C-c ^	picture-movement-up	Sets default drawing direction to up.
C-c .	picture-movement-down	Sets default drawing direction to down.

Table 6-6. Picture Mode Commands (continued)

Keystrokes	Command Name	Action
C-c >	picture-movement-right	Sets default drawing direction to right.
C-c <	picture-movement-left	Sets default drawing direction to left.
C-c `	picture-movement-nw	Sets default drawing direction to northwest.
C-c '	picture-movement-ne	Sets default drawing direction to northeast.
C-c /	picture-movement-sw	Sets default drawing direction to southwest.
C-c \	picture-movement-se	Sets default drawing direction to southeast.
C-c C-f	picture-motion	Moves cursor forward in default drawing direction.
C-c C-b	picture-motion-reverse	Moves cursor backward in default drawing direction.
C-f	picture-forward-column	Moves the cursor to the right one character.
C-b	picture-backward-column	Moves the cursor to the left one character.
C-n	picture-move-down	Moves the cursor down one character.
C-p	picture-move-up	Moves the cursor up one character.
C-d	picture-clear-column	Blanks out character under the cursor; doesn't move remaining text to the left.
C-c C-d	delete-char	Deletes character under the cursor and moves remaining text to the left.
C-k	picture-clear-line	Deletes text on current line; doesn't delete line if used twice.
C-o	picture-open-line	Inserts blank line.
C-j	picture-duplicate-line	Duplicates current line on the next line.
C-c C-w *r*	picture-clear-rectangle-to-register	Saves rectangle to register *r*.
C-c C-x *r*	picture-yank-rectangle	Inserts rectangle saved in register *r* at cursor position.

Using Outline Mode

When you're writing something, whether it's a book, a long memo, or a technical specification, it's often hard to get a sense for organization as you go along. Therefore, it is often difficult to "grow" an outline smoothly into a much larger paper or to reorganize a paper as you go along. The words get in the way of your headings, making it hard to "see the forest for the trees."

Outline mode provides a built-in solution to this problem. It gives you the ability to hide or display text selectively, based upon its relationship to the structure of your document. For example, you can hide all of your document's text except for its headings; this will give you a feel for the document's shape. When you're looking at the headings, you can focus on structure without being concerned about the individual words; then when you've solved your structural problems, you can make the words reappear.

Outline mode is more useful for documents with several levels of headings (or for long programs) than for plain outlines containing very little text. The longer a document is, the harder it is to get a quick feel for the overall structure, and this is where outline mode's ability to hide and show portions of the text comes in very handy.

Outline mode requires that you follow some special conventions in your outline or document. On the left, we show a "traditional" outline; on the right, we show the same outline, after being prepared for outline mode:

Traditional Outline	Outline Mode
All About the Universe	All About the Universe
I. Preface	*Preface
A. Scope of book	**Scope of book
This book is all-inclusive	This book is all-inclusive
B. Intended audience	**Intended audience
Universe dwellers	Universe dwellers
II. Chapter 1	*Chapter 1
A. Universe basics	**Universe basics

While traditional outlines use a hierarchical scheme of roman numerals, upper-case letters, numbers, and lowercase letters for heading levels 1 through 4, outline mode by default expects to see one asterisk (*) for a first-level header, two for a second-level header, and so on. Lines that don't start with an *, such as "This book is all-inclusive," are referred to as *body* lines. Notice that Emacs expects to see the asterisk in the first column. You can use traditional outline indentation, provided that the asterisks start in the first column.

In the sample outline, there are only two body lines. As we developed the book, though, we'd gradually add more and more body: "This book is all-inclusive" would be replaced by a substantial chunk of the preface, and other body lines later in the outline would turn into the text for chapter one. When used properly, outline mode removes the distinction between outlining and writing. As your outline grows and becomes more detailed, it can gradually become your paper.[4]

Entering Outline Mode

Outline mode is really just a group of commands that are only loaded when outline mode is switched on. To start outline mode, type **ESC-x outline-mode RETURN**. "Outline" appears on the mode line.

Once you are in outline mode, you can use special commands to move quickly from one part of the outline to another. **C-c C-n** moves to the next heading or subheading; **C-c C-p** moves to the previous one. **C-c C-f** moves to the next heading of the same level, so you can use this to move from one first-level heading to another throughout the outline, or from one second-level heading to another within a given entry. **C-c C-b** moves backward to the previous heading of the same level. If you want to move from a second-level header to its first-level header, up a level in the outline structure, you type **C-c C-u**. (If you are on a first-level header already, **C-c C-u** beeps since it can't move to a higher level.) Figure 6-5 illustrates how these cursor commands would work on our sample outline.

---

[4] Of course, formatting is a problem. If you are using a formatter like **troff** or TeX, you can use a query-replace to change the asterisk-style headers into headers that are appropriate for your macro package. To strip the asterisks out of the file once you've finished writing, use a regular expression replace, as discussed in Chapter 11, Emacs LISP Programming. Alternatively, if you're ambitious, you can customize outline mode so that it works directly on the headers that your document processor recognizes. Customizing outline mode isn't for the faint of heart. But if you take this route, you can achieve complete integration between writing and outlining.

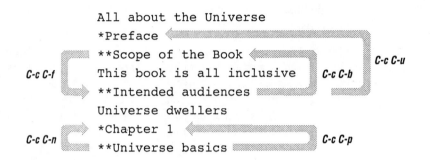

Figure 6-5. Moving Around in Outline Mode

These commands make it easy to solve a lot of organizational problems. If you often think, "I know I'm writing about widgets, but I can't remember the bigger point I'm trying to make," type **C-c C-u** to get to the next higher level of the outline. If you want to figure out how widgets relate to the other topics within the section, use **C-c C-b** and **C-c C-f** to move backwards and forwards to your other headings.

Hiding and Showing Text

The most important feature of outline mode is the ability to selectively hide or show different portions of your text. The ability to see a skeletal view of a long document with outline mode is its best feature; it's much easier to evaluate the structure of a document when you can hide everything but the headings and see whether it is coherent or in need of some reorganization.

Although it sounds like something out of a detective story, **ESC-x hide-body** hides all the body (or text) lines but leaves all the headers (lines that begin with an asterisk) visible. Wherever Emacs hides text, it places an ellipsis (...) on the corresponding header line. The ellipsis tells you that some hidden text is present. The buffer itself is *not* modified; you'll notice, if you watch the left side of the mode line, that the asterisks that indicate a modified buffer don't appear. If you save a file and exit while some text is hidden, Emacs saves the hidden text along with what you see displayed on the screen; hiding text in no way implies losing text. The next time you read the file, Emacs shows all text that was hidden.

Hide-body is a good way to get a feel for the structure of a long document. Copy the file, then do a search and replace that marks first-level headers with *, second-level headers with **, and so forth. You can then type **ESC-x hide-body**

RETURN and see only the headings without the text. For example, let's start with the simple outline we gave above and hide the body.

Type: **ESC-x hide-body RETURN**

```
All About the Universe
*Preface█
**Scope of book...
**Intended audience...
*Chapter 1
**Universe basics
```

Body hidden; the two "body" lines are represented by ellipses.

To show all the hidden text in a file, whether headers or body, type **ESC-x show-all RETURN**. These two commands, **hide-body** and **show-all,** are the only ones that work on the outline as a whole; the rest of the commands (and there are lots of them) work only on the particular part of the outline the cursor is on. You don't have to learn all the commands at first; start with a few and then add more as you need them. In working with outline mode, we use the **hide-body** and **show-all** commands 90 percent of the time.

The **hide-subtree** command can be used to hide all the subheadings and text for a particular header. The cursor can be anywhere on the heading or the text that's associated with it. Let's start with the original outline again, and hide the "preface" subtree.

Type: **ESC-x hide-subtree RETURN**

```
All About the Universe
*Preface█ ...
*Chapter 1
**Universe basics
```

The ellipsis shows that text is hidden.

Note what's happened. When we used the **hide-body** command, the two body lines disappeared, and was replaced by ellipses. When we used the **hide-subtree** command, an entire section of the outline (including lower-level headings) disappeared and was replaced by an ellipsis.

The **show-subtree** command does exactly the opposite. If the cursor is on a header that has some hidden text associated with it, **ESC-x show-subtree RETURN** displays all hidden text, whether body or subhead.[5] The command

---

[5] Both **hide-subtree** and **show-subtree** have default bindings, but these don't work properly on some systems; if you type **C-c C-h** (**hide-subtree**) or **C-c C-s** (**show-subtree**), the command doesn't take effect until you type some kind of key sequence that affects the display (for example, **C-v** to scroll). Using the command's full name does not produce this error.

ESC-x **hide-entry** RETURN hides the text that is directly underneath a given heading. It leaves the other subheadings, together with their text, untouched. To show the text that is hidden with **hide-entry**, give the command ESC-x **show-entry** RETURN.

If, as is useful in reviewing overall structure, you want to see only subheadings but no text, type ESC-x **show-branches** RETURN. The command ESC-x **hide-leaves** RETURN hides only body text and not subheadings, making it look like a real outline with no text attached to the entries. If you used **hide-leaves** on the outline above, it would look like the following screen.

Type: ESC-x **hide-leaves** RETURN

```
All About the Universe
*Preface
**Scope of book ...
**Intended audience ...█
*Chapter 1
**Universe basics
```

Hide-leaves hides the text lines associated with the Preface and its subheadings but shows the subheadings themselves.

If you only want to see the next lower-level of subheadings for a given header, first type ESC-x **hide-subtree** RETURN, and then type ESC-x **show-children** RETURN. All text remains hidden and only the next lower-level of header is shown. For example, if the cursor is on a second-level header, **show-children** gets you all the third-level headers underneath it.

Table 6-7 shows the commands for hiding and showing text and headers.

Table 6-7. Outline Mode's Hiding and Showing Commands

Use this command	To hide
hide-body	All body lines.
hide-subtree	Subheads and bodies associated with a given header.
hide-entry	Body associated with a particular header (not subheads and their bodies).
hide-leaves	Bodies of a particular header and bodies of all its subheads.

Use this command	To show
show-all	Everything that's hidden.
show-subtree	Subheads and text associated with a given header.

Table 6-7. Outline Mode's Hiding and Showing Commands (continued)

Use this command	To show
show-entry	Body associated with a particular header (not subheads and their bodies.
show-branches	Bodies of a header and all bodies of all its subheads.
show-children	Next level of subheads associated with a particular header (none of body text).

Editing While Text is Hidden

Now that you know how to hide and show text, let's discuss some of the properties of hidden text. It's often very useful to edit a document while some of it is hidden—it's a great way to make major changes in document structure—but there are some dangers that you should be aware of. Let's say you've hidden all text with outline mode and only the headers are showing, giving you a true "outline" of your document. If you move a header that has hidden text and headers associated with it, everything that is hidden moves when you move the visible text. Later, when you "show" all of the document, the hidden text appears in its new location—underneath the header that you moved. Similarly, if you delete a header, you delete all hidden text as well.

This makes moving blocks of text easy. However, there are some things to watch out for. If you delete the ellipsis following an entry, Emacs deletes the hidden information as well. To its credit, Emacs tries to keep you from doing this; it does not allow you to delete the ellipsis using the DEL key or use normal cursor commands like **C-b** to move the cursor onto it. If you delete the ellipsis with **C-d**, Emacs brings the hidden text onto the screen intact. Still, with persistence or bad luck, it is possible to delete the ellipsis and lose text in the process (using, for example, **C-k**). Although typing **C-y** restores the ellipsis, when you show the text, some of it may be missing. You cannot restore the information by retyping the ellipsis, either; it must be recovered from an auto-save file (of the form *#filename#*) or backup file (of the form *filename˜*).

Another limitation of working with hidden text is that you can only move text to another buffer if both buffers are in outline mode. If you try moving hidden text from an outline to a buffer that isn't in outline mode, you will see text that is basically garbage with ^M's inserted at intervals. Some of the text may even be missing. If you put both buffers in outline mode, you should be able to move text between windows without trouble.

Finally, you can certainly add headings and text when various parts of the document are hidden. But be careful not to type on top of an ellipsis; whatever you type will be inserted into the hidden text. (You can probably predict what will happen, but it's not worth the effort.)

Customizing Outline Mode

It's instructive to think a bit about how outline mode works. (This is going to get ugly—if you're new to Emacs, skip to the next section.) Outline mode is controlled by a single variable, **outline-regexp**, whose value is a regular expression. This regular expression has to match any header line. The length of the match determines the level of the header. For example, the default value for **outline-regexp** is essentially `*+` (it's actually a bit more complicated, but this is close enough). That is, it matches one or more asterisks. Outline mode considers a single `*` to be a first-level heading because it matches one character; `**` indicates a second-level heading because it matches two characters; and so on. The actual number of characters that match isn't important, but longer matches *always* indicate lower-level headings.

If you are clever enough, you can take advantage of this and make outline mode work for practically anything. Consider this regular expression:

    \\(\\.11\\)\\|\\(\\.1e2\\)\\|\\(\\.lev3\\)\\|\\(\\.level4\\)

Ugly enough? It could be expressed more economically, but at even greater cost to clarity. It uses a few features that are described in Chapter 11. Now, this regular expression matches the following headers:

.l1	First level
.le2	Second level
.lev3	Third level
.level4	Fourth level

This is beginning to look like **troff**, if you're familiar with it. Now, all you need is to translate these headers into some **troff** header macros that you're familiar with.[6] Then add a line like this to your *.emacs* file:

    (setq outline-regexp "the-ugly-thing-you-just-saw")

and you can use outline mode on regular **troff** text. Users of TeX or Scribe could concoct something similar.

---

[6] Not a subject for this book, but eminently do-able. It requires you know at least one sleazy **troff** trick: although **troff** only allows two-character macro names, when it sees something like .level4, it treats it as an invocation of the macro .le, with "vel4" as the first argument. So write a .le macro that tests the first argument to see whether it's "2," "v3," "vel4," etc.

7

Using Emacs with UNIX Text Formatters

Marking Up Text for troff and nroff
Marking Up Text for TeX and LaTeX
Marking Up Text for Scribe

So far, the formatting described in this book has only used the capabilities inherent in Emacs, which is not a text formatter. Text processing systems often separate file editing (Emacs' job) and text formatting. You write a file containing *markup* that describes how you want the output to be formatted; a separate program reads this file as input and creates output for your laser printer. Three formatters are common under UNIX and Emacs supports all three:

- **troff** is the traditional text formatter of the UNIX world. **nroff** is an equivalent program that formats output for an ASCII terminal; **nroff** is the basis for the **man** command. The Free Software Foundation has created a troff-lookalike called **groff**.

- Scribe is a commercially available text formatter that was very popular in the early- and mid-80's. Scribe's usage is waning now.

- TeX is a formatter that was developed by Donald Knuth for generating his books. Of the three processors we're discussing here, it's the most elaborate. LaTeX is essentially a set of predefined commands for TeX, designed to make it similar to Scribe. TeX and LaTeX are available from the American Mathematical Society for the cost of distribution.

If you use one or more of these formatters, Emacs has several major modes that help you insert formatting commands, or markup, into your text. While the amount of help that Emacs offers varies, using the mode designed for your text formatter will streamline your work.

Comments

nroff mode shares one important feature with TeX and Scribe modes—and, indeed, with the programming language modes that will be discussed in Chapter 10, *Emacs for Programmers*. It understands comments. By way of review, if the characters **.\ "** appear at the beginning of a line, the entire line is treated as a comment (i.e., ignored). If the characters **\ "** appear in the middle of a line, the remainder of the line is ignored. At least to our taste, there are some problems with Emacs' support for comments in **nroff**, but you should still experiment with this feature; despite the problems, you will probably find it useful.

Assume that you have auto-fill mode (a minor mode) enabled. As you are typing, you decide to insert a comment anywhere on the line. Emacs detects the comment marker (**\ "**). When you type beyond the right margin and Emacs starts a new line, it assumes that you want to continue the comment on the new line. To make it easy for you, Emacs automatically inserts the comment marker **\ "** at the beginning of the new line. Emacs only inserts the comment marker when it starts the new line. If you aren't in auto-fill mode, or if you type **RETURN** yourself, it won't do anything special.

Unfortuantely, Emacs omits the initial period. As a result, **troff** will add an unwanted blank line to your output. We don't see any obvious way to correct this problem, aside from going back and inserting periods by hand. It would be easy to define a macro, using a regular expression search-and-replace, that would correct initial comment markers automatically. (That's an exercise we'll leave to you.)

When you're in nroff mode, the command **ESC-;** (for **indent-for comment**)[1] automatically inserts a comment marker (**\ "**) at the end of the current line. If there's nothing else on the line, **indent-for-comment** goes through a rather strange behavior. The first time you press **ESC-;** it inserts **\ "** at the beginning of the line. The second time, it replaces the previous comment marker with **. \ "** (note the space between the dot and backslash). The third time, you get **.\ "**.

---

[1] **indent-for-comment** really isn't part of nroff mode; it actually works in almost any mode, provided that the concept of a *comment* is reasonable. For example, you can use it in Scribe mode, TeX mode, C mode, FORTRAN mode, and so on. It always inserts the appropriate comment marker for whatever language you're using.

Depending on your tastes, you might find that typing **ESC-;** repeatedly is more convenient than typing a comment marker by hand.

Finding Headings

You may find it convenient to redefine the **page-delimiter** variable to help you find section headings. This variable is a regular expression that defines a page boundary; commands like **C-x]** (for **forward-page**) use **page-delimiter** to determine when the next page begins. By default, **page-delimiter** looks for formfeed (**C-l**) characters; but you can just as easily set it to find **troff** section delimiters. Of course, these sections have nothing to do with the way your document is paginated; but Emacs doesn't care.

For example, assume that you're using the "ms" macro package. Documents using the ms package use the macro **.NH** to start new sections. Therefore, setting the **page-delimiter** variable to **"^\.NH"** tells Emacs that it should consider **.NH**, appearing at the beginning of a line, to start a new page. Once you have made this setting, you can use the "page" commands to move between sections of your **troff** document.

To set **page-delimiter**, give the command **ESC-x set-variable RETURN page-delimiter RETURN "^\.NH" RETURN**. To make this setting permanent, add the following line to your *.emacs* file:

```
(setq nroff-mode-hook '(lambda () (setq page-delimiter "^\\.NH")))
```

(Note that you need two backslashes in this case.) If you are using a different macro package, you'll have to develop your own setting for **page-delimiter**. See Chapter 11, *Emacs LISP Programming*, for a complete discussion of regular expressions.

Note that **page-delimiter** isn't a feature of nroff mode; you can perform similar tricks no matter what kind of document you're editing.

Marking Up Text for troff and nroff

nroff mode is just like text mode, but with a few conveniences thrown in. For the purposes of this discussion, there is no difference between **nroff** and its relatives **troff** and **groff**; the commands discussed here work for the whole **troff** family.

To enter nroff mode, type **ESC-x nroff-mode RETURN**. nroff appears on the mode line. nroff mode provides four substantial features:

- It redefines the meaning of a paragraph by resetting the **paragraph-separate** variable. With this setting, the **fill-paragraph** command (**ESC-q**) works correctly.

- It provides some special commands for navigating in a **troff** document. Using these commands, you can move forward and backward, jumping over all **troff** commands.

- A special "electric nroff mode" (a minor mode associated with nroff mode) automatically supplies "matching pairs" of certain formatting commands.

- It provides some features for working with comments (which we described earlier).

Paragraph Formatting

We'll take these features one at a time. First, paragraph separation: if you do a lot of text editing and get used to using **fill-paragraph**, **troff** documents will cause you misery. Emacs usually determines when a paragraph ends by looking for blank lines. **troff** documents usually don't have any blank lines, so Emacs tries to reformat the entire file, creating a big mess.

troff formatting commands (usually called requests or macros) must all begin at the left margin, and they all begin with a dot (.) or a single right quote ('). Whatever **fill-paragraph** does, it must leave these lines untouched. Therefore, nroff mode simply defines a paragraph so that any line beginning with either a dot or an apostrophe starts a paragraph, in addition to the usual Emacs definition of blocks of text separated by blank lines. For example, consider the following text.

Initial state:

```
.H1 "Various Ways of Questioning about the Thing"
.H2 "Philosophical and Scientific Questioning"
.PP
From the range of the basic questions
of metaphysics we shall
here ask this
.I
one
.R
question:  What is a thing?
.PP
-----Emacs:  heidegger          (Nroff Fill)--Top-------------
```

Initial **troff** text.

Here's some text prepared for **troff**. To reformat the first paragraph ("From the range"), move the cursor into the paragraph and type **ESC-q**. In any other mode, this would create havoc; it would make the entire file a single long paragraph. In nroff mode, the result looks like the following screen.

Type: **ESC-q**

```
.H1 "Various Ways of Questioning about the Thing"
.H2 "Philosophical and Scientific Questioning"
.PP
From the range of the basic questions of metaphysics
we shall here ask this
.I
one
.R
question:  What is a thing?
.PP
-----Emacs:  heidegger          (Nroff Fill)--Top-------------
```

Reformatted text, with the middle paragraph filled.

Emacs does not try to "fill" the whole document, or even the whole paragraph. It only reformats the text between the .PP macro and the following .I macro.

Navigation

When you're working on a file that's liberally sprinkled with **troff** commands, getting from one place to another can be a pain; you're always jumping around macros. nroff mode offers a convenient way to move from one text line to the next, skipping any macros in between. **ESC-n** moves the cursor to the next text line, and **ESC-p** moves the cursor to the previous text line, as shown in Figure 7-1.

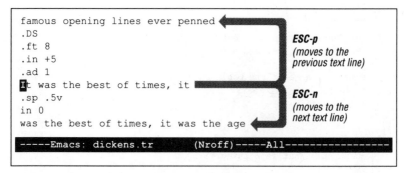

```
famous opening lines ever penned
.DS
.ft 8
.in +5
.ad l
It was the best of times, it
.sp .5v
in 0
was the best of times, it was the age
-----Emacs: dickens.tr          (Nroff)-----All----------------
```

ESC-p
(moves to the previous text line)

ESC-n
(moves to the next text line)

Figure 7-1. Moving Around in nroff Mode

Because files that are marked up can seem so much longer, nroff mode also provides a command to count the number of "real" text lines. The command **ESC-?** counts the number of text lines (excluding mark-up lines) in a given region. If you want to find out how many text lines are in the file, type **C-x h** to mark the buffer, then press **ESC-?** to count the number of text lines.

Macro Pairs

Electric nroff mode provides one additional feature. **troff** macros often come in "start/end" pairs. For example, .TS starts a table and .TE ends a table. In electric nroff mode, Emacs automatically supplies the "second part" of the pair; you only have to type the first part.

To enter electric nroff mode, first enter nroff mode, and then type **ESC-x electric-nroff-mode**. The electric mode is really a minor mode that provides an enhancement to "vanilla" nroff mode, rather than an independent major mode. Therefore, you can't enter electric nroff mode directly.

Once you have entered electric nroff mode, you can type a pair of "matched" commands by typing the first command and typing **C-j** (or **LINEFEED**). Emacs supplies the other command and puts a blank line in between; it then puts the cursor on the blank line, between the two. This allows you to continue typing text without moving the cursor; it is especially useful for those who mark up their files as they write.

The following screen shows how to use electric nroff mode to finish a .DS/.DE pair.

Type: **.DS**

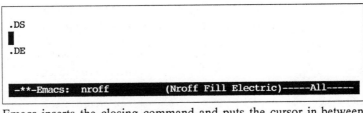

```
.DS█




─**─Emacs:  nroff        (Nroff Fill Electric)─────All─────
```

You type the opening command of a command pair.

Type: **C-j**

```
.DS
█
.DE


─**─Emacs:  nroff        (Nroff Fill Electric)─────All─────
```

Emacs inserts the closing command and puts the cursor in between them.

Electric nroff mode can "complete" most of the pairs that are defined by -ms, -me, and -mm macro packages, in addition to a few **troff** primitives that are usually paired. Table 7-1 shows the **troff** macros that electric nroff mode recognizes.

Table 7-1. Electric nroff Mode Command Pairs

Starting macro (typed)	Ending macro (supplied by Emacs)	Used by
.(b	.)b	me macro package
.(l	.)l	me macro package
.(c	.)c	me macro package
.(x	.)x	me macro package
.(z	.)z	me macro package
.(d	.)d	me macro package
.(q	.)q	me macro package
.(f	.)f	me macro package
.LG	.NL	ms macro package
.MS	.NL	ms macro package
.LD	.DE	ms macro package
.CD	.DE	ms macro package
.BD	.DE	ms macro package
.DS	.DE	ms macro package
.DF	.DE	ms macro package

181

Table 7-1. Electric nroff Mode Command Pairs (continued)

Starting macro (typed)	Ending macro (supplied by Emacs)	Used by
.FS	.FE	ms, mm macro package
.KS	.KE	ms macro package
.KF	.KE	ms macro package
.LB	.LE	mm macro package
.AL	.LE	mm macro package
.BL	.LE	mm macro package
.DL	.LE	mm macro package
.ML	.LE	mm macro package
.RL	.LE	mm macro package
.VL	.LE	mm macro package
.RS	.RE	ms macro package
.TS	.TE	tbl preprocessor
.EQ	.EN	eqn preprocessor
.PS	.PE	pic preprocessor
.BS	.BE	mm macro package
.na	.ad b	troff primitive
.nf	.fi	troff primitive
.de	..	troff primitive

Making nroff Mode Part of Your Startup

If you use **troff** heavily, you may want to make nroff mode your default major mode. Since nroff mode is really text mode with a few extra commands thrown in, it works well for almost everything you do. To make nroff mode part of your startup, put this line at the top of your *.emacs* file:

```
(setq default-major-mode 'nroff-mode)
```

If you have a line in your *.emacs* file that sets something else (like text mode) as your default major mode, delete it. To have the new line take effect, save the file and re-enter Emacs. Table 7-2 summarizes the commands available in nroff mode.

Table 7-2. nroff Mode Commands

Keystrokes	Command	Function
(none)	nroff-mode	Enters nroff mode.
ESC-n	forward-text-line	Moves the cursor to the next text line.
ESC-p	backward-text-line	Moves the cursor to the previous text line.
ESC-?	count-text-lines	Counts the text lines in a region.
(none)	electric-nroff-mode	Enters a minor mode in which you type the first in a pair of nroff commands, press C-j, and Emacs inserts the second command of the pair.
C-j	electric-nroff-newline	In electric nroff mode only, supplies the troff macro that "completes" the pair started on the the current line.
ESC-;	indent-for-comment	Inserts a comment marker in the text.

Marking Up Text for TeX and LaTeX

GNU Emacs provides much fuller support for marking up TeX files than it does for **troff** files. Both TeX and LaTeX modes are major modes; once you turn them on, all kinds of special behavior kicks in to help you mark up and process these files from within Emacs. Many of the features of TeX mode also apply to LaTeX; LaTeX users should read this section first, then go on to read about the distinctives of LaTeX mode.

To enter TeX mode, type **ESC-x tex-mode RETURN**. Emacs looks at the file to see if it looks like TeX or LaTeX and puts you in the correct mode. If you want to specify TeX mode particularly, type **ESC-x plain-tex-mode RETURN**; similarly, to start LaTeX mode, type **ESC-x latex-mode RETURN**.

Matching Braces

TeX commands often take the form \keyword{text}. TeX mode doesn't try to figure out if you're using the "right" keywords, since TeX is extensible and you may have defined your own keywords. It does, however, provide support for avoiding the most common TeX error: mismatched curly braces and dollar signs.

In TeX, curly braces ({}) and dollar signs ($$) should always appear in pairs; Emacs checks to make sure that each opening brace or dollar sign also has a counterpart. When you type a closing brace or dollar sign, the cursor moves quickly to its counterpart (provided that it is on the screen; it shows the context in the minibuffer if it is not), then back again. This visual check doesn't actually affect the cursor's location in the file; if you type while it is moving back to the opening brace, the text appears in the normal spot. It won't let you type in the wrong place.[2]

Curly braces are often nested, so the cursor may not move to the nearest opening brace, but to the one that corresponds with the closing brace. For example, here are three levels of braces on one line:

```
\keyword{this is some \boo{funny text with \bar{many} nested} braces}
         1                2                      3      3       2      1
```

Emacs won't warn you if there is no matching brace, and of course there's no way for Emacs to tell whether the brace it finds is the "right" matching brace. You have to watch to make sure that Emacs finds the other brace, and that the brace it finds is correct. Emacs also won't search the whole buffer to find the matching brace; this would take too much time. It searches back a finite amount, and then gives up. So if the matching brace is very far back in the file, you may never see it.

NOTE

Unfortunately, TeX mode isn't smart enough to distinguish literal braces and dollar signs (ones that appear in your text) from braces and dollar signs that are part of the formatting machinery. Braces and dollar signs in the text aren't necessarily matched properly. Therefore, it's easy to confuse Emacs' checking mechanism.

Emacs also helps to generate braces in "matching pairs." The command **ESC-{** inserts two braces and positions the cursor so that your next text will fall between the braces.

---

[2] "Moving back to the opening element" is standard Emacs behavior for parentheses and square brackets (for more on this topic, see Chapter 10, *Emacs for Programmers*). Even though parentheses and square brackets don't factor into TeX formatting, Emacs continues to match parentheses and square brackets in this mode as well. Because Emacs' own error messages often refer to mismatched parentheses, we'll often use "parentheses" as the generic term for curly braces, dollar signs, square brackets, and parentheses in the following discussion.

Type: **ESC-{**

```
Blah, blah, blah blah{}


-**--Emacs:          tekblahs (TeX Fill)--All----------------
```

Typing **ESC-}** moves you past the "right" brace. It always finds the correct closing brace, given your current position. For example, if the cursor was on the word "funny" and you pressed **ESC-}**, it would move to the closing brace (following the word "nested").

Type: **ESC-}**

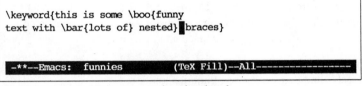

```
\keyword{this is some \boo{funny
text with \bar{lots of} nested} braces}


-**--Emacs:  funnies         (TeX Fill)--All----------------
```

ESC-} jumps out of the current bracing level.

If the cursor were on the word "boo" or earlier, **ESC-}** would move the cursor just past the last brace on the second line. If there is no closing brace, you get an error message that says "unbalanced parentheses." You also get this error message if you type **ESC-}** while the cursor is in a section that is not surrounded by braces, which can be a little confusing.

To check for mismatched curly braces and dollar signs, you can type **ESC-x validate-TeX-buffer RETURN**.[3] This command checks the entire buffer for unbalanced parentheses, curly braces, dollar signs and the like, starting at the end. When you first run this command, you may find its behavior strange. It stops briefly at the end of each paragraph containing an error and displays a message: "Mismatch found in paragraph starting here." After it has finished, it moves the cursor back to its initial position. Since this message inevitably appears at the end of a paragraph, it sounds strange. Emacs sets the mark at the end of the last paragraph it believes to be correct.

What use, you might ask, is setting the mark repeatedly and only letting you just glimpse where it was set as the command runs? There is a way to get back to each error after the command is done, using an Emacs feature called the *mark ring*.

---

[3] Emacs commands are always case-sensitive. This is not usually a problem since most commands are in lowercase. **validate-TeX-buffer** is an exception. You must use the capitalization you see here or Emacs will say the command doesn't exist.

Remember the kill ring (from Chapter 2), where Emacs stores many of the deletions you make during a session. The mark ring is similar. Emacs stores the last 16 "marked" locations in the mark ring. Ordinarily, this might not be very useful since so many commands (besides the straightforward **set-mark**) set the location of the mark. With **validate-TeX-buffer**, however, using the mark ring is the only way to get back to the places where Emacs found mismatched parentheses in your file. You can step through the errors using the mark ring by typing **C-u C-@**. Emacs moves the cursor to the mark position and moves the mark to its previous location.

Sometimes a mismatched parenthesis early in the buffer can start a chain reaction of "errors" through the rest of the file. If you suspect that one of the corrections you make may have fixed most of the rest of the errors, simply run **validate-TeX-buffer** again.

When you're stepping through errors, **ESC-}** (described earlier) provides a good way to check where the closing brace for a given opening brace is. Position the cursor right after the opening brace and press **ESC-}**.

A final note: we hear that this command isn't perfect, so don't be surprised if it doesn't find every error you think it should.

Quotation Marks and Paragraphing

TeX mode also has features for handling quotation marks and paragraph separation. Typing quotation marks (") in TeX or LaTeX mode causes Emacs to insert either opening (``` `` ```) or closing ('') quotes. These characters are really two single quotes used to simulate double left and double right quotation marks; "left" and "right" quotation marks are not part of the standard ASCII character set. If you need to type a literal " for any reason, simply use the quote-character command preceding the quotation mark, like this: **C-q "** (for **TeX-insert-quote**).

Pressing **C-j** (or **LINEFEED**) inserts the correct paragraph separation for TeX and LaTeX: two hard returns. It also checks the previous paragraph for mismatched parentheses. For example, if you press **C-j** and there is an opening brace with no closing brace in the previous paragraph, Emacs says: "Paragraph being closed appears to contain a mismatch." This lets you check each paragraph as you write it rather than waiting to check the whole buffer at once, making it easier to find errors if there are any.

Comments

In TeX mode **C-x ;** inserts a comment marker (a percent sign, **%**) at the end of the current line.

Processing and Printing Text

In addition to marking up files for TeX, you can actually process them and see your errors without leaving Emacs. To process a whole buffer, type **C-c C-b**. The messages that would appear on screen are channeled to a buffer called ***TeX shell***, which Emacs displays on your screen. If the buffer isn't on the screen, **C-c C-l** will automatically display it.

Processing part of a TeX buffer requires a special trick. TeX files consist of a header that does a lot of setup work, followed by a "body" that contains the text and its markup. Therefore, to process part of a buffer, Emacs needs to find the header, send it to TeX first, and then send the part of the file that you've selected. To make it possible for Emacs to find the header, surround it with the following strings:

```
%**start of header
%**end of header
```

Since leading percent signs are comment syntax to TeX, these lines won't interfere with the processing of your file.

For example, on a typical file you would have a header that defines typestyles and so forth for the various keywords in the file, followed by marked-up text. Once you insert the strings above, you would have:

```
%**start of header
TeX header stuff
%**end of header
Regular text
The region you want to print
More regular text
```

For TeX files, these strings tell Emacs where the header is. Set the mark at one end of the region you want to print, move to the other end, and press **C-c C-r**. To kill the processing before it's complete, type **C-c C-k**.

Using either of these commands to process a TeX (or LaTeX) file generates a *.dvi* file, which is an intermediate, "device-independent" file that still needs to be translated into printer commands. To print the *.dvi* file, give the command **C-c C-p**; this translates the *.dvi* file and sends it to your default printer. **C-c C-q** displays the print queue so you know when to go to the printer to look for your processed output.

Several important variables tell Emacs how to print a TeX file. You need to know about them if **C-c C-p** or **C-c C-q** don't work correctly; this probably means that, for some reason, the configuration of TeX on your system is nonstandard. The variable **TeX-command** (note the capitalization) determines the command that is used to run TeX. Its default value is simply "TeX." The variable **TeX-dvi-print-command** determines the command that is used to print a *.dvi* file; its default is "lpr -d". For print queues, the command used to show the print queue is controlled by the **TeX-show-queue-command** variable. By default, **TeX-show-queue-command** is set to "lpq". These default settings are fairly reasonable, but be forewarned: TeX configuration varies quite a bit, so don't be surprised if you need some customization to make TeX mode work correctly.

Differences for LaTeX Mode

LaTeX is an "easier" version of TeX which was created to make TeX imitate the commercial product Scribe, which is discussed in the next section. Everything that we've said about TeX mode applies to LaTeX mode as well, so you should read the sections about TeX mode above before reading this section.

LaTeX mode offers one additional capability: you can close pairs of commands by typing **C-c C-f**.

Type: **\begin{document} C-c C-f**

```
\begin{document}
█
\end{document}



-**---Emacs:         scratch (Latex)---------All--------------
```

If you type the beginning of a LaTeX formatting pair, and then type **C-c C-f**, Emacs inserts the second part of the pair automatically.

C-c C-f works with any keyword, regardless of what it is. Because LaTeX (like TeX) is very customizable, Emacs can't check to make sure that it's a valid LaTeX keyword or even that it's been defined. For example, if you typed **\begin{eating} C-c C-f**, Emacs inserts **\end{eating}**. It's up to you to make sure you use valid keywords.

If you want to print a portion of a LaTeX buffer, you don't need to "mark" the header in any special way. LaTeX headers are fairly uniform, so it's possible for Emacs to figure out where the header begins and ends without any help.

Table 7-3 summarizes the special commands available for LaTeX and TeX.

Table 7-3. TeX and LaTeX Commands

Keystrokes	Command Name	Action
(none)	tex-mode	Enters TeX or LaTeX mode according to file's contents.
(none)	plain-tex-mode	Enters TeX mode.
(none)	latex-mode	Enters LaTeX mode.
C-j	TeX-terminate-paragraph	Inserts two hard returns (standard end of paragraph) and checks syntax of paragraph.
ESC-{	TeX-insert-braces	Inserts two braces and puts cursor between them.
ESC-}	up-list	If you are within braces, puts the cursor following the closing brace.
(none)	validate-TeX-buffer	Checks buffer for syntax errors.
C-c C-b	TeX-buffer	Process buffer in TeX or LaTeX.
C-c C-l	TeX-recenter-output-buffer	Put the message shell on the screen, showing (at least) the last error message.
C-c C-r	TeX-region	Process region in TeX or LaTeX.
C-c C-k	TeX-kill-job	Kill TeX or LaTeX processing.
C-c C-p	TeX-print	Print TeX or LaTeX output.
C-c C-q	TeX-show-print-queue	Show print queue.

Marking Up Text for Scribe

Scribe is another powerful text formatter that was commonly used under UNIX. Of the three, it is probably the least commonly used today—which is unfortunate, because it was probably the best designed. (Pardon the editorializing.) Scribe was relatively easy for nontechnical people to use, and was extremely good at enforcing a uniform "look" for documents. Like the other formatters, Scribe is completely customizable. A system administrator (or some other honcho) defines environments (often called styles or components in word processing and desktop publishing software) that specify fonts, sizes, and other characteristics of output. For example, a system administrator might define the style of a chapter opening;

when you put the code "@Chapter" in your file, the characteristics and "look" that the system administrator has defined will appear in your final output.

To start Scribe mode, simply type **ESC-x scribe-mode RETURN**. "Scribe" appears on the mode line. Since Scribe mode is a major mode, you can exit it by entering another major mode such as text mode; to re-enter text mode, type **ESC-x text-mode RETURN**.

Marking Environments

Scribe mode makes it easy to mark up Scribe files. It offers specialized commands for marking up text. Table 7-4 shows some commands that allow you to insert common environments.

Table 7-4. Scribe Environments

Keystrokes	Command Name	What Emacs Inserts
C-c [	scribe-begin	@Begin[ ]
C-c]	scribe-end	@End[ ]
C-c s	scribe-subsection	@SubSection[ ]
C-c S	scribe-section	@Section[ ]
C-c c	scribe-chapter	@Chapter[ ]
C-x ;	indent-for-comment	@Comment[ ]

These environments should be valid in any Scribe document. After you give any of these commands, Emacs positions the cursor so you can start typing without repositioning the cursor.

Type: **C-c S**

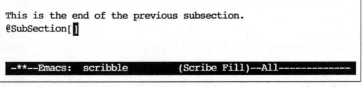

```
This is the end of the previous subsection.
@SubSection[█]


-**--Emacs:  scribble          (Scribe Fill)--All------------
```

Emacs inserts "@SubSection," and positions you to type the subsection's title.

Emacs also lets you mark up a "region" and put "@begin" and "@end" formatting commands around it. Define a region by setting the mark at one end and moving the cursor to the other end; type **C-c C-e**; and Emacs asks you to type an environment name in the minibuffer. For example, the following screen shows how to mark a quotation.

Initial state:

```
It was the best of times, it was the worst
of times, it was the age of wisdom, it was the age of
foolishness, it was the epoch of belief, it was the
epoch of incredulity, it was the season of Light, it
was the season of Darkness, ...

-**--Emacs:  dickens        (Scribe)--All-------------------
```

Initial text, at beginning of quotation.

Set the mark on "I" and move to the end of the region.

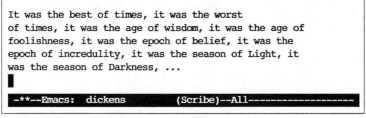

```
It was the best of times, it was the worst
of times, it was the age of wisdom, it was the age of
foolishness, it was the epoch of belief, it was the
epoch of incredulity, it was the season of Light, it
was the season of Darkness, ...


-**--Emacs:  dickens        (Scribe)--All-------------------
```

Mark the beginning of the paragraph, then move to the end of the quotation.

Type: **C-c C-e**

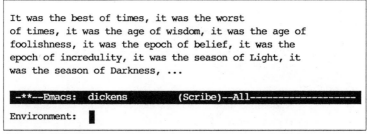

```
It was the best of times, it was the worst
of times, it was the age of wisdom, it was the age of
foolishness, it was the epoch of belief, it was the
epoch of incredulity, it was the season of Light, it
was the season of Darkness, ...

-**--Emacs:  dickens        (Scribe)--All-------------------
Environment:
```

After **C-c C-e**, Emacs asks you for the name of an environment.

Type: **quotation**

```
@begin(quotation)
It was the best of times, it was the worst
of times, it was the age of wisdom, it was the age of
foolishness, it was the epoch of belief, it was the
epoch of incredulity, it was the season of Light, it
was the season of Darkness, ...
@end(quotation)
```
```
-**--Emacs: dickens         (Scribe)--All-------------------
```

Emacs inserts @begin(quotation) and @end(quotation) for you.

The cursor should be in the first column (i.e., on the left margin) of the line following the quote when you give the **C-c C-e** command. Remember that Emacs does not check to make sure that the environment you request is valid.

Emacs can also insert the markup you need before you type the text. To do so, type **C-c C-e** and then type the name of the environment in the minibuffer. Emacs inserts the formatting commands and puts the cursor in between them so you can type the appropriate text.

Initial state:

```
Later, we'll stick in a quotation here:
▮


-**--Emacs: dickens         (Scribe)--All-------------------
```

Initial text.

Type: **C-c C-e**

```
Later, we'll stick in a quotation here:



-**--Emacs: dickens         (Scribe)--All-------------------
Environment: ▮
```

Emacs prompts for an environment.

Type: **quotation RETURN**

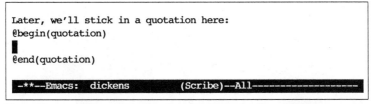

```
Later, we'll stick in a quotation here:
@begin(quotation)
█
@end(quotation)
```
`-**--Emacs:  dickens          (Scribe)--All------------------`

Emacs inserts the markup, leaving the cursor in the middle.

Again, the cursor should be on the left margin when you give this command. Emacs does not check for correctness.

Marking Fonts

Scribe mode provides a set of commands for adding font markup (italic, bold, and so on). For example, you can italicize a word by putting the cursor on the word or on the space immediately following it, and pressing **C-c i**.

Type: **C-c i**

```
It was the best of times, it was the @i[wors█]
```
`-**--Emacs:  dickens          (Scribe)--All------------------`

Emacs inserts @ i [   ] around the current word.

Emacs italicizes the word that the cursor is on, or the word immediately before the cursor. This helps you to type naturally: you can type a word, italicize it with **C-c i**, and then continue typing. You don't need any intermediate commands to move the cursor.

In general, **C-c** followed by the first letter of the font name tells Emacs what font you want to make a given word. This means that you use **C-c i** for italic (as we've seen), **C-c u** for underline, and **C-c b** for bold, as summarized in Table 7-5. This is one case in which Emacs can check for correctness; it will complain if you type an invalid font name.

Table 7-5. Scribe Fonts

Keystrokes	Command Name	What Emacs Inserts
C-c u	scribe-underline-word	@u[...]
C-c b	scribe-bold-word	@b[...]
C-c i	scribe-italicize-word	@i[...]

Tabs, Quotation Marks, and Parentheses

When you press **TAB** in Scribe mode, Emacs inserts the Scribe tab character, @\. To create a normal text mode tab, press **ESC-TAB**.

Left and right double quotes are a problem for Scribe, as they are for any text processing program. Because left and right double quotes aren't in the ASCII character set, you won't find them on your keyboard; `` and '' are the customary alternatives. Scribe mode inserts the appropriate double quotes automatically if you set the variable **scribe-electric-quote** to **t**. To do so, either use the **ESC-x set-variable** command,[4] or add the following line to your *.emacs* file:

```
(setq scribe-electric-quote t)
```

In Scribe, all bracketing units are created equal: there's no difference between square brackets, parentheses, curly braces and so on. (Of course, you can't match a square bracket with a curly brace and so on; but otherwise, there's no inherent difference between the bracket types.) Emacs checks for balanced parentheses and brackets in Scribe mode, but doesn't complain if it suspects an error. By checking, we mean that when you type a closing parenthesis or bracket, the cursor moves quickly to its counterpart (provided that it is on the screen; it shows the context in the minibuffer if it is not), then back again. This visual check doesn't actually affect the cursor's location in the file; if you type while it is moving back to the opening bracket, the text appears in the normal spot. It won't let you type in the wrong place.

The command **ESC-}** (**up-list**) helps you to find corresponding opening and closing brackets. If you are in a block of text, somewhere following the opening bracket and want to find the corresponding closing bracket, pressing **ESC-}** moves you to the space immediately following the closing bracket. If there is no closing

---

[4] The **set-variable** command only enables "electric quotes" for your current Emacs session. You must set the variable *after* entering Scribe mode.

bracket, or if the cursor is not within a section surrounded by brackets, you get an error message that says "unbalanced parentheses." This feature works for nested parentheses and brackets as well as for simpler cases.

Scribe mode also has an "electric parenthesis" feature. If you set the variable **scribe-electric-parenthesis** to **t**, Scribe will automatically provide a closing parenthesis of the correct type (i.e., either a bracket, an angle bracket, a curly brace, or a parenthesis) whenever you type anything of the form "@command." For example, if you type "@title[," Emacs automatically adds a right bracket ("]").

Type: **@title[**

```
@title[]



-**--Emacs:  dickens          (Scribe)--All--------------------
```

Emacs supplies the right parenthesis, and positions the cursor so you can continue typing.

Again, Emacs can't tell whether the "title" environment (or whatever you happen to type) is valid. To set **scribe-electric-parenthesis** to **t**, add the following line to your *.emacs* file:

```
(setq scribe-electric-parenthesis t)
```

Table 7-6 summarizes the special commands for Scribe mode.

Table 7-6. Scribe Mode Commands

Keystrokes	Command	Action
(none)	scribe-mode	Enters Scribe mode.
C-c [	scribe-begin	Inserts markup for begin (@Begin[ ]).
C-c]	scribe-end	Inserts markup for end (@End[ ]).
C-c s	scribe-subsection	Inserts markup for subsections (@SubSection[ ]).
C-c S	scribe-section	Inserts markup for sections (@Section[ ]).
C-c c	scribe-chapter	Inserts markup for chapters (@Chapter[ ]).

Table 7-6. Scribe Mode Commands (continued)

Keystrokes	Command	Action
C-c C-e	scribe-bracket-region-be	Surrounds region with correct markup for a specified environment.
C-c e	scribe-insert-environment	Inserts correct markup for a specified environment.
C-c u	scribe-underline-word	Underlines word cursor is on or follows.
C-c b	scribe-bold-word	Bolds word cursor is on or follows.
C-c i	scribe-italicize-word	Italicizes word cursor is on or follows.
TAB	scribe-tab	Inserts Scribe tab, @\ .
ESC-TAB	tab-to-tab	Inserts a normal tab.
ESC-}	up-list	If you are within brackets, puts the cursor following the closing bracket.

8

Writing Macros

What is a Macro?
Defining a Macro
Adding to an Existing Macro
Naming and Saving Your Macros
Building More Complicated Macros
Beyond Macros

What is a Macro?

What is a macro? In Emacs, a *macro* is simply a group of recorded keystrokes that you can play back over and over again. Macros are a great way to save yourself from repetitive work. For example, let's say you want to delete the third column of a table. Normally, you would go to the first line; move over to the third column; delete it; then go to the second line; give the same set of commands; and so on, until you finish, your fingers wear out, or you get too bored. Emacs lets you record the keystrokes that you used to work on the first line of the table, and then "play these back" repeatedly until the job is done.

Any command or action that you do within Emacs, from typing text to editing to switching buffers, can be done within a macro. The key to using macros well is, not too surprisingly, recognizing when you're doing repetitive work: sensing that you have pressed more-or-less the same sequence of keys several times in a row. Once you can do this, you have a good feel for when to use macros. The next talent that you'll need is, given that you've recognized a cycle of "almost identical" keystrokes, figuring out how to make that cycle *exactly identical* that is, figuring out a set of keystrokes that, if repeated exactly, will do exactly what you want. Neither of these is particularly difficult; with a little practice, you'll be using macros all the time.

If this sounds like "lazy man's programming," it is: macros give you a simple way to do very complicated things without learning LISP and without learning any customization tricks. If the task you build the macro for is something you have to do frequently, you can even save macros and load them when you want to use them. This way, you can build up a set of convenient macros, which become your own "special commands" for editing your files. You're not just limited to the commands Emacs gives you; you can make your own!

What you use macros for will depend on the kind of work you do in Emacs. We've used macros to:

- Mark up text for formatting.

- Copy headings from one buffer to another to create an outline.

- Do complex search and replace type operations that query-replace can't quite handle.

- Create index entries.

- Reformat files that were imported from another kind of application.

- Change tables from one format to another.

- Compile, run, and test the output from a program with a single command.

You'll be able to think of many more things to do with macros once you learn the few basic commands you need to use them.

Defining a Macro

To start defining a macro, type **C-x (**. The abbreviation "Def" appears on the mode line, showing that you are in macro definition mode. In this mode, Emacs records all the keystrokes that you type, whether they are commands or literal text, so that you can "replay" them later. To end the macro, type **C-x)**; you leave the macro definition mode, and Emacs stops recording your keystrokes. Emacs also stops recording your keystrokes automatically if you give it an illegal command or if you press **C-g**.

While you're defining a macro, Emacs acts on your keystrokes as well as recording them: that is, anything you type while in macro definition mode is treated as a regular command and executed. While you're defining a macro, you're doing completely normal editing. That way you can see that the macro does exactly what you want it to and can cancel it (with **C-g**) if you notice that it really isn't quite what you want. Unfortunately, it's very difficult to edit a macro in Emacs. If you make a mistake, your only real option is to cancel the macro and start again.[1]

To execute your macro, type **C-x e** (for **call-last-kbd-macro**). Emacs then replays your keystrokes exactly as you gave them. You can only have one active macro at a time. If you define another one, it becomes the active macro and overwrites any that you defined before.

Here's a quick example that shows how to define and execute a macro. We like to read printouts that are double-spaced and there's no easy way to print a standard ASCII text file this way under UNIX. This macro can be used to double-space all the text in the buffer.

Keystrokes	Result
C-x (	Starts the macro; Def appears on the mode line.
C-e	Moves to the end of the current line.
RETURN	Inserts a blank line.
C-f	Moves forward one character (beginning of the next line).
C-x)	Ends the macro definition.

You might want to try it on a copy of a file.

---

[1] This isn't quite true. If you can "undo" your mistake by using the "undo" command, deleting and retyping a few characters, or moving the cursor around a bit, you can continue with your macro definition as if nothing happened. Macros execute very quickly, so a few extra commands won't hurt much. However, such macros are more likely to have hidden problems. Remember that macros are only useful if they are re-usable.

Initial state:

```
It was the best of times, it was the worst of times, it

was the age of wisdom, it was the age of foolishness,
incredulity, it was the epoch of belief, it was the
epoch of it was the season of Light, it was the season
of Darkness, it was the spring of hope, it was the
winter of despair, we had everything before us, we had
nothing before us, we were all going direct to Heaven,
we were all going direct the other way--in short, the
period was so far like the present period, that some of
its noisiest authorities insisted on its being
received, for good or for evil, in the superlative
degree of comparison only.

-**-Emacs:  dickens        (Text Fill)-----All---------------
```

In defining the macro, you double-spaced the first line, leaving the cursor on the second line.

Now let's be brave and assume the macro works; we'll try repeating it four times. Of course, in real-life, you'd be better off trying it once before doing anything so bold.

Type: **C-u C-x e**

```
It was the best of times, it was the worst of times, it

was the age of wisdom, it was the age of foolishness,

incredulity, it was the epoch of belief, it was the

epoch of it was the season of Light, it was the season

of Darkness, it was the spring of hope, it was the

winter of despair, we had everything before us, we had
nothing before us, we were all going direct to Heaven,
we were all going direct the other way--in short, the
period was so far like the present period, that some of
its noisiest authorities insisted on its being
received, for good or for evil, in the superlative
degree of comparison only.
-**-Emacs:  dickens        (Text Fill)-----All---------------
```

Now we've done the first five lines: one by defining the macro, and four more by executing it.

The macro works well, so we can double-space the rest of the buffer with confidence: type **C-u** several times, then **C-x e**. Or, if you like to be precise, use **ESC-x count-lines-region RETURN** to find out how many lines are in the area you want to double-space. For example, if you only want to double-space the current paragraph, **count-lines-region** shows that there are six lines remaining, give the command **ESC-6 C-x e**.

Here are some common errors you should try to avoid:

- Don't forget to type **C-x)** when you've finished the macro. If you try to execute a macro before it has been defined, Emacs will complain and will forget the macro's definition.

- Remember that **C-g** terminates a macro, causing Emacs to forget its definition.

- Remember that virtually any error automatically terminates a macro. If Emacs beeps at you, you'll have to start over.

- Remember that Emacs executes the keystrokes *exactly* as you typed them, with no intelligence whatsoever. Avoid making assumptions like, "Of course I'll be at the beginning (or end) of the line when I execute the macro."

If you invoke a macro and it does the wrong thing, you can use **C-x u** (the normal "undo" command) to undo it. Emacs is smart enough to realize that "undo the last command" means "undo the entire macro" rather than "undo the last command within the macro."

Tips for Creating Good Macros

It's easy to learn how to record and re-use your keystrokes. However, if you're a typical new user, you'll make a few mistakes: you'll create a macro, use it, and then find out that it didn't do exactly what you thought. With a little care, it's easy to make your macros more useful and less vulnerable to mistakes.

Good macros are ones that work in all the situations that you want them to. This means that, within a macro, you should use commands that are absolute rather than relative. For example, if you write a macro that puts a formatting string around the word the cursor is on, you want the macro to work no matter how long the word is. This means that you would use an absolute command such as **ESC-f** (**forward-word**) rather than a few **C-f**s to move forward one character at a time. Similarly, commands such as **C-e** and **C-a** are good for defining the beginning or end of a line rather than moving the cursor forward or backward.

Often, macros start with a search command that brings you to the place in the file you want the macro to start. It's a good idea to type the search argument (as in **C-s** *searchstring*) rather than using the command to repeat the last search (**C-s** **C-s**). You may have changed the search string between the time you defined the macro and when you executed it, and **C-s** **C-s** remembers only what the last search string was.

It is often a good idea to add extra commands (typically **C-a** and **C-e**) that aren't strictly necessary, just to make sure that you're positioned correctly on the line. The fewer assumptions that a macro makes, the better off you'll be. So, if a sequence of commands will only work right if you start from the beginning of the line, start the macro with **C-a** even if you already "know" that you'll "only want to give the command when you're at the beginning of the line."

Finally, while we're reciting rules and cautions, here's one more: keep in mind that you will probably want to execute your macros repeatedly. That is, you'll certainly type **C-u C-x e** (execute it four times in a row); **C-u C-u C-x e** (16 times); or even **C-u C-u C-u C-u C-u C-x e** (1024 times). With a little foresight, you'll be able to create macros that can be executed in long chains without problems.

In general, good macros have three parts:

1. They find the place you want the macro to start working (often using search).

2. They do the work that needs to be done on the text.

3. They prepare themselves to repeat.

How can a macro prepare itself to repeat? For example, assume that you're writing a macro to delete the third column of table. After deleting the column, the macro should position itself at the beginning of the next line (or wherever it needs to be) so you don't have to reposition yourself before re-using it.

Here's a slightly more complex example. If you start a macro with a search, you have to make sure that the end of the macro moves the cursor past the last spot you searched for. If you don't, the macro will keep finding the same place in the file and never go on to the next occurrence of what you're searching for. As a general rule, if your macro operates on a line of text, it should end by moving to the beginning of the next line. Remember that your goal is to create a sequence of keystrokes that can be executed many times in a row, with no interruption.

Ending gracefully is another good quality to strive for in your macros. This is usually a matter of what keystrokes you choose to record. For example, **C-n** is one Emacs command that does not stop and beep when the end of the buffer is reached; it merrily adds new lines to the end of the file. If you have a macro with **C-n** in the wrong spot and you repeat it a few hundred times, it won't stop when it's done. Rather than moving to the beginning of the next line by typing **C-a C-n**, try **C-e C-f**—this has the same effect but doesn't add more lines to your file.

A More Complicated Macro Example

Sometimes you may want to find all the references to a particular topic in a file. This macro takes every sentence in the buffer that contains the word "Emacs" and copies it to another buffer. If you try this macro, you'll need to type some text about Emacs into a buffer (or copy what's on the sample screen following the macro).

Keystrokes	Result
C-x (	Starts macro definition; Def appears on the mode line.
C-s emacs	Finds the word Emacs.
ESC	Stops the search after it is successful.
ESC-a	Moves to the beginning of the sentence.[3]
C-@	Sets the mark.
ESC-e	Moves to the end of the sentence.
ESC-w	Copies the sentence to the kill ring.
C-x b emacsrefs RETURN	Moves to a buffer called emacsrefs.
C-y	Inserts the sentence.
RETURN	Starts the next sentence on a new line.
C-x b RETURN	Moves back to the original buffer.
C-x)	Ends the macro definition; Def is removed from the mode line.

Now, assume that you've already constructed this macro and that you can invoke it with **C-x e**. The following screen shows what happens when you run it.

---

[3] **ESC-a**'s conception of a "sentence" is controlled by the variable **sentence-end**, which is a fairly complex regular expression. By default, a sentence ends with a period, question mark, or exclamation mark, optionally followed by a quotation mark or parenthesis (including brackets or braces), and followed by two or more spaces or a linefeed.

Type: **C-u C-x e**

```
    Some Sentences about Editors

    TECO is an archaic editor.  Emacs is a modeless
    editor.  vi is a modal editor.  EDT is a
    proprietary editor.  GNU Emacs was written by
    Stallman.  Unipress Emacs was written by Gosling.█
-**-Emacs:  emacstext          (Text Fill)-----All-----------
    Emacs is a modeless
    editor.
    GNU Emacs was written by
    Stallman.
    Unipress Emacs was written by Gosling.
-**-Emacs:  emacsrefs          (Text Fill)-----All-----------
```

By executing the macro, we've created a buffer that contains all of this text's references to the Emacs editor.

The "emacsrefs" buffer may not be visible when you've finished, but that's no problem: just type **C-x b emacsrefs** to display the new buffer.

As in the previous example, you can jump back and forth between an unlimited number of buffers while defining a macro. Macros don't need to be confined to one buffer. Macros that work with several buffers *are* more difficult to debug; when several buffers are involved, it becomes harder for you to keep track of where the cursor and the mark are. And it is easy to make mistaken assumptions about what buffer you're visiting—hence, it's a good idea to specify the buffer name explicitly (as we did in the example). However, once you get accustomed to working with multiple buffers, you'll be amazed at how much work you can do with almost no effort.

Windows are sometimes useful in macros, but, again, you have to watch out. It's better to start out a macro with one window on the screen and then have the macro open other windows, and finally close all but one (**C-x 1**). If you write a macro with two windows on the screen and later try to execute it with four windows on the screen, the results will be unpredictable at best!

Adding to an Existing Macro

You can't edit macros, but you can add some commands to the end of a macro by typing **C-u C-x (. C-u C-x (** executes the macro you've written so far, then waits for you to add more keystrokes. When you've finished adding keystrokes, type **C-x)** to end the macro definition.

This command is especially useful when you write a macro, then realize that it isn't quite complete. You can either type the extra keystrokes yourself each time you execute the macro, or append those keystrokes to the end of the macro. You may want to do this if you realize that the macro you've written doesn't set itself up to be executed again. In the example above of copying references to Emacs to another buffer, we originally left off the command that moves back to the first buffer, then added it in later.

For example, let's assume that you decide that you only want to collect the first occurrence of "Emacs" in each section of your document. The document happens to be written in **troff** (UNIX's built-in typesetting system), and you can recognize sections because they begin with ".NH." Let's change the macro to add this feature.

Keystrokes	Result
C-u C-x (	Start adding to the current macro.
C-s .NH	We've found "Emacs" and are back to the original buffer. Now search for the begining of the next section.
ESC	Stop the search after it is successful.
C-x)	Ends the macro definition; Def is removed from the mode line.

Naming and Saving Your Macros

Often, a macro is just a temporary solution to a one-time problem. It saves you some work, but isn't general enough to save and use again. Other times, you'll build a macro that does a task that you have to do often and will want to save. For example, if you're a writer, you often need to put a word or a phrase in some other font, like bold. Although the exact commands you need depend on which text formatting package you're using, creating a macro to put a word in boldface type should be easy. However, no matter how easy it is to create the macro, you'll eventually get tired of retyping it all the time. If you do a lot of writing, you'll want to use this macro frequently, in many different editing sessions; you won't want it to disappear when you quit Emacs, or whenever you need to define some other macro.

Going further, you might want a collection of "permanent" macros that put words, sentences, paragraphs, and so on in bold or italic type; if you're a programmer, you might want some macros that help you format comments properly (note that Emacs has some built-in features to handle this; see Chapter 10, *Emacs for Programmers*).

In this section, we'll describe how to save macros so that you can use them in different editing sessions.

To save a macro, follow these steps:

1. Define the macro (if you've already done this, you don't have to do it again).

2. Type **ESC-x name-last-kbd-macro** and press **RETURN**. Now type a name for your macro and press **RETURN** again. A non-Emacs sounding name is best so that Emacs doesn't confuse it with one of its own commands. Once you've done this, Emacs will remember the macro for the rest of the editing session. To use it again, type the command **ESC-x** *name* (where *name* is the name you've chosen).

3. If you want to save the macro definition permanently, you must go further: insert the macro definition into a file. Type **C-x C-f** *filename* **RETURN** to find the file to insert the definition in and move to the end of it by typing **ESC->**. If you want the macro to be available every time you run Emacs, find your *.emacs* file. Otherwise, you may want to give the file the same name you gave the macro or have a file called macros that contains all your macro definitions.

4. Type **ESC-x insert-kbd-macro RETURN** *macroname* **RETURN**. Emacs inserts LISP code that represents your macro into the buffer. You don't need to understand the code.

5. Save the file by typing **C-x C-s**.

Now you have a permanent file that contains your macro.

If you're feeling adventurous, you can modify your macro by editing the file by hand. However, we discourage you from doing this. The record that Emacs saves is nothing more than a transcript of your keystrokes. It isn't particularly easy to edit, and it is particularly easy to get things fouled up.

Executing a Macro You've Named

Once you have given a macro a name, you can execute it by typing the command **ESC-x** *macroname* **RETURN**. Emacs executes the macro. You can repeat the macro *n* times by typing **ESC-***n* **ESC-x** *macroname* **RETURN**. You can have any number of named macros in use; you aren't limited to one, as you are with keyboard macros.

If you save the macro in your *.emacs* file, it's easy to execute; it will always be available whenever you're running Emacs. Simply type **ESC-x** *macroname* **RETURN**.

If you save the macro in some other file, it won't be loaded automatically. Before executing the macro, you need to make Emacs read your macro definition file by using the command **ESC-x load-file**. For example, let's say that you have defined a macro called "bold-word" and placed it in the file *nroff.macs*, in the directory ~/*emacs* (the *emacs* subdirectory of your home directory). To make this macro available, give the command **ESC-x load-file ~/emacs/nroff.macs RETURN**. You can load this file automatically by adding the line:

```
(load-file "/emacs/nroff.macs")
```

to your *.emacs* file. Once you've done this, you can give the command **ESC-x bold-word RETURN** to your heart's content.

Here's a trick that you might find find useful. Assume that you've saved a macro called "make-double-spaced-text." Of course, typing **ESC-x make-double-spaced-text RETURN** whenever you want to use the macro is time-consuming and, frankly, more work than adding carriage returns by hand. How do you solve this problem? You can define a keyboard macro that executes your permanent macro.

Keystrokes	Action
C-x (	Start keyboard macro definition.
ESC-x make-double-spaced-text RETURN	Execute your saved macro.
C-x)	End keyboard macro definition.

Now you can execute the "double-space" macro merely by typing **C-x e**.

Taking it one step further, you can simply bind the macro command to a key; Chapter 9, *Customizing Emacs*, talks about this. For example, to bind **make-double-spaced-text** to **C-c C-d**, type **ESC-x local-set-key C-c C-d make-double-spaced-text RETURN**.

Building More Complicated Macros

So far, we've covered the basics of writing, executing, and saving keyboard macros. Now let's discuss a couple of more advanced features Emacs lets you add to your macros: pausing a macro for keyboard input and inserting a query in a macro.

Pausing a Macro for Keyboard Input

Sometimes it's useful to pause a macro briefly so you can type something. For example, if you write a lot of memos, you could have a macro that prints out a template, and then pauses for you to fill in variables (such as the date and the recipient's name). You can do this (and similar tasks) by inserting a recursive edit into a macro. A recursive edit is just a fancy way to say, "Stop and let me type a while, then pick up the macro where I left off."

When you're defining a macro, type **C-u C-x q** at the point that you want the recursive edit to occur. Emacs enters a recursive edit. (You can tell you're in a recursive edit because square brackets appear on the mode line.) Nothing you type during the recursive edit becomes a part of the macro. You can type whatever you want to, then press **ESC-C-c** to exit the recursive edit. Notice how the square brackets disappear when you type **ESC-C-c**. When the square brackets are no longer on the screen, you have left the recursive edit. Anything you type now will become part of the macro.

You can put as many "pauses" in your macros as you want to.

Example

Here's an example of a macro that puts a memo template on the screen and uses recursive edits to let you type the date, recipient's name, and sender's name.

Keystrokes	Action
C-x (	Starts keyboard macro definition.
Memorandum	Displays Memorandum on the screen.
ESC-s	Centers the word "Memorandum."
RETURN RETURN	Moves the cursor down two lines.
Date: TAB	Displays Date: on the screen.
C-u C-x q	Enters a recursive edit, during which the keystrokes you type are not recorded as part of the macro.
ESC-C-c	Exits the recursive edit.
RETURN RETURN	Moves the cursor down two lines.
To: TAB	Displays To: on the screen.
C-u C-x q	Enters a recursive edit.
ESC-C-c	Exits the recursive edit.
RETURN RETURN	Moves the cursor down two lines.
From: TAB	Displays From: on the screen.
C-u C-x q	Enters a recursive edit.
ESC-C-c	Exits the recursive edit.
RETURN RETURN	Moves the cursor down two lines.
ESC-78 -	Draws a line of hyphens across the screen.

Keystrokes	Action
RETURN	Inserts a blank line.
C-x)	Ends keyboard macro definition.

The following screen shows what this macro looks like when you run it.

Type: **C-x e**

```
                         Memorandum

        Date:  █




     -**-Emacs:   memo         [(Text Fill)]----------All-------------
```

The macro pauses so that you can type the date.

Type: **10/31/91** ESC-**C-c**

```
                         Memorandum

        Date:   10/31/91

        To:  █



     -**-Emacs:   memo         [(Text Fill)]----------All-------------
```

The macro pauses so you can type the recipient's name.

Type: **Fred ESC-C-c**

```
                      Memorandum

Date:  10/31/91

To:   Fred

From: █



-**-Emacs:   memo         [(Text Fill)]---------All------------
```

The macro pauses so you can type the sender's name.

Type: **Maurice ESC-C-c**

```
                      Memorandum

Date:  10/31/91

To:   Fred

From:  Maurice

--------------------------------------------------

█
-**-Emacs:   memo          (Text Fill)----------All------------
```

The macro inserts a line of hyphens to separate the heading of the
memo from the body.

Now the macro has finished editing; you can type the body of the memo, or you
can go back and edit any of the fields you've already filled in.

Adding a Query to a Macro

The more complex the task your macro does, the more difficult it is to make the
macro general enough to work in every case. Although macros can do a lot of
things, they aren't full programs: you can't have if statements, loops, and the
other things you associate with a program. In particular, a macro can't get input
from the user, and then take some action on the basis of that input. If you really
need this feature, read Chapter 11, *Emacs LISP Programming*.

However, one feature lets a macro get input, in a very limited way, from the user. You can create a macro that queries the user while it is running; it works much like a query-replace. To create this kind of a macro, type **C-x q** while you are defining the macro. Nothing will happen immediately; go on defining the macro as you normally would.

Things get interesting later, when you execute the macro. When it gets to the point in the macro where you typed **C-x q**, Emacs prints a query in the minibuffer, asking: "Proceed with macro? (SPACE, DEL, C-d, C-r, or C-l)." The query responses listed below are analogous to those in query-replace, which we discussed in Chapter 3, *Search and Replace Operations*:

- Pressing **SPACE** means "continue executing."

- Pressing **C-d** means to stop executing the macro and cancel any repetitions.

- Pressing **DEL** means to stop this macro, but go on to the next repetition, if any.

- Pressing **C-r** starts a recursive edit, which lets you do any editing or moving around you may want to and then resume the macro by exiting the recursive edit. To exit a recursive edit, press **ESC-C-c**. Emacs again asks if you want to proceed with the macro, and you type **SPACE** for yes or **DEL** or **C-d** for no.

- Pressing **C-l** puts the line the cursor is on in the middle of the screen (this is good for getting a feel for the context). Similar to **C-r**, Emacs again asks if you want to proceed with the macro and you have to answer with **SPACE**, **DEL**, or **C-d**. Pressing **C-g** doesn't cancel this type of query; you have to use one of the prescribed responses.

Example

Let's say that you write a macro that copies comments from a program to another buffer. The comments in the program are all surrounded by lines of asterisks, so you start the macro with a search for a string of asterisks. However, not all strings of asterisks are followed by a comment and not all comments are worth copying. Following the search with a query lets you decide case-by-case whether the search has found a comment you want to copy.

Here's the macro definition.

Keystrokes	Action
C-x (	Starts the macro definition.
C-s ******	Searches for a string of asterisks.
ESC	Stops the search when it is successful.

Keystrokes	Action
C-x q	Inserts a query in the macro; Emacs will ask you if you want to proceed at this point when you run the macro.
C-n	Moves down to the next line.
C-a	Moves to the beginning of the line.
C-@	Sets the mark.
C-s ***** ESC	Finds the closing string of asterisks.
C-p	Moves up a line.
C-e	Moves to the end of the line.
ESC-w	Copies the comment to the kill ring.
C-n C-n	Moves down past this comment.
C-x b comments	Moves to a buffer called comments.
C-y	Inserts the comment in the buffer.
RETURN	Inserts a blank line.
C-x b	Moves back to the original buffer.
C-x)	Ends the macro definition.

Beyond Macros

Macros are an extremely important tool for streamlining repetitive editing. They let you write your own commands for performing complex tasks, without needing to know anything more than you already know: the basic Emacs commands for moving around and manipulating text. Even if you're an Emacs novice, you should be able to use macros with little difficulty.

However, Emacs is almost infinitely flexible, and macros cannot do everything. In many situations, there's no substitute for writing a LISP function that will do exactly what you want. If you know LISP or would like to learn some, you can write your own LISP functions to do more complex tasks than keyboard macros can handle. Chapter 11 covers the basics of writing LISP functions.

Table 8-1 summarizes the macro commands we discussed in this chapter.

Table 8-1. Macro Commands

Keystrokes	Command Name	Action
C-x (	start-kbd-macro	Starts macro definition.
C-x)	end-kbd-macro	Ends macro definition.
C-x e	call-last-kbd-macro	Executes last macro defined.
ESC-*n* C-x e	digit-argument and call-last-kbd-macro	Executes the last macro defined *n* times.
C-u C-x (	start-kbd-macro	Executes the last macro defined, then lets you add keystrokes to it.
(none)	name-last-kbd-macro	Lets you name the last macro you created (a preface to saving it).
(none)	insert-last-keyboard-macro	Inserts the macro you named into a file.
(none)	load-file	Loads a file containing command definitions; used to load macro files you've saved.
(none)	*macroname*	Executes a keyboard macro you've saved.
C-x q	kbd-macro-query	Inserts a query in a macro definition.
C-u C-x q	(none)	Inserts a recursive edit in a macro definition.
ESC-C-c	exit-recursive-edit	Exits a recursive edit.

9

Customizing Emacs

Keyboard Customization
Terminal Support
Emacs Variables
Emacs LISP Packages
Auto-mode Customization

It is possible to customize Emacs in just about any way you can imagine. Almost everything you see on the screen, every command, keystroke, message, etc., can be changed. As you may imagine, most customizations involve the Emacs startup file *.emacs*.

Some changes require a knowledge of Emacs LISP programming (see Chapter 11), while others are simple enough without such knowledge. In this chapter, we will cover a variety of useful customizations that require no programming knowledge. For now, however, you will need to know this: every Emacs command corresponds to a LISP *function*, which has the form:

```
(function-name arguments)
```

For example, if you want to move the cursor forward by a word, you type **ESC-f**. What you are actually doing is running the LISP function:

```
(forward-word 1)
```

This chapter covers a wide variety of topics relating to customization and advanced Emacs usage. We will start with two common things that users want or need to learn about in relation to Emacs: keyboards and terminals. You will find out how to customize your keyboard commands, make special keys on your keyboard useful, and set up your terminal so that it works properly with Emacs. The remainder of the chapter discusses how you can modify and extend Emacs' behavior through its *variables* and through the use of *packages* that add extra functionality. Comprehensive lists of useful variables and packages are contained in Appendix C, *Emacs Variables*, and Appendix D, *Emacs LISP Packages*. For information on even more advanced customization techniques, see Chapter 11, *Emacs LISP Programming*.

Before we go on to these topics, two important comments concerning .*emacs* files are in order. First, if you are inserting code into your .*emacs* file, you may end up putting in something that causes Emacs to fail or behave strangely. If this happens, there is a way to invoke Emacs without running your .*emacs* file: simply invoke Emacs with the command-line option **-q**, and Emacs will not run your .*emacs* file. Then you can examine the file to figure out what went wrong.

The other comment is perhaps the most important piece of advice we can give you concerning customizing your Emacs environment: *steal mercilessly from other users*. In particular, if you are dealing with a messy situation involving terminal configuration or flow-control problems or a subtle point about some specialized mode, it is possible that some other user may have solved the problem(s) already. This is not "dishonest" or "subversive" in any way; rather, it is *encouraged* by the makers of GNU Emacs, who would much rather that software be shared than kept to oneself. Emacs even provides an easy way to try out other users' .*emacs* files: invoke Emacs with the option **-u** *username*, and *username*'s .*emacs* file will be run instead of yours.

Keyboard Customization

Perhaps the most common things that Emacs users want to customize are the keystrokes that cause commands to be run. We say that keystrokes are associated with commands via *key bindings*.

Actually, *every* keystroke runs a command in Emacs. Printable character keys (letters, numerals, punctuation, and space) run the command **self-insert-command**, which merely causes the key just pressed to be inserted at the cursor in the current buffer. (You could play a nasty April Fool's joke on a naive Emacs user by changing the bindings of their printable characters.)

The default set of key bindings is adequate for most purposes, of course, but there are various cases in which you may want to add or change key bindings. Emacs contains literally hundreds of commands, only some of which have key bindings.

As you know, you can access those that don't have bindings by typing **ESC-x** *command-name* **RETURN**. But if you intend to use such a command often, you may want to bind it to a keystroke sequence for convenience. You may want to set special keys on your terminal, such as arrow, numeric keypad, or function keys, to perform commands you use often. You may need to rebind commands that are bound to keys that are inaccessible because of flow-control problems. We will cover examples of all of these instances of key bindings and rebindings.

The other important concept you need to know now is that of a *keymap*, which is an array of key bindings. The most basic default key bindings in Emacs are kept in a keymap called **global-map**. There is also the concept of a *local* keymap, which is specific to a single buffer. Local keymaps are used to implement commands in modes (like C mode, text mode, shell mode, etc.), and each such mode has its own keymap that it installs as the local mode when invoked. When you type a key, Emacs first looks it up in the current buffer's local map (if any). If it doesn't find an entry there, it looks in **global-map**. If an entry for the key is found, its associated command is run.

But what happens with commands that are bound to multiple keystrokes, as in **ESC-d** (for **kill-word**)? The answer is that the keys **C-x**, **ESC**, and **C-c** are actually bound to special internal functions that cause Emacs to wait for another key to be pressed and then to look up that key's binding in another map; they also cause messages like "C-x-" to appear in the minibuffer if more than a second passes before the next key is pressed. The additional keymaps for **C-x** and **ESC** are called **ctl-x-map** and **esc-map** respectively, while **C-c** is reserved for local keymaps associated with modes like C mode and shell mode.

For example, here is what happens when you type **ESC-d**. When **ESC** is typed, Emacs looks it up in the buffer's local map. We will assume it doesn't find an entry there. Then Emacs searches **global-map**; there it finds an entry for **ESC** with a special function (called **ESC-prefix**) that waits for the next keystroke and uses **esc-map** to determine which command to execute. When **d** is typed, **ESC-prefix** looks up the entry for **d** in **esc-map**, finds **kill-word**, and runs it.

You can create your own key bindings by adding entries in keymaps (or overriding existing ones). There are three functions available for doing this: **define-key**, **global-set-key**, and **local-set-key**. Their forms are:

```
(define-key keymap "keystroke" 'command-name)
(global-set-key "keystroke" 'command-name)
(local-set-key "keystroke" 'command-name)
```

Notice the double quotes around "keystroke" and the single quote preceding *command-name*. This is just LISP syntax; for more details, see Chapter 11. The "keystroke" is one or more characters, either printable or special characters. For the latter, use the conventions in Table 9-1.

Table 9-1. Special Character Conventions

Special Char	Definition
\C-x	C-x (where x is any letter)
\C-[or \e	ESC
\C-j or \n	LINEFEED
\C-m or \r	RETURN
\C-i or \t	TAB

Thus, the string "abc\C-a\ndef" is equal to abc, C-a, LINEFEED, and def, all concatenated into one string. Note that control characters are "case-insensitive," e.g., \C-A is the same thing as \C-a.

The function **define-key** is the most general, since it can be used to bind keys in any keymap. **global-set-key** is used to bind keys in the global map only; since there is only one **global-map**, (**global-set-key** ...) is the same as (**define-key global-map** ...). **Local-set-key** is used to bind keys in the local map of the *current buffer*; thus, it is only really useful for specifying temporary key bindings during an Emacs session.

Here is an example of a simple keyboard customization. Let's say you are writing code in a programming language. You compile it and get error messages that contain the line number of the error, and you want to go to that line in the source file to correct the error.[1] You would want to use the **goto-line** command, which is not bound by default to any keystroke. Say you want to bind it to **C-x l**. The command to put into your *.emacs* file is:

```
(define-key ctl-x-map "l" 'goto-line)
```

This binds the "l" slot in **ctl-x-map** to the command **goto-line**. Alternatively, you can use *either one* of the following:

```
(define-key global-map "\C-xl" 'goto-line)
(global-set-key "\C-xl" 'goto-line)
```

These have the same effect but are less efficient—Emacs has to figure out that what you really want to do is bind the "l" slot in **ctl-x-map**.

---

[1] There is a better way of dealing with this situation, which we will cover in the next chapter.

Other examples of key rebindings include binding **C-x ?** to **help-command** and **C-h** to **backward-char**, as in Chapter 1, and binding **ESC-.** to **set-mark-command** as in Chapter 2. This is shown in the following:

```
(global-set-key "\C-x?" 'help-command)
(global-set-key "\C-h" 'backward-char)
(global-set-key "\." 'set-mark-command)
```

Notice that these could also be done as:

```
(define-key ctl-x-map "?" 'help-command)
(define-key global-map "\C-h" 'backward-char)
(define-key esc-map "." 'set-mark-command)
```

After you put a key binding (or any other code) in your *.emacs* file, you will need to "run" (or *evaluate*) the file for the change to take effect. The command for this is **ESC-x eval-current-buffer RETURN**. If you do not use this command, the changes will not take effect until the next time you invoke Emacs.

Getting Around Flow-control Problems

Another common reason for customizing keystrokes is the *flow-control* problem that occurs in some situations involving terminals (as opposed to PCs or workstations). Some operating systems and data communications devices (terminals, modems, networks, etc.) use the characters **C-s** and **C-q** to act as "stop" and "go" signs for terminal input and output, to prevent buffer overflow.

Many more modern systems use other means of flow control, such as extra hardware, but others still use the **C-s**/**C-q** convention. This is especially likely in situations where there are multiple data communications devices between you and the actual computer (for example, a terminal talking to a modem, talking to another modem, talking to a terminal server, talking to a local area network, talking to a computer, remotely logged into another computer ...).

In general, the more pieces of hardware between you and the computer, the more likely that **C-s** and **C-q** are used as flow-control characters; this means that those two characters are not accessible to Emacs. To find out whether this situation affects you, simply invoke Emacs and type **C-s**. If you see the "Isearch:" prompt in the minibuffer, all is probably well. Otherwise, nothing will happen and your terminal will appear to hang—any other keys you type will have no effect. Actually, you will have told some piece of hardware not to accept any more input. To get out of this, just type **C-q**. Any keys you hit in between will then take effect.

An easy way to get around this problem is to bind different keystroke sequences to the commands normally bound to **C-s** and **C-q**, i.e., **isearch-forward** and **quoted-insert** respectively. It will also be necessary to reset the "forward search repeat" character to something other than **C-s**. For example, you could use **ESC-s** for **isearch-forward**, **ESC-q** for **quoted-insert**, and **C-f** forward search repeat. To do this, put the following in your *.emacs* file:

```
(define-key esc-map "s" 'isearch-forward)
(define-key esc-map "q" 'quoted-insert)
(setq search-repeat-char ?\C-f)
```

The last of these is not a **define-key** command, for the following reason: the search repeat character is not really a key bound to a command, but rather an "option" within the **isearch-forward** command. The latter uses an Emacs *variable* (see below) to determine the search repeat character. The **setq** command causes the variable **search-repeat-character** to be set to the single character **C-f**; the LISP syntax for specifying single character values is described later in this chapter.

There are certain pathological cases in which flow-control problems can be even worse. If Emacs has to do lots of continuous terminal output (e.g., if you are scrolling through a file with lots of long lines of text), the operating system or some piece of data communications hardware might start sending **C-s/C-q** pairs to the computer to stem the flood of data. When this happens, Emacs will usually try to interpret the flow-control characters as an incremental search command (since **C-s** is normally bound to **isearch-forward**).

You can prevent Emacs from interpreting **C-s/C-q** as a command by removing the two keys' bindings with the **global-unset-key** function,[2] and by overriding the option in which any control character can be used to exit incremental search. Just put the following lines in your *.emacs*:

```
(global-unset-key "\C-s")
(global-unset-key "\C-q")
(setq search-exit-option nil)
```

The last of these lines sets the variable **search-exit-option**, which is described in the table of Emacs variables in Appendix C. Under this setting, you can only use **ESC** to end an incremental search; this is necessary so that any **C-s/C-q**'s the hardware sends won't cause incremental search to terminate.

This LISP code will solve most but not all of your problems. For example, you may be in the middle of an "interactive" command that does lots of I/O (such as **query-replace** or incremental search), and a stray **C-s/C-q** might have annoying effects. For example, if you are in the middle of an incremental search, you might hear a "beep" and see "^S^Q" (for **C-s C-q**) appended to your search string in the minibuffer. You can counteract this by doing the following: press any key

---

[2] There is also an analogous **local-unset-key** function that applies to the keymap in the current buffer only.

(since **C-q** is the "quote" character in incremental search), and that key will appear in place of the "^Q". Then press DEL twice to delete the key you pressed and the preceding "^S" from your search string. Once you have done this, you can resume your search or query-replace.

Special Keys

A more complicated keyboard customization task is binding commands to special keys, such as arrow, numeric keypad, or function keys, on your terminal. This level of customization takes some work, but if you like using special keys, it is well worth the effort.

Special keys on any terminal generate *character codes*, which are sequences of characters, often starting with a special character such as ESC. So the first thing you need to do is to discover what character codes the special keys on your terminal generate. For example, many terminals conform to the ANSI standard, which means that they have numeric keypads that can be put into "application mode" so that they generate complex code sequences rather than the normal digits and punctuation (period, comma, and dash). Application mode keypad keys all produce a prefix of **ESC-O** followed by some other character, e.g., **ESC-O w** for the 7 key.

You can look up the character codes for your terminal's special keys in the terminal's manual. If this information is not available, you can use the **quoted-insert** command to find the character codes. Just switch to a clean buffer, such as `*scratch*`, and type **C-q**[3] followed by each special key. Control characters will show up with a caret (^) in front, e.g., ^**X** for **C-x**;[4] Certain special characters will show up as control characters, as follows:

ESC   ^[
RETURN   ^M
LINEFEED   ^J

TAB just appears as a tab, i.e., one or more spaces. Thus, the ANSI keypad-7 key will appear as "^[Ow."

On some terminals, the special keys will not be useful for customizing in Emacs because they generate character codes that merely duplicate the bindings for basic Emacs commands. For example, the arrow keys of the Wyse WY-50

---

[3] Or **ESC-q** if you have the flow-control problem described above.

[4] Notice that control characters take up one *character position*, even though they take two spaces to display; for example, typing **C-f** when the cursor is on a control character will cause the cursor to move forward two spaces.

generate **C-k** (up), **C-j** (down), **C-h** (left), and **C-l** (right); it would be unwise indeed to rebind these keystrokes! Some terminals also have numeric keypads but no "application mode"—that is, their keypad keys can only generate digits and punctuation. These are obviously not useful for Emacs customization either. As a general rule, special keys can be customized in Emacs if they can be made to generate character codes that start with a special character (such as ESC) and are at least three characters long.

If your terminal's special keys satisfy this requirement, you can write LISP code to put in your *.emacs* file that binds the keys to commands of your choice. The code should create a keymap corresponding to the common prefix of a set of special keys and then bind each key to a command. For example, here is some LISP code that sets up bindings for arrow, function, and keypad keys on an ANSI compatible terminal such as the DEC VT100 or VT200:

```
(setq term-file-prefix nil)
(send-string-to-terminal "\e=")

(setq SS3-map (make-keymap))    ;set up the keymap for the keypad
(define-key global-map "\eO" SS3-map)

(define-key SS3-map "A" 'previous-line)      ; up arrow
(define-key SS3-map "B" 'next-line)          ; down-arrow
(define-key SS3-map "C" 'forward-char)       ; right-arrow
(define-key SS3-map "D" 'backward-char)      ; left-arrow

(define-key SS3-map "M" 'isearch-forward)    ; Enter

(define-key SS3-map "P" 'other-window)       ; PF1
(define-key SS3-map "Q" 'query-replace)      ; PF2
(define-key SS3-map "R" 'replace-string)     ; PF3
(define-key SS3-map "S" 'suspend-emacs)      ; PF4

(define-key SS3-map "l" 'delete-char)        ; ,

(define-key SS3-map "n" 'delete-next-word)      ; .
(define-key SS3-map "p" 'isearch-backward)      ; 0
(define-key SS3-map "q" 'beginning-of-line)     ; 1
(define-key SS3-map "r" 'find-file)             ; 2
(define-key SS3-map "s" 'end-of-line)           ; 3
(define-key SS3-map "t" 'backward-word)         ; 4
(define-key SS3-map "v" 'forward-word)          ; 6
(define-key SS3-map "w" 'beginning-of-buffer)   ; 7
(define-key SS3-map "x" 'save-buffer)           ; 8
(define-key SS3-map "y" 'end-of-buffer)         ; 9
```

The semicolons denote the start of comments (which Emacs ignores); anything between a semicolon and the end of the line is a comment.

The first two lines of this code bear some explanation. Emacs has some built-in LISP code that facilitates binding of special keys on certain types of terminals (particularly DEC VT100 and VT200 types and various workstations) but not others. The first line of the above code cancels out the effects of the built-in code (if any), assuring that the rest of this code will work properly for all terminal types.

The second line is particularly for VT100/200-style terminals, whose keypads can be set to work in two modes, "application" and "numeric." In the latter mode, the keypad keys merely act as duplicates of the numerals, dash, comma, and period. Clearly this is not useful in our case, so the idea is to force the terminal into application mode. Sending the terminal the sequence **ESC-=** does this; thus the **send-string-to-terminal** command. *If your terminal is not a VT100 or VT200 or equivalent, do not use this line.*

The next two lines are for creating the keymap and "hooking it up" to the global map so it can be activated. The first one creates a keymap called **SS3-map**; while you can name your keymaps whatever you want, this is so named because DEC documentation refers to the **ESC-O** prefix as "SS3." The second line binds this map to the **ESC-O** sequence in the global keymap.[5] Notice that keymaps, not just commands, can be bound (recursively) to slots in keymaps. Thus, this LISP command causes the global map to pass control to **SS3-map** whenever **ESC-O** is typed, i.e., whenever a key that generates a character sequence starting with **ESC-O** is typed.

The rest of the LISP commands above bind specific arrow and keypad keys to Emacs commands. The four arrow keys are bound to the expected cursor motion commands, and the rest of the keypad is set up as shown in the following diagram.

---

[5] Actually, it binds **SS3-map** to the "O" slot in **esc-map**; see the explanation of keymaps at the beginning of this chapter.

F1 other- window	F2 query- replace	F3 replace- string	F4 suspend- emacs
7 beginning- of-buffer	8 save- buffer	9 end- of-buffer	-
4 backward- word	5	6 forward- word	, delete- char
1 beginning- of-line	2 find- file	3 end- of-line	ENTER isearch-
0 isearch- backward		. delete- word	forward

Notice that the 5 and dash keys are not bound. As an exercise, see if you can figure out what LISP code you would need to write to bind these keys to two commands that you use often.

Terminal Support

There are lots of different display devices in the world—terminals, PCs, graphics workstations, etc. Emacs is capable of running on all but the "dumbest" of them, but whether it actually does or not depends on a couple of features of UNIX.

The first of these is called an *environment variable*. When you log onto a UNIX system, several of these are set up for you. They have values, usually character strings, that the UNIX Shell keeps around and passes to each command you invoke as an indication of various features of your computing environment.

By convention, environment variables are named in all capital letters. Typical ones include **PATH**, which tells UNIX which directories to look for commands in, and **SHELL**, whose value is the name of the shell you are using. We are concerned with the environment variable **TERM**, which tells UNIX and certain programs (such as Emacs) which kind of terminal you are using.

TERM is usually set when you log on, either by some system-wide shell initialization file or by your own *.profile* file (*.login* for C Shell users). On some systems, you may even be prompted for your terminal type when you log on. To check the value of **TERM**, type **echo $TERM** at the UNIX prompt; the dollar sign means "value of." To set it, type **TERM=termname** (for Bourne, Korn, or **bash**

Shell; note the lack of spaces on either side of the equal sign) or **setenv TERM termname** (for C Shell). If you don't know what your terminal type is, try asking your system administrator. If he or she doesn't know, read on and you will see how you can find out for yourself.

The other UNIX feature relating to terminals is **termcap** (for "terminal capability"), a file in the /etc directory. It contains descriptions of terminals that consist of their physical characteristics, such as width and height in characters, and the hardware commands they support, such as scrolling, reverse video, and cursor motion.

Some versions of UNIX (derived from AT&T's System V) use **terminfo** instead of **termcap**; consult your system administrator to find out if yours is one. **Terminfo** uses a more sophisticated database instead of a single file for terminal descriptions, but otherwise it is similar to (and mostly upwardly compatible with) **termcap**.

The language in which **termcap** entries are written is terse and incomprehensible to non-experts, while **terminfo** entries are compiled into non-human-readable form. However, the names of terminals supported are easy enough to discern.

If your version of Emacs uses **termcap** (as the majority do), you can search the file /etc/termcap using the UNIX **grep** utility. Make a guess at your terminal type, based on its make and model, and type:

```
% grep -i guess /etc/termcap
```

The **-i** option tells **grep** to ignore case distinctions. Say your terminal is a DEC VT100, and you type **grep vt100 /etc/termcap**. If you are successful, **grep** will print one or more lines that look like this:

```
d0|vt100|vt100-am|dec vt100:\
```

Any of the strings within vertical bars will do as a value for **TERM**. Most entries include a number of synonyms for the terminal name.

If your version of Emacs uses **terminfo**, you can search for your terminal type in the **terminfo** database. It is organized as a tree of directories under the directory /usr/lib/terminfo. This contains several (sub)directories, one for each numeral and letter of the alphabet. Under these are files, one for each particular terminal type whose name begins with that letter or numeral. For example, the entry for the VT100 is in the file /usr/lib/terminfo/v/vt100. These files are individual terminal descriptions.

There are two ways to discover the **terminfo** name of your terminal. The first is to **cd** to the subdirectory of /usr/lib/terminfo corresponding to the first letter of your guess for the terminal's name. Then type **ls** to get the list of terminal description files, and choose an appropriate-looking one. Use the filename as your terminal type, and set the **TERM** environment variable to that name.

Another way to search the **terminfo** database is to use the UNIX **find** command. Just type:

```
% find /usr/lib/terminfo -name "guess" -print
```

where "guess" must be surrounded by double quotes and can contain file-matching wildcard characters such as * and ?. If you are successful, **find** will print one or more lines with names of terminal description files; just use one of them (sans its directory prefix, of course) as your value of **TERM**.

The contents of **termcap** files (and **terminfo** databases) vary from system to system. In the earlier days of UNIX as a commercial product (about ten years ago), it was possible to be on a UNIX system whose **termcap** file didn't support various popular terminals. But as UNIX has come of age, **termcap** files have grown—typical ones support a few hundred terminal types. However, it is still possible that your terminal is not listed in **termcap** or **terminfo**, especially if it is from an "independent" maker (WYSE, for example). Such terminals tend to be clones of more common ones (the VT100 is most often emulated) or can be configured as such. You may need to set up your terminal to emulate a more common one and then set **TERM** to be that type. In general, your terminal would be rare indeed if most **termcap**s and **terminfo** databases didn't support it somehow.[6]

Most modern terminals can do lots of things in hardware that make Emacs' life easier, such as character insertion and partial-screen scrolling. Emacs takes advantage of such features where they exist but is capable of simulating them in software where they don't. Emacs even knows how to do without certain basic features like reverse video (for mode lines). There is only one feature that your terminal absolutely must have: the ability to position the cursor. If you invoke Emacs and you get a message saying that your terminal is not powerful enough, then either your **TERM** environment variable is not set correctly or your terminal is just too "dumb." Nowadays, the latter possibility is very remote.

A few final notes about terminals. You may have found that **termcap** or **terminfo** contains several entries that seem to apply to your terminal. In that case (if you have **termcap**), it is most likely that the entry that comes first is the correct one, or at least a reasonable default—**termcap** files are usually designed that way.

---

[6] For a more complete explanation of **termcap** and **terminfo** databases, see the Nutshell Handbook, *termcap and terminfo*, by John Strang, Linda Mui, and Tim O'Reilly.

You may have a terminal that acts like a well-known one (such as the VT100) but has extra features. If so, Emacs may run more efficiently if you specify the actual terminal type instead of relying on the "lowest common denominator." It is worth your while to make the effort to search **termcap** or **terminfo** for an entry that takes advantage of extra features.

Emacs Variables

Now we will get into ways to affect Emacs' behavior—not just its user interface. The easiest way to do this is by setting **variables** that control various things. We already saw examples of this like **auto-save-interval** in Chapter 2, *Editing Files*. To set the value of a variable, use the **setq** function in your *.emacs*, as in:

```
(setq auto-save-interval 800)
```

Although **auto-save-interval** takes an *integer* (number) value, many Emacs variables take "true" or "false" values, called *Boolean* in computer parlance. In Emacs LISP, **t** is the true value, while **nil** is false—though in most cases, anything other than **nil** is taken to mean true. There are other types of values that Emacs variables can take; here is how to specify them:

- *Strings* of characters are surrounded by double quotes. We saw examples of strings in the arguments to key-binding commands earlier in this chapter.

- *Characters* are specified like strings but with a **?** preceding them, and they are not surrounded by double quotes. Thus, **?x** and **?\C-c** are character values, x and C-c respectively.

- *Symbols* are given by a single quote followed by a symbol name—for example, **'never** (see the variable **version-control** in Appendix C, *Emacs Variables*).

A list of useful Emacs variables, grouped by category, appears in Appendix C with descriptions and default values. There are several dozen Emacs variables—many more than those covered in Appendix C. If there is something about Emacs that you want to customize, there may be a variable that controls the feature (especially if what you want to change involves a number or a true-or-false condition). To find out whether there are any variables that relate to what you want to do, you can use the **apropos** command described in Chapter 13, *Online Help*, and look through its output for variables and their descriptions.

Several Emacs variables can have different values for each buffer (*local* values) as well as a *default* value. Such variables assume their default values in buffers where the local values are not specified. Accordingly, you can set both the default and local values of such variables. When you set the value of a variable such as **left-margin** or **case-fold-search**, you are actually setting the local value. The way to set default values is to use **setq-default** instead of **setq**, as in:

```
(setq-default left-margin 4)
```

Unfortunately, there is no general way to tell whether a variable just has one global value or has default and local values (except, of course, by looking at the LISP code for the mode). Therefore the best strategy is to use a plain **setq**, *unless* you find by experience that a particular variable doesn't seem to take on the value you **setq** it to—in which case you should use **setq-default**. For example, if you put the line:

```
(setq case-fold-search nil)
```

in your *.emacs* file, you will find that Emacs will still ignore case differences in search commands as if this variable were still **t**; instead, you should use **setq-default**.

Emacs LISP Packages

Emacs contains lots of LISP code; in fact, as we will see in Chapter 11, the majority of Emacs' built-in functionality is written in LISP. Emacs also comes with several extra LISP *packages* (also known as *libraries*) that you can "bring in" (or *load*) to add more features. LISP packages are being added to Emacs all the time, and sometimes your system administrator will add packages obtained from sources other than the Free Software Foundation.

Therefore, we have included a table of the most useful *built-in* LISP packages, along with explanations of how to use them, in Appendix D, *Emacs LISP Packages*. Briefly, Emacs' built-in packages do the following kinds of things:

- Support programming in C, LISP, FORTRAN, and several other languages (see Chapter 10, *Emacs for Programmers*).

- Support word processing with TeX, **nroff, troff,** and Scribe (see Chapter 7, *Using Emacs with UNIX Text Formatters*).

- Emulate other editors (**vi, EDT,** and Gosling Emacs).

- Interface to UNIX utilities such as the shell and mail (see Chapter 5, *Emacs as a Work Environment*) as well as **ftp, kermit, telnet,** and the **MH** mail system.

- Provide editing support functions, such as spell checking (Chapter 3, *Search and Replace Operations*) and outline editing (Chapter 6, *Simple Text Formatting and Specialized Editing*) as well as text sorting, command history editing, Emacs variable setting (Appendix C, *Emacs Variables*), and much more.

- Play various games and provide other forms of amusement.

See Appendix D, *Emacs LISP Packages*, for more details.

Auto-mode Customization

The tables in Appendix D list several major modes that are automatically invoked when you visit a file whose name ends in the appropriate suffix. Look for "suffix" in the right-hand columns of the tables to see many of the associations between filename suffixes and major modes that Emacs sets up by default. These associations are contained in the special Emacs variable **auto-mode-alist**. **Auto-mode-alist** is a list of pairs (*regexp, mode*), where *regexp* is a regular expression (see Chapters 3 and 11) and *mode* is the name of a function that invokes a major mode. When Emacs visits a file, it searches this list (from the beginning) for a match to the regular expression. If it finds one, it runs the associated mode function. Notice that *any* part of a file's name can actually be associated with a major mode—not just its suffix.

You can add your own associations to **auto-mode-alist**, although the syntax is weird if you are not used to LISP (see Chapter 11 for the gory details). Let's say you are programming in the Ada language, and your Ada compiler expects files with suffix *.a* (some compilers expect *.ada*). To get Emacs to put Ada files in Ada mode whenever you visit them, put the following line in your *.emacs* file:

```
(setq auto-mode-alist (cons '("\.a$" . ada-mode) auto-mode-alist))
```

Make sure you include the single quote after the **cons** and the dot between "**\.a$**" and **ada-mode**. The notation '(x . y) is just LISP syntax for "make a pair out of x and y." The string "**\.a$**" is a regular expression that means "anything with *.a* at the end of it," i.e., $ matches the end of the string (as opposed to end of line, which is what it matches during regular expression search and replace). The entire line of LISP basically means "add the pair ("**\.a$**", 'ada-mode) to the front of the auto-mode-alist." Note that, since Emacs searches **auto-mode-alist** from the beginning and stops when it finds a match, you can use the above **cons** construct to override existing mode associations.[7]

---

[7] LISP programmers will understand that there are other ways to add to **auto-mode-alist**, such as **append**.

As another example, let's say you save certain mail messages in files whose names begin with *msg-* and you want to edit these files in text mode. Here is the way to do it:

```
(setq auto-mode-alist (cons '("^msg-" . text-mode) auto-mode-alist))
```

Notice that in this case we are matching the *beginning*, rather than the end, of the filename. The regular expression operator " ^ " means beginning of string, so the entire regular expression means "anything beginning with msg-."

Finally, if the name of a file you are editing does not match any of the regular expressions in **auto-mode-alist**, Emacs will put it into the mode whose name is the value of the variable **default-major-mode**. This is normally fundamental mode, a basic mode without special functionality. However, many people like to set their default mode to text mode; this is the code to do it:

```
(setq default-major-mode 'text-mode)
```

We have covered many useful ways to customize Emacs in this chapter, but we have really only scratched the surface. To find out more, turn to Chapter 11 and find out about LISP programming, the key to getting Emacs to do just about anything you want.

10

Emacs For Programmers

Language Modes
C Mode
The LISP Modes
FORTRAN Mode
Compiling Programs

As many programmers know, the task of programming usually breaks down into a cycle of think-write-debug. If you have used UNIX (or various other operating systems) for programming, you have probably become accustomed to using a set of disjoint tools for each phase of the cycle, e.g., a text editor for writing, a compiler for compiling, and the operating system itself for running programs. You would undoubtedly find an environment much more productive if the boundaries between the cycle phases—and the tools that support them—were erased.

Emacs provides considerable support for writing, running, and debugging programs written in a wide variety of languages, and it integrates this support into a smooth framework. Since you never have to leave Emacs when developing programs, you will find it easier to concentrate on the actual programming task (i.e., the "think" part of the cycle) because you won't have to spend lots of time going from one tool to another.

When you write code, you can use one of Emacs' *programming language modes*; these turn Emacs into rudimentary "syntax-directed" or "language-sensitive" editors that have knowledge about the syntax of the language and that make it easy for you to write code in a uniform, easy-to-read, customizable style. Language modes exist for several different programming languages.

Emacs also supports running and debugging programs. The shell mode, which we saw in Chapter 5, allows you to use Emacs as a windowing system so that you can run your code while editing it. There is a powerful facility for interfacing to many compilers and the UNIX **make** command: Emacs can interpret compilers' error messages and visit files where errors occur, at the appropriate line number.

In this chapter, we will cover the features of language modes in general. Then we will examine three particular language modes—C, LISP, and FORTRAN. After the discussion of C mode, we will look at the **etags** facility, which is a great help to C programmers who work on large, multi-file projects. Finally, we will discuss the compiler/**make** interface.

Language Modes

We have already seen various examples of Emacs modes, including text mode (Chapter 2, *Editing Files*, and Chapter 6, *Simple Text Formatting and Specialized Editing*) and shell mode (Chapter 5, *Emacs as a Work Environment*). Special functionality like **list-buffers** (Chapter 4, *Using Buffers and Windows*) and **dired** (Chapter 5) are actually modes as well. All modes have two basic components: an Emacs LISP *package* that implements the mode and a *function* that invokes it.

The version of Emacs on which this book is based (Version 18) comes with language modes for Ada, C, FORTRAN, ICON, LISP, MIM, Modula-2, PROLOG, Scheme, and Simula; future versions should add more. Many—but not all—of the language modes are "hooked" into Emacs so that if you visit a file with the proper filename suffix, you will automatically be put in the correct mode. To find out whether Emacs does this for the language you are using, look up your language in the table of Emacs LISP packages in Appendix D. If one or more suffixes are listed in the right-hand column, then Emacs will invoke the mode for files with those suffixes.

However, if no suffix is listed (or if your compiler supports a different suffix than the ones listed), here is how you can set up Emacs to invoke the mode automatically when you visit your source files. There are two things you need to do: first, look again at the right-hand column in the package table entry for your language, and you will find the name of the function that invokes the mode (e.g., **ada-mode**, **modula-2-mode**). Second, you need to put code in your *.emacs* file that tells Emacs to automatically load the proper package whenever you visit a file with the suffix for the language in question.

There are two lines of code you need to write for this. The first uses the **autoload** command, which tells Emacs where to look for commands it doesn't already know about. It sets up an association between a function and the package that implements the function, so that when the function is invoked for the first time, Emacs will load the package to get the code. In our case, we need to create an association between a function that invokes a language mode and the package that implements the mode. The format of **autoload** is:

```
(autoload 'function "filename")
```

Note the single quote preceding "function" and the double quotes around "filename"; for more details on this LISP syntax, see Chapter 11, *Emacs LISP Programming*. Let's say you are an Ada programmer; you would put the following line in your *.emacs*:

```
(autoload 'ada-mode "ada")
```

This tells Emacs to load the "ada" package when the function **ada-mode** is invoked for the first time.

The second line of code necessary completes the picture by creating an association between the suffix for source files in your language and the mode-invoking function, so that the function is automatically invoked when you visit a file with the proper suffix. This involves the Emacs global variable **auto-mode-alist**, which we saw in Chapter 9, *Customizing Emacs*; it is a list of such associations that Emacs uses to put visited files in modes according to their names. Here is how to create such an association for **ada-mode**, so that Emacs puts all files with the suffix *.a* in that mode; refer to Chapter 9 for a more complete explanation:

```
(setq auto-mode-alist (cons '("\.a$" . ada-mode) auto-mode-alist))
```

These two lines of LISP code set up the following chain of events when you visit a file whose suffix indicates source code in your programming language. Let's say you visit the file *pgm.a*. First, Emacs reads the file. Then it finds an entry corresponding to the *.a* suffix in the **auto-mode-alist** and tries to invoke the associated function **ada-mode**. It notices that the function **ada-mode** doesn't exist but that there is an **autoload** association between it and the "ada" package. So it loads that package and, finding the **ada-mode** command, runs it. After this, your buffer is in Ada mode. If you put the above code in your *.emacs* file, Emacs will "recognize" the language in question during all subsequent sessions.

Syntax

Language modes differ in exact functionality, of course, but they all support the same basic concepts. The most important of these involves knowledge about the *syntax* of the language in question, i.e., its characters, vocabulary, and certain aspects of its grammar. We have already seen that Emacs has knowledge about syntactic aspects of human language. When you edit regular text, Emacs knows about words, sentences, and paragraphs: you can move the cursor and delete text with respect to those units. It also knows about certain kinds of punctuation, such as parentheses: when you type a right parenthesis, it will "flash" the matching left parenthesis by moving the cursor there for a second and then returning.[1] This is a convenient way of ensuring that your parentheses match correctly.

Emacs has knowledge about programming language syntax that is analogous to its knowledge of human-language syntax. In general, it keeps track of the following basic syntactic elements:

- *Words*, which correspond to *identifiers* and *numbers* in most programming languages.

- *Punctuation*, which includes such things as *operators* (e.g., +, −, <, and >) and *statement separators* (e.g., semicolons).

- *Strings*, which are strings of characters to be taken literally and surrounded by *delimiters* (such as quotation marks).

- *Parentheses*, which can include such things as square brackets ([and]) and curly braces ({ and }) as well as regular parentheses.

- *Whitespace*, such as spaces and tabs, which are to be ignored.

- *Comments*, which are strings of characters to be taken literally and surrounded by delimiters that depend on the language (e.g., /* and */ for C, or semicolon (;) and LINEFEED for LISP).

Emacs keeps this information internally in the form of *syntax tables*; like keymaps (as described in Chapter 9), Emacs has a *global* syntax table used for all buffers, as well a *local* table for each buffer, which varies according to the mode the buffer is in. In addition, language modes know about more advanced language-dependent syntactic concepts like statements, statement blocks, functions, subroutines, LISP S-expressions (syntactic expressions), etc.

Formatting

In addition to syntactic knowledge, Emacs language modes contain various features to help you produce nicely-formatted code. These features implement standards of indentation, commenting, and other aspects of programming style, thus ensuring consistency and readability, getting comments to line up, and so on. Perhaps more importantly, they relieve you of the tiresome burden of supplying

---

[1] Actually, there is a limit to how far back (in characters) Emacs will search for a matching open parenthesis: this is the value of the variable **blink-matching-paren-distance**, which defaults to 4000.

correct indentation and even of remembering what the current indentation is. The nicest thing about these standards is that they are usually customizable.

We have already seen that, in text mode, you can type **LINEFEED** (or **C-j**, instead of **RETURN**) at the end of a line and Emacs will indent the next line properly for you. This indentation is controlled by the variable **left-margin**, whose value is the column to indent to. Much the same thing happens in programming language modes, but the process is more flexible and complex.

As in text mode, **LINEFEED** will indent the next line properly in language modes. You can also indent any line properly after it has been typed in by pressing TAB with the cursor anywhere on the line. Most language modes have sets of variables that control indentation style (and, of course, that you can customize). Table 10-1 lists a few other commands relating to indentation that work according to the rules set up for the language in question.

Table 10-1. Basic Indentation Commands

Keystrokes	Command Name	Action
ESC C-\	indent-region	Indent each line between cursor and mark.
ESC-m	back-to-indentation	Move to the first non-blank character on the line.
ESC-^	delete-indentation	Join this line to the previous one.

The following is an example of what **ESC C-** does. This example will be in C, and subsequent examples will refer to it. The concepts in all examples in this section are applicable to most other languages, and we will cover analogous LISP and FORTRAN features in the sections on modes for those languages.

Suppose you have typed in the following C code:

```
int times (x, y)
int x, y;
{
int i;
int result = 0;

for (i = 0; i < x; i++)
{
result += y;
}
}
```

If you set mark at the beginning of this code, put the cursor at the end, and type **ESC C-** Emacs will format it like this:

```
int times (x, y)
    int x, y;
{
  int i;
  int result = 0;

  for (i = 0; i < x; i++)
    {
      result += y;
    }
}
```

The **ESC C-** command is also handy for indenting an entire file according to your particular indentation style: you can just type **C-x h** (for **mark-whole-buffer**) followed by **ESC C-**.

The **ESC-m** command is handy for moving to the beginning of the actual code on a line. For example, assume your cursor is positioned like this:

```
int res█lt = 0;
```

If you type **ESC-m**, it will move to the beginning of the `int`:

```
█nt result = 0;
```

As an example of the **ESC-^** command, let's say you want the opening curly brace for the for statement to appear on the same line as the `for`. Put the cursor anywhere on the line with the opening curly brace, type **ESC-^**, and the code will look like this:

```
for (i = 0; i < x; i++) {
    result += y;
  }
```

Most language modes provide additional indentation commands that relate to specific features of the language.

Since all programming languages have comment syntax, Emacs provides a few features that deal with comments in general; these are made language-specific in each language mode. The universal comment command for all language modes is **ESC-;** for **indent-for-comment**.[2] When you type **ESC-;**, Emacs moves to a column equal to the value of the variable **comment-column**; if the text on the line goes past that column, it moves to one space past the last text character. Then it

---

[2] The key binding is mnemonic for LISP programmers, since comments in LISP start with semicolons.

inserts a comment delimiter (or a pair of opening and closing delimiters, as in /* and */ for C) and puts the cursor after the opening delimiter.

For example, if you want to add a comment to the statement in the for-loop body of the above multiply function, put the cursor anywhere on the line containing that statement and type **ESC-;**. The result will be:

```
result += y;                /* ▊*/
```

You can then type your comment in between the delimiters. If you were to do the same thing on a longer line of code, say:

```
q_i = term_arr[i].num_docs / total_docs;
```

the result would be:

```
q_i = term_arr[i].num_docs / total_docs; /* ▊*/
```

You can customize the variable **comment-column**, of course, by putting the appropriate code in your *.emacs* file. This is the most useful way if you want to do it permanently. But if you want to reset **comment-column** temporarily within the current buffer, you can just move the cursor to where you want the comment column to be and type **C-x ;** for **set-comment-column**. Note that this will only affect the value of **comment-column** in the current buffer; its value in other buffers—even other buffers in the same mode—will not be changed.

When you are typing a comment and you want to continue it on the next line, **ESC-j** (for **indent-new-comment-line**) will do it. This command will start a new comment on the next line (though some language modes allow you to customize it so that it continues the same comment instead). Say you have typed in the text of the comment for the statement in the for-loop body in the "times" function, and the cursor is at the end of the text:

```
result += y;            /* add the multiplicand▊*/
```

Now you want to extend the comment to another line. If you type **ESC-j**, you will get the following:

```
result += y;            /* add the multiplicand */
                        /* ▊*/
```

Then you can type in the second line of your comment. You can also use **ESC-j** to split existing comment text into two lines. Assume your cursor is positioned like this:

```
result += y;            /* add the ▊multiplicand */
```

If you type **ESC-j** now, the result will be:

```
result += y;            /* add the */
                        /* ▋ultiplicand */
```

You can easily get rid of *single-line* comments by using **ESC-x kill-comment RETURN** (not bound to keystrokes by default), which will delete any comment on the current line. The cursor does not have to be within the comment. Each language mode has special features relating to comments in the particular language, usually including variables that let you customize commenting style.

Having covered the concepts general to all language modes, we will now look at specific modes for C, LISP, and FORTRAN. The next three sections will deal in turn with these modes; at the end of the section on C mode, we will examine the **etags** facility, which helps C programmers who work on large, multi-file programs. There is no need for you to read all three sections if you are only interested in one or two of these langugages. If you program in another language for which Emacs has a mode, you may want to read one of the sections below to get the "flavor" of a language mode; since all language modes have the same basic concepts, this should get you off to a good start.

C Mode

Emacs automatically enters C mode when you visit a file whose suffix is *.c*, *.h*, or *.y* (for **yacc** grammars). You can also put any file in C mode manually by typing **ESC-x c-mode RETURN**. Emacs also invokes C mode for C++ files, whose suffix is *.cc*. There is no separate C++ mode at this writing, but C mode is a fairly acceptable substitute when editing C++ code.[3]

In C mode, Emacs understands the syntax elements described earlier in this chapter. In addition to the standard Emacs commands for words and sentences (which are mainly useful only inside multi-line comments), C mode contains advanced commands that know about functions.[4] A summary of these commands appears in Table 10-2.

---

[3] If you are a C++ programmer, you may be able to get a third-party C++ mode from a friend or colleague, or from a network bulletin board such as NETNEWS. Consult your system administrator for details.

[4] These commands have "defun" in their names because they are actually adaptations of analogous commands in LISP mode; a "defun" is a function definition in LISP.

Table 10-2. C Function Commands

Keystrokes	Command Name	Action
ESC C-a	beginning-of-defun	Move to beginning of function body.
ESC C-e	end-of-defun	Move to end of function.
ESC C-h	mark-c-function	Put cursor at beginning of function, mark at end.

C statement and statement block delimiter characters are bound to commands that, in addition to inserting the appropriate character, also provide proper indentation. These characters are {, }, ;, and : (for labels and **switch** cases). For example, if you are closing out a statement block or function body, you can press **LINEFEED** (or **RETURN**) and type }, and Emacs will line it up with its matching {. This eliminates the need for you to scroll back through the code to find out what column the { is in.

Since } is a parenthesis-type character, Emacs will attempt to "flash" a matching { when you type it. If the matching { is outside of the text displayed in your window, Emacs will instead print the line containing the { in the minibuffer. Furthermore, if there is only whitespace (blanks or tabs) following the { on its line, Emacs will also print a ^J (for **C-j** or **LINEFEED**) followed by the next line, thus giving a better idea of the context of the {.

Recall the "times" example from before. Let's say you are typing in a } to end the function, and the { that begins the function body is off-screen. Since there is no code on the line following the beginning {, you will see the following in the minibuffer after you type }:

```
Matches {^J    int i;
```

Emacs provides several variables that enable you to set the overall indentation style to your liking. (See Chapter 9, *Customizing Emacs*, for how to set variables.) Table 10-3 contains a list of these variables, which will be followed by examples that show how most of them can be used.

Table 10-3. C Mode Indentation Variables

Variable	Default	Description
c-indent-level	2	Indentation of statements within the surrounding context (statement block or function body).
c-continued-statement-offset	2	Extra indentation of multi-line statements after the first line; this includes such things as the (one-statement) "then" clause of an **if** statement or "do" clause of a **while**.
c-argdecl-indent	5	Indentation for type declarations of function arguments.
c-brace-offset	0	Extra indentation for any line that starts with **{**; negative values used to "counteract" **c-indent-level** (see examples below).
c-continued-brace-offset	0	Extra indentation of **{** used to start statement blocks used as substatements for **if, while**, etc. Cumulative with **c-continued-statement-offset**.
c-brace-imaginary-offset	0	If a **{** directly follows other text (e.g., **if (. . .)**), assume it would be indented this far if it were on a line by itself.
c-label-offset	-2	Extra indentation for lines containing a colon (**:**, as in **case, default,** or **goto** labels). Negative values are used to "counteract" **c-indent-level**; see below.
c-auto-newline	nil	If non-**nil**, insert a newline and indent before and after **{** and **}**, and after **;** and **:**.

The default values conform to the standards that were used by the authors of Emacs. Here are some examples of the effects of changing their values.

Recall, once again, the "times" function from earlier in the chapter. When it is indented with all indentation variables set to defaults, it looks like this:

```
int times (x, y)
      int x, y;
{
  int i;
  int result = 0;

  for (i = 0; i < x; i++) {
    result += y;
  }
}
```

The most "basic" indentation variable is **c-indent-level**. In Kernighan and Ritchie's *The C Programming Language* (hereafter referred to as "K&R"), lines in example code are indented in multiples of 5 spaces. If we set **c-indent-level** to 5 instead of the default 2, the result would resemble code that appears in K&R:

```
int times (x, y)
      int x, y;
{
     int i;
     int result = 0;

     for (i = 0; i < x; i++) {
          result += y;
     }
}
```

Since the for-loop body is only one statement, we could, of course, remove the curly braces. The resulting code is then considered to be a single statement, and thus the `result += y` line would be indented according to the value of the variable **c-continued-statement-offset** (instead of **c-indent-level**). Since its value is still 2, we get the following if we indent it properly (e.g., by going to its line and pressing **TAB**):

```
     for (i = 0; i < x; i++)
       result += y;
```

We would have to set **c-continued-statement-offset** to 5 to achieve the correct K&R indentation, which would be the same as if the statement had curly braces around it.

Next, notice that the type declarations of the function's arguments are indented. Many C programmers prefer the K&R style, in which type declarations are not indented. To get this behavior, we need to set **c-argdecl-indent** to 0. This has the result:

```
int times (x, y)
int x, y;
```

Another common stylistic difference among C programmers is whether to put left curly braces used to open statement blocks on separate lines. If you do this, you will find the **c-auto-newline** feature useful. If you set it to **t** (or any value other than **nil**), whenever you type an opening **{** Emacs will insert newlines both *before* and *after* it and do proper indentation. Say you are typing in the for statement, and your cursor is in this position:

```
for (i = 0; i < x; i++)█
```

When you type **{**, the *immediate* result will be:

```
for (i = 0; i < x; i++)
    {
      █
```

That is, you will be put on an empty line after the line with the **{**. Notice, however, that the **{** is offset by 5, due to **c-continued-statement-offset**. Most C programmers like to have the **{** line up with the **for**; this is the convention K&R uses. The variable **c-brace-offset** can take care of this: if you set it to -5, it will counteract **c-continued-statement-offset**, resulting in the expected:

```
for (i = 0; i < x; i++)
{
  █
```

when you type the **{**. In addition, the **c-auto-newline** feature automatically newlines-and-indents when you type **;** or **:**. The auto-indent function of the semicolon combines with **c-continued-statement-offset** to produce a useful "side effect:" if you type in a statement, press **;** and find that Emacs indents the statement too far, chances are that you forgot a semicolon in a previous statement. This is a good way of discovering missing semicolons—a common mistake in C programming.

Finally, some programmers differ in how they like their case (and goto) labels indented. The K&R convention is to have them line up with the switch statement, as in:

```
switch (ch) {
case 'a':
```

The variable **c-label-offset** can be used to achieve this in a way similar to **c-brace-offset**—by counteracting **c-indent-level**. Just set it to the negative of **c-indent-level**, which according to K&R standards would be -5.

Here is a summary of the code you need to put in your *.emacs* file if you want C mode's indentation style to conform to K&R:

```
(setq c-indent-level 5)
(setq c-continued-statement-offset 5)
(setq c-argdecl-indent 0)
(setq c-brace-offset -5)
(setq c-label-offset -5)
```

C mode also provides support for comments; earlier in the chapter, we saw examples of this support. There is, however, another feature. You can customize the **ESC-j** (**indent-new-comment-line**) feature so that Emacs continues the same comment on the next line instead of creating a new pair of delimiters. The variable **comment-multi-line** controls this: if it is set to **nil** (the default), Emacs will generate a new comment on the next line, as in the example from earlier in the chapter:

```
result += y;                    /* add the multiplicand */
                                /* █ /
```

This is the result of typing **ESC-j** after "multiplicand", and it shows that the cursor is positioned so that you can type in the text of the second comment line. However, if you set **comment-multi-line** to **t** (or any value other than **nil**), you will get this instead:

```
result += y;                    /* add the multiplicand
                                █/
```

Etags

Another feature of Emacs that applies to C programmers is the **etags** facility.[5] If you work on large, multi-file C programming projects, you will find **etags** to be an enormous help. **Etags** is basically a multi-file search facility that knows about C function definitions as well as searching in general. With it, you can find a function anywhere in an entire directory without having to remember in which file the function is defined, and you can do searches and query-replaces that span multiple files. **Etags** uses *tag tables*, which contain lists of function names for each file in a directory along with information on where the functions' definitions are located within the files. Many of the commands associated with **etags** involve regular expressions (see Chapter 3, *Search and Replace Operations*) in search

---

[5] Users of **ex** and **vi** will recognize **etags** to be similar to **ctags**. **etags** only knows about C functions (not C typedefs and not Pascal or FORTRAN), but it is a bit more flexible; for example, it allows for multiple functions with the same name.

strings. If you are not comfortable using regular expressions, remember that you can always use "normal" search strings as long as you stick to non-"special" characters such as letters, digits, and underscore (_).

To use **etags**, first you must invoke the separate **etags** program in your current directory to create the tag table. Its arguments are the files for which you want tag information. The usual way to invoke it is *etags *.[ch]*, i.e., build a tag table from all files ending in *.c* or *.h*. You can run **etags** from within Emacs from shell mode or with the command **ESC-! (shell-command)**. The output of **etags** is the file *TAGS*, which is the tag table. When you are writing code, you can update your tag table to reflect new files and function definitions by invoking **etags** again.

Once you have created the tag table, you need to make it known to Emacs. To do this, type **ESC-x visit-tags-table RETURN**. This prompts you for the name of the tag table file; the default is *TAGS* in the current directory, as you would expect. After you do this, you can use the various Emacs tags commands.

The most important tag command is **ESC-. (find-tag)**. This prompts you for a string to use in searching the tag table for a function whose name contains the string. Supply the search string, and Emacs will visit the file containing the matching function name in the current window and go to the first line of the function's definition. A variation of **ESC-.** is **C-x 4 . (find-tag-other-window)**, which uses another window instead of replacing the text in your current window.

A nice feature of **ESC-.** is that it will pick up the word the cursor is on and use it as the default search string. For example, if your cursor is anywhere on the string "my_function", **ESC-.** will use "my_function" as the default. This means that when you are looking at a C statement that calls a function, you can type **ESC-.** to see the code for that function.

If you have multiple functions with the same name, **ESC-.** will find the function in the file whose name comes first in alphabetical order. To find the others, you can use the command **ESC-, (tags-loop-continue)** to find the next one (or complain if there are no more). This is especially useful if your directory contains more than one program, i.e., if there is more than one function called "main." **ESC-,** also has other uses, as we will see.

You can use the tag table to search for more than just function definitions. The command **ESC-x tags-search RETURN** prompts for a regular expression; it searches through all files listed in the tag table (e.g., all *.c* and *.h* files) for *any* occurrence of the regular expression, whether a function name or not. This gives you a capability similar to the **grep** facility discussed at the end of this chapter. Once you have invoked **tags-search**, you can find additional matches by typing **ESC-,**.

There is also an analogous query-replace capability. The command **ESC-x tags-query-replace RETURN** does a *regular expression* query-replace on all files listed in the tag table. See Chapter 3, *Search and Replace Operations*, for a discussion of regular expression query-replace. As with the regular **query-replace-regexp** command, if you precede **tags-query-replace** with a prefix argument (i.e., **C-u ESC-x tags-query-replace RETURN**), it will only replace matches that are entire words. This is useful, for example, if you want to replace occurrences of `printf` without disturbing occurrences of `fprintf`. If you exit a **tags-query-replace** with **ESC** or **C-g**, you can resume it later by typing **ESC-,**.

The command **ESC-x tags-apropos** rounds out the search facilities of **etags**. If you give it a regular expression argument, it will produce a buffer ***Tags List***, in an associated window, that contains a list of all tags in the tag table (including names of files as well as functions) that match the regular expression. For example, if you want to find out the names of output routines in a multiple-file C program, you could invoke **tags-apropos** with the argument `print` or `write`.

Finally, you can use the command **ESC-x list-tags RETURN** to list all the tags in the table—i.e., all the functions—for a given C file. Supply the filename at the prompt, and you will get a buffer ***Tags List*** showing the names of functions defined in that file along with their return types (if any). Note that if you move your cursor to this list, you can use **ESC-.** to look at the actual code for the function: since **ESC-.** picks up the word the cursor is on as the default function name, you can just move the cursor to the name of the function you want to see and press **ESC-.** followed by **RETURN** to see it.

The LISP Modes

There are actually three LISP modes, listed here by their **ESC-x** command names:

emacs-lisp-mode
> Used for editing Emacs LISP code, as covered in Chapter 11 (filename *.emacs* or suffix *.el*).

lisp-mode
> Used for editing LISP code intended for another LISP system (suffix *.l* or *.lisp*).

lisp-interaction-mode
> Used for editing and running Emacs LISP code.

All three modes all have the same basic functionality; they differ only in the support they give to running LISP code.

All three LISP modes understand the basic syntax elements common to all language modes. In addition, they have various commands that apply to the more advanced syntactic concepts of S-expressions, lists, and defuns. An *S-expression* (or syntactic expression) is any syntactically correct LISP expression, be it an atom (number, symbol, variable, etc.) or parenthesized list. *Lists* are special cases of S-expressions, and *defuns* (function definitions) are special cases of lists. There are several commands that deal with these syntactic concepts; you will most likely become comfortable with a subset of them.

Table 10-4 shows the commands that handle S-expressions.

Table 10-4. S-expression Commands

Keystrokes	Command Name	Action
ESC C-b	backward-sexp	Move backward by one S-expression.
ESC C-f	forward-sexp	Move forward by one S-expression.
ESC C-t	transpose-sexps	Transpose the two S-expressions around the cursor.
ESC C-@	mark-sexp	Set mark to the end of the current S-expression, cursor to the beginning.
ESC C-k	kill-sexp	Delete the S-expression following the cursor.
(none)	backward-kill-sexp	Delete the S-expression preceding the cursor.

Since an S-expression can be a wide variety of things, the actions of commands that handle S-expressions are determined by where your cursor is when you invoke them. If your cursor is on a (or whitespace preceding one, the S-expression in question is taken to be the list that starts with that (. If it is on some other character such as a letter or number (or preceding whitespace), then the S-expression is taken to be an atom (symbol, variable, or constant).

For example, suppose your cursor is in this position:

```
(mary bob█(dave (pete)) ed)
```

If you type ESC C-f, the cursor will move like this:

```
(mary bob (dave (pete))█ed)
```

That is, you are moving forward past the S-expression (dave (pete)), which is a list. However, say your cursor is positioned like this:

(mary █ob (dave (pete)) ed)

When you type **ESC C-f**, it will move here:

(mary bob█(dave (pete)) ed)

In this case, the S-expression is the atom **bob**.

The commands handling lists are shown in Table 10-5.

Table 10-5. Commands for Moving in Lists

Keystrokes	Command Name	Action
ESC C-n	forward-list	Move forward by one list.
ESC C-p	backward-list	Move backward by one list.
ESC C-d	down-list	Move forward and down one parenthesis level.
(none)	up-list	Move forward out of one parenthesis level.
ESC C-u	backward-up-list	Move backward out of one parenthesis level.

As a mnemonic device, you can think of lists as analogous to lines and S-expressions as analogous to characters; thus, **C-n** and **C-p** appear in list motion commands, while **C-f** and **C-b** appear in S-expression motion commands. **ESC C-n** and **ESC C-p** work similarly to **ESC C-f** and **ESC C-b** respectively, except that the cursor must be positioned so that there is a list in front or back of it to move across—i.e., there must be an opening or closing parenthesis on, after, or before the cursor. If there is not, Emacs will signal an error. For example, if your cursor is positioned like this:

(fred bob (dave (pete))█ed)

and you type **ESC C-n**, Emacs will complain with the message: "Containing expression ends prematurely." However, if your cursor is here:

(fred█ bob (dave (pete)) ed)

then the "next list" is actually (dave (pete)), and the cursor will end up like this if you type **ESC C-n**:

(fred bob (dave (pete))█ed)

The commands for moving up or down lists enable you to get inside or outside them. For example, say your cursor is here:

▌fred bob (dave (pete)) ed)

typing **ESC C-d** will move the cursor here:

(▌red bob (dave (pete)) ed)

This is because `fred` is the next level down after its enclosing list. Typing **ESC C-d** again has this result:

(fred bob (▌ave (pete)) ed)

You are now inside the list (dave (pete)). At this point, typing **ESC C-u** will do the opposite of **ESC C-u**, i.e., move the cursor back and outside of the two lists. But if you type **ESC-x up-list RETURN**, you will move *forward* as well as out, resulting in this:

(fred bob (dave (pete))▌ed)

The commands for defuns listed in Table 10-6 are much more straightforward.

Table 10-6. Commands for Working with Functions

Keystrokes	Command Name	Action
ESC C-a	beginning-of-defun	Move to the beginning of the current function.
ESC C-e	end-of-defun	Move the the end of the current function.
ESC C-h	mark-defun	Put cursor at beginning of function, mark at end.

These commands only work properly when the (`defun` that starts the current function is at the beginning of a line.

The LISP modes provide "flashing" of matching left parentheses; if the matching parenthesis is outside of the current window, the line it is on will appear in the minibuffer. The LISP modes also provide indentation via the TAB key and LINEFEED (**C-j**) for newline-and-indent (except in LISP interaction mode; see below). The indentation style supported by the LISP modes "knows" a lot about LISP keywords and list syntax; unfortunately it is not easily customized.[6]

---

[6] The indentation style is bound up in the Emacs LISP code for LISP mode. If you are an experienced LISP hacker, you can examine the code for **lisp-mode.el** in the Emacs LISP directory and determine how to customize indentation the way you wish. A good place to start looking is the function **lisp-indent-line**.

Here is an example, a LISP equivalent of the "times" C function shown earlier in the chapter, that should show various features of the indentation style:

```
(defun times (x y)
  (let ((i 0)
        (result 0))
    (while (< i x)
      (setq result (+ result y)
            i (1+ i)))
    result))
```

The basic indentation value is 2; this is used whenever code on the next line goes down a level in nesting. For example, the body of the function, after the line containing **defun**, is indented by 2. The "**(while . . .**" and "**result))**" lines are indented by 2 with respect to the **let** because they are the body of the block **let** introduces.

Things like **defun**, **let**, and **while** are function calls, even though they act like "keywords." The indentation convention for function calls is that if there are arguments on lines after the line where the function name and first argument are, the additional arguments are made to line up with the first one. In other words, this has the form:

```
function-name arg1
              arg2
              arg3
              ...)
```

The multiple arguments to **setq** in the above function provide another example of this.

However, the indentation of the line **(result 0)** shows that something a bit different happens with lists that are not function calls. The list in question is actually **((i 0) (result 0))**, which is a list with two elements (both of which are also lists). The indentation style supported by the LISP modes lines up these two elements.

Even though keyword-like terms such as **let** and **while** are actually function calls, the LISP modes "understand" these functions to the extent that special indentation conventions are set up for them. For example, if we were to put the condition for the while-loop on a separate line and press **TAB** to indent it properly, the result would be this:

```
(while
    (< i x)
  (setq result (+ result y)
        i (1+ i)))
```

Similar things happen with **if** and **cond** control structures; Chapter 11, *Emacs LISP Programming*, contains properly indented examples.

Another remark about indentation conventions: the LISP modes are geared toward a style in which multiple right parentheses are put on the same line immediately following each other, instead of on separate lines. For example, the line `i (1+ i)))` contains right parentheses that close off the `1+` function, the `setq`, and the `while` respectively. If you prefer, you can put your closing parentheses on separate lines, but if you press **TAB** to indent them, they will *not* line up properly with their matching open parentheses; you will have to indent them manually.

In addition to the TAB and LINEFEED commands for indentation, the LISP modes support the command **ESC C-q** (**indent-sexp**), which indents every line in the S-expression just *following* the cursor. You can use this, for example, to indent an entire function definition: just put the cursor right before the `defun` and type **ESC C-q**.

Comments in the LISP modes are handled by the universal comment command **ESC-;**, which indents out to **comment-column** (or, if there is text there, one space past the last character), inserts a semicolon, and puts the cursor just past it. If you want a comment to occupy an entire line (or to start anywhere other than at **comment-column**), you must move to where you want the comment to start and type the semicolon yourself. Note that if you press **TAB** on any line that only contains a comment, the comment will move out to **comment-column**. To get around this, use *two or more* semicolons instead of a single one; this causes TAB to leave the comments where they are. The LISP modes also support the other comment commands discussed earlier in the chapter, including **ESC-j** to extend a comment to another line and **ESC-x kill-comment RETURN** to get rid of a single-line comment.

Those are the features common to all three LISP modes; next, we will discuss the features unique to each.

Emacs LISP mode was designed to be used with code meant to run within Emacs itself, so it facilitates running the code you type in. Since LISP is an interpreted (as opposed to purely compiled) language, it is possible to blur the line between the "write" and "run/debug" phases of LISP programming; Emacs LISP mode takes some advantage of this opportunity, while LISP interaction mode goes even further—as we'll see later. In Emacs LISP mode, the command **ESC C-x** (**eval-defun**) picks up the function definition around or after the cursor and evaluates it—meaning that it parses the function and stores it so that Emacs "knows" about the function when you invoke it.

Emacs LISP mode also includes the command **ESC-TAB** (**lisp-complete-symbol**), which does *completion* on the symbol (variable, function name, etc.) preceding the cursor, as described in Chapter 13, *Online Help*. That is, you can type in the shortest unambiguous prefix for the symbol and type **ESC-TAB**, and Emacs will try to complete the symbol's name for you as far as it can. If it completes the symbol name, you can go on with whatever you are doing. If it doesn't, you haven't provided an unambiguous prefix. You can type in more characters (to disambiguate further), or you can type **ESC-TAB** again, and a help window showing the choices will pop up. Then you can type in more characters and complete the symbol yourself, or you can try for completion again.

LISP mode (as opposed to Emacs LISP mode) is meant for use with LISP processors other than the Emacs LISP interpreter. Therefore it includes a couple of commands for interfacing to an external LISP interpreter. The LISP mode command **C-c C-l (run-lisp)** starts up your system's LISP interpreter as a subprocess and creates the buffer `*lisp*` (with an associated window) for input and output.[7] If a LISP subprocess already exists, **C-c C-l** uses it rather than creating a second one. You can send function definitions to the LISP subprocess by putting the cursor anywhere within a function's definition and using **ESC C-x**, which in this case stands for **lisp-send-defun**. This causes the functions you define to become known to the LISP interpreter so that you can invoke them later.

Emacs LISP mode is probably the best thing to use if you are editing entire files of Emacs LISP code, e.g., if you are programming your own mode (as described in Chapter 11, *Emacs LISP Programming*) or modifying an existing one. However, if you are editing "little" pieces of LISP code (e.g., making additions or modifications to your *.emacs* file), Emacs has more powerful features you can use that further blur the line between writing and running code.

The first of these is the command **ESC-ESC** (for **eval-expression**). This enables you to type in a one-line LISP expression of any kind in the minibuffer; the expression is evaluated, and the result is printed in the minibuffer. This is an excellent, quick way to check the values of Emacs variables and to experiment with "internal" Emacs functions that aren't bound to keys and/or that require arguments. You can use the symbol completion command **ESC-TAB** while you are using **eval-expression**.

Unfortunately (or fortunately, depending on your point of view), Emacs doesn't normally let you use **eval-expression**. If you try pressing **ESC-ESC**, you will see the message "loading novice ..." in the minibuffer. Then a window will pop up and you will see a message on the order of, "you didn't really mean to type that, did you?". You get three options: press **SPACE** to try the command once only, **y** to try it and enable it for future use with no questions asked, or **n** to do nothing.

---

[7] This LISP mode command (**run-lisp**) was designed to run with the **franz** LISP system on BSD UNIX systems, though it should work with other LISP interpreters.

If you want to use **eval-expression**, type **y**. This actually results in the following line being put in your *.emacs* file:

```
(put 'eval-expression 'disabled nil)
```

If you are a knowledgeable LISP programmer, you will understand that this sets the property **disabled** of the symbol **eval-expression** to **nil**. In other words, Emacs considers certain commands to be *verboten* to novice users and thus allows commands to be *disabled*. If you want to skip this entire procedure and just use **eval-expression**, simply put the above line in your *.emacs* yourself (make sure you include the single quotes).

The other, even more powerful feature for editing Emacs LISP code is LISP interaction mode. This is the mode the default buffer `*scratch*` is in. Filenames with no suffixes normally cause Emacs to go into LISP interaction mode, though you can change this using the technique involving the variable **auto-mode-alist** described earlier in this chapter and (in more detail) in Chapter 9, *Customizing Emacs*. You can also put any buffer in LISP interaction mode by typing **ESC-x lisp-interaction-mode RETURN**; to create an extra LISP interaction buffer, just type **C-x b** (for **switch-to-buffer**), supply a buffer name, and put it in LISP interaction mode.

LISP interaction mode is identical to Emacs LISP mode except for one important feature: **LINEFEED (C-j)** is bound to the command **eval-print-last-sexp**. This takes the S-expression just before point, evaluates it, and prints the result right there in the buffer. To get the usual **newline-and-indent** functionality attached to **LINEFEED** in other modes, you must press **RETURN** followed by **TAB**.

Remember that an S-expression is any syntactically valid expression in LISP. Therefore, you can use **LINEFEED** in LISP interaction mode to check the values of variables, enter function definitions, run functions, etc. For example, if you type **auto-save-interval** and press **LINEFEED**, the value of that variable (300 by default) will appear. If you type in a **defun** and press **LINEFEED** after the last right parenthesis, Emacs will store the function defined (for future invocation) and print its name; in this case, **LINEFEED** is similar to **ESC C-x (eval-defun)** except that the cursor must be *after* (as opposed to before or in the middle of) the function being defined. If you type in a call to a function, Emacs will evaluate (run) the expression and respond with whatever value the function returns.

LINEFEED in LISP interaction mode gives you an excellent way to play around with, incrementally develop, and debug Emacs LISP code, and since Emacs LISP is "true" LISP, it is even useful for developing some bits of code for other LISP systems.

FORTRAN Mode

Emacs goes into FORTRAN mode when you visit a file with suffix *.f*. FORTRAN mode has several features that relate to the language's column-oriented format. It understands the syntactic elements common to all language modes; in addition, it supports the commands listed in Table 10-7 that deal with statements and subprograms.

Table 10-7. FORTRAN Mode Motion Commands

Keystrokes	Command Name	Action
C-c C-n	fortran-next-statement	Move forward one statement.
C-c C-p	fortran-previous-statement	Move backward one statement.
ESC C-a	begin-ning-of-fortran-subprogram	Move to the beginning of the current subprogram.
ESC C-e	end-of-fortran-subprogram	Move to the end of the current subprogram.
ESC C-h	mark-fortran-subprogram	Put the cursor at beginning of subprogram, mark at end.

The **C-c C-n** and **C-c C-p** commands differ from the normal **C-n** and **C-p** commands in that they skip over continuation and comment lines.

FORTRAN mode supports the indentation and comment commands common to all language modes, with some modifications that will be described shortly. In addition to the universal comment command **ESC-;**, the command **ESC C-q** (for **fortran-indent-subprogram**) properly indents the subprogram surrounding the cursor, and **C-c ;** (**fortran-comment-region**) comments out the region between the cursor and mark.

Just about every aspect of FORTRAN mode indentation, continuation and comment style is customizable,[8] via several Emacs variables. Table 10-8 lists these variables, followed by some examples of how to use them.

Table 10-8. Fortran Mode Variables

Variable	Default	Description
fortran-minimum-statement-indent	6	Indentation so that statements begin at the start of the statement field (e.g., indent by 6 out to column 7).
fortran-do-indent	3	Additional indentation used within **do** blocks.
fortran-if-indent	3	Analogous for **if** blocks.
fortran-continuation-char	$	Character placed in column 6 of continuation lines.
fortran-continuation-indent	5	Indentation for continuations of statements (e.g., indent by 5 out to column 6).
fortran-comment-line-column	6	Indentation used for comments that take up an entire line; used with the **ESC-;** comment command.
fortran-comment-indent-style	'fixed	Values can be **nil**, **'fixed**, or **'relative** (note the single quotes preceding the latter two); see examples below.
comment-start	nil	String for starting comments that appear on the same lines as code; see example below. If **nil**, do not allow this kind of comment.
fortran-line-number-indent	1	Maximum indentation for line numbers so that they don't reach column 5 (continuation column). See the explanation of electric line numbering below.
fortran-comment-region	"c$$$"	String inserted in each line by **fortran-comment-region (C-c ;)** command.

---

[8] In fact, it is possible to customize FORTRAN mode so far out that the compiler won't accept the code!

A few examples should illustrate some of these features. Let's say you want to write a function "times" that is analogous to the C function from earlier in the chapter:

```
      integer function times (i, j)
      times = 0
      do 10 k = 1, i
         times = times + j
10    continue
      return
      end
```

As you type in each line of code, press **TAB** first to move out to column 7, the start of the statement field (i.e., indent by the number of columns given by **fortran-minimum-statement-indent**). Emacs will indent the bodies of do and if statements according to the value of the variables **fortran-do-indent** and **fortran-if-indent** respectively.[9] Note that when you type the `continue`, it will initially be indented as if it were part of the do-loop body. You must press **TAB** again *afterwards*, so that Emacs can adjust its indentation outwards to line up with the matching do. The same holds true for continue statements that end if blocks. (FORTRAN mode also understands `enddo` and `end do` to end do blocks, as well as `else`, `elseif`, `endif`, and `end if` for if blocks.) Also note that statement blocks cannot share common `continue`s; each if or do must have its own `continue` for the indentation to work properly.

FORTRAN mode provides assistance in dealing with line numbers with a feature called *electric line numbering*. If you type a digit before any actual FORTRAN code in a line, FORTRAN mode assumes you are typing a line number and it indents the digit and any subsequent ones properly: it moves the digit to column 2 (i.e., indents by the value of **fortran-line-number-indent**) and then moves the cursor to column 7 so you can type in the FORTRAN statement for that line. Additional digits "join" the line number, and the cursor moves back to column 7.

To illustrate this, say you are typing the line with the **10** on it. Your cursor starts out at the beginning of the line. Then, when you type **1**, the result is this:

    1   █

And when you type **0**, it joins the **1** like this:

    10   █

---

[9] FORTRAN mode requires at least one space after the **do** or **if** for this feature to work, even though most compilers don't require it.

Notice that your cursor will still return to column 7 for the statement that is to go on that line. You can type up to five digits for line numbers; on the fifth digit, the indentation will move back to column 1 to make room, as in:

```
12345 █
```

If you try to type a line number with more than 5 digits, FORTRAN mode will print a warning in the minibuffer.

FORTRAN mode supports two kinds of commenting styles: the standard style, in which full-line comments are denoted by a **c** in column 1, as well as comments on the same line as statements, in which a **!** after the statement signals the start of a comment. Note that some compilers do not allow the latter style. By default, FORTRAN mode does not allow it either, but you can turn it on by setting **comment-start** to the string **" ! "**.

If you have set **comment-start** to **" ! "**, and you type **ESC-;** to start a comment on a line that contains code, Emacs will indent out to **comment-column** (or, if text is there, one space past the last text character), insert a **!** and put the cursor after it. Furthermore, if you type **ESC-j** to extend the comment to the next line, Emacs will open a new line, indent out to **comment-column**, and insert another **!**. However, if **comment-start** is **nil** and you type **ESC-;** on a line of code, Emacs will instead open up a new line *above* the current one and put a **c** in column 1 for a full-line comment.

You can control the indentation style for full-line comments via the variable **fortran-comment-indent-style**. Normally, when you type **ESC-;** on an empty line, Emacs inserts a **c** and indents out to column 7 for the comment text. Furthermore, if you try to type comment text before column 7, Emacs will re-indent it to column 7 if you type **TAB** (or **ESC C-q** to indent an entire subprogram). This behavior is represented by the default value of **fortran-comment-indent-style**, which is **'fixed** (note the single quote).

However, your compiler may allow comment text to occupy columns before column 7. If you want to take advantage of this, set **fortran-comment-indent-style** to **nil**. Then you can type in comment text anywhere after the **c**, and Emacs won't touch your indentation if you type **TAB** or **ESC C-q**. Another option: if you want your comment text indented out *past* column 7, set **fortran-comment-indent-style** to **'relative**. Under this setting, typing **ESC-;** results in indentation out to column 7 *plus* the value of **fortran-minimum-statement-indent**, i.e., out 6 more columns to column 13.

Another feature of FORTRAN mode is its table of *abbrevs* (see Chapter 3, *Search and Replace Operations*), which are abbreviations for FORTRAN keywords that you can use as "shorthand." FORTRAN mode actually extends the usual functionality of abbrevs by attaching special significance to the **;** character. To avoid confusion with any abbrevs you might have set up, FORTRAN mode's abbrevs all begin with **;**, and if you type **;?** you will get a ***Help*** window containing a list of all FORTRAN abbrevs.

To use abbrevs in FORTRAN mode, first type **ESC-x abbrev-mode RETURN** to turn on abbrevs. Then you can type an abbreviation and press **SPACE** to expand it. There are abbreviations for every FORTRAN keyword; Table 10-9 shows just a few examples.

Table 10-9. Some FORTRAN Mode Abbreviations

Abbrev	Keyword
;c	continue
;dp	double precision
;dw	do while
;f	format
;fu	function
;g	goto
;in	integer
;p	print
;rt	return
;su	subroutine

For example, if you are starting a function (and you are in abbrev-mode), type **;fu** and press **SPACE**. If you pause while typing the **;fu**, Emacs will remind you that you are using an abbreviation by printing the characters you type in the mini-buffer. After you type **SPACE**, the **;fu** will disappear and be replaced by "function."

A few miscellaneous commands round out FORTRAN mode. **ESC C-j (fortran-split-line)** does the opposite of **ESC ^** (join this line to the previous one): it splits up the current line at the cursor, inserts a continutation character and provides additional indentation of 6 columns. **C-c C-r (fortran-column-ruler)** prints a two-line "ruler" above the current line that looks like this:

```
0    4 6  10        20       30       40       50       60       70
[    ]|{   |    |    |    |    |    |    |    |    |    |    |    |}
```

The ruler is only temporary; press any key to erase it. Finally, **C-c C-w (fortran-window-create)** shrinks the current window horizontally to 72 columns, to help ensure that your lines aren't too long. This can be a guidline for when to press **ESC C-j** to split the current line.

Compiling Programs

As mentioned at the beginning of this chapter, Emacs' support for programmers does not end when you are done writing the code. A typical strategy for using Emacs when working on a large programming project is to log in, go to the directory where your source files reside, and invoke Emacs on all source files (e.g., **emacs Makefile *.[ch]** for C programmers). While you are editing your code, you can compile it using the commands described below—as you will see, you need not even worry about saving your changes. You can also test your compiled code in a shell window using shell mode (described in Chapter 5, *Emacs as a Work Environment*) if you are using a terminal or other display device without a windowing system. The bottom line is that you should rarely—if ever—have to leave Emacs throughout your login session.

Emacs provides a more direct and powerful way to interface to compilers and the UNIX **make** utility. At the heart of this facility is the command **ESC-x compile RETURN**. This causes a series of things to happen. First, it prompts you for a compilation command. The default command is **make -k**,[10] but if you type in another command, that becomes the default for subsequent invocations during your Emacs session. You can change the default by setting the variable **compile-command** in your *.emacs* file.

Once you have typed the command, Emacs offers to save all unsaved file buffers, thus relieving you of the responsiblity of making sure your changes have been saved. Then it creates a buffer called `*compilation*` and an associated window. It runs the compilation command (as a subprocess, just like the shell in shell mode), with output going to the `*compilation*` buffer.

Now the fun begins. If the compilation resulted in an error, you can type **C-x `** (for **next-error**; note that the second character is a backquote, not a single quote); Emacs will read the first error message, figure out the file and line number of the error, and visit the file at that line number. Once you have corrected the error, you can type **C-x `** again to visit subsequent error locations. Each time you type **C-x `**, Emacs scrolls the `*compilation*` window so that the current error message appears at the top. To start at the first error message again, type **C-x** with a prefix argument (i.e, **C-u C-x `**). A nice thing about **C-x `** is that you can use it as soon as an error is encountered; you do not have to wait for the compila-

---

[10] The **-k** option overrides **make**'s default of stopping after a job returns an error. Instead, **make** will continue on branches of the dependency tree that do not depend on the branch where the error occurred.

tion job to finish. When you have fixed all of the errors, you can type **ESC-x compile RETURN** to repeat the process.

How does Emacs interpret the error message? It uses the variable **compilation-error-regexp**, which is a regular expression designed to match the error messages of a wide variety of compilers;[11] its value is:

```
"\\([^ :\n]+\\(:  *\\|, line \\|(\\)[0-9]+\\)\\|\\([0-9]+ *of *[^ \n]+\\)"
```

This is rather incomprehensible, but it basically stands for the following: a filename, followed by a colon or ", line", then a line number; alternatively, a line number followed by "of" and a filename. Whitespace (blanks and newlines) is allowed between these things. Most compilers print error messages that contain one of these possibilities.

This regular expression was designed with various C compilers in mind. It should also work with compilers for languages for which Emacs has language modes, such as FORTRAN, Ada, and Modula-2. There is a *chance* that it won't work with certain compilers. You can find out by trying **ESC-x compile** on some code that you know contains an error; if you type **C-x `** and Emacs claims that there are "no more errors," then the **next-error** feature does not work with your compiler.

If this is the case, we do *not* recommend substituting your own regular expression for **compilation-error-regexp** unless you are a very experienced Emacs LISP hacker. This is because the regular expression is designed to interface with some LISP code in the **compile** package that builds up a complex LISP data structure when parsing the error messages. Instead, we recommend that you report the situation as a "bug" to the Free Software Foundation (see Appendix E, *Bugs and Bug Fixes*, for how to report bugs); be sure to include the language, name of the compiler, your machine and operating system, as well as a sample error message.

The **compile** package also includes similar support for the UNIX **grep** (search files) command. This effectively gives Emacs a multi-file search capability. If you type **ESC-x grep**, you will be prompted for arguments to send to **grep**, i.e., a search pattern and filename(s). Emacs will run **grep** with the **-n** option, which tells it to print filenames and line numbers of matching lines.[12] The same things will happen as with **ESC-x compile**; you can type **C-x `** to have Emacs visit the next matched line in its file.

---

[11] Unfortunately, Emacs will not understand error messages generated by **make** itself, such as from syntax errors in your *makefile*.

[12] If **grep -n** is run on only one file, it just prints line numbers; Emacs forces it to print the filename as well in this case by appending the dummy file */dev/null* to the **grep** command.

11

Emacs LISP Programming

Introduction to LISP
LISP Primitive Functions
Useful Built-in Emacs Functions
Programming a Major Mode
Customizing Existing Modes
Building Your Own LISP Library

If you have been using Emacs for a while and have been taking advantage of some of its more advanced features, chances are that you have found something that Emacs doesn't do. Although Emacs has hundreds and hundreds of built-in commands, dozens of packages and modes, and so on, everyone eventually runs into some functionality that Emacs doesn't have—by default. Whatever functionality you find missing, you can program it using Emacs LISP.

Before you plunge in, however, note that this chapter is not for everyone. It is intended for people who have already become comfortable using Emacs and who have some programming experience, though not necessarily with LISP *per se*. If you have no such experience, you may want to skip this chapter; if there is something specific you would like Emacs to do, you might try to find a friendly Emacs LISP hacker to help you write the necessary code.

In addition, we will not cover LISP in its entirety in this chapter. That would require a full book. Instead, we will cover the basics of the language and other features that are very often useful in writing Emacs code. If you wish to go beyond this chapter, turn to the *Gnu Emacs LISP Reference Manual*, available from the Free Software Foundation (their address is given in Appendix A), or any of the various LISP textbooks available (Winston and Horn's *LISP*, Addison-Wesley, 1984, is a good choice).

Emacs LISP is a full-blown LISP implementation;[1] thus it is more than the usual "macro" or "script" language found in many text editors. (One of the authors has written a small expert system entirely in Emacs LISP.) In fact, you could even think of Emacs itself as a LISP system with lots of built-in functions, many of which happen to pertain to text manipulation, window management, file I/O, and other things useful to text editing. The source code for Emacs, written in C, implements the LISP interpreter, LISP primitives, and only the most basic commands for text editing; a large layer of built-in LISP code on top of that implements the rest of Emacs' functionality. A current version of Emacs comes with over 60,000 lines of LISP.

This chapter starts with an introduction to the aspects of LISP that resemble common programming languages like C and Pascal. These features will be enough to enable you to write many Emacs commands. Then we will deal with how to interface LISP code with Emacs so that the functions you write can become Emacs commands. We will see various built-in LISP functions that are very useful for writing your own Emacs commands, including those that use regular expressions; we give an explanation of regular expressions that extends the introduction in Chapter 3, *Search and Replace Operations*, and is oriented toward LISP programming. We will return to the basics of LISP for a little while, covering the unique features of the language that have to do with lists, and then show you how to program a simple major mode that should tie many of the chapter's concepts together. After that, you will see how easy it is to customize Emacs' built-in major modes without having to change (or even look at) the code that implements them. We finish the chapter by describing how to build your own library of LISP packages.

Introduction to LISP

You may have heard of LISP as a language for artificial intelligence (AI). If you aren't into AI, don't worry. LISP may have an unusual syntax, but many of its basic features are just like those of more "conventional" languages you may have seen, such as C or Pascal. We will emphasize such features in this chapter. After introducing the basic LISP concepts, we will proceed by building up various example functions that you can actually use in Emacs. In order to try out the

---

[1] Experienced LISP programmers should note that Emacs LISP most closely resembles MacLISP, with a few Common LISP features added. More complete Common LISP emulation can be had by loading the package **cl** (see Chapter 9, *Customizing Emacs*, and Appendix D, *Emacs LISP Packages*).

examples, you should be familiar with Emacs LISP mode and LISP interaction mode, which were discussed in Chapter 10, *Emacs for Programmers.*

Basic LISP Entities

The most basic things in LISP that you need to know for now are *functions, variables*, and *atoms*. Functions are the only "program units" in LISP, covering the notions of procedures, subroutines, programs, and even operators in other languages.

Functions are defined as lists of the above entities, usually as lists of calls to other, existing functions. All functions have *return values* (as with C or Pascal functions); a function's return value is simply the value of the last item in the list, usually the value returned by the last function called. A function call within another function is equivalent to a *statement* in other languages, and we will use "statement" interchangeably with "function call" in this chapter. The syntax for function calls is:

```
(function-name argument1 argument2 ...)
```

This is equivalent to:

```
function_name (argument1, argument2, ...);
```

in C or Pascal. This syntax is used for all functions, including those equivalent to arithmetic or comparison operators in other languages. For example, to add 2 and 4 in C or Pascal, you would use the expression 2 + 4, whereas in LISP you would use:

```
(+ 2 4)
```

Similarly, where you would use 4 >= 2 (greater than or equal), the LISP equivalent is:

```
(>= 4 2)
```

Variables in LISP are similar to those in any other language, except that they do not have *types*. A LISP variable can assume any type of value.

Atoms are values of any type, including integers, characters, strings, Boolean truth values, symbols, and special Emacs types such as buffers, windows, and processes. The syntax for various kinds of atoms is:

- **Integers** are what you would expect: signed whole numbers in the range -2^{24} to $2^{24}-1$.

- **Characters** are preceded by a question mark, e.g., ?a. ESC, LINEFEED, and TAB are abbreviated \e, \n, and \t respectively; other control characters are denoted with the prefix \C-, so that (for example) **C-a** is denoted as ?\C-a.[2]

- **Strings** are surrounded by double quotes; quote marks within strings need to be preceded by a backslash. For example, "Jane said, \"See Dick run.\"" is a legal string.

- **Booleans** are **t** for true and **nil** for false, though most of the time, if a Boolean value is expected, any non-**nil** value will be assumed to mean true. **nil** is also used as a null or non-value in various situations, as we will see.

- **Symbols** are names of things in LISP, e.g., names of variables or functions. Sometimes it is important to refer to the *name* of something instead of its value, and this is done by preceding the name with a single quote ('). For example, the **define-key** function, described in Chapter 9, *Customizing Emacs*, uses the *name* of the command (as a symbol) rather than the command itself.

A simple example that ties many of these basic LISP concepts together is the function **setq**. As you may have figured out from previous chapters, **setq** is a way of assigning values to variables, as in:

```
(setq auto-save-interval 800)
```

Notice that **setq** is a function, unlike in other languages in which special syntax such as = or := is used for assignment. **setq** takes two arguments: a variable name and a value. In this example, the variable **auto-save-interval** (the number of keystrokes between auto-saves) is set to the value 800.

Setq can actually be used to assign values to multiple variables, as in:

```
(setq thisvar thisvalue
      thatvar thatvalue
      theothervar theothervalue)
```

The return value of **setq** is simply the last value assigned, in this case *theothervalue*.

There are other ways of setting the values of variables, as we'll see, but **setq** is the most widely applicable.

---

[2] Integers are also allowed where characters are expected. The ASCII code (on most machines) is used.

Defining Functions

Now it's time for an example of a simple function definition. If you are at a terminal, you may want to invoke Emacs without any arguments; this puts you into the buffer `*scratch*`, an empty buffer in LISP interaction mode (see Chapter 10, *Emacs for Programmers*), so that you can actually try this and subsequent examples.

Before we get to the example, however, some more comments on LISP syntax are necessary. First, you will notice that the dash (-) is used as a "break" character in names of variables, functions, etc. This is simply a widely-used LISP programming convention; thus the dash takes the place of the underscore (_) in languages like C and Ada. A more important issue has to do with all of the parentheses in LISP code. LISP is an *old* language that was designed before anyone gave much thought to language syntax, so its syntax is not exactly programmer-friendly. Yet LISP's heavy use of lists—and thus its heavy use of parentheses—has its advantages, as we'll see towards the end of this chapter.

The main problem a programmer faces is how to keep all those parentheses balanced properly. Compounding this is the usual programming convention of putting multiple right parentheses at the end of a line, rather than the more readable technique of placing each right parenthesis directly below its matching left parenthesis. Your best defense against this is the support the Emacs LISP modes give you, particularly the TAB key for proper indentation and the flash-matching-parenthesis feature.

Now for our example function. Suppose you are a student or journalist who needs to keep track of the number of words in a paper or story you are writing. Emacs has no built-in way of counting the number of words in a buffer, so we'll write a LISP function that does the job:

```
1. (defun count-words-buffer ()
2.   (let ((count 0))
3.     (goto-char (point-min))
4.     (while (< (point) (point-max))
5.       (forward-word 1)
6.       (setq count (1+ count)))
7.     (message "buffer contains %d words." count)))
```

Let's go through this function line by line and see what it does. (Of course, if you are trying this at a terminal, don't type the line numbers in.)

The **defun** on line 1 defines the function by its name and arguments. Notice that **defun** is itself a function—one that, when called, defines a new function. (**defun** returns the name of the function defined, as a symbol.) The function's arguments appear as a list of names inside parentheses; in this case, the function has no arguments. Arguments can be made *optional* by preceding them with the keyword

&optional. If an argument is optional and not supplied when the function is called, its value is assumed to be **nil**.

Line 2 contains a **let** construct, whose general form is:

```
(let ((var1 value1) (var2 value2) ... )
  statement-block)
```

The first thing **let** does is define the variables *var1*, *var2*, etc., and set them to the initial values *value1*, *value2*, etc. Then **let** executes the *statement block*, which is a sequence of function calls or values, just like the body of a function.

It is useful to think of **let** as doing three things:

1. *Define* (or *declare*) a list of variables.

2. *Set* the variables to initial values, as if with **setq**.

3. Create a *block* in which the variables are known. The **let** block is known as the *scope* of the variables.

If a **let** is used to define a variable, its value can be reset later within the **let** block with **setq**. Furthermore, a variable defined with **let** can have the same name as a global variable; all **setq**s on that variable within the **let** block act on the local variable, leaving the global variable undisturbed. However, a **setq** on a variable that is *not* defined with a **let** is assumed to be global. It is advisable to avoid using global variables as much as possible, since their names might conflict with those of existing global variables.

So, in our example function, we use **let** to define the local variable **count** and initialize it to 0. As we will see, this variable is used as a loop counter.

Lines 3 through 7 are the statements within the **let** block. The first of these calls the built-in Emacs function **goto-char**, which we first saw in Chapter 2, *Editing Files*. The argument to **goto-char** is a (nested) function call to the built-in function **point-min**. *Point* is Emacs' internal name for the position of the cursor, and we'll refer to the cursor as point throughout the remainder of this chapter. **point-min** returns the value of the first character position in the current buffer, which is almost always 1; then, **goto-char** is called with the value 1, which has the effect of moving point to the beginning of the buffer.

The next line sets up a **while** loop, which is similar to the same construct in languages like C and Pascal. The **while** construct has the general form:

```
(while condition
  statement-block)
```

Like **let, while** sets up another statement block. **Condition** is a value (an atom, a variable, or a function returning a value). This value is tested; if it is **nil**, the condition is considered to be false, and the **while** loop terminates. If the value is other than **nil**, the condition is considered to be true, the statement block gets executed, the condition is tested again, and the process repeats.

Of course, it is possible to write an infinite loop. If you write a LISP function with a while loop and try running it, and your terminal hangs, chances are that you have made this all-too-common mistake; just type **C-g** to abort it.

In our sample function, the condition is the function **<**, which is a less-than function with two arguments, analogous to the < operator in Pascal or C. The first argument is another function that returns the current character position of point; the second argument returns the maximum character position in the buffer, i.e., the length of the buffer. The function **<** (and other conditional functions) returns a Boolean value, **t** or **nil**.

The loop's statement block consists of two statements. Line 5 moves point forward 1 word (i.e., as if you had typed **ESC-f**). Line 6 increments the loop counter by 1; the function **1+** is shorthand for (**+ 1 variable-name**). Notice that the third right parenthesis on line 6 balances the left parenthesis preceding **while**. So, the while-loop causes Emacs to go through the current buffer a word at a time while counting the words.

The final statement in the function uses the built-in function **message** to print a message in the minibuffer saying how many words the buffer contains. The form of the **message** function will be familiar to C programmers. The first argument to **message** is a format string, which contains text and special formatting instructions of the form %x, where x is one of a few possible letters. For each of these instructions, in the order they appear in the format string, **message** reads the next argument and tries to interpret it according to the letter after the percent sign. The letters mean the following:

%s   String or symbol

%c   Character

%d   Integer

For example,

```
(message "\"%s\" is a string, %d is a number, and %c is a character"
         "hi there" 142 ?q)
```

will cause the message:

```
"hi there" is a string, 142 is a number, and q is a character
```

to appear in the minibuffer.[3]

Turning LISP Functions into Emacs Commands

The **count-words-buffer** function that we've just finished will work, but it has a few problems. If you have typed it in, try it yourself by typing (**count-words-buffer**) in your LISP interaction window. Move your cursor to just after the last closing parenthesis in the function and type **C-j** (or **LINEFEED**)—the "evaluate" key in LISP interaction mode—to run it.

If there was some text after your cursor (i.e., where you typed **C-j**) in your window, you will have noticed that the function causes Emacs to move point to the end of the buffer—it will not return point to where it was. As you might guess, this is a common problem in Emacs LISP commands, so there is a simple way to get around it: the **save-excursion** function, which has the form:

```
(save-excursion
  statement-block)
```

This causes the statements in the block to be run, but with the cursor motion generated by the statements kept internal to Emacs and not shown on the screen, and with point and mark preserved. In addition to preventing inconvenience, **save-excursion** can also function as a "stack" for saving and retrieving point and mark positions in arbitrary levels of nesting within LISP functions. **Save-excursion**'s return value is the return value of the last statement in the block.

So, if a function contains cursor motion commands that you don't want the user to see, you need to surround them with a **save-excursion** block, as in:

```
(defun count-words-buffer ()
  (save-excursion
    (let ((count 0))
      (goto-char (point-min))
      (while (< (point) (point-max))
        (forward-word 1)
        (setq count (1+ count)))
      (message "buffer contains %d words." count))))
```

---

[3] This is analogous to the C code:

```
printf ("\"%s\" is a string, %d is a number, and %c is a character\n",
        "hi there", 142, 'q');
```

Now that you can execute the function correctly from a LISP interaction window, i.e., try executing the function with **ESC-x**, like any other Emacs command. Try typing **ESC-x count-words-buffer RETURN** and see what happens: you will get the error message "[No match]." This is because you need to "register" a function with Emacs to make it available for interactive use. The function to do this is **interactive**, which has the form:

```
(interactive "prompt-string")
```

This should be the first statement in a function, i.e., right after the line containing the **defun** and the documentation string (see next page). Using **interactive** causes Emacs to register the function as a command, to add the function's documentation to its online help facility, and to prompt the user for the arguments declared in the **defun** statement. The prompt string is optional.

The prompt string has a special format: for each argument you want to prompt the user for, you provide a substring of prompt-string. The substrings are separated by LINEFEEDs (\n). The first letter of each substring is a code for the type of argument you want. There are many choices; the most commonly used are listed in Table 11-1.

Table 11-1. Argument Codes for Interactive Function

Code	Function
b	Name of an existing buffer.
f	Name of an existing file.
n	Number (integer).
s	String.

Each of these have uppercase variations:

B	Name of a buffer that may not exist.
F	Name of a file that may not exist.
N	Number, unless command is invoked with a prefix argument, in which case use the prefix argument.
S	Symbol.

With the **b** and **f** options, Emacs signals an error if the buffer or file given does not already exist. Another useful option to **interactive** is r, which we will see later. There are many others; consult the documentation for function **interactive** for the details. The rest of each substring is the actual prompt that appears in the minibuffer.

The way **interactive** is used to fill in function arguments is somewhat complicated and best explained through an example. A simple example is in the function **goto-percent**, which we will see shortly. It contains the statement:

```
(interactive "nPercent: ")
```

The **n** in the prompt string tells Emacs to prompt for an integer; the string "Percent: " will appear in the minibuffer.

As a slightly more complicated example, let's say we want to write a simplified version of the **replace-string** command. Here's how we would do the prompting:

```
(defun replace-string (from to)
  (interactive "sReplace string: \nsReplace with: ")
  ...)
```

The prompt string consists of two substrings, "sReplace string: " and "sReplace with: ", separated by a LINEFEED. The initial **s** in each means that a string is expected. When this command is invoked, first the prompt "Replace string:" will appear in the minibuffer. When the user types a string and presses **RETURN**, then the prompt "Replace with:" appears, and the user types in another string and presses **RETURN** again. The two strings the user types in are used as values of the function arguments **from** and **to** (in that order), and the command runs to completion. Thus, **interactive** supplies values to the function's arguments in the order of the substrings of the prompt string.

The use of **interactive** does not preclude calling the function from other LISP code; in this case, the calling function needs to supply values for all arguments. For example, if we wanted to call our version of **replace-string** from another LISP function that needs to replace all occurrences of "Bill" with "Deb" in a file, we would use:

```
(replace-string "Bill" "Deb")
```

Since the function is not being called interactively in this case, the **interactive** statement has no effect; the argument **from** is set to "Bill," and **to** is set to "Deb."

Getting back to our **count-words-buffer** command: it has no arguments, so its **interactive** command does not need a prompt string. The final modification we will want to make to our command is to add a *documentation string* (or *doc string* for short), which will be shown by online help facilities such as **describe-function (C-h f)**. Doc strings are just LISP strings; they are optional and can be arbitrarily many lines long. Remember that any double quotes inside a string need to be preceded by backslashes.

With all of the fixes taken into account, the complete function looks like this:

```
(defun count-words-buffer ()
  "Count the number of words in the current buffer;
print a message in the minibuffer with the result."
  (interactive)
  (save-excursion
    (let ((count 0))
      (goto-char (point-min))
      (while (< (point) (point-max))
        (forward-word 1)
        (setq count (1+ count)))
      (message "buffer contains %d words." count))))
```

LISP Primitive Functions

Now that you've seen how to write a working function, we'll discuss LISP's primitive functions. These are the building blocks from which you'll build your own functions. As mentioned above, LISP uses functions where other languages would use operators, i.e., for arithmetic, comparison, and logic. Table 11-2 shows some LISP primitive functions that are equivalent to these operators.

Table 11-2. LISP Primitive Functions

Arithmetic	+, -, *, / % (remainder) 1+ (increment) 1- (decrement) max, min
Comparison	>, <, >=, <= /= (not equal) = (for integers and characters) equal (for strings and other complex objects)
Logic	and, or, not

All of the arithmetic functions except **1+**, **1-**, and **%** can take arbitrarily many arguments, as can **and** and **or**.

It may seem inefficient or syntactically ugly to use functions for everything. However, one of the main merits of LISP is that the core of the language is very small and very easy to interpret efficiently. And the syntax is not as much of a problem if you have support tools such as Emacs' LISP modes to help you.

Statement Blocks

We have seen that a statement block can be defined using the **let** function. We also saw that **while** includes a statement block in its format. There are other important constructs that define statement blocks: **progn** and other forms of **let**.

progn, the most basic, has the form:

```
(progn
  statement-block)
```

progn is a simple way of making a block of statements "look like" a single one, somewhat like the **begin** and **end** of Pascal or the curly braces of C. The value returned by **progn** is the value returned by the last statement in the block. **progn** is especially useful with control structures like **if** (see below) that, unlike **while**, do not include statement blocks.

There are other forms of the **let** function. The simplest is:

```
(let (var1 var2 ...)
  statement-block)
```

In this case, instead of a list of (**var value**) pairs, there is simply a list of variable names. As with the other form of **let**, these become local variables accessible in the statement block. However, instead of initializing them to given values, they are all just initialized to **nil**.

In the form of **let** we saw first, the initial values for the local variables can be function calls (remember that all functions return values). All such functions are evaluated *before* any values are assigned to variables. However, there may be cases in which you want the values of some local variables to be available for computing the values of others. This is where **let***, the final version of **let**, comes in.

For example, let's say we want to write a function **goto-percent** that allows you to go to a place in the current buffer expressed as a percentage of the text in the buffer. Here is one way to write this function:

```
(defun goto-percent (pct)
  (interactive "nGoto percent: ")
  (let* ((size (point-max))
         (charpos (/ (* size pct) 100)))
    (goto-char charpos)))
```

As we saw earlier, the **interactive** function is used to prompt users for values of arguments. In this case, it prompts for the integer value of the argument **pct**. Then the **let*** function initializes **size** to the size of the buffer in characters, then uses that value to compute the character position **charpos** that is **pct** percent of the buffer's size. Finally, the call of **goto-char** causes point to be moved to that character position in the current window.

The important thing to notice is that if we had used **let** instead of **let***, the value of **size** would not be available when computing the value of **charpos**. **Let*** can also be used in the (**var1 var2 ...**) format, just like **let**.

We should also note that a more efficient way to write **goto-percent** is this:

```
(defun goto-percent (pct)
  (interactive "nPercent: ")
  (goto-char (/ (* pct (point-max)) 100)))
```

Control Structures

We already saw that the **while** function acts as a control structure like similar statements in other languages. There are two other important control structures in LISP: **if** and **cond**.

The **if** function has the form:

```
(if condition
    true-case
  false-block)
```

Here, the condition is evaluated; if it is non-**nil**, **true-case** is evaluated; if **nil**, **false-block** is evaluated. Note that **true-case** is a *single statement*, while **false-block** is a statement block. **False-block** is optional.

As an example, let's recall the customization of a terminal's special keys from Chapter 9, *Customizing Emacs*. If you use more than one terminal, you will want to have code in your *.emacs* that figures out what terminal type you are currently on and then sets up the appropriate key bindings.

This code should illustrate a few other important Emacs LISP features. For brevity, we will deal with arrow keys on ANSI-type terminals such as DEC VT100/200s and the **xterm** terminal emulator for the X Window System. Table 11-3 shows the character codes output by these keys.

Table 11-3. Character Codes for ANSI Arrow Keys

Arrow	Character Code
up	ESC O A
down	ESC O B
right	ESC O C
left	ESC O D

Here is the code that sets up the keymap and bindings. The semicolons are comment markers; everything from the semicolon to the end of the line is a comment:

```
(setq termtype (getenv "TERM"))

(if (or (equal termtype "vt200")        ;all of these have ANSI keypads
        (equal termtype "vt100")
        (equal termtype "xterm"))
    (progn
      (setq term-file-prefix nil)          ;override default key mappings
      (send-string-to-terminal "\e=")    ;force application keypad
      (setq SS3-map (make-keymap))       ;set up the keymap for the keypad
      (define-key global-map "\eO" SS3-map)

      (define-key SS3-map "A" 'previous-line)   ; up arrow
      (define-key SS3-map "B" 'next-line)       ; down arrow
      (define-key SS3-map "C" 'forward-char)    ; right arrow
      (define-key SS3-map "D" 'backward-char))  ; left arrow

  (if (equal termtype other-term-type...)
      (progn
        code for binding keys on other terminal)))
```

The first statement uses the built-in function **getenv**, which is an interface to the UNIX operating system that returns the value of the given *environment variable* (see Chapter 9, *Customizing Emacs*) as a string. In this case, the UNIX environment variable **TERM** describes the type of terminal you are on (if set properly ...).

The condition in the **if** clause tests to see if **termtype** is equal to any of the three given. If so, the code in the **progn** block gets executed. Remember that the "true" part of the **if** function is only one statement, so **progn** is necessary to make a statement block. We saw the first four lines of the block in Chapter 9. The remaining lines in the block bind the arrow keys to the expected cursor motion functions.

The second **if** is actually the "false" clause of the first **if**. It is like an "else if" in Pascal or C. In this **if** clause, we can test for another terminal type and do the key bindings for that type in the **progn** block.

A more general conditional control structure is the **cond** function, which has the form:

```
(cond
 (condition1
  statement-block1)
 (condition2
  statement-block2)
 ...)
```

C and Pascal programmers can think of this as a sequence of *if then else if then else if...*, or as a kind of generalized "case" or "switch" statement. The conditions are evaluated in order, and when one of them evaluates to non-**nil**, the corresponding statement block is executed; the **cond** function terminates and returns the last value in that statement block.[4]

We can rewrite the above **if** example using **cond**. Here we assume that we are concerned with three different terminal types, the last of which is the default:

```
(setq termtype (getenv "TERM"))

(cond ((or (equal termtype "vt200")          ;all of these have ANSI keypads
           (equal termtype "vt100")
           (equal termtype "xterm"))
       (setq term-file-prefix nil)           ;override default key mappings
       (send-string-to-terminal "\e=")       ;force application keypad
       (setq SS3-map (make-keymap))          ;set up the keymap for the keypad
       (define-key global-map "\eO" SS3-map)

       (define-key SS3-map "A" 'previous-line)  ;up arrow
       (define-key SS3-map "B" 'next-line)      ;down arrow
       (define-key SS3-map "C" 'forward-char)   ;right arrow
       (define-key SS3-map "D" 'backward-char)) ;left arrow

      ((equal termtype other-term-type...)
       (code for binding keys on other terminal))

      (t
       (code for binding keys of third terminal type)))
```

The third conditional expression is simply the atom **t** (true), which causes the code for the third terminal type to execute if the terminal is not of the first two types.

---

[4] Statement blocks are actually optional; some programmers like to omit the final statement block, leaving the final "condition" as an "otherwise" clause to be executed if all of the preceding conditions evaluate to **nil**. If the statement block is omitted, the value returned by **cond** is simply the value of the condition.

Useful Built-in Emacs Functions

Many of the Emacs functions that exist and that you may write involve searching and manipulating the text in a buffer. Such functions are particularly useful in specialized modes, like rmail and the programming language modes described in the previous chapter. There are many built-in Emacs functions that relate to text in strings and buffers; the most interesting ones take advantage of Emacs' regular expression facility, which we introduced in Chapter 3, *Search and Replace Operations*.

We will first describe the basic functions relating to buffers and strings that don't use regular expressions. Afterwards, we will discuss regular expressions in more depth than Chapter 3, concentrating on the features that are most useful to LISP programmers, and we will describe the functions that Emacs makes available for dealing with regular expressions.

Buffers, Text, and Regions

Table 11-4 shows some basic Emacs functions relating to buffers, text, and strings that are only useful to LISP programmers and thus aren't bound to keystrokes. We already saw a couple of them in the **count-words-buffer** example.

Table 11-4. Buffer and Text Functions

Function	Value or Action
point	Character position of point.
mark	Character position of mark.
point-min	Minimum character position (usually 1).
point-max	Maximum character position (usually size of buffer).
bolp	Whether point is at beginning of line (**t/nil**).
eolp	Whether point is at end of line.
bobp	Whether point is at beginning of buffer.
eobp	Whether point is at end of buffer.
insert	Insert any number of arguments (strings or characters) into buffer after point.
int-to-string	Convert an integer argument to a string.
char-to-string	Convert a character argument to a string.
concat	Concatenate arbitrarily many string arguments together.

Table 11-4. Buffer and Text Functions (continued)

Function	Value or Action
substring	Given a string and two integer indices *start* and *end*, return the substring starting after *start* and ending at *end*. Indices start at 0. For example, (substring "appropriate" 2 5) returns "pro."
aref	Array indexing function that can be used to return individual characters from strings; takes an integer argument and returns the character as an integer, using the ASCII code (on most machines). For example, (aref "appropriate" 3) returns 114, the ASCII code for "r."

There are many, many functions other than those in Table 11-4 that deal with buffers and text, including some that you should be familiar with as user commands. Several commonly-used Emacs functions use *regions*, which are areas of text within a buffer. When you are using Emacs, you delineate regions by setting the mark and moving the cursor. However, region-oriented functions (such as **kill-region**, **indent-region**, and **shell-command-on-region**—really, any function with *region* in its name) are actually more flexible when used within Emacs LISP code. They typically take two integer arguments that are used as the character positions of the boundaries for the region on which they operate. These arguments default to the values of **point** and **mark** when the functions are called interactively.

Obviously, this method is more general (and thus more desirable) than one in which only point and mark can be used to delineate regions. The **r** option to the **interactive** function makes it possible. For example, if we wanted to write the function **translate-region-into-German**, here is how we would start:

```
(defun translate-region-into-German (start end)
  (interactive "r")
  ...
```

The **r** option to **interactive** fills in the two arguments **start** and **end** when the function is called interactively, but if it is called from other LISP code, both arguments must be supplied. The usual way to do this is like this:

```
(translate-region-into-German (point) (mark))
```

But you need not call it in this way. If you wanted to use this function to write another function called **translate-buffer-into-German**, you would only need to write the following as a "wrapper":

```
(defun translate-buffer-into-German ()
   (translate-region-into-German (point-min) (point-max)))
```

In fact, it is best to *avoid* using point and mark within LISP code unless it is really necessary; use local variables instead. Try not to write LISP functions as if they were users—that sort of behavior is better suited to macros (see Chapter 8, *Writing Macros*).

Regular Expressions

Regular expressions (regexps) provide much more powerful ways of dealing with text. Although most Emacs users tend to avoid commands that use regexps, like **replace-regexp** and **re-search-forward**, regular expressions are very widely used within LISP code. Such modes as rmail, dired, and programming language modes would be *unthinkable* without them. Regular expressions require time and patience to learn about and become comfortable with, but it is well worth the effort for LISP programmers, because you have the opportunity to edit and test your regular expressions (you can't debug when using a user regexp command).

We will introduce the various features of regular expressions by way of a few examples of search and replace situations; such examples are easy to explain without introducing lots of extraneous details. Afterwards, we will describe LISP functions that go beyond simple search and replace capabilities with regular expressions. The following are examples of searching and replacing tasks that the normal search/replace commands can't handle or handle poorly:

1. You are developing code in C, and you want to combine the functionality of the routines *read* and *readfile* into a new routine called *get*. You want to replace all references to these routines with references to the new one.

2. You are writing a **troff** document using outline mode, as described in Chapter 6, *Simple Text Formatting and Specialized Editing*. In outline mode, headers of document sections have lines that start with one or more asterisks. You want to write a function called **remove-outline-marks** to get rid of these asterisks so that you can run **troff** on your file.

3. You want to change all occurrences of *program* in a document, including *programs* and *program's*, to *module/modules/module's*, but *without* changing *programming* to *moduleming* or *programmer* to *modulemer*.

4. You are working on documentation for some C software that is being rewritten in Ada. You want to change all of the filenames in the documentation

from *filename.c* to *filename.a*, since *.a* is the extension your Ada compiler requires.

We will soon show how to use regular expressions to deal with these examples, which will be referred to by number. Note that this discussion of regular expressions, while more comprehensive than that in Chapter 3, does not cover every feature; those that it doesn't cover are redundant with other features or relate to concepts that are beyond the scope of this book. It is also important to note that the regular expression syntax described here is for use with *LISP strings only*; there is an important difference between the regexp syntax for LISP strings and the regexp syntax for user commands (like **replace-regexp**), as we will see.

Basic Operators

Regular expressions began as an idea in theoretical computer science, but they have found their way into many nooks and crannies of everyday, practical computing. The syntax used to represent them may vary, but the concepts are very much the same everywhere. You probably already know a subset of regular expression notation: the "wildcard" characters used by the UNIX shell to match filenames. The Emacs notation is a bit different—it is more similar to those used by editors like **ed** and **vi** and UNIX software tools like **lex** and **grep**. So let's start with the Emacs regular expression operators that resemble UNIX shell wildcard characters; these are listed in Table 11-5.

Table 11-5. Basic Regular Expression Operators

Emacs Operator	UNIX Shell Equivalent	Function
.	?	Matches any character.
.*	*	Matches any string.
[abc]	[abc]	Matches a, b, or c.
[a-z]	[a-z]	Matches any lowercase letter.

For example, to match all filenames beginning with **program** in the UNIX shell, you would specify **program***. In Emacs, you would say **program.***. To match all filenames beginning with **a** through **e** in UNIX, you would use [a-e]* or [abcde]*; in Emacs, it's [a-e].* or [abcde].*. In other words, the dash within the brackets specifies a *range* of characters.[5] More on ranges and bracketed character sets shortly.

To specify a character that is used as a regular expression operator, you need to precede it with a double-backslash, as in `\\*` to match an asterisk. Why a *double* backslash? The reason has to do with the way Emacs LISP reads and decodes strings. When Emacs reads a string in a LISP program, it decodes the backslash-escaped characters, and thus turns double backslashes into single backslashes. If the string is being used as a regular expression—i.e., if it is being passed to a function that expects a regular expression argument—that function will use the single backslash as part of the regular expression syntax. For example, given the following line of LISP:

```
(replace-regexp "fred\\*" "bob*")
```

the LISP interpreter decodes the string `fred\\*` as `fred\*` and passes it to the **relace-regexp** command. Then the **replace-regexp** command understands `fred\*` to mean `fred` followed by a (literal) asterisk. Notice, however, that the second argument to **replace-regexp** is *not* a regular expression, so there is no need to backslash-escape the asterisk in **bob*** at all. Also notice that if you were to invoke the above as a user command, you would not need to double the backslash, i.e., you would type **ESC-x replace-regexp RETURN** followed by **fred*** and **bob***. Emacs decodes strings read from the minibuffer differently.

The `*` regular expression operator in Emacs (by itself) actually means something different from the `*` in the UNIX shell: it means "zero or more occurrences of whatever is before the `*`." Thus, since `.` matches any character, `.*` means "zero or more occurrences of any character," i.e., any string at all. Anything can precede a `*`: for example, `read*` matches "rea" followed by zero or more d's; `file[0-9]*` matches "file" followed by zero or more digits.

There are two operators closely related to `*`. The first is `+`, which matches *one* or more occurrences of whatever precedes it. Thus, `read+` will match "read" and "readdddd" but not "rea," and `file[0-9]+` requires that there be at least one digit after "file." The second is `?`, which matches *zero or one* occurrence of whatever precedes it (i.e., makes it optional). `read?` matches "rea" or "read," and `file[0-9]?` matches "file" followed by one optional digit.

Before we move on to other operators, a few more comments about character sets and ranges are in order. First, you can specify more than one range within a single character set. The set `[A-Za-z]` can thus be used to specify all

---

[5] Emacs uses ASCII codes (on most machines) to build ranges, but you shouldn't depend on this fact; it is better to stick to dependable things, like all-lowercase or all-uppercase alphabet subsets or `[0-9]` for digits, and avoid potentially non-portable things, like `[A-z]` and ranges involving punctuation characters.

alphabetic characters; this is better than the non-portable [A-z]. It is also possible to combine ranges with lists of characters in sets; for example, [A-Za-z_] means all alphabetic characters plus underscore, i.e., all characters allowed in the names of identifiers in C. If you give ^ as the first character in a set, it acts as a "not" operator; the set will match all characters that *aren't* the characters after the ^. For example, [^A-Za-z] matches all *non*-alphabetic characters.

A ^ anywhere other than first in a character set has no special meaning; it's just the caret character. Conversely, - has no special meaning if it *is* given first in the set; the same is true for]. However, we don't recommend that you use this shortcut; instead, you should double-backslash-escape these characters just to be on the safe side. A double backslash preceding a non-special character *usually* means just that character—but watch it! A few letters and punctuation characters are used as regular expression operators, some of which are covered below. "Booby-trap" characters that become operators when double-backslash-escaped are listed later. The ^ character has a different meaning when used outside of ranges, as we'll see soon.

Grouping and Alternation

If you want to get *, +, or ? to operate on more than one character, you can use the \\(and \\) operators for grouping. Notice that, in this case (and others to follow), the backslashes are part of the operator. (All of the non-basic regular expression operators include backslashes so as to avoid making too many characters "special.") As we saw before, these need to be *double*-backslash-escaped so that Emacs will decode them properly. If one of the basic operators *immediately* follows \\), it will work on the entire group inside the \\(and \\). For example, \\(read\\)* matches the empty string, "read," "readread," etc. and read\\(file\\)? matches "read" or "readfile." Now we can handle the first of the examples given at the beginning of this section with this LISP code:

```
(replace-regexp "read\\(file\\)?" "get")
```

The alternation operator \\| is a "one or the other" operator; it matches *either* whatever precedes it *or* whatever comes after it. \\| treats parenthesized groups differently from the basic operators. Instead of requiring parenthesized groups to work with subexpressions of more than one character, its "power" goes out to the left and right as far as possible, until it reaches the beginning/end of the regexp, a \\(, a \\), or another \\|. Some examples should make this clearer:

- read\\|get matches read or get.
- readfile\\|read\\|get matches readfile, read, or get.

- \\(read\\|get\\)file matches readfile or getfile.

In the first example, the effect of the \\| extends to both ends of the regular expression. In the second, the effect of the first \\| extends to the beginning of the regexp on the left and to the second \\| on the right. In the third, it extends to the backslash-parentheses.

Context

Another important category of regular expression operators has to do with specifying the *context* of a string, i.e., the text around it. In Chapter 3, *Search and Replace Operations*, we saw the **word-search** commands, which are invoked as options within incremental search. These are special cases of context specification; in this case, the context is word-separation characters, e.g., spaces or punctuation, on both sides of the string.

The simplest context operators for regular expressions are ^ and $, two more basic operators that are used at the beginning and end of regular expressions respectively. The ^ operator causes the rest of the regular expression to match *only* if it is at the beginning of a line; $ causes the regular expression preceding it to match only if it is at the end of a line. In Example 2, we need a function that matches occurrences of one or more asterisks at the beginning of a line; this will do it:

```
(defun remove-outline-marks ()
  "Remove section header marks created in outline-mode."
  (interactive)
  (replace-regexp "^\\*+" ""))
```

This function finds lines that begin with one or more asterisks (the * is a literal asterisk and the + means "one or more"), and it replaces the asterisk(s) with the empty string "", thus deleting them.

Note that ^ and $ *cannot* be used in the middle of regular expressions that are intended to match strings that span more than one line. Instead, you can put \n (for LINEFEED) in your regular expressions to match such strings. Another such character you may want to use is \t for TAB. When ^ and $ are used with regular expression searches on *strings* instead of buffers, they match beginning and end of string respectively; the function **string-match**, described later in this chapter, can be used to do regular expression search on strings.

Here is a real-life example of a complex regular expression that covers the operators we have seen so far: **sentence-end**, a variable that Emacs uses to recognize the ends of sentences for sentence motion commands like **forward-sentence** (**ESC-e**). Its value is:

```
"[.?!][]\"')}]*\\($\\|\t\\|  \\)[ \t\n]*"
```

Let's look at this piece by piece. The first character set, [**. ? !**], matches a period, question mark, or exclamation mark (the first two of these are regular expression operators, but they have no special meaning within character sets). The next part, [ ]\ " ') }] *, consists of a character set containing right bracket, double quote, single quote, right parenthesis, and right curly brace. A * follows the set, meaning that zero or more occurrences of *any* of the characters in the set will match. So far, then, this regexp will match a sentence-ending punctuation mark followed by zero or more ending quotes, parentheses, or curly braces. Next, there is the group \\($\\|\t\\| \\), which matches any of the three alternatives $ (end of line), TAB, or *two* spaces. Finally, [\t\n]* matches zero or more spaces, tabs, or LINEFEEDs. Thus the sentence-ending characters can be followed by end-of-line or a combination of spaces (at least two), tabs, and LINEFEEDs.

There are other context operators besides ^ and $; two of them can be used to make regular expression search act like word search. The operators \\< and \\> match the beginning and end of a word respectively. With these we can go part of the way toward solving Example 3. The regular expression \\<program\\> will match "program" but not "programmer" or "program-ming" (it also won't match "microprogram"). So far so good; however, it won't match "program's" or "programs." For this, we need a more complex regular expression:

```
\\<program\\('s\\|s)?\\>
```

(You can probably get away with omitting the final \\>.) This means, "a word beginning with `program' followed optionally by apostrophe-s or just s." This does the trick as far as matching the right words goes.

Retrieving Portions of Matches

However, there is still one piece missing: the ability to replace "program" with "module" while leaving any **s** or **'s** untouched. This leads to the final regular expression feature will will cover here: the ability to retrieve portions of the matched string for later use. The above regular expression is indeed the correct one to give as the search string for **replace-regexp**. As for the replace string, the answer is **module\\1**; in other words, the required LISP code is:

```
(replace-regexp "\\<program\\('s\\|s\\)?\\>" "module\\1")
```

The \\1 means, in effect, "substitute the portion of the matched string that matched the subexpression inside the \\(and \\)." It is the only regular-expression-related operator that can be used in replacements. In this case, it means to use 's in the replace string if the match was "program's," s if the match was "programs," or nothing if the match was just "program." The result is the correct substitution of "module" for "program," "modules" for "programs," and "module's" for "program's."

Another example of this feature solves Example 4. To match filenames *filename.c* and replace them with *filename.a*, use the LISP code:

```
(replace-regexp "\\(filename\\)\\.c" "\\1.a")
```

Remember that \\. means a literal dot (.). Note that **filename** was surrounded by \\(and \\) in the search string for the *sole purpose* of retrieving it later with \\1.

Actually, the \\1 operator is only a special case of a more powerful facility (as you might have guessed, if you are clever). In general, if you surround a portion of a regular expression with \\(and \\), the string matching the parenthesized subexpression will be saved. When you specify the replace string, you can retrieve the saved substrings with \\N, where N is the number of the parenthesized subexpression from left to right, starting with 1. Parenthesized expressions can be nested; their corresponding \\N numbers are assigned in order of \\(from left to right.

LISP code that takes full advantage of this feature tends to contain very complicated regular expressions. For example, here is a slightly simplified version of the regular expression Emacs' floating-point arithmetic package uses to match floating-point numbers:

```
"[ \t]*\\(-?\\)\\([0-9]*\\)\
\\(\\.\\([0-9]+\\)\\)?\
\\(\\([Ee]\\)\\(-?\\)\\([0-9]+\\)\\)?"
```

This regexp matches floating-point numbers like 3.1459, -0.679, .7, 84.0e7, 932E-14, etc. The backslashes at the ends of the first two lines serve as continuation characters, i.e., as signals that the regexp is to be continued uninterrupted on the next line. Basically, the first line of this regexp matches the integer part of the floating-point number (after optional spaces or tabs), the second line matches the optional fractional (decimal) part, and the third line matches the optional exponent (power of 10).

There are a *lot* of parentheses in this monster (8 pairs); they are used in the floating-point package to extract relevant parts of matched numbers for conversion to an internal format. Here is what each parenthesized group means; examine the regexp and see if you can verify the meanings.

Group	Meaning
1	Optional minus sign for integer part.
2	Digits of integer part (zero or more).
3	Optional fractional part.
4	Digits of fractional part (one or more).
5	Optional exponent.
6	"E" or "e" preceding exponent.
7	Optional minus sign for exponent.
8	Digits of exponent (one or more).

If this regexp were used as the search argument in a **replace-regexp** function, then, for example, \\1 could be used in the replace string to substitute the optional minus sign for the integer part (it would substitute an empty string if there is no minus sign); \\2 could be used to substitute the integer part (or an empty string if there are no digits); \\8 could be used to substitute the exponent (or an empty string if there is no exponent).

Regular Expression Operator Summary

Table 11-6 concludes our discussion of regular expression operators with a reference list of all the operators covered.

Table 11-6. Regular Expression Operators

Operator	Function
.	Match any character.
*	Match 0 or more occurrences of preceding char or group.
+	Match 1 or more occurrences of preceding char or group.
?	Match 0 or 1 occurrences of preceding char or group.
[. . .]	Set of characters; see below.
\\(	Begin a group.
\\)	End a group.
\\|	Match the subexpression before or after \\|.
^	At beginning of regexp, match beginning of line or string.
$	At end of regexp, match end of line or string.
\n	Match LINEFEED within a regexp.
\t	Match TAB within a regexp.

Table 11-6. Regular Expression Operators (continued)

Operator	Function
\\<	Match beginning of word.
\\>	Match end of word.
The following operators are meaningful within character sets:	
^	At beginning of set, treat set as chars not to match.
-	Specify range of characters.
The following is also meaningful in regexp replace strings:	
\\N	Substitute portion of match within the Nth \\(and \\), counting from left \\(to right, starting with 1.

Finally, the following characters are operators (not discussed here) when double-backslash-escaped: **b, B, w, W, s, S, '**, and **`**. Thus, these are "booby-traps" when double-backslash-escaped.

Functions that Use Regular Expressions

The functions **re-search-forward**, **re-search-backward**, **replace-regexp**, **query-replace-regexp**, **isearch-forward-regexp**, and **isearch-backward-regexp** are all user commands that use regular expressions, and they can all be used within LISP code (though it is hard to imagine incremental search being used within LISP code). The section on customizing major modes later in this chapter contains an example function that uses **re-search-forward**.

There are other such functions that aren't available as user commands. Perhaps the most widely-used one is **looking-at**. It takes a regular expression argument and does the following: it returns **t** if the text after point matches the regular expression (**nil** otherwise); if there was a match, it saves the pieces surrounded by \\(and \\) for future use, as above. The function **string-match** is similar: it takes two arguments, a regexp and a string. It returns the starting index of the portion of the string that matches the regexp, or **nil** if there is no match.

The functions **match-beginning** and **match-end** can be used to retrieve the saved portions of the matched string. Each takes as argument the number of the matched expression (as in \\N in **replace-regexp** replace strings) and returns the character position in the buffer marking the beginning (for **match-beginning**) or end (for **match-end**) of the matched string. With the argument 0, the character position marking the beginning/end of the *entire* string matched by the regular expression is returned.

Two more functions are needed to make the above useful: we need to know how to convert the text in a buffer to a string. No problem: **buffer-string** returns the entire buffer as a string; **buffer-substring** takes two integer arguments, marking the beginning and end positions of the substring desired, and returns the substring.

An example should tie these functions together. Say there is a floating-point number in a buffer, and you want to extract its exponent only, as a string. The following code will do it:

```
(if (looking-at floating-point-regexp)
    (buffer-substring (match-beginning 8) (match-end 8)))
```

The code for the calculator mode later in this chapter contains a few other examples of **looking-at**, **match-beginning**, and **match-end**.

Finding Other Built-in Functions

Emacs contains hundreds of built-in functions that may be of use to you in writing LISP code. Yet finding which one to use for a given purpose is not so hard.

The first thing to realize is that you will often need to use functions that are already accessible as keyboard commands. You can use these by finding out what their function names are via the **C-h k (describe-key)** command (see Chapter 13, *Online Help*). This gives the command's full documentation, as opposed to **C-h c** (**describe-key-briefly**), which only gives the command's name. Be careful: in a few cases, some common keyboard commands require an argument when used as LISP functions. An example is **forward-word**; to get the equivalent of typing **ESC-f**, you have to use (**forward-word 1**).

Another powerful tool for getting the right function for the job is the **command-apropos (C-h a)** help function. Given a regular expression, it will search for all commands that match it and display their key bindings (if any) and documentation in a help window. This can be a great help if you are trying to find a command that does a certain "basic" thing. For example, if you want to know about commands that operate on words, type **C-h a** followed by *word*, and you will see documentation on about a dozen and a half commands having to do with words.

The limitation with **command-apropos** is that it only gives information on functions bound as keyboard commands. Even more powerful is **apropos**, which is not accessible via any of the help keys (you must type **ESC-x apropos RETURN**). Given a regular expression, **apropos** displays all functions, variables, and other symbols that match it. Be warned, though: **apropos** can take a long time to run and can generate *very* long lists if you use it with a general enough concept (such as *buffer*). You should be able to use the **apropos** commands on a small number of well-chosen keywords and find the function(s) you need. Because, if a function seems general and basic enough, the chances are excellent that Emacs has it built-in.

Once you have found the function you are interested in, you may find that the **apropos** documentation does not give you enough information about what the function does, its arguments, how to use it, or whatever. The best thing to do at this point is to search Emacs' LISP source code for examples of the function's use. Your system should have the LISP source code installed in some directory called *emacs-source/lisp*, where *emacs-source* is the root of the Emacs source code on your system. Use **grep** or some other search facility to find examples, then edit the files found to look at the surrounding context. Although most of Emacs' built-in LISP code is not very profusely documented, the examples of function use that it provides should be helpful—and may even give you ideas for your own functions.

By now, you should have a framework of Emacs LISP that should be sufficient for writing many useful Emacs commands. Examples of various kinds of functions, both LISP primitives and built-in Emacs functions, have been covered. You should be able to extrapolate many others from the ones given in this chapter along with help techniques such as those above. In other words, you are well on your way to becoming a fluent Emacs LISP programmer.

To test yourself, start with the code for **count-words-buffer** and try writing the following functions:

count-lines-buffer   Print the number of lines in the buffer.

count-words-region   Print the number of words in a region.

what-line   Print the number of the line point is currently on.

Programming a Major Mode

Once you get comfortable with Emacs LISP programming, you may find that that "little extra something" you want Emacs to do takes the form of a major mode. In previous chapters, we covered major modes for text entry, word processor input, and programming languages. Many of these modes are quite complicated to program, so we'll provide a simple example of a major mode, from which you can learn the concepts needed to program your own. Then, in the following section, you will learn how you can customize existing major modes without changing any of the LISP code that implements them.

We'll develop **calc-mode**, a major mode for an integer calculator whose functionality will be familiar to you if you have used the UNIX **dc** (desk calculator) command. It is a Reverse Polish (stack-based) calculator of the type made popular by Hewlett-Packard. After explaining some of the principal components of major modes and some interesting features of the calculator mode, we will give the mode's complete LISP code.

Components of a Major Mode

A major mode has various components that integrate it into Emacs. Some of these are:

• The *symbol* that is the name of the function that implements the mode.

• The *name* of the mode that appears in the mode line in parentheses.

• The *local keymap* that defines key bindings for commands in the mode.

• *Variables* and *constants* known only within the LISP code for the mode.

• The special *buffer* the mode may use.

Let's deal with these in order. The mode symbol is set by assigning the name of the function that implements the mode to the global variable **major-mode**, as in:

```
(setq major-mode 'calc-mode)
```

Similarly, the mode name is set by assigning an appropriate string to the global variable **mode-name**, as in:

```
(setq mode-name "Calculator")
```

The local keymap is defined using functions discussed in Chapter 9, *Customizing Emacs*. In the case of the calculator mode, there is only one key to bind (the LINEFEED or **C-j** key), so we use a special form of the **make-keymap** command called **make-sparse-keymap** that is more efficient with a small number of key bindings. To use a keymap as the local map of a mode, we call the function **use-local-map**, as in:

```
(use-local-map calc-mode-map)
```

As we saw above, variables can be defined by using **setq** to assign a value to them, or by **let** to define local variables within a function. The more "official" way to define variables is the **defvar** function, which allows documentation for the variable to be integrated into online help facilities such as **C-h v** (**describe-variable**). The format is:

```
(defvar varname initial-value "description of the variable")
```

A variation on this is **defconst**, with which you can define constant values (that never change). For example:

```
(defconst operator-regexp "[-+*/%]"
   "Regular expression for recognizing operators.")
```

defines the regular expression to be used in searching for arithmetic operators.

It is also desirable to make variables *local* to the mode, so that they are only known within a buffer that is running the mode.[6] To do this, use the **make-local-variable** command, as in:

```
(make-local-variable 'stack)
```

Notice that the *name* of the variable, not its value, is needed; therefore a single quote precedes the variable name, turning it into a symbol.

Finally, various major modes use special buffers that are not attached to files. For example, the **C-x C-b** (**list-buffers**) command creates a buffer called `*Buffer List*`. To create a buffer in a new window, we use the **pop-to-buffer** function, as in:

```
(pop-to-buffer "*Calc*")
```

There are a couple of useful variations on **pop-to-buffer**. We won't use them in our mode example, but they are useful in other circumstances:

switch-to-buffer Same as the **C-x b** command covered in Chapter 5, *Emacs as a Work Environment*; can also be used with a buffer name argument in LISP.

set-buffer Used only within LISP code to set the buffer for editing. The best thing to use for creating a temporary "work" buffer within a LISP function.

---

[6] Unfortunately, since such variables are defined *before* they are made local to the mode, there is still a problem with name clashes with global variables. Therefore, it is still important to use names that aren't already used for global variables. A good strategy for avoiding this is to use variable names that start with the name of the mode.

More LISP Basics: Lists

A Reverse Polish calculator uses a data structure called a *stack*. Think of a stack as being similar to a spring-loaded dish stack in a cafeteria. When you enter a number into a Reverse Polish calculator, you *push* it onto the stack. When you apply an operator such as plus or minus, you *pop* the top two numbers off the stack, add or subtract them, and push the result back on.

A fundamental concept of LISP, the *list*, is a natural for implementing stacks. The list is the main concept that sets LISP apart from other programming languages. It is a data structure that has two parts: the *head* and *tail*. These are known in LISP jargon, for purely historical reasons, as **car** and **cdr** respectively. Think of these as "the first thing in the list" and "the rest of the list." The functions **car** and **cdr**, when given a list argument, return the head and tail of it respectively.[7] Two functions are often used for making lists. **Cons** (construct) takes two arguments, which become the head and tail of the list respectively. **List** takes a list of elements and makes them into a list. For example:

```
(list 2 3 4 5)
```

makes a list of the numbers from 2 to 5, and:

```
(cons 1 (list 2 3 4 5))
```

makes a list of the numbers from 1 to 5. Then **car** applied to that list would return **1**, while **cdr** would return the list **(2 3 4 5)**.

These concepts are important because stacks, such as that used in the calculator mode, are very easily implemented as lists. To push the value of **x** onto the stack **stack**, we can just say:

```
(setq stack (cons x stack))
```

If we want to get at the value at the top of the stack,

```
(car stack)
```

will return it. To pop the top value off the stack, we say:

```
(setq stack (cdr stack))
```

Bear in mind that the elements of a list can be *anything*, including other lists. (This is why a list is called a *recursive* data structure.) In fact (ready to be confused?) just about everything in LISP that is not an atom is a list. This includes

---

[7] Experienced LISP programmers should note that Emacs LISP does not supply standard contractions like **cadr**, **cdar**, etc.

functions, which are basically lists of function name, arguments, and expressions to be evaluated. The idea of functions as lists will come in handy very soon.

The Calculator Mode

The complete LISP code for the calculator mode appears at the end of this section; you should refer to it while reading the following explanation. If you type the code in, you can use the calculator by typing **ESC-x calc-mode RETURN**. You will be put in the buffer ***Calc***. You can type a line of numbers and operators and then type **C-j** to evaluate the line. There are three special commands:

=   Print the value at the top of the stack.
p   Print the entire stack contents.
c   Clear the stack.

Blank spaces are not necessary, except to separate numbers. For example, typing:

```
4 17*6/=
```

followed by **C-j**, evaluates (4 * 17) / 6 and causes the result 11 to be printed (integer division truncates the remainder).

The heart of the code for the calculator mode is the functions **calc-eval** and **next-token**. (See the code below for these.) **Calc-eval** is bound to the **C-j** key in calculator mode. Starting at the beginning of the line preceding **C-j**, it calls **next-token** to grab each *token* (integer, operator, or command letter) in the line and evaluate it.

Next-token uses a **cond** construct to see if there is an integer, operator, or command letter at point by using the regular expressions **integer-regexp**, **operator-regexp**, and **command-regexp**. According to which regular expression was matched, it sets the variable **proc-fun** to the name (symbol) of the function that should be run (**push-number**, **operate**, or **command**), and it sets **tok** to the result of the regular expression match.

Back in **calc-eval**, we see where the idea of a function as list comes in. The **funcall** function reflects the fact that there is very little difference between *code* and *data* in LISP. It is possible to put together a list consisting of a symbol and a bunch of expressions and evaluate it as a function, using the symbol as the function name and the expressions as arguments; this is what **funcall** does. In this case,

```
(funcall proc-fun tok)
```

treats the symbol value of **proc-fun** as the name of the function to be called and calls it with the argument **tok**. Then the function does one of three things:

- If the token is an integer, **push-number** pushes the integer onto the stack.

- If the token is an operator, **operate** performs the operation on the top two numbers on the stack (see below).

- If the token is a command, **command** performs the appropriate command.

The function **operate** takes the idea of functions as lists of data a step further by converting the token from the user *directly* into a function (an arithmetic operator). This is accomplished by the function **read**, which takes a character string and converts it into a symbol. Thus, **operate** uses **funcall** and **read** in combination as follows:

```
(defun operate (tok)
  (let ((op1 (pop))
        (op2 (pop)))
    (fpush (funcall (read tok) op2 op1))))
```

This function takes the name of an arithmetic operator (as a string) as its argument. As we saw above, the string **tok** is a token extracted from the `*Calc*` buffer, in this case an arithmetic operator such as + or *. The function pops the top two arguments off the stack using the **pop** function, which is similar to the use of **cdr** above. **Read** converts the token to a symbol, and thus to the name of an arithmetic function. So, if the operator is +, then **funcall** is called as:

```
(funcall '+ op2 op1)
```

This means that the function **+** is called with the two arguments, which is exactly equivalent to simply (**+ op2 op1**). Finally, the result of the function is pushed back onto the stack.

All this voodoo is necessary so, for example, the user can type a plus sign and LISP will automatically convert it into a plus *function*. We could have done the same thing less elegantly—and less efficiently—by writing **operate** with a **cond** construct (as in **next-token**), which would look like this:

```
(defun operate (tok)
  (let ((op1 (fpop))
        (op2 (fpop)))
    (cond ((equal tok "+")
           (+ op2 op1))
          ((equal tok "-")
           (- op2 op1))
          ((equal tok "*")
           (* op2 op1))
          ((equal tok "/")
           (/ op2 op1))
```

```
        (t
          (% op2 op1)))))
```

The final thing to notice in the calculator mode code is the function **calc-mode**, which starts the mode. It creates (and pops to) the ***Calc*** buffer. Then it kills all existing local variables in the buffer, initializes the stack to **nil** (empty), and creates the local variable **proc-fun** (see above). Finally it sets **calc-mode** as the major mode, sets the mode name, and activates the local keymap.

LISP Code for the Calculator Mode

Now you should be able to understand all of the code for the calculator mode. You will notice that there really isn't that much code at all! This is testimony to the power of LISP and the versatility of built-in Emacs functions. Once you understand how this mode works, you should be ready to start rolling your own. Without any further ado, here is the code:

```
;;    Integer calculator mode.
;;
;;    Supports the operators +, -, *, /, and % (remainder).
;;    Commands:
;;    c       clear the stack
;;    =       print the value at the top of the stack
;;    p       print the entire stack contents
;;

(defvar calc-mode-map nil
  "Local keymap for calculator mode buffers.")

; set up the calculator mode keymap with
; C-j (linefeed) as "eval" key
(if calc-mode-map
    nil
  (setq calc-mode-map (make-sparse-keymap))
  (define-key calc-mode-map "\C-j" 'calc-eval))

(defconst integer-regexp "-?[0-9]+"
  "Regular expression for recognizing integers.")

(defconst operator-regexp "[-+*/%]"
  "Regular expression for recognizing operators.")

(defconst command-regexp "[c=ps]"
  "Regular expression for recognizing commands.")

(defconst whitespace "[ \t]"
  "Regular expression for recognizing whitespace.")
```

```lisp
;; beep and print an error message
(defun error-message (str)
  (beep)
  (message str)
  nil)

;; stack functions
(defun push (num)
  (if (integerp num)
      (setq stack (cons num stack)))))

(defun top ()
  (if (not stack)
      (error-message "stack empty.")
    (car stack)))

(defun pop ()
  (let ((val (top)))
    (if val
        (setq stack (cdr stack)))
    val))

;; functions for user commands:
(defun print-stack ()
  "Print entire contents of stack, from top to bottom."
  (if stack
      (progn
        (insert "\n")
        (let ((stk stack))
          (while stack
            (insert (int-to-string (pop)) " "))
          (setq stack stk)))
    (error-message "stack empty.")))

(defun clear-stack ()
  "Clear the stack."
  (setq stack nil)
  (message "stack cleared."))


(defun command (tok)
  "Given a command token, perform the appropriate action."
  (cond ((equal tok "c")
         (clear-stack))
        ((equal tok "=")
         (insert "\n" (int-to-string (top))))
        ((equal tok "p")
         (print-stack))
        (t
         (message (concat "invalid command: " tok)))))

(defun operate (tok)
```

```
  "Given an arithmetic operator (as string), pop two numbers
off the stack, perform operation tok (given as string), push
the result onto the stack."
  (let ((op1 (pop))
        (op2 (pop)))
    (push (funcall (read tok) op2 op1))))

(defun push-number (tok)
  "Given a number (as string), push it (as integer)
onto the stack."
  (push (string-to-int tok)))


(defun invalid-tok (tok)
  (error-message (concat "Invalid token: " tok))
  (sit-for 0))          ;make sure message is displayed

(defun next-token ()
  "Pick up the next token, based on regexp search.
As side effects, advance point one past the token,
and set name of function to use to process the token."
  (let (tok)
    (cond ((looking-at integer-regexp)
           (goto-char (match-end 0))
           (setq proc-fun 'push-number))
          ((looking-at operator-regexp)
           (forward-char 1)
           (setq proc-fun 'operate))
          ((looking-at command-regexp)
           (forward-char 1)
           (setq proc-fun 'command))
          (t
           (setq proc-fun 'invalid-tok)))
    ;; pick up token and advance past it (and past whitespace)
    (setq tok (buffer-substring (match-beginning 0) (point)))
    (if (looking-at whitespace)
        (goto-char (match-end 0)))
    tok))


(defun calc-eval ()
  "Main evaluation function for calculator mode.
Process all tokens on an input line."
  (interactive)
  (beginning-of-line)
  (while (not (eolp))
    (let ((tok (next-token)))
      (funcall proc-fun tok)))
  (insert "\n"))

(defun calc-mode ()
  "Calculator mode.  6-digit precision, postfix notation.
Understands the arithmetic operators +, -, *, / and %,
```

```
plus the following commands:
    c    clear stack
    =    print top of stack
    p    print entire stack contents (top to bottom)
Linefeed (C-j) is bound to an evaluation function that
will evaluate everything on the current line.  No
whitespace is necessary, except to separate numbers."
  (interactive)
  (pop-to-buffer "*Calc*" nil)
  (kill-all-local-variables)
  (make-local-variable 'stack)
  (setq stack nil)
  (make-local-variable 'proc-fun)
  (setq major-mode 'calc-mode)
  (setq mode-name "Calculator")
  (use-local-map calc-mode-map))
```

The following are some possible extensions to the calculator mode, offered as exercises. If you try them, you will increase your understanding of the mode's code and Emacs LISP programming in general.

1. Add an operator ^ for "power" (e.g., 4 5 ^ evaluates to 1024). Note that there is no built-in power function in Emacs LISP, so you will have to write your own.

2. Add support for octal (base 8) and/or hexadecimal (base 16) numbers. An octal number has a leading "0," and a hexadecimal has a leading "0x"; thus, 017 equals decimal 15, and 0x17 equals decimal 23.

3. Add operators \+ and * to add/multiply *all* of the numbers on the stack, not just the top two (e.g., 4 5 6 \+ evaluates to 15, and 4 5 6 * evaluates to 120).[8]

Customizing Existing Modes

Now that you understand some of what goes into programming a major mode, you may decide you want to customize an existing one. Luckily, in most cases, you don't have to worry about changing any mode's existing LISP code to do this—you may not even have to *look* at the code. All Emacs major modes have "hooks" for letting you add your own code to them. Appropriately, these are called **mode-hooks**. Every built-in major mode in Emacs has a mode hook called

---

[8] APL programmers will recognize these as variations of that language's "scan" operators.

mode-name-**hook**, where *mode-name* is the name of the mode or the function that invokes it. For example, C mode has **c-mode-hook**, shell mode has **shell-mode-hook**, etc.

What exactly is a hook? It is a variable whose value is some LISP code to run when the mode is invoked. When you invoke a mode, you run a LISP function that typically does many things (e.g., set up key bindings for special commands, create buffers, and local variables, etc.); the last thing a mode-invoking function usually does is run the mode's hook if it exists. Thus, hooks are "positioned" to give you a chance to override anything the mode's code may have set up. For example, any key bindings you define will override the mode's default bindings.

We saw earlier that LISP code can be used as the value of a LISP variable; this comes in handy when you create hooks. Before we show you exactly how to create a hook, we need to introduce yet another LISP primitive function: **lambda**. **lambda** is very much like **defun** in that it is used to define functions, the difference being that **lambda** defines functions that don't have names (or, in LISP parlance, "anonymous functions"). The format of **lambda** is:

```
(lambda (args)
  code)
```

where *args* are arguments to the function and *code* is the body of the function. To assign a lambda function as the value of a variable, you need to "quote" it to prevent it from being evaluated (run). That is, you use the form:

```
(setq var-name
     '(lambda ()
        code))
```

Therefore, to create code for a mode hook, you use the form:

```
(setq mode-name-hook
     '(lambda ()
        code for mode hook))
```

The simplest thing you can do with mode hooks is to change one or more of the key bindings for a mode's special commands. Here is an example: in Chapter 6, *Simple Text Formatting and Specialized Editing*, we saw that picture mode is a useful tool for creating simple line drawings. There are several commands in picture mode that set the default drawing direction. The command to set the direction to "down," **picture-movement-down**, is bound to **C-c .**. This is not as mnemonic a binding as **C-c <** for **picture-movement-left** or **C-c ^** for **picture-movement-up**, so let's say you want to make **C-c v** the binding for **picture-movement-down** instead. The keymap for picture mode is, not surprisingly, called **picture-mode-map**, so the code you need to do this key binding is:

```
(define-key picture-mode-map "\C-cv" 'picture-movement-down)
```

The hook for picture mode is called **edit-picture-hook** (since **edit-picture** is the command that invokes picture mode). So, to put this code into the hook for picture mode, the following should go into your *.emacs*:

```
(setq edit-picture-hook
      '(lambda ()
         (define-key picture-mode-map "\C-cv" 'picture-movement-down)))
```

This creates a lambda function with the one key binding command as its body. Then, whenever you enter picture mode (starting with the next time you invoke Emacs), this binding will be in effect.

As a slightly more complex example, let's say you use **nroff** or **troff** to format text. You use nroff mode (see Chapter 7, *Using Emacs with UNIX Text Formatters*), but you find that there are no Emacs commands that enter standard **nroff/troff** font change commands (\fB, \fI, and \fR for boldface, italic, and roman (or "regular") respectively). You want to write your own functions to insert these strings, and you want to bind them to keystrokes in nroff mode.

To do this, first you need to write the functions that insert the font-change strings. These are very simple:

```
(defun nroff-insert-bold ()
  (interactive)
  (insert "\\fB"))

(defun nroff-insert-italic ()
  (interactive)
  (insert "\\fI"))

(defun nroff-insert-roman ()
  (interactive)
  (insert "\\fR"))
```

Remember that the double backslashes are necessary in the insert strings so that Emacs interprets them as single backslashes, and that the **(interactive)** commands are necessary so that Emacs can use these functions as user commands.

The next step is to write code that binds these functions to keystrokes in nroff mode's keymap, which is called **nroff-mode-map**, using the techniques described in Chapter 9, *Customizing Emacs*. Assume you want to bind these functions to **C-c C-b** (bold), **C-c C-i** (italic), and **C-c C-r** (roman). Again, this is no problem:

```
(define-key nroff-mode-map "\C-c\C-b" 'nroff-insert-bold)
(define-key nroff-mode-map "\C-c\C-i" 'nroff-insert-italic)
(define-key nroff-mode-map "\C-c\C-r" 'nroff-insert-roman)
```

Finally, you need to convert these lines of LISP into a value for **nroff-mode-hook**. Here is the code to do this:

```
(setq nroff-mode-hook
    '(lambda ()
        (define-key nroff-mode-map "\C-c\C-b" 'nroff-insert-bold)
        (define-key nroff-mode-map "\C-c\C-i" 'nroff-insert-italic)
        (define-key nroff-mode-map "\C-c\C-r" 'nroff-insert-roman)))
```

If you put this code in your *.emacs*, together with the function definitions above, then you will get the desired functionality whenever you use nroff mode.

Here is a third example. Let's say you program in C, and you want a LISP function that counts the number of C function definitions in a file. The following function does the trick; it is somewhat similar to the **count-lines-buffer** example earlier in the chapter. The function goes through the current buffer looking for (and counting) C function definitions by searching for `{` at the beginning of a line:

```
(defun count-functions-buffer ()
"Count the number of C function definitions in the buffer."
  (interactive)
  (save-excursion
    (goto-char (point-min))
    (let ((count 0))
      (while (re-search-forward "^{" nil t)
        (setq count (1+ count)))
      (message "%d functions defined." count))))
```

The **re-search-forward** call in this function has two extra arguments; the third (last) of these means "if not found, just return **nil**, don't signal an error." The second argument must be set to **nil**, its default, so that the third argument can be supplied.[9]

---

[9] The second argument to **re-search-forward**—and other search functions—bounds the search: if given an integer value N, don't search past character position N. **Nil**, the default, means don't bound the search.

Now assume we want to bind this function to **C-c f** in C mode. Here is how we would set the value of **c-mode-hook**:

```
(setq c-mode-hook
      '(lambda ()
         (define-key c-mode-map "C-cf" 'count-functions-buffer)))
```

Put this code and the above function definition in your *.emacs*, and this functionality will be available to you in C mode.

Building Your Own LISP Library

Once you have become proficient at Emacs LISP programming, you will want a library of LISP functions and packages that you can call up from Emacs at will. Of course, you can define a few small functions in your *.emacs* file, but if you are writing bigger pieces of code for more specialized purposes, you will not want to clutter up your *.emacs*—nor will you want Emacs to spend all that time evaluating the code each time you start it up. The answer is to build your own LISP library, analogous to the *lisp* directory that comes with Emacs and contains all of its built-in LISP code. Once you have created a library, you can load whatever LISP packages you need at a given time and not bother with the others.

There are two simple steps you need to take to create a library. First, create a directory (with the UNIX **mkdir** command) in which your LISP code will reside. Most people create a *lisp* subdirectory of their home directory. LISP files are expected to have names ending in *.el* (your *.emacs* file is an exception). The second step is to make your directory known to Emacs, so that when you try to load a LISP package Emacs will know where to find it. Emacs keeps track of such directories in the global variable **load-path**, which is a list of strings that are directory names.

The initial value for **load-path** is just the name of the LISP directory that comes with Emacs, e.g., */usr/local/emacs/lisp*. You will need to add the name of your own LISP directory to **load-path**. One way to do this is to use the LISP function **append**, which concatenates any number of list arguments together. For example, if your LISP directory is ˜*yourname/lisp*, you would put the following in your *.emacs* file:

```
(setq load-path (append load-path (list "~yourname/lisp")))
```

The function **list** is necessary because all of the arguments to **append** must be lists. This line of code must precede any commands in your *.emacs* that load packages from your LISP directory.

When you load a library, Emacs searches directories in the order in which they appear in **load-path**; therefore, in this case, Emacs will search its default LISP directory first. If you want your directory to be searched first, you should use the **cons** function described earlier instead of **append**, as follows:

```
(setq load-path (cons "~yourname/lisp" load-path))
```

This form is useful if you want to replace one of the standard Emacs packages with one of your own. For example, you'd use this form if you've written your own version of C mode and want to use it instead of the standard package. Notice that the directory name here is *not* surrounded by a call to **list** because **cons'** first argument is an atom (a string in this case). This is similar to the use of **cons** for pushing values onto stacks, as in the calculator mode described earlier.

If you want Emacs to search the directory you happen to be in at any given time, simply add **nil** to **load-path**, either by prepending it via **cons** or by appending it via **append**. This is analogous to putting **.** in your UNIX **PATH** environment variable.

Once you have created a private LISP library and told Emacs where to find it, you're ready to load and use the LISP packages that you've created. There are several ways of loading LISP packages into your Emacs. The first of these should be familiar from Chapter 9, *Customizing Emacs*:

1. Type **ESC-x load-library RETURN** as a user command, as described in Chapter 9.

2. Put the line (**load** *"package-name"*) within LISP code. Putting a line like this into your *.emacs* file will make Emacs load the package whenever you start it.

3. Invoke invoke Emacs with the command-line option "-l *package-name*." This loads the package *package-name* to be loaded.[10]

4. Put the line (**autoload** *'function "filename"*) within LISP code (typically your *.emacs* file), as described in Chapter 10, *Emacs for Programmers*. This causes Emacs to load the package when you execute the given *function*.

---

[10] There is also the option "-f *function-name*" which causes Emacs to run the function *function-name* on invocation.

Byte-compiling LISP Files

Once you have created your LISP directory, you can make loading your LISP files more efficient by *byte-compiling* them, or translating their code into *byte code*, a more compact, machine-readable form. Byte-compiling the LISP file *filename.el* creates the byte code file *filename.elc*. Byte code files are typically 40 to 75 percent the size of their non-byte-compiled counterparts.

Although byte-compiled files are more efficient, they are not strictly necessary. The **load-library** command, when given the argument "filename," first looks for a file called *filename.elc*. If that doesn't exist, it tries *filename.el*, i.e., the non-byte-compiled version. If *that* doesn't exist, it finally tries just *filename*. This means that you can byte-compile your *.emacs* file, which may result in faster startup if your *.emacs* is large.

You can byte-compile a file by invoking **ESC-x byte-compile-file RETURN** and supplying the filename. If you omit the *.el* suffix, Emacs will append it and ask for confirmation. Then you will see an entertaining little display in the mini-buffer as the byte-compiler does its work: the names of functions being compiled will flash by. The byte-compiler creates a file with the same name as the original LISP file but with *c* appended; thus, *filename.el* becomes *filename.elc*, and *.emacs* becomes *.emacsc*.

Finally, if you develop a directory with several LISP files and you make changes to some of them, you can use the **byte-recompile-directory** command to recompile only those LISP files that have been changed since being byte-compiled (analogously to the UNIX **make** utility). Just type **ESC-x byte-recompile-directory RETURN** and supply the name of the LISP directory or just press **RETURN** for the default, which is the current directory.

12

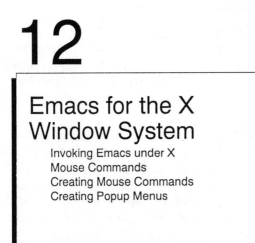

Emacs for the X Window System

Invoking Emacs under X
Mouse Commands
Creating Mouse Commands
Creating Popup Menus

The X Window System is a windowing system that was originally developed at MIT. Like Emacs, X has been ported to a wide variety of hardware and operating systems, including many flavors of UNIX as well as MS-DOS and the Macintosh. It serves as a fast, flexible basis for taking full advantage of graphics workstations. Yet X is only as good as the software that runs on top of it. Many people think of X as an "assembly language" for writing programs that use its standardized facilities; high level window managers (such as those that come with the OpenLook and Motif graphics toolkits) are implemented on top of X.

Emacs is another program that can take advantage of the X Window System. If you use a workstation and your Emacs has been built with its X interface included, you will find that Emacs has several features that make it even more powerful. These include:

- Using a mouse as a pointing device or "second cursor."

- Cutting and pasting text between Emacs and other windows.

- Using popup menus for help and other purposes.

We will cover all of these features in this chapter.[1] We will also describe how you can set up your own mouse commands, in the manner of the key bindings discussed in Chapter 9, *Customizing Emacs*, and how you can create your own X mouse commands and popup menus. The discussion of the latter two topics, i.e., the last two sections of this chapter, assumes that you are familiar with the LISP programming material in Chapter 11, *Emacs LISP Programming*. If you aren't a LISP programmer, you can get along fine without reading these sections.

We should note at this point that the features listed above all *add* to the functionality of Emacs when it is run as an X window. However, there is one feature that Emacs' X interface *leaves out*: the ability to suspend Emacs via **C-z** or **C-x C-z**. When you are running X and you want to leave Emacs to do something else, you can of course just switch windows, so this functionality becomes unnecessary. Both **C-z** and **C-x C-z** are unbound when Emacs is run as an X window.

This chapter is obviously not for you if you don't use a workstation that runs the X Window System. Yet even if you do, there is a chance that your Emacs does not have the X interface included; this is an option that your system administrator can choose when building Emacs. To check this, simply invoke Emacs from an X terminal window. You should see a *new* window appear with Emacs in it; exactly how the window appears is a function of the window manager you are using on top of X. However, if your X terminal window *becomes* an Emacs window, then your Emacs does not include an X interface. You can certainly still use Emacs this way, though you will not be able to use the mouse and Emacs will not "understand" if you change the size of your window.

Invoking Emacs under X

When you invoke Emacs under X, there are various options you can supply that relate to the size and shape of the window, the font used to display text, colors to use (if you have a color display), and various other things. There are two different ways to specify these options.

---

[1] The information in this chapter is based on Version 11 of X.

Command Line and .X11Startup Options

The best strategy is to figure out how you want to set the options (if you want to override the defaults) and put the resulting command line in the X startup file *.X11Startup* in your login directory. (This file simply consists of commands that invoke X programs. If you weren't aware of this file, type **ls -a** to see if you have one; your system administrator may have set one up for you.) Make sure the line you put in this file ends in **&** so that the job is put in the background.

Here are the options that you can use:

-geometry Tells X what size to make your Emacs window and where to put it on the screen. The argument has the form "*widthxheight+X+Y*". *Width* and *height* are the width and height of the screen in *text characters* (not pixels); the default is 24 by 80, which is the same as a standard CRT screen. *X* and *Y* are the screen coordinates of the upper-left corner of the window, where (0, 0) means the top-left corner of the screen. The default depends on the window manager you have running on top of X. See the example below.

-wn *name* Name to use in the title bar of the window. The default is *emacs @ hostname*, where *hostname* is the name of your machine.

-r Put the window in reverse video.

-i Use a "kitchen sink" figure as an icon when iconifying Emacs. When you *iconify* a window, it disappears and a small picture (*icon*) appears elsewhere on the screen. Exactly how to iconify a window depends on your window manager. Once your window has been iconified, you can click the left-hand mouse button on the icon to get Emacs back. If **-i** is not specified, a standard icon will be used instead.

-font *font* Use the font *font* as the type font to use in the window. Emacs requires that you use *fixed-width* fonts, which include the font *fixed.pcf* and any fonts with names of the form *WxH.pcf*, where *W* is the width and *H* is the height in pixels (e.g., *8x13.pcf*). There will also be several fonts with long, complex names on your system; the names have fields separated by dashes, and any font whose name has **m** or **c** as its 11th field is also fixed width. Use the command **xlsfonts** to get a list of all such fonts, i.e., type **xlsfonts '*-m-*'** or **xlsfonts '*-c-*'**, and consult the man page for this command for more information. The default font is whatever X is using when Emacs is invoked.

-b *width*   Set the window's outside border to *width* pixels wide. The default is 1 pixel.

-ib *width*   Set the window's inside border to *width* pixels wide. The default is 1 pixel.

-nw   Don't start up a new window for Emacs. If you use this option when invoking Emacs from an X terminal window, it will just use the terminal window instead.

There are also several options you can set if you are using a color display. Each one of these takes an argument *color*, which is the name of a color chosen from those listed in the file */usr/lib/X11/rgb.txt*:

-fg *color*   Set the color for text characters.

-bg *color*   Set the color for the window's background.

-bd *color*   Set the color for the window's border.

-cr *color*   Set the color for the text cursor.

-ms *color*   Set the color for the mouse arrow.

Here is an example Emacs/X invocation. You can type this command into an X terminal window or put it in your *.X11Startup* file:

```
emacs -geometry 80x50+524+90 -i -wn "GNU Emacs" -fg red &
```

This command line does the following:

- Makes the Emacs window 80 characters wide by 50 high, almost the size of an 8-1/2 by 11 sheet of paper.

- Puts its upper-left corner at screen coordinates (524, 90), which on a 19-inch display with 768 by 1024 resolution is all the way over to the right and down a bit less than an inch from the top of the screen.

- Uses the "kitchen sink" figure as an icon.

- Puts "GNU Emacs" on the title bar at the top of the window.

- Makes the text characters appear in red (for color displays only; this has no effect on monochrome displays).

.Xdefaults File

If you use more than one Emacs window at a time and you want them all configured in the same way, there is an easier way to specify options. The *.Xdefaults*
file in your home directory can contain default options for any application that
runs under X. To use this with Emacs, put lines of the form:

```
emacs.option: value
```

in the file. *Option* is a keyword that is equivalent to a command-line option (as
described at the beginning of this section), as shown in Table 12-1.

Table 12-1. Options for .Xdefaults File

Option	Equivalent	Values
geometry	-geometry	(see above)
title	-wn	String to appear in title bar.
reverseVideo	-r	On or off.
bitmapIcon	-i	On or off.
font	-font	Name of font.
borderWidth	-b	Number of pixels.
internalBorder	-ib	Number of pixels.
For color displays only:		
foreground	-fg	Color name.
background	-bg	Color name.
borderColor	-bd	Color name.
cursorColor	-cr	Color name.
pointerColor	-ms	Color name.

For example, you would put the following lines in your *.Xdefaults* file to set the
same options as the command example for the *.X11Startup* file given earlier:

```
emacs.geometry: 80x50+524+90
emacs.font: 8x13
emacs.bitmapIcon: on
emacs.title: GNU Emacs
emacs.borderWidth: 3
emacs.foreground: red
```

However, it is not wise to specify placement coordinates in your *.Xdefaults* file if you anticipate using multiple Emacs windows. You can specify the window size only by using a line like this:

```
emacs.geometry:80x50
```

This way, whenever a new Emacs window is created, its upper-left corner will be placed by your window manager at some "reasonable" position.

Note that if you make changes to your *.Xdefaults* file, you will have to restart your X session for them to take effect, because X needs to read the contents of your *.Xdefaults* file into its internal *resource database*, and it normally does this at startup time. However, some window managers have commands that allow you to tell X to reconfigure the resource database on the fly.

Mouse Commands

If you use a workstation with a windowing system and a mouse, there are certain things you would think Emacs ought to be able to do. For example, it seems natural that, if you move the mouse arrow to some spot in an Emacs text window and you click a mouse button, the Emacs cursor should move there. There should also be no reason why the text you cut and paste in Emacs using mouse commands should not be available for cutting and pasting from and to other X windows. Furthermore, Emacs should be able to react to window-resizing commands in an appropriate way.

Emacs' X interface was designed to do exactly these things, and more. If you resize the X window containing Emacs, Emacs will "understand" this by shrinking or enlarging its own windows proportionally. Emacs also understands mouse buttons; they are bound to Emacs commands in much the same way as keystrokes are bound to commands (as described in Chapter 9, *Customizing Emacs*).

Emacs assumes you are using a standard three-button mouse that looks like Figure 12-1.

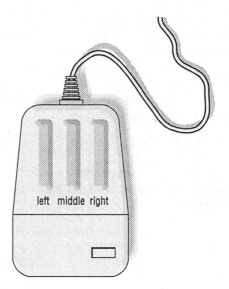

Figure 12-1. Three-button Mouse

A mouse *click* is the result of clicking a mouse button, perhaps with the CON-
TROL and/or SHIFT keys held down at the same time. We will use **boldface** when
describing mouse clicks; **C** means CONTROL and **S** means SHIFT; for example,
C-S-right means "hold down CONTROL and SHIFT while clicking the right
mouse button."[2] Table 12-2 lists all of the mouse commands supported by Emacs'
X interface, which we will follow with explanations and examples. The right-
hand column shows, where applicable, the standard Emacs commands to which
the mouse commands are similar.

Table 12-2. Mouse Commands

Mouse Click	Command Name	Standard Emacs Equivalent
left	x-mouse-set-point	(move cursor to where arrow is)
middle	x-paste-text	yank (**C-y**)
right	x-cut-text	copy-region-as-kill (**ESC-w**)
C-middle	x-cut-and-wipe-text	kill-region (**C-w**)
C-right	x-mouse-select-and-split	split-window-vertically (**C-x 2**)
S-middle	x-cut-text	copy-region-as-kill (**ESC-w**)

[2] If your keyboard has a META key, Emacs can also deal with it during mouse clicks; for example,
C-M-left means "hold down CONTROL and META while clicking the left mouse button." However,
there are no default bindings for mouse clicks involving the META key.

Table 12-2. Mouse Commands (continued)

Mouse Click	Command Name	Standard Emacs Equivalent
S-right	x-paste-text	yank (**C-y**)
C-S-left	x-buffer-menu	(creates menu; see below)
C-S-middle	x-help	(creates menu; see below)
C-S-right	x-mouse-keep-one-window	delete-other-windows (**C-x 1**)

Notice that **S-middle** and **S-right** duplicate **middle** and **right** respectively, and that **C-left** and **S-left** are unbound. Later in this chapter, we will show how you can bind your own mouse commands.

The most basic mouse command, and the one you are likely to use most often, is **left**, which just moves the Emacs cursor to where the mouse is pointing (this can include changing Emacs windows). To cut a region of text, simply move the Emacs cursor to one end of it, move the mouse to the other end and click **C-middle**. To copy the text to the kill ring, use **right** or **S-middle** instead.

In other words, the mouse arrow acts as a "second cursor" that is used as if it were a "mark" when you cut and paste. To get cut text back, simply move the *mouse* (not the Emacs cursor) to where you want the text to go and click **middle** or **S-right**. We recommend that you use **right** for copying regions to the kill ring and **middle** for pasting them, since this creates the somewhat natural sequence of **left-right-middle** for point-copy-paste, and it avoids having to use the CONTROL and SHIFT keys.

Here is an example of how cutting and pasting with the mouse works. Let's say we have this text:

```
Here is a sentence, the middle
of which we want to delete,
but the end of which we want to keep.
```

We move the mouse to the beginning of the first **the** and click **left**; then the Emacs cursor and the mouse both point there:

```
Here is a sentence, the middle
of which we want to delete,
but the end of which we want to keep.
```

Now we move the mouse to the "the" after the "but":

```
Here is a sentence, the middle
of which we want to delete,
but the end of which we want to keep.
```

The Emacs cursor doesn't move, even though the mouse does. Next, we click **C-middle** to cut the text:

Here is a sentence, ▮he end of which we want to keep.

The text "the middle of which we want to delete, but" is now in the kill ring; it can be yanked via **middle** or the standard **C-y**.

The beauty of the mouse commands for cutting and pasting is that they don't just duplicate the corresponding standard Emacs commands; they also interface to X *cut buffers*, which are used for cutting and pasting text between X windows. That is, the **x-cut-text** and **x-cut-and-wipe-text** commands put a copy of the cut text into an X cut buffer and another copy into the Emacs kill ring; **x-paste-text** inserts the text in the X cut buffer where the mouse is.

This means that if you cut a region using the mouse commands, you can go to another X window, click **middle**, and the cut text will be pasted in to that window. Similarly, if you highlight a region of text in another X window (e.g., in an **xterm** window by clicking **left** and holding it down while moving it), you can paste this text into an Emacs window by clicking **middle**. This can be extremely useful; for example, if you are reading mail in a mail window, you can use Emacs to compose replies that contain portions of the original messages by cutting and pasting those portions from the mail window to the Emacs window.

The commands **C-right** and **C-S-right** are convenient ways to manipulate windows. They have the same effects as the standard Emacs commands noted in the table above, except that **C-right** command first selects the window to which the mouse is pointing. In other words: if you want one of your windows split vertically, move the mouse to the window you want to split and click **C-right**. Emacs will split that window, whether or not the Emacs cursor was in it.

The remaining two mouse commands take advantage of Emacs' ability to build popup X menus. **C-S-left** (**x-buffer-menu**) produces a popup menu of all the current buffers in your Emacs session, rather like the **C-x C-b** (**list-buffers**) command, and it allows you to select a buffer with the mouse. Hit **C-S-left** and hold it down for a second; a window that looks like Figure 12-2 will appear.

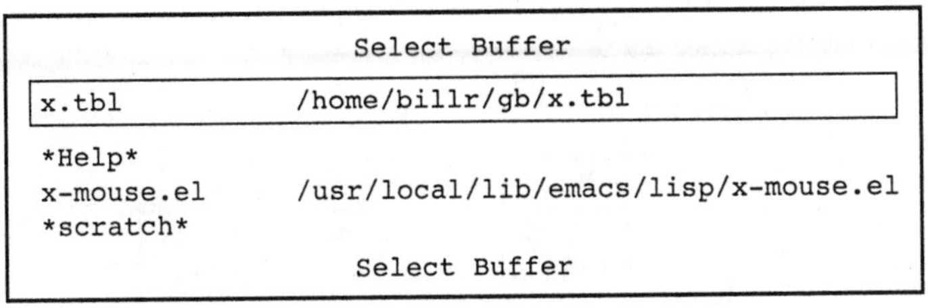

```
                     Select Buffer
 ┌────────────────────────────────────────────────────────┐
 │ x.tbl            /home/billr/gb/x.tbl                    │
 └────────────────────────────────────────────────────────┘
   *Help*
   x-mouse.el      /usr/local/lib/emacs/lisp/x-mouse.el
   *scratch*
                     Select Buffer
```

Figure 12-2. Select Buffer

After the popup menu appears, you can let go of the mouse button. To select a buffer to go in the current window, move the mouse to the desired buffer and click any mouse button. To cancel this command, simply move the mouse outside the popup menu and click any button.

An even more powerful feature is **C-S-middle** (**x-help**). This gives you a "stack" (or *card deck*) of popup menus that duplicate the various **C-h** help commands described in the next chapter. The stack looks like Figure 12-3.

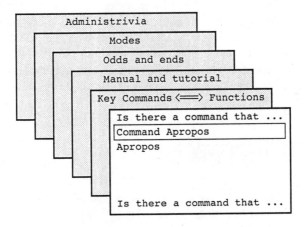

Figure 12-3. Command Apropos

If you move the mouse towards the upper left along the title bars of each card in the deck, the card will pop up to the front and you will see its complete list of options. For example, the card titled "Key Commands <==> Functions" looks like Figure 12-4.

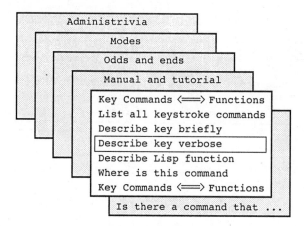

Figure 12-4. Key Commands—Functions

As with the buffer menu above, you can let go of the mouse button once the help menu stack appears. Move the mouse along the tops of the cards to get at the card you want, then move the mouse down to get the option you want. Hit any mouse button to select that option. For example, if you move your mouse down to the "Describe key verbose" line and click a button, you will be prompted in the minibuffer for a keystroke sequence. Say you type **C-w**; you will see a ***Help*** window (an Emacs window, not an X popup window) with the full description of the **kill-region** command. For a full description of this and other help commands, most of which are available as options on X help stack menus, see the next chapter.

Creating Mouse Commands

You can create your own mouse commands in a way very similar to the key binding technique covered in Chapter 9, *Customizing Emacs*. Recall that we used the function **define-key** to bind commands to keystrokes; we can use the same function to bind commands to mouse clicks. Key bindings involve *keymaps*, or arrays of (keystroke, command) pairs; mouse bindings involve the special keymap **mouse-map**.

Whereas the standard key bindings use character strings to specify keystrokes, Emacs' X interface uses a set of special variables to specify mouse clicks. These variables have names beginning with **x-button** and ending with descriptions of the particular mouse button. For example, the variable for **left** is **x-button-left**; for **C-right** it's **x-button-c-right**; for **C-S-middle** it's **x-button-c-s-middle**.[3]

Here is the format of the commands you would put in your *.emacs* to bind mouse clicks:

```
(define-key mouse-map x-button-click 'command-name)
```

Note the single quote preceding **command-name**. For example, the default binding for **right** looks like this:

```
(define-key mouse-map x-button-right 'x-cut-text)
```

But let's say you want to change it so that **right** kills like **C-w** rather than copying like **ESC-w**. You would put the following in your *.emacs* file:

```
(define-key mouse-map x-button-right 'x-cut-and-wipe-text)
```

Then let's say you want to bind **C-middle**, the original binding of **x-cut-and-wipe-text**, to the **save-buffer** command. This line in your *.emacs* will do it:

```
(define-key mouse-map x-button-c-middle 'save-buffer)
```

This has one little problem: it will save the buffer corresponding to the window the *Emacs cursor* is in, regardless of where the mouse is. Here is a simple LISP function you can use to solve this problem:

```
(defun x-mouse-save-buffer (arg)
   "Select Emacs window mouse is on and offer to save its buffer."
   (if (x-mouse-select arg)
       (save-buffer)))
```

Notice that it isn't necessary to put an **(interactive)** line in the definition of an X mouse function. Even if you aren't a LISP programmer, you can use this function by typing it into your *.emacs*; follow it with this line to bind it to **C-middle**:

```
(define-key mouse-map x-button-c-middle 'x-mouse-save-buffer)
```

If you do know LISP (and/or if you have read Chapter 11, *Emacs LISP Programming*), then read on and you will see how this function can serve as a blueprint for writing simple mouse commands of your own.

The argument **arg** is passed to all mouse commands when the mouse button is clicked; it is nothing more than the X and Y coordinates of the mouse relative to the top-left of the entire Emacs X window. The function **x-mouse-select** selects the Emacs window where the mouse is and moves the Emacs cursor there; it returns the mouse's coordinates relative to that window, or **nil** if the select failed

---

[3] If your keyboard has a META key, you can use such things as **x-button-c-m-right**. The **m** goes after **c** (if any) and before **s** (if any) in mouse button names.

for some reason. If the **x-mouse-select** succeeds, then the above function offers to save the buffer in the selected window in the normal way.

Here are a few more ideas for simple mouse functions that you can try by adapting **x-mouse-save-buffer**. The first two are direct adaptations, while the third is a bit more complex:

x-mouse-enlarge-window

> Select the window the mouse is in and enlarge it as if **C-x ^** (**enlarge-window**) were clicked.

x-mouse-delete-window

> Select the window the mouse is in and delete it as if **C-x 0** (**delete-window**) were clicked.

x-mouse-buffer-another-window

> Take the buffer in the window the *Emacs cursor* is in and display it in another window, that which the *mouse* is in. Hint: the function (**current-buffer**) returns the buffer displayed in the current window, i.e., the one the Emacs cursor is in.

Of course, you can create arbitrarily complex mouse functions if you are an ambitious LISP hacker. There are a few functions other than **x-select-window** that you might find useful. For example, **x-store-cut-buffer** takes a string argument and stores it in the X cut buffer, while **x-get-cut-buffer** does the opposite—it gets the text in the X cut buffer and returns it as a string. Consult the file *x-mouse.el* in your system's Emacs LISP directory for more information.

Creating Popup Menus

If you are really ambitious, you may want to create your own popup menus. Emacs provides a single function, **x-popup-menu**, to enable you to build menus in the card stack style used in the help menu system described above. The format of its arguments is a bit complex, but once you understand it, you will find it easy to create menus. The format looks like this:

```
(x-popup-menu arg
        '("title"
          ("title for card 1"
           ("item 1" . value-1)
           ("item 2" . value-2)
           (...))
          ("title for card 2"
           ("item 1" . value-1)
```

```
("item 2" . value-2)
(...))
(...)))
```

Be sure to include the single quote before ("title" and the dots (periods) between each pair of (item, value). The first argument to this function, **arg**, is the same as in the functions described above—it contains the X and Y coordinates of the mouse arrow when the menu is invoked. The initial *title* is the string to be used as the title of the entire menu (card stack), though this doesn't actually appear when the menu is displayed. Each *title for card N* is the title to be used in the top and bottom of each menu card. The rest of the description for each card is a list of *dot-pairs* (*item, value*), where *item* is a string that goes on the menu card and *value* is the value that the entire **x-popup-menu** function returns (as a LISP symbol) when that item is selected.

As a simple example, we'll construct a two-card menu with several commands that have to do with window manipulation:

```
(x-popup-menu
 arg
 '("Window Command Menu"
   ("Vertical Window Commands"
    ("Split window" . split-window-vertically)
    ("Enlarge window" . enlarge-window)
    ("Shrink window" . shrink-window)
    ("One window" . delete-other-windows))
   ("Horizontal Window Commands"
    ("Split window" . split-window-horizontally)
    ("Enlarge window" . enlarge-window-horizontally)
    ("Shrink window" . shrink-window-horizontally)
    ("One window" . delete-other-windows))))
```

When you use this menu and select an item, **x-popup-menu** returns the function selected; for example, if you click the mouse on the line **Enlarge window** of the first card (**Vertical Window Commands**), **x-popup-window** will return the function **enlarge-window** as a symbol. It will not *run* this function—yet. We need to surround **x-popup-menu** with some more LISP code to get that to happen. Specifically, we need the function **call-interactively**, which takes a LISP symbol and runs the function that the symbol names.[4] The following code defines a function that does the trick:

```
(defun x-window-command-menu (arg)
  (let ((menu-selection
          (x-popup-menu
            arg
            '("Window Command Menu"
              ("Vertical Window Commands"
               ("Split window" . split-window-vertically)
               ("Enlarge window" . enlarge-window)
               ("Shrink window" . shrink-window)
               ("One window" . delete-other-windows))
              ("Horizontal Window Commands"
               ("Split window" . split-window-horizontally)
               ("Enlarge window" . enlarge-window-horizontally)
               ("Shrink window" . shrink-window-horizontally)
               ("One window" . delete-other-windows))))))
    (if (and menu-selection (x-mouse-select arg))
        (call-interactively menu-selection))))
```

In this function, the **let** block runs the function **x-popup-menu** and stores the result—the selected menu item—in the variable **menu-selection**. If the menu selection fails for any reason (e.g., the user decides to abort the process by clicking the mouse outside the menu), **x-popup-menu** returns **nil**. Then, **x-mouse-select** is called to select the Emacs window the mouse is on. If this and the **x-popup-menu** call both succeeded, the latter's return value is called as a function.

Finally, we need to bind this function to a mouse button, for example, to **C-right**:

```
(define-key mouse-map x-button-c-right 'x-window-command-menu)
```

If you put this and the above function in your *.emacs*, you will have the popup menu available the next time you invoke Emacs. When you click **C-right**, you will see a card stack menu that looks like Figure 12-5.

---

[4] The LISP primitive function **funcall** is really the most basic way to do this; **call-interactively** is more general because it also allows the user to supply arguments to the function (from the minibuffer or via a prefix argument) according to its (**interactive** ...) declaration. See Chapter 11, *Emacs LISP Programming*, for details.

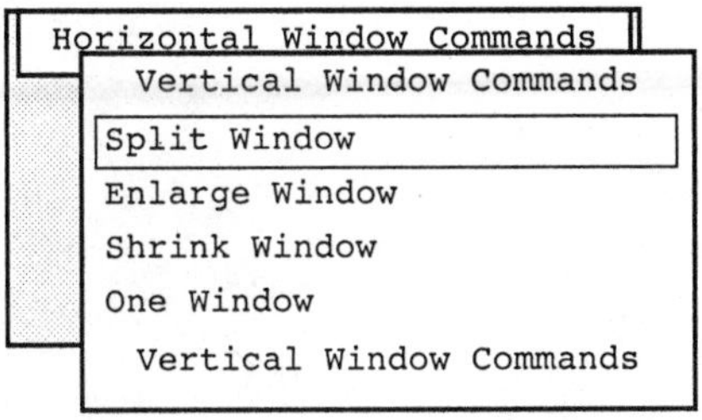

```
┌─────────────────────────────────────┐
│ Horizontal Window Commands │        │
│ ┌──────────────────────────────────────┐
│ │   Vertical Window Commands           │
│ │ ┌──────────────────────────────────┐ │
│ │ │ Split Window                     │ │
│ │ └──────────────────────────────────┘ │
│ │   Enlarge Window                     │
│ │   Shrink Window                      │
│ │   One Window                         │
│ │                                      │
│ │     Vertical Window Commands         │
│ │                                      │
│ └──────────────────────────────────────┘
```

Figure 12-5. Window Command Menu

It is important to realize that this example used string constants for all of its menu items. Of course, you can use any string values at all—including functions that return string values. For example, the function **x-buffer-menu** that is bound to the mouse button **C-S-left** constructs a menu by getting a list of currently active buffers and their associated files, and formatting them into a menu. It uses such built-in Emacs functions as **buffer-list** (return a list of all active buffers), **buffer-name** (return the name of a buffer as a string), and **buffer-file-name** (return the name of a buffer's associated file). For more details, and for more ideas for your own mouse and menu commands, you may want to look at the file *x-mouse.el* in your system's Emacs LISP directory.

13

Online Help

Completion
Help Commands
Help in Complex Emacs Commands

Emacs has the most comprehensive online help facility of any text editor—and one of the best such facilities of any program at all. In fact, Emacs' online help facilities probably cut down the time it took for us to write this book by an order of magnitude. There are three basic aspects of Emacs' online help:

- *Completion*, in which Emacs helps you finish typing names of things (such as filenames).

- The help key (normally **C-h**), which allows you to get help on a wide variety of topics and gives you access to such tools as the **info** database and the Emacs tutorial.

- Help facilities of complex commands like **query-replace** and **dired**.

This chapter will deal with all of these in turn.

Completion

We saw an example of Emacs' completion facility in Chapter 1, *Emacs Basics*. Completion is more than just a feature—it is a general principle in the design of Emacs. It can be articulated as follows:

> *If you have to type in the name of something, and that name is one of a finite number of possibilities, Emacs should figure out what you mean after the smallest possible number of keystrokes.*

In other words, you can type in the *shortest unambiguous prefix* and tell Emacs to figure out the rest of the name. By "shortest unambiguous prefix," we mean "enough of the name, starting from the beginning, to distinguish it from the other possibilities." Several important things in Emacs have names that are chosen from a finite number of possibilities, including:

- Commands

- Files in a given directory

- Buffers

- Emacs variables

Most of the time, completion is available when you are prompted for a name of something in the minibuffer. While you are typing in the name, there are three characters you can use to tell Emacs to help complete it for you: **TAB**, **SPACE**, and question mark (**?**). These do the following things:

TAB   Complete the name as far as possible.

SPACE   Complete the name out to the next puncutation character.

?   List the choices at this point in a `*Completion*` window.

You will probably find TAB to be the most useful.

As a running example, assume you have typed **C-x C-f** to visit a file, and the file you want to visit is a C program called *program.c*. Let's say you type **pro** and press **TAB**; Emacs will respond by completing the name to the full *program.c*. If you press **SPACE**, Emacs will only complete as far as *program*. After Emacs completes the name, you can press **RETURN** to visit the file.

How much of the name do you need to type in before you can use completion? That depends on the other possible choices in the given situation. If *program.c* were the only file in your directory, you could just type **p** and press **TAB**.[1] If there were other files in your directory and none of them have names beginning with **p**, you could do the same thing. But if you had a file called *problem.c*, you would have to type **prog** before you press **TAB**; in this case, "prog" is the shortest unambiguous prefix. If you just type in **pro** and press **TAB**, Emacs will respond with a `*Completion*` window containing a list of the completion choices, in this case *program.c* and *problem.c*, and return your cursor to the minibuffer so that you can finish typing the filename. The same thing would happen if you typed a question mark instead of TAB. At this point, you can type **g** and press **TAB** again; Emacs will complete the name to *program.c*.

As another example, let's say you have documentation for your C program in the file *program.doc*, and you want to visit it. You press **C-x C-f** and type **prog** at the prompt, followed by **TAB**. Emacs will complete out to *program.*. At this point, you can type **d** and press **TAB** again; Emacs will complete the entire *program.doc*. In other words, you can use completion repeatedly—not just once—when specifying a name.

Finally, let's say you also have a file in your directory just called *program*, which is the result of compiling your C file; but you still want to visit the documentation file. You type in **prog** and press **TAB**; Emacs completes out to *program*. At this point, TAB and SPACE do different things. If you press **TAB** again, Emacs will respond with the message "[Complete, but not unique]" in the minibuffer, but if you press **SPACE**, Emacs will assume that you aren't interested in the file *program* and will attempt to complete further. Since you have the files *program.c* and *program.doc*, Emacs will only complete out to *program.* and you will have to type **d** and press **TAB** again.

Completion works the same way with buffer names, e.g., when you type **C-x b** to switch to another buffer in the current window. It also works with command names when you type **ESC-x**—but with one added feature. Notice that when you specify a file or buffer name, it is possible that the file/buffer you want doesn't already exist (for example, when you want to create a new file). In this case, of course, you must type in the entire file/buffer name and press **RETURN**. But when you type **ESC-x** for a command, there is no possibility of the command not existing. Therefore Emacs will automatically attempt to do completion on command names when you press **RETURN**.

For example, if you want to put a buffer for a text file in fill mode (see Chapter 2, *Editing Files*), you can type **ESC-x auto-f** and press **RETURN** instead of typing the entire **ESC-x auto-fill-mode**. If you type in a non-unique (ambiguous) prefix

---

[1] You can't just press **TAB** without typing the **p** because the current and parent directories, named **.** and **..** respectively, are also file choices. Normally, Emacs runs **dired** if you visit a file that is a directory.

of a command name— e.g., if you type **ESC-x aut**—and press **RETURN**, then RETURN will act just like TAB; in this case, it will complete out to "auto-". If you press **RETURN** again, Emacs will respond with a `*Completion*` window listing the choices, which in this case are **auto-fill-mode** and **auto-save-mode**. To get **auto-fill-mode**, you will have to type **f** and press **RETURN** again.

Completion on command names with RETURN is *very* convenient. After you have used Emacs for a while, you will become familiar with the shortest unambiguous prefixes for commands you use often, and you can save a considerable amount of typing by using these prefixes instead of the full names.[2]

Emacs can also do completion on the names of Emacs variables. In Chapter 2, *Editing Files*, and elsewhere, we saw how you can use **ESC-x set-variable** to change the values of Emacs variables. The RETURN feature described above works on variables as well as commands; therefore you can use completion, including RETURN, when doing **ESC-x set-variable**. Actually, commands and variables are both special kinds of Emacs LISP *symbols*, and Emacs can do completion with RETURN on all kinds of LISP symbols. Completion on LISP symbols will come in handy when you are using some of the help commands described later in this chapter.

Customizing Completion

If you have read Chapter 9, *Customizing Emacs*, and you are comfortable with setting Emacs variables, you should know that there are a few variables you can set to customize the way Emacs does completion. The variable **completion-auto-help** determines whether a `*Completion*` window automatically appears when you try to use SPACE or TAB on an ambiguous prefix. Its default is **t**, meaning that such windows will automatically appear. If you set it to **nil**, instead of a completion window appearing, Emacs just displays the message "[Next char not unique]" for a couple of seconds in the minibuffer.

If you are a programmer or if you use text formatters like TeX, you will be creating files that are not meant for humans to read, such as object files created by compilers and print files created by text formatters. Ideally, you wouldn't want Emacs to bother with these files when you are doing completion; for example, if you have the files *program.c* and *program.o* (object-code output from the compiler), you will only want Emacs to recognize the former. Emacs does have a feature that deals with this—indeed, you may already have noticed that in this kind of situation, if you type "program" and press **TAB**, Emacs ignores *program.o* and

---

[2] For example, if you make changes to your *.emacs* file regularly, you will appreciate that **ESC-x eval-c** is an acceptable prefix for **ESC-x eval-current-buffer**.

completes out to *program.c*. The variable **completion-ignored-extensions** controls this; it is a list of filename suffixes that Emacs ignores during filename completion. By default, the list includes tilde (˜) for Emacs backup files, *.o* for programmers, various suffixes for TeX users, *.elc* (byte-compiled Emacs LISP) for Emacs customizers, and others. (Of course, if you really want to look at these files, you can type in their names manually.)

You can add your own "ignored" suffix to the list by putting a line of this form in your *.emacs* file:

```
(setq completion-ignored-extensions
      (cons "suffix" completion-ignored-extensions))
```

For example, let's say you are doing text processing with a printer that prints PostScript, and your text processor produces print files with the suffix *.ps*. You don't want to look at these files, so you put the following line in your *.emacs*:

```
(setq completion-ignored-extensions
      (cons ".ps" completion-ignored-extensions))
```

Finally, you can tell Emacs to ignore case distinctions when doing completion by setting the variable **completion-ignore-case** to **t** (or any value other than **nil**). Its default value is **nil**, meaning that Emacs will respect case distinctions.

Help Commands

Emacs has many, many help commands, which are available as standard Emacs commands or as options to the **C-h** help key.[3] They can be used to find information about commands, keystrokes, variables, modes, and various things about Emacs in general. The most basic help command is **C-h C-h (help-for-help)**; the second keystroke is **C-h** even if you have rebound your help key. This causes Emacs to print the message:

A B C F I K L M N S T V W C-c C-d C-n C-w. Type C-h again for more help:

in the minibuffer. The listed keystrokes are all those that invoke help commands. For example, if you type **K** (or **k**) at this point, you will be invoking the **describe-key** command; as we will see, this is as if you just typed **C-h k** at any time.

---

[3] If you have rebound your help key, you will need to mentally substitute the new binding for **C-h** throughout the remainder of this chapter—with a few exceptions, which will be noted.

But if you type **C-h** again at this point—it must be **C-h** even if your help key is rebound—you will see a `*Help*` buffer in a window with descriptions of all the help commands, and the message:

```
A B C F I K L M N S T V W C-c C-d C-n C-w or Space to scroll:
```

in the minibuffer. You can type any one of these help keys, or if you press **SPACE**, the `*Help*` window will scroll down as if you press **C-v**. Any other key will abort the whole process. If you scroll to the bottom of the help documentation, you can type a help key or any other key to abort.

The keys listed in the above minibuffer messages are those that, when appended to your help key, run Emacs' help commands at any time. Now we will discuss each of these. Help commands divide into two general categories: those that provide answers to specific questions and those that give general information about Emacs.

You will find the help commands in the former category to be invaluable after you have become comfortable with Emacs. Because it is so large and functionally rich, there will be times when you need to look up a detail such as a keystroke or command name, or when you need to do something with Emacs that you don't know exactly how to do. As we've repeated again and again throughout this book, Emacs probably does what you want; you just need to figure out how. The help commands let you find these things out immediately, without leaving Emacs and without being a slave to your reference manual.

Detail Information

Let's start with the help commands that are useful when you need to look up a specific detail. You will probably use the commands listed in Table 13-1, most often.

Table 13-1. Detail Information Help Commands

Keystrokes	Command Name	Question Answered
C-h c	describe-key-briefly	What command does this keystroke sequence run?
C-h k	describe-key	What command does this keystroke sequence run, and what does it do?
C-h l	view-lossage	What are the last 100 characters I typed?
C-h w	where-is	What is the key binding for this command?

Table 13-1. Detail Information Help Commands (continued)

Keystrokes	Command Name	Question Answered
C-h f	describe-function	What does this function do?
C-h v	describe-variable	What does this variable mean, and what is its value?
C-h m	describe-mode	Tell me about the mode the current buffer is in.
C-h b	describe-bindings	What are all the key bindings for this buffer?
C-h s	describe-syntax	What is the syntax table for this buffer?

Perhaps the most common situation that calls for online help is when you press the wrong key and something happens to your buffer—but you're not sure what. Usually, the safest thing to do is to press **C-x u** (**undo**). But there are several cases in which this won't help, e.g., a runaway **replace-string**. If you remember what you typed, you can use **C-h c** (**describe-key-briefly**) to see what command was run; just retype the offending keystroke(s) at the prompt and Emacs will respond with the name of the command bound to the key(s) in the minibuffer. If the command name alone doesn't help, **C-h k** (**describe-key**) will pop up a `*Help*` window with a description of the command as well as its name and key binding. However, if you don't know what keys you pressed, you can type **C-h l** (**view-lossage**). This will pop up a `*Help*` window showing the last 100 keystrokes you typed; the offending ones will likely be near the end, and you can use **C-h c** or **C-h k** with those keystrokes.

Now suppose you want information on a command that isn't bound to keystrokes. Type **C-h f** (**describe-function**) and enter the name of the command at the prompt, and Emacs will respond with a `*Help*` window containing the documentation for that command. If you remember the name of a command but forget its binding, type **C-h w** (**where-is**). This is the "opposite" of **C-h c**; it shows the key binding for a given command in the minibuffer, or the message "*command-name* is not on any keys" if the command has no binding.

You may forget a detail that involves the value of a variable; for example: will Emacs respect or ignore case during a search (the variable **case-fold-search**)? How often are my buffers being auto-saved (**auto-save-interval**)? If you type **C-h v** (**describe-variable**) followed by the name of the variable, Emacs will put its value as well as its documentation in a `*Help*` window. **C-h f, C-h w,** and **C-h v** all allow you to use completion when typing command/variable names. **C-h f** and **C-h v** are also especially useful to Emacs LISP programmers; note that

C-h f can give you information on *all* functions, not just those bound to key-strokes as commands.

Another common help situation arises when you use a special mode, such as shell mode or a mode for a programming language or text processor, and you forget a command specific to that mode or some other characteristic such as indentation conventions. If you type **C-h m (describe-mode)** in a buffer running the mode, Emacs will pop up a `*Help*` window showing the mode's documentation. Documentation for a mode usually includes all of its local key bindings (i.e., all the commands special to the mode and their associated keystrokes), customization variables, and other interesting characteristics.

The last two help commands in Table 13-1 are not particularly useful except to high-powered Emacs customizers. **C-h b (describe-bindings)** gives you a `*Help*` window showing *all* key bindings active in the current buffer, including local (buffer-specific) as well as global ones. **C-h s (describe-syntax)** produces a `*Help*` window with a description of the *syntax table* (see Chapter 10, *Emacs for Programmers*) active in the current buffer.

Apropos Commands

Another type of help command applies when you want Emacs to do something but you're not sure exactly what command to use or what variable to set. This is the *apropos* command, which resembles a rudimentary information retrieval system of the type found at many libraries. There are two forms of the apropos command, shown in Table 13-2.

Table 13-2. Apropos Commands

Keystrokes	Command Name	Question Answered
C-h a	command-apropos	What commands involve this concept?
(none)	apropos	What functions and variables involve this concept?

Both of these commands prompt for *regular expressions* (see Chapter 3, *Search and Replace Operations*). When you type **C-h a** followed by a regular expression, Emacs finds all the commands that match it; it displays their key bindings (if any) and the first lines of their documentation in a `*Help*` window. (Documentation of Emacs commands and variables is usually written so that the first line is a summary and the rest is elaboration.) As always, if you are leery of using regular expressions, you can use regular search strings as long as you stick to non-special characters. For example, if you want to know what replace commands Emacs supports, press **C-h a** and then type **replace**; Emacs will display a list of information on the following commands:

- **query-replace**

- **query-replace-regexp**

- **replace-buffer-in-windows**

- **replace-regexp**

- **replace-string**

- **tags-query-replace**

If you have ever used an information retrieval system, you already know that some skill is needed to use such a system effectively. You need to choose your concepts (search strings) carefully, so that they aren't too general (too much output to wade through) or too specific (too little output, making it less likely that you get the information you want). This problem is compounded when you use the **apropos** command, which is the same as **command-apropos** except that it reports on *all* functions (including internal Emacs functions) and variables as well as commands. If you type in a search string that is too general, not only will Emacs produce an enormous buffer of help information but it will take a long time to do so. For example, invoking **apropos** with the argument "file" or "buffer" causes Emacs to "crunch" for quite a while (depending on the speed of your computer) and results in output listing well over a hundred Emacs objects. In general, you may have to invoke **apropos** or **command-apropos** a few times to get the information you want (in terms of size as well as relevance).

Apropos is usually overkill—unless you are an Emacs LISP programmer who needs information on non-command functions. However, you must use it if you want information on variables. There is no **variable-apropos** command. But we think one should be included, so here is LISP code for such a function; it was adapted directly from the code for **command-apropos**. There is also a line of LISP that binds this command to **C-h C-v**. If you like, you can put this code verbatim into your *.emacs* file and have the command available in future Emacs sessions:

```
(defun variable-apropos (string)
  "Like apropos but lists only symbols that are names of variables
that are user-modifiable."
  (interactive "sVariable apropos (regexp): ")
  (let ((message
          (let ((standard-output (get-buffer-create *Help*)))
            (print-help-return-message 'identity))))
    (apropos string 'user-variable-p)
    (and message (message message)))))

(define-key help-map "C-v" 'variable-apropos)
```

As an example of this command, you can type **C-h C-v** and type **auto-save** at the prompt; Emacs will respond with information about the variables **auto-save-default**, **auto-save-interval**, **auto-save-visited-file-name**, and **delete-auto-save-files**. To find the value and full description of one of these variables, use **C-h v**.

General Information

The rest of the help commands provide general information about Emacs. These are shown in Table 13-3.

Table 13-3. General Information Help Commands

Keystrokes	Command Name	Action
C-h t	help-with-tutorial	Run the Emacs tutorial.
C-h i	info	Start the info documentation reader.
C-h n	view-emacs-news	View news about changes in Emacs from older versions.
C-h C-c	describe-copying	View the Emacs General Public License. (See Appendix F.)
C-h C-d	describe-distribution	View information on ordering Emacs from FSF. (See Appendix A.)
C-h C-w	describe-no-warranty	View the (non-)warranty for Emacs. (See the "NO WARRANTY" section of Appendix F.)

The most important of these for beginning users is **C-h t** (**help-with-tutorial**), which deletes all extra windows (leaving just one) and starts up a learn-by-doing tutorial. Actually, it displays a file called *TUTORIAL* in the window. If you are just starting Emacs, you can use the tutorial to get experience with the following Emacs features:

- Basic cursor motion

- Delete and yank

- Visiting and saving files

- Buffers

- Text and auto-fill modes

- Incremental search

- Basic help commands

You might want to use the tutorial along with Chapter 1, *Emacs Basics*, and Chapter 2, *Editing Files*. It is helpful, but of necessity it covers only the most basic information.

Much more comprehensive general documentation can be obtained by typing **C-h i** (**info**), which starts up the **info** documentation reader. This is a browser for lots of information about Emacs (and other GNU software) that looks a bit like a modern hypertext system.[4] That is, it is organized as *trees* of information *nodes*. If you want information on a certain topic, you can select its tree; the nodes of the tree contain information on subtopics, sub-subtopics, etc., organized hierarchically.

When you type **C-h i**, you will see a read-only buffer containing the *directory node* of the **Info** system in a window in Info mode. Complete details about using this system are beyond the scope of this book, but **Info** is largely self-documenting. If you press **h** while in **Info**, you will get a tutorial on **Info** analogous to the one described above for basic Emacs commands. You can also type **C-h m** (**describe-mode**) to get help on Info mode; this will summarize the commands available.

Perhaps the most important of the remaining Emacs help commands for hard-core users and customizers is **C-h n** (**view-emacs-news**), which visits the file *NEWS* that comes with Emacs. This contains a history of changes made to Emacs since the last major version; for example, all changes in Version 18 (with respect to Version 17) and all changes to Version 18 up to the latest minor version (which in our case is Version 18.57).[5] This can be a very *long* file if there have been several minor releases since the last major version—in our case, the file is over 1600 lines long. If you want to look through it for changes to a specific aspect of Emacs, use an appropriate search command. But if you just want to skim it, note that this file was intended for use with outline mode: topics are introduced on lines beginning with *, and subtopics are introduced on lines beginning with **. Use outline mode to skim the file; see Chapter 6, *Simple Text Formatting and Specialized Editing*, for information.

Help in Complex Emacs Commands

Many of the more complicated Emacs commands include their own sets of keystroke functions. These commands will often have their own "help" functionality,

---

[4] In fact, it is one of the earliest sucessful examples of a working hypertext system.

[5] This does not, however, mean that 57 minor versions were publicly released since Version 18!

but help is invoked with **?** rather than the standard help key. Here is a summary of some popular complex commands and what **?** does within each of them:

dired (C-x d)

> You will see a list of the most often-used available commands in the mini-buffer. *This list is not complete.* Type **C-h m** (**describe-mode**) for more comprehensive documentation.

query-replace (ESC-%)

> You will see a `*Help*` window listing the available commands. Typing **C-h** (even if your help key is rebound) does the same thing. This also works with **query-replace-regexp**.

list-buffers (C-x C-b)

> You will see a `*Help*` window giving information on buffer menu mode. This has the same effect as typing **C-h m** (**describe-mode**).

Completion

> When you are responding to a minibuffer prompt with the name of some-thing on which Emacs can do completion, typing **?** at any time will give you a `*Completion*` window with the choices available at that point. Completion is explained earlier in this chapter.

A

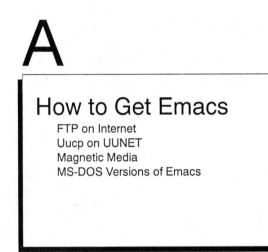

How to Get Emacs

FTP on Internet
Uucp on UUNET
Magnetic Media
MS-DOS Versions of Emacs

As we discussed in the preface, Emacs is "free." This doesn't necessarily mean that it won't cost you any money, but the Free Software Foundation is committed to making Emacs as easy to obtain as possible. If you get it from FSF, they do charge—but a fraction of the price of other similar software, and only to cover their media, shipping, and handling costs. Yet FSF *encourages* you to get a copy from a friend if this is more convenient. If you are in an environment with lots of machines (such as a large company or a university department), and someone else already has Emacs, you are more than welcome to get it from him or her.

If no one in your organization has Emacs already, but you have access to Internet or UUNET, you can still get it without the expense and inconvenience of magnetic media by copying the software from a machine at MIT called "prep". We will give step-by-step instructions for both networks. Before you follow them, go to the directory where you want the software to reside, and *make sure you have at least 25 megabytes of disk storage available.*

To get Emacs via Internet, you need to use the File Transfer Protocol (FTP) utility. In particular, you will use anonymous FTP; machines that support this allow anyone to connect to them, although with some (understandable) access restrictions. The following UNIX session will demonstrate how to do this; the commands you type appear in **boldface** and responses appear in regular font. We assume that **$** is your UNIX prompt. NOTE: at the password prompt, type anything you want, but don't just press **RETURN**.

```
$ ftp prep.ai.mit.edu
Connected to prep.ai.mit.edu.
220 aeneas FTP server (Version 4.136 Mon Oct 31 23:18:38 EST 1988) ready.
Name (prep.ai.mit.edu:): anonymous
331 Guest login ok, send ident as password.
Password:
230 Guest login ok, access restrictions apply.
ftp> binary
200 Type set to I.
ftp> cd /pub/gnu
250 CWD command successful.
ftp> ls emacs-[0-9][0-9].[0-9][0-9].tar.Z
200 PORT command successful.
150 Opening data connection for /bin/ls (128.119.40.122,2653) (0 bytes).
emacs-18.57.tar.Z
226 Transfer complete.
remote: emacs-[0-9][0-9].[0-9][0-9].tar.Z
19 bytes received in 0.023 seconds (0.79 Kbytes/s)
```

Note: the above *emacs-18.57.tar.Z* may vary; in the following, substitute whatever FTP actually lists:

```
ftp> get emacs-18.57.tar.Z
200 PORT command successful.
150 Opening data connection for emacs-18.57.tar.Z (128.119.40.122,2654) (3988838 bytes)
```

At this point, expect a wait of ten minutes or so as the file is sent to you. It is a large compressed **tar** archive. The next steps are to quit FTP and uncompress the archive:

```
226 Transfer complete.
local: emacs-18.57.tar.Z remote: emacs-18.57.tar.Z
4009261 bytes received in 3.6e+02 seconds (11 Kbytes/s)
ftp> quit
221 Goodbye.
$ uncompress emacs-18.57.tar
```

This will create the file *emacs-18.57.tar*, without the *.Z*, which is the uncompressed archive. Depending on your machine, this may take several minutes. Finally, you need to "unpack" the files from the archive:

```
$ tar xvf emacs-18.57.tar
x emacs-18.57/
x emacs-18.57/ChangeLog, 954 bytes, 2 blocks
x emacs-18.57/etc/
x emacs-18.57/etc/3B-MAXMEM, 1913 bytes, 4 blocks
x emacs-18.57/etc/APOLLO, 1836 bytes, 4 blocks
x emacs-18.57/etc/APPLE, 3102 bytes, 7 blocks
x emacs-18.57/etc/CCADIFF, 6938 bytes, 14 blocks
. . .
```

This list of created files goes on for a while—about 700 files for Version 18.57. If you don't want to see the list, omit the **v** from the tar command.

You are now finished getting all of the files for Emacs. In the top-level directory (*emacs-18.57* in this example), you will find files called *INSTALL* and *README*; these are the ones for you (or your system administrator) to read next so that you can build and install Emacs on your machine.

Uucp on UUNET

You can also get GNU Emacs via anonymous **uucp** from UUNET. UUNET maintains a large database of publicly available software, including the source code for many BSD UNIX utilities. To use their services, you must either subscribe or dial in to their system using a 900 number.[1] As of this printing, you will be billed at $0.40/minute for using the 900 number. Subscribers may use an 800 number to access the system.

In either case, contact the following address for more information about UUNET and the services it provides:

> UUNET Communications Services
> 3110 Fairview Park Drive, Suite 570
> Falls Church, VA 22042
> phone: 703 876 5050
> e-mail: info@uunet.uu.net

Setting up a connection to UUNET involves nothing more than setting up a standard UUCP connection; for information about how to do this, see the Nutshell Handbook, *Managing UUCP and Usenet*, by Grace Todino and Tim O'Reilly.

---

[1] The number is 900-468-7727; the account name is **uucp**, and there's no password.

Once you have set up a connection, you should first retrieve an index that shows you where the publicly available files are:

```
$ uucp uunet\!~/ls-1R.Z ~uucp
```

The file will eventually arrive in your UUCP home directory (usually */usr/spool/uucppublic*). To minimize transfer time and save disk space, this file is encoded. To convert it into a readable representation, give the following command:[2]

```
$ uncompress ls-1R
```

You don't need the *.Z* suffix; **uncompress** supplies it automatically, and removes the suffix from the decoded file's name. When you have a human-readable version of this file, look through it (which may be a bit painful) to find where the GNU Emacs sources are stored. You're looking for something like this:

```
/usr/spool/ftp/gnu/emacs:
total 4455
-rw-rw-r-- 1 kyle         100000 Mar  1 14:29 18.57.Z.00
-rw-rw-r-- 1 kyle         100000 Mar  1 14:29 18.57.Z.01
-rw-rw-r-- 1 kyle         100000 Mar  1 14:29 18.57.Z.02
-rw-rw-r-- 1 kyle         100000 Mar  1 14:29 18.57.Z.03
-rw-rw-r-- 1 kyle         100000 Mar  1 14:29 18.57.Z.04
-rw-rw-r-- 1 kyle         100000 Mar  1 14:29 18.57.Z.05
...
-rw-rw-r-- 1 kyle         100000 Mar  1 14:29 18.57.Z.36
-rw-rw-r-- 1 kyle         100000 Mar  1 14:29 18.57.Z.37
-rw-rw-r-- 1 kyle         100000 Mar  1 14:29 18.57.Z.38
-rw-rw-r-- 1 kyle          88838 Mar  1 14:29 18.57.Z.39
```

The directory */usr/spool/ftp/gnu/emacs* probably won't change, but you never know. The version number and the number of files most certainly will change. Once you've found the filenames, give a command like this:

```
$ uucp uunet\!~/gnu/emacs/18.57.Z.[0-3][0-9] ~uucp
```

When the transfer is complete (and this may take a very long time—hours if you only have a 1200 baud modem), there will be 40 or so files in your UUCP direc-

---

[2] Many UNIX systems have the **compress** and **uncompress** utilities, but some don't. If yours doesn't, you can also get these from UUNET. Give these commands:

```
$ uucp uunet\!~/compress.tar ~uucp
```
...wait for the transfer to complete, then...
```
$ tar xvf compress.tar
```

The **tar** command unpacks the source code for **uncompress** and **compress**. Instructions for building and using these utilities should be included in the archive.

tory. Move them to some more satisfactory place. Then start reassembling them. First, use **cat** to create a single gigantic file:

```
% cat *.Z.* >> emacs.tar.Z
```

This command is fairly risky. It is easier than listing all the filenames in order (from 00 to 39), but it's often a mistake to trust the shell's sense of numeric order. In this case, it should work; but it may not if the next version of Emacs follows different naming conventions. Now uncompress the whole mess:

```
% uncompress emacs.tar
```

This creates a giant file, which is a **tar** archive. Use **tar** to unpack it:

```
% tar xvf emacs.tar
```

This command unpacks all of the Emacs source files and directories into your current directory. Once you've done this, you're ready to begin building Emacs. Look at the *Install* and *README* files that come with the distribution to find out how.

Magnetic Media

If you don't have access to UUNET or Internet, and you can't get Emacs from anyone you know, you will have to buy it from the Free Software Foundation. They will ship it to you in any of the following formats:

- 1600 bpi reel-to-reel tape, **tar** format.

- 1600 bpi reel-to-reel tape, VAX/VMS **backup** format.

- 1/4-inch Sun cartridge tape, **tar** format.

- 1/4-inch QIC-24 DC600A cartridge tape for IBM RS/6000 systems, in AIX distribution format.

They can also sell you copies of the *GNU Emacs Reference Manual*, and, of course, all other GNU software.

Prices will vary; *at this writing*, a reel-to-reel **tar** tape costs $200. The tape includes Emacs, the Emacs Lisp Reference Manual (as *Texinfo* source, meaning that you can use TeX to format it), two Scheme interpreters, **bison** (a freeware version of the popular **yacc** parser generator), and a couple of games. You can also order formatted copies of the Emacs reference manual for $20 each, or $13 each if you order six or more.

For more information or to place an order, contact the FSF at:

> Free Software Foundation
> 675 Massachusetts Avenue
> Cambridge, MA 02139
> (617)876-3296

MS-DOS Versions of Emacs

If you are a user of MS-DOS, an editor named Freemacs is available. It claims to be compatible with GNU Emacs; we have no experience with it, and can't verify this claim. It is available under the same terms (i.e., the general public license), although it isn't a Free Software Foundation product.

Freemacs is available from the FTP site **rape.ecs.clarkson.edu** under the directory */e/freemacs*; use the procedure described above to run FTP. Freemacs sources are also available from UUNET; use the UUCP procedure given above to transfer it to your system.

If you can't get Freemacs via FTP or UUNET, you should be able to contact the author at one of the following mail addresses: **nelson@gnu.ai.mit.edu** or **nelson@clutx.clarkson.edu**. He is willing to make a DOS floppy disk for a $15 copying fee. NOTE: although Russ has a "GNU" mail address, please don't ask the Foundation itself for information about Freemacs.

Epsilon is another MS-DOS version of Emacs that deserves mention. Epsilon is a commercial product available from:

> Lugaru Software Ltd.
> 5843 Forbes Avenue
> Pittsburgh, PA 15217
> TEL: 412-421-5911
> FAX: 412-421-6371

While the authors haven't used it, Epsilon is reputed to be the best of the MS-DOS Emacs implementations.

B

Making Emacs Work the Way You Think It Should

The most frustrating part of learning Emacs is sitting down at a terminal and finding out that some "helpful" administrator has changed all the commands. At this point, you're helpless: you can't delete the global customization file, the Emacs you have doesn't match the manual (or this book), and the administrator probably didn't even think of documenting the changes.

Similar problems arise if the administrator who set up your account also gave you a "useful" private *.emacs* file. This private file may indeed be great for experienced users—but if it prevents you from learning the editor, it isn't really much help at all.

Fortunately, there is a way out. If you find yourself in this situation, delete or rename any *.emacs* file you already have. Then create a one-line *.emacs* file in your home directory. It should look exactly like this:

```
(setq inhibit-default-init t) ; no global initialization
```

Then start Emacs again.

This file prevents Emacs from reading its global initialization file.

There's still one awkward situation: what if you're sitting down at someone else's keyboard? You start Emacs, and all of a sudden you're faced with someone else's "private" keybindings and features. Even in this situation, there's a solution:

* Try using the command **emacs -q**. The **-q** option tells Emacs not to read the user's *.emacs* file before starting. By doing this, you'll avoid the user's private customizations.

* However, you still don't have your own customizations. If you want to make Emacs read your own *.emacs* file, even when you're using someone else's account, give the command **emacs -u** *yourname*. For example: **emacs -u deb** starts Emacs with the user Deb's initialization file (*˜deb/.emacs*).

The **-u** option may not work if you're on a network. It assumes either that you have the same home directory on every system, or that you have a different home directory on every system and you have an up-to-date *.emacs* file in all of your home directories. There are certainly networks that don't meet either condition. However, network configuration is not a topic we can discuss in this book. If you're interested, see the Nutshell Handbook, *Managing NFS and NIS*, by Hal Stern; it discusses the problem of networked home directories in detail.

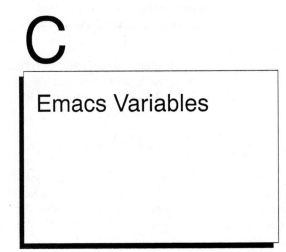

C

Emacs Variables

In this appendix, we will list several useful Emacs variables. These are grouped by category, and the variables' default values are shown (where practical to do so). For more details on specific variables, see the chapters referred to at the beginning of each table. For information on variables used in programming language modes, see Chapter 10, *Emacs for Programmers*.

Table C-1. Backups, Auto-save, and Versioning (Chapter 2)

Variable	Default	Description
make-backup-files	t	If **t**, create a backup version of the current file before saving it for the first time.

Table C-1. Backups, Auto-save, and Versioning (Chapter 2) (continued)

Variable	Default	Description
backup-by-copying	nil	If **t**, create backup files by *copying* rather than *renaming* the file being saved to a backup version. The default is renaming, which is more efficient. Copying is slightly safer; for example, a disk crash during a copy shouldn't hurt you, while a very badly-timed crash during a **mv** may destroy your backup file.[1]
version-control	nil	If **t**, create numbered versions of files as backups (with names of the form *filename⁻N⁻*). If **nil**, only do this for files that have numbered versions already. If **'never** (note the leading single quote), never make numbered versions.
kept-new-versions	2	Number of latest versions of a file to keep when a new numbered backup is made.
kept-old-versions	2	Number of oldest versions of a file to keep when a new numbered backup is made.
trim-versions-without-asking	nil	If **t**, trim excess versions (not those kept according to the above variables) without asking for confirmation first.
auto-save-default	t	If **t**, do auto-saving of every file visited.
auto-save-visited-file-name	nil	If **t**, auto-save to the file being visited rather than to a special auto-save file.
auto-save-interval	300	Number of keystrokes between auto-saving; if 0, turn off auto-saving.
delete-auto-save-files	t	Non-**nil** means delete auto-save files whenever the "real" file is saved.

---

[1] NOTE: Since backing up a file creates a new version, it will create one that is owned by you. Thus, if this variable is **nil** and the original file is not owned by you, the renamed version will be owned by you. This may be a problem if you are logged in as "root" and you are changing files that are not owned by root, such as **uucp** configuration files.

Table C-1. Backups, Auto-save, and Versioning (Chapter 2) (continued)

Variable	Default	Description
buffer-offer-save	nil	Non-**nil** means offer to save current buffer when exiting Emacs, even if the buffer is not a file.

Table C-2. Searching and Replacing (Chapter 3)

Variable	Default	Description
case-fold-search	t	If non-**nil**, treat upper and lowercase letters as the same when searching.
case-replace	t	If non-**nil**, preserve the original case of letters when doing replaces (even if **case-fold-search** is on).
search-repeat-char	?C-s	Keystroke to repeat an incremental search forward.
search-reverse-char	?C-r	Keystroke to repeat an incremental search backward.
search-slow-speed	1200	If terminal is communicating at this speed or slower, use "slow-style" incremental search, in which a one-line window shows partial search results.[2]
search-yank-line-char	?C-y	Keystroke to cause search to yank rest of line in current buffer into search string.
search-yank-word-char	?C-w	Keystroke to cause search to yank next word in current buffer into search string.
search-delete-char	DEL	Keystroke to delete a character from an incremental search string.

---

[2] Unfortunately, this option depends on the computer "thinking" that your terminal is communicating at the slow speed. If you are going through a LAN, terminal server, or other data communications device, chances are that the computer will be talking to it at high speed and thus be "ignorant" that your terminal is slow speed.

Table C-2. Searching and Replacing (Chapter 3) (continued)

Variable	Default	Description
search-exit-char	ESC	Keystroke to stop an incremental search.
search-exit-option	t	If non-**nil**, any control character can be used to exit incremental search.
search-quote-char	?C-q	Keystroke to quote special characters during incremental search.

Table C-3. Display (Chapters 2, 4, 6)

Variable	Default	Description
next-screen-context-lines	2	Number of lines to retain when scrolling forward or backward by **C-v** or **ESC-v**.
scroll-step	0	When moving the cursor out of the current window, scroll this many lines forward or backward. If 0, scroll enough lines to place the cursor at center of window after scrolling.
tab-width	8	Width of tab stops. When set, becomes local to the current buffer.
truncate-lines	nil	If non-**nil**, do not "wrap" long lines; instead, truncate them and use **$** to show that the line continues off-screen.
truncate-partial-width-windows	t	If non-**nil**, truncate long lines (as above) in all windows that are not full screen wide.
window-min-height	4	Minimum allowable height of windows (in lines).
window-min-width	10	Minimum allowable width of vertically-split windows (in columns).
ctl-arrow	t	Non-**nil** means display control characters using ^{X}, where X is the letter being "controlled." Otherwise, use octal (base 8) ASCII notation for display.

Table C-3. Display (Chapters 2, 4, 6) (continued)

Variable	Default	Description
display-time-day-and-date	nil	If non-**nil**, **ESC-x display-time RETURN** will also show the day and date.
visible-bell	nil	If non-**nil**, "flash" the screen instead of beeping when necessary.
track-eol	nil	If non-**nil**, whenever the cursor is at end of line, "stick" to end of line when moving the cursor up or down; otherwise, stay in the column where the cursor is.
blink-matching-paren	t	If **t**, blink matching open parenthesis-type character when a corresponding close parenthesis is typed.
blink-matching-paren-distance	4000	Maximum number of characters to search through to find a matching open parenthesis character when a close parenthesis is typed.
echo-keystrokes	1	Echo prefixes for unfinished commands (e.g., **ESC-**) in minibuffer after user pauses for this many seconds; 0 means don't do echoing at all.
insert-default-directory	t	If non-**nil**, insert current directory in minibuffer when asking for a file name.
inverse-video	nil	If non-**nil**, use reverse video for the entire display (normal video for mode lines).
mode-line-inverse-video	t	Non-**nil** means use reverse video for mode lines.

Table C-4. Modes (Chapters 2, 5, 6, 9, 11)

Variable	Default	Description
major-mode	fundamental-mode	Default mode for new buffers, unless set by virtue of the filename. When setting this variable, remember to precede the mode name with a single quote (the value is a *symbol*).
auto-mode-alist	(see Chapter 9)	List of associations between file names and major modes.
left-margin	0	Number of columns to indent when typing **C-j** in fundamental mode and text mode.
indent-tabs-mode	t	If non-**nil**, allow the use of tab characters (as well as spaces) when indenting with **C-j**.
find-file-run-dired	t	When visiting a file, run **dired** if the filename is a directory and this is non-**nil**.
shell-file-name	$SHELL	Filename of shell to run with functions that use one, such as **list-directory**, **dired**, and **compile**. Taken from value of the UNIX environment variable SHELL.
explicit-shell-file-name	$ESHELL	Filename of shell to run in shell mode. If the UNIX environment variable ESHELL does not exist, the value of the environment variable SHELL is used.
load-path	("*emacs-source*/lisp")	List of directories to search for LISP packages to load. See Chapter 11. Default is *lisp* subdirectory of directory where Emacs source code is installed on your system.

Table C-5. Mail (Chapter 5)

Variable	Default	Description
mail-self-blind	nil	If non-**nil**, automatically insert your own name in the BCC (blind copy) field. This ensures that you save a copy of your mail.
mail-default-reply-to	nil	Character string to insert in Reply-to field of mail messages by default.
mail-use-rfc822	nil	If non-**nil**, use the full RFC822 parser on mail addresses, which takes longer but increases the odds that complex net addresses will be parsed correctly.
rmail-primary-inbox-list	nil	List of files containing incoming (unread) mail. If **nil**, use the list ("~/**mbox**" "/**usr/spool/mail**/*your-name*").
rmail-file-name	"~/RMAIL"	File where **rmail** puts mail messages.
mail-archive-file-name	nil	Character string used as name of file to save all outgoing messages in; if **nil**, don't save all outgoing messages.
rmail-dont-reply-to-names	nil	Regular expression specifying names to omit when constructing lists of addresses to reply to. If **nil**, omit yourself from reply list.
rmail-delete-after-output	nil	If non-**nil**, automatically delete a message if it is saved in a file.

Table C-6. Text Editing (Chapter 2, 3, 6, 7, 11)

Variable	Default	Description
sentence-end	(see Chapter 11)	Regular expression that matches ends of sentences.
paragraph-separate	"^[\t\C-l]*$"	Regular expression that matches lines that separate paragraphs.
page-delimiter	"\C-l"	Regular expression that matches page breaks.
TeX-command	"tex"	Character string used as command to run TeX on a file in TeX mode.
TeX-dvi-print-command	"lpr -d"	Character string used as command to print a file in TeX mode with **C-c C-p**.
TeX-show-queue-command	"lpq"	Character string used as command to show the print queue with **C-c C-q** in TeX mode.
scribe-electric-quote	nil	If non-**nil**, turn double quotes into `` or '' in Scribe mode.
scribe-electric-parenthesis	nil	In Scribe mode, whenever a left parenthesis-type character is typed, insert a matching right parenthesis if this is non-**nil**.
outline-regexp	"[*\C-l]+"	Regular expression used to match heading lines in outline mode.
selective-display-ellipses	t	If **t**, display "..." in place of hidden text in outline mode; otherwise don't display anything.

Table C-7. Completion (Chapter 13)

Variable	Default	Description
completion-auto-help	t	If non-**nil**, provide help if a completion (via TAB or RETURN in minibuffer) is invalid or ambiguous.
completion-ignored-extensions	(see Chapter 13)	List of filename suffixes that Emacs ignores when doing completion on filenames.
completion-ignore-case	nil	If non-**nil**, ignore case distinctions when doing completion.

Table C-8. Miscellaneous

Variable	Default	Description
spell-command	"spell"	UNIX command to use with **spell-word**, **spell-string**, etc. For example, to use your own private list of words not to flag as misspelled, set this to "spell +*mywordlist*". See the UNIX man page for **spell** for more details.
kill-ring-max	30	Keep this many pieces of deleted text in kill ring before throwing away oldest kills.
require-final-newline	nil	If a file being saved is missing a final LINEFEED: **nil** means don't add one; **t** means add one automatically; otherwise ask whether to add a LINEFEED.[3]

---

[3] Note that some programs (like **troff**) require files to end in a LINEFEED.

D

Emacs LISP Packages

The tables in this appendix list the most useful LISP packages that come with Emacs. All LISP packages are located in the directory *emacs-source/lisp*, where *emacs-source* is the directory in which you placed the Emacs source distribution. We have omitted all of the packages that provide "basic" Emacs support; likewise, we have omitted many packages whose function is unspeakably obscure. While some of the packages below are described in some detail in this book, most aren't; you will have to rely on GNU Emacs' online help for precise descriptions of what the package does. See Chapter 13 for details on online help; the most important help commands you will need for finding out about the functionality of LISP packages are **C-h f** (**describe-function**) and **C-h m** (**describe-mode**).

Wherever it is reasonable, the tables give commands that "start" the package. This has the following meanings:

- If the package implements a major mode, the startup-command is the function that puts Emacs into this major mode.

- If the package implements a major mode that is automatically loaded when you visit a file with a certain suffix, we list "suffix *suffixname*" in addition to the startup-command.

- If the package implements a minor mode, the startup-command is the function that puts Emacs into this minor mode.

- If the package implements a set of general-purpose functions, we've tried to pick the most "typical" of these functions. For example, the *studly* package implements three commands. We arbitrarily picked **studlify-region** as one way to invoke this package. If there isn't any reasonable choice, we list "many."

Finally, a word on using the packages. Some packages are automatically loaded when Emacs starts; some are loaded when you visit a file with the appropriate suffix (such as many of the modes for programming languages); some are automatically loaded whenever you give the appropriate command (for example, **esc-x shell RETURN** loads the package *shell.el* for **shell-mode**); and some are never automatically loaded. Although Emacs comes with a standard configuration of packages that are loaded, auto-loaded, or not loaded at all, your system administrator is very likely to have customized this. So how do you know which is which?

Really, you don't care. In the tables, the "Startup" column tells you what command (or commands) put the package to work. Start Emacs, and give this command (**ESC-x** *startup-command* **RETURN**). If Emacs complains "no match," then the package wasn't loaded automatically; you need to load the package "by hand." To do so during an Emacs session, use the command **ESC-x load-library** *name* **RETURN**, where the package's "name" is given in the first column of the table. You can also tell Emacs to load packages automatically at startup time by putting lines in your *.emacs* that have this form:

```
(load "name")
```

Now, without further ado, here are the tables of LISP packages.

Table D-1. Support for C Programming

Package	Description	Startup
c-mode	Major mode for editing C source files.	**c-mode,** suffixes *.c, .h, .y, .cc*
c-fill	Minor mode; additional formatting for multi-line C comments.	**c-comment**
cmacexp	Function for using cpp to expand macros in C source code.	**c-macro-expand**
gdb	Major mode for working with the gdb debugger.	**gdb-mode**

Table D-2. Support for General Programming

Package	Description	Startup
ada	Major mode for editing Ada source code.	**ada-mode**
fortran	Major mode for editing FORTRAN source code.	**fortran-mode,** suffix *.f*
icon	Major mode for editing ICON source code.	**icon-mode**
mim	Major mode for editing MIM source code.	**mim-mode**
modula-2	Major mode for editing Modula-2 source code.	**modula-2-mode**
prolog	Major mode for editing Prolog source code.	**prolog-mode,** suffixes *.pl, .prolog*
scheme	Major mode for editing Scheme source code.	**scheme-mode,** suffix *.scm*
simula	Major mode for editing Simula source code.	**simula-mode**
compile	Function for compiling programs and running **make**.	**compile**

Table D-3. Support for LISP Programming

Package	Description	Startup
lisp-mode	Major modes for LISP, Emacs LISP, and LISP interaction.	**lisp-mode,** **emacs-lisp-mode,** **lisp-interaction-mode**[1]
cl	Functions and macros for Emacs LISP compatibility with Common LISP.	many
debug	Functions for debugging Emacs LISP programs.	**debug**
disass	Function to disassemble Emacs LISP code.	**disassemble**
float	Set of functions for floating-point arithmetic.	many

---

[1] LISP mode is automatically invoked for files with suffixes *.l, .lsp, .lisp,* and *.ml*; Emacs LISP mode is automatically invoked for files with suffixes *.el* and *.emacs.* LISP interaction mode is the mode for buffer `*scratch*`.

Table D-4. Support for Text Processing

Package	Description	Startup
text-mode	Major mode for editing unprocessed text files.	**text-mode**[2]
nroff	Major mode for editing **nroff** and **troff** text files.	**nroff-mode**
scribe	Major mode for editing Scribe text files.	**scribe-mode**
tex-mode	Major mode for editing TeX and LaTeX text files.	**tex-mode,** **latex-mode**[3]
bibtex	Major mode for editing LaTeX bibliography files.	**bibtex-mode**

Table D-5. Emulations for Other Editors

Package	Description	Startup
edt	Function to set key bindings to emulate the VAX/VMS **EDT** editor.	**edt-emulation-on**
gosmacs	Function to set key bindings for compatibility with Gosling Emacs.	**set-gosmacs-bindings**
mlconvert	Function to convert Gosling Emacs "mocklisp" code to Emacs LISP.	**convert-mocklisp-buffer**
vi	Major mode for emulating the **vi** editor.	**vi-mode**
vip	Another major mode for emulating **vi**.	**vip-mode**

Table D-6. Interfaces to Other UNIX Utilities

Package	Description	Startup
shell	Major mode for interacting with the UNIX shell.	**shell-mode**
ftp	Set of functions to perform remote file transfer using **FTP** (Internet File Transfer Protocol).	many

---

[2] Text mode is automatically invoked for files with suffixes for files whose names *begin* with /tmp/Re (Mail messages) and /tmp/fol (for some news readers), and files whose names *contain* "Message."

[3] TeX mode is automatically invoked for files with suffixes *.tex* and *.TeX*; LaTeX mode is automatically invoked for files with suffixes *.sty* and *.bbl*.

Table D-6. Interfaces to Other UNIX Utilities (continued)

Package	Description	Startup
kermit	Functions to help run the **kermit** file transfer program within shell mode.	many
mh-e	Various functions for use with the **MH** mail system.	**mh-rmail, mh-smail**
rmail	Major mode for reading and editing mail.	**rmail**
telnet	Major mode for using the Internet Telnet protocol.	**telnet-mode**
uncompress	Function to temporarily uncompress compressed files while you are visiting them.	**uncompress-while-visiting**

Table D-7. General Editing Packages

Package	Description	Startup
chistory	Function that lets you edit and repeat previous commands.	**repeat-matching-complex-command**
echistory	Major mode for editing and repeating previous commands.	**electric-command-history**
compare-w	Function for comparing two Emacs windows.	**compare-windows**
options	Functions to list and set Emacs variables.	**list-options, edit-options**
saveconf	Functions to save buffer/window configurations for future editing sessions.	**save-context, recover-context, kill-emacs**[4]
sort	Functions for sorting various kinds of text files.	**sort-lines, sort-columns, sort-fields**
spell	Functions for checking your spelling.	**spell-word, spell-region, spell-buffer**
outline	Major mode for outline editing.	**outline-mode**
underline	Function to underline text in a buffer	**underline-region**

---

[4] If you load the library *saveconf.el*, your window/buffer configuration will be saved automatically when you exit Emacs.

Table D-8. Games

Package	Description	Startup
blackbox	Major mode; plays the "blackbox" game.	**blackbox-mode**
dissociate	Function to randomly scramble text.	**dissociated-press**
doctor	Major mode for playing psychiatrist.	**doctor**
flame	Function to generate a random insult.	**flame**
hanoi	Function to play the "Towers of Hanoi" game.	**hanoi**
life	Major mode that plays the "life" (reproductive patterns) game.	**life**
spook	Functions for attracting the CIA's attention to your mail.	**spook**
studly	Functions to randomly capitalize letters.	**studlify-region**
yow	Print a random quotation from Zippy the Pinhead.	**yow**

Table D-9. Miscellaneous

Package	Description	Startup
cal	Function to display a 3-month calendar.	**cal**
emacsbug	Function to mail a bug report to the FSF.	**report-emacs-bug**
time	Function for displaying current time in the mode line.	**display-time**

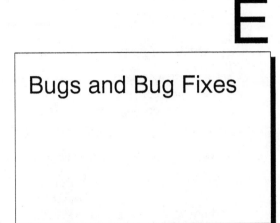

E

Bugs and Bug Fixes

There are no perfect programs. GNU Emacs is very thoroughly debugged, but it is certainly possible to find things that don't work right. While writing this book, the authors managed to make Emacs "dump core" at least once. And—time for a confession—like most users, we never reported the problem: we went on with our work.

The Free Software Foundation is very responsive to problem reports. However, they need to be real problem reports: simple differences of opinion about how something should work are not bugs. If you think that a certain command should work differently, remember that Emacs has been around for a long time and has many users; it can't be changed to satisfy a single user. In the *GNU Emacs Manual*, the Free Software Foundation publishes some excellent guidelines for reporting bugs, which we'll summarize very quickly:

- You most certainly have a bug if you run into some kind of system error (Emacs dumps core, terminates with a segmentation fault, or does something else antisocial).

- When reporting bugs, be as specific as possible. A few commands will help you report exactly what was happening when things went awry. **C-h l** (for

view-lossage) reports the last 100 or so keystrokes you made; **ESC-ESC** (**open-dribble-file** "*filename*") saves every keystroke you type in the specified *filename*; and **ESC-ESC** (**open-termscript** "*filename*") saves every key you type and every character sent to the screen in the specified *filename*.

- The Free Software Foundation discourages you from trying to "interpret" bugs in the bug report. "I did thus-and-such and this happened" is useful, particularly if the problem is repeatable; "I think there's a problem with terminal handling" doesn't give any useful information at all.

- Always report which version of Emacs you are using. The command **ESC-x emacs-version** will give you the relevant information.

- Always report the contents of the file you were editing (if it makes a difference), the contents of your *.emacs* file, which mode you were in, and any LISP libraries (custom or otherwise) that you have to load in order to create the problem.

We will add one very important guideline:

- Although we have taken every effort to write a book that is accurate, we can't claim to be perfect. We rather suspect that we're somewhat less than perfect. And, with that in mind, please DO NOT cite this book as an authority when reporting a bug. While we haven't asked, the Free Software Foundation would be completely justified in rejecting any bug reports based on a third-party publication. If you suspect a bug, use the *GNU Emacs Manual* or the online help facility to find out what the command that's giving you trouble is really supposed to do. In doing so, you may find out that this book is incorrect; if you do, please report the problem via electronic mail to **nuts@ora.com**.

If you have access to Internet or USENET mail, you can send bug reports to the following mail addresses:

bug-gnu-emacs@prep.ai.mit.edu (Internet)

or

... !ucbvax!prep.ai.mit.edu!bug-gnu-emacs (USENET).

F

Public Statements

The GNU General Public License
GNU Manifesto
The League for Programming Freedom

This appendix covers two important documents that you should be familiar with: the GNU General Public License and the GNU Manifesto. The General Public License defines the terms under which GNU Emacs, other Free Software Foundation products, and many privately written programs are distributed. We print two versions of the license in its entirety. The GNU Manifesto is a larger document that states why the Free Software Foundation exists.

Following this material, we have a brief description of the League for Programming Freedom, an unrelated organization that may be of interest. We tell you where to get the League's two position papers, and print a membership form from one of the position papers.

The GNU General Public License

All copies of GNU Emacs are distributed under the terms of the General Public License, which is commonly known as a "copyleft." In essence, the General Public License states that anyone who receives GNU Emacs has the right to give copies of Emacs to others; that anyone who receives Emacs may not place further restrictions on its distribution; and if you distribute any improvements to Emacs, they must be distributed under the same terms as the original program itself. You are allowed to charge for distributing Emacs, so "free software" isn't necessarily cheap in that sense. However, you cannot restrict anyone's (including your customers') ability to use the program or to give it away. The license was crafted to make sure that GNU Emacs and other programs would remain free.

The General Public License has become an important part of the UNIX culture. It prevents a practice that's unfortunately common in the industry: a vendor finds a good piece of public domain software, improves it in some way, and then makes the improved program proprietary. By preventing this practice, the license goes much further towards protecting the author's intent in sharing the program than simply placing the program in the public domain. It is increasingly common for programmers who want to share their software to "copyleft" it (i.e., distribute it under the terms of the General Public License).

The Free Software Foundation has designed the general public license so that any program can use it easily. Following the license *proper*, the Free Software Foundation tells you how to make it apply to your own software. The license is updated periodically, and is currently in a state of flux. Below, we print Version 1, which applies to GNU Emacs as of this printing; following it, we print Version 2, which will become effective in the very near future. Several clarifications were published prior to this version, and a special version addresses some issues related to "copylefting" libraries.

Despite these many versions, the General Public License is an amazingly clear piece of legal work. And, as the license promises, any future versions will maintain the spirit of the version we have published below. You may see some changes in the details, but you will not see any changes to the fundamental rights guaranteed to you as a user.

General Public License, Version 1

GNU GENERAL PUBLIC LICENSE
Version 1, February 1989

Copyright (C) 1989 Free Software Foundation, Inc.
675 Mass Ave, Cambridge, MA 02139, USA

Everyone is permitted to copy and distribute verbatim copies of this license document, but changing it is not allowed.

Preamble

The license agreements of most software companies try to keep users at the mercy of those companies. By contrast, our General Public License is intended to guarantee your freedom to share and change free software—to make sure the software is free for all its users. The General Public License applies to the Free Software Foundation's software and to any other program whose authors commit to using it. You can use it for your programs, too.

When we speak of free software, we are referring to freedom, not price. Specifically, the General Public License is designed to make sure that you have the freedom to give away or sell copies of free software, that you receive source code or can get it if you want it, that you can change the software or use pieces of it in new free programs; and that you know you can do these things.

To protect your rights, we need to make restrictions that forbid anyone to deny you these rights or to ask you to surrender the rights. These restrictions translate to certain responsibilities for you if you distribute copies of the software, or if you modify it.

For example, if you distribute copies of a such a program, whether gratis or for a fee, you must give the recipients all the rights that you have. You must make sure that they, too, receive or can get the source code. And you must tell them their rights.

We protect your rights with two steps: (1) copyright the software, and (2) offer you this license which gives you legal permission to copy, distribute and/or modify the software.

Also, for each author's protection and ours, we want to make certain that everyone understands that there is no warranty for this free software. If the software is modified by someone else and passed on, we want its recipients to know that what they have is not the original, so that any problems introduced by others will not reflect on the original authors' reputations.

The precise terms and conditions for copying, distribution and modification follow.

GNU GENERAL PUBLIC LICENSE
TERMS AND CONDITIONS FOR COPYING, DISTRIBUTION AND MODIFICATION

0. This License Agreement applies to any program or other work which contains a notice placed by the copyright holder saying it may be distributed under the terms of this General Public License. The "Program", below, refers to any such program or work, and a "work based on the Program" means either the Program or any work containing the Program or a portion of it, either verbatim or with modifications. Each licensee is addressed as "you".

1. You may copy and distribute verbatim copies of the Program's source code as you receive it, in any medium, provided that you conspicuously and appropriately publish on each copy an appropriate copyright notice and disclaimer of warranty; keep intact all the notices that refer to this General Public License and to the absence of any warranty; and give any other recipients of the Program a copy of this General Public License along with the Program. You may charge a fee for the physical act of transferring a copy.

2. You may modify your copy or copies of the Program or any portion of it, and copy and distribute such modifications under the terms of Paragraph 1 above, provided that you also do the following:

> a) cause the modified files to carry prominent notices stating that you changed the files and the date of any change; and

> b) cause the whole of any work that you distribute or publish, that in whole or in part contains the Program or any part thereof, either with or without modifications, to be licensed at no charge to all third parties under the terms of this General Public License (except that you may choose to grant warranty protection to some or all third parties, at your option).

> c) If the modified program normally reads commands interactively when run, you must cause it, when started running for such interactive use in the simplest and most usual way, to print or display an announcement including an appropriate copyright notice and a notice that there is no warranty (or else, saying that you provide a warranty) and that users may redistribute the program under these conditions, and telling the user how to view a copy of this General Public License.

> d) You may charge a fee for the physical act of transferring a copy, and you may at your option offer warranty protection in exchange for a fee.

Mere aggregation of another independent work with the Program (or its derivative) on a volume of a storage or distribution medium does not bring the other work under the scope of these terms.

3. You may copy and distribute the Program (or a portion or derivative of it, under Paragraph 2) in object code or executable form under the terms of Paragraphs 1 and 2 above provided that you also do one of the following:

> a) accompany it with the complete corresponding machine-readable source code, which must be distributed under the terms of Paragraphs 1 and 2 above; or,

> b) accompany it with a written offer, valid for at least three years, to give any third party free (except for a nominal charge for the cost of distribution) a complete machine-readable copy of the corresponding source code, to be distributed under the terms of Paragraphs 1 and 2 above; or,

c) accompany it with the information you received as to where the corresponding source code may be obtained. (This alternative is allowed only for noncommercial distribution and only if you received the program in object code or executable form alone.)

Source code for a work means the preferred form of the work for making modifications to it. For an executable file, complete source code means all the source code for all modules it contains; but, as a special exception, it need not include source code for modules which are standard libraries that accompany the operating system on which the executable file runs, or for standard header files or definitions files that accompany that operating system.

4. You may not copy, modify, sublicense, distribute or transfer the Program except as expressly provided under this General Public License. Any attempt otherwise to copy, modify, sublicense, distribute or transfer the Program is void, and will automatically terminate your rights to use the Program under this License. However, parties who have received copies, or rights to use copies, from you under this General Public License will not have their licenses terminated so long as such parties remain in full compliance.

5. By copying, distributing or modifying the Program (or any work based on the Program) you indicate your acceptance of this license to do so, and all its terms and conditions.

6. Each time you redistribute the Program (or any work based on the Program), the recipient automatically receives a license from the original licensor to copy, distribute or modify the Program subject to these terms and conditions. You may not impose any further restrictions on the recipients' exercise of the rights granted herein.

7. The Free Software Foundation may publish revised and/or new versions of the General Public License from time to time. Such new versions will be similar in spirit to the present version, but may differ in detail to address new problems or concerns.

Each version is given a distinguishing version number. If the Program specifies a version number of the license which applies to it and "any later version", you have the option of following the terms and conditions either of that version or of any later version published by the Free Software Foundation. If the Program does not specify a version number of the license, you may choose any version ever published by the Free Software Foundation.

8. If you wish to incorporate parts of the Program into other free programs whose distribution conditions are different, write to the author to ask for permission. For software which is copyrighted by the Free Software Foundation, write to the Free Software Foundation; we sometimes make exceptions for this. Our decision will

be guided by the two goals of preserving the free status of all derivatives of our free software and of promoting the sharing and reuse of software generally.

NO WARRANTY

9. BECAUSE THE PROGRAM IS LICENSED FREE OF CHARGE, THERE IS NO WARRANTY FOR THE PROGRAM, TO THE EXTENT PERMITTED BY APPLICABLE LAW. EXCEPT WHEN OTHERWISE STATED IN WRITING THE COPYRIGHT HOLDERS AND/OR OTHER PARTIES PROVIDE THE PROGRAM "AS IS" WITHOUT WARRANTY OF ANY KIND, EITHER EXPRESSED OR IMPLIED, INCLUDING, BUT NOT LIMITED TO, THE IMPLIED WARRANTIES OF MERCHANTABILITY AND FITNESS FOR A PARTICULAR PURPOSE. THE ENTIRE RISK AS TO THE QUALITY AND PERFORMANCE OF THE PROGRAM IS WITH YOU. SHOULD THE PROGRAM PROVE DEFECTIVE, YOU ASSUME THE COST OF ALL NECESSARY SERVICING, REPAIR OR CORRECTION.

10. IN NO EVENT UNLESS REQUIRED BY APPLICABLE LAW OR AGREED TO IN WRITING WILL ANY COPYRIGHT HOLDER, OR ANY OTHER PARTY WHO MAY MODIFY AND/OR REDISTRIBUTE THE PROGRAM AS PERMITTED ABOVE, BE LIABLE TO YOU FOR DAMAGES, INCLUDING ANY GENERAL, SPECIAL, INCIDENTAL OR CONSEQUENTIAL DAMAGES ARISING OUT OF THE USE OR INABILITY TO USE THE PROGRAM (INCLUDING BUT NOT LIMITED TO LOSS OF DATA OR DATA BEING RENDERED INACCURATE OR LOSSES SUSTAINED BY YOU OR THIRD PARTIES OR A FAILURE OF THE PROGRAM TO OPERATE WITH ANY OTHER PROGRAMS), EVEN IF SUCH HOLDER OR OTHER PARTY HAS BEEN ADVISED OF THE POSSIBILITY OF SUCH DAMAGES.

END OF TERMS AND CONDITIONS

Appendix: How to Apply These Terms to Your New Programs

If you develop a new program, and you want it to be of the greatest possible use to humanity, the best way to achieve this is to make it free software which everyone can redistribute and change under these terms.

To do so, attach the following notices to the program. It is safest to attach them to the start of each source file to most effectively convey the exclusion of warranty; and each file should have at least the "copyright" line and a pointer to where the full notice is found.

<one line to give the program's name and a brief idea of what it does.> Copyright (C) 19yy <name of author>

This program is free software; you can redistribute it and/or modify it under the terms of the GNU General Public License as published by the Free Software Foundation; either version 1, or (at your option) any later version.

This program is distributed in the hope that it will be useful, but WITHOUT ANY WARRANTY; without even the implied warranty of MERCHANTABILITY or FITNESS FOR A PARTICULAR PURPOSE. See the GNU General Public License for more details.

You should have received a copy of the GNU General Public License along with this program; if not, write to the Free Software Foundation, Inc., 675 Mass Ave, Cambridge, MA 02139, USA.

Also add information on how to contact you by electronic and paper mail.

If the program is interactive, make it output a short notice like this when it starts in an interactive mode:

Gnomovision version 69, Copyright (C) 19xx name of author Gnomovision comes with ABSOLUTELY NO WARRANTY; for details type `show w'. This is free software, and you are welcome to redistribute it under certain conditions; type `show c' for details.

The hypothetical commands `show w' and `show c' should show the appropriate parts of the General Public License. Of course, the commands you use may be called something other than `show w' and `show c'; they could even be mouseclicks or menu items—whatever suits your program.

You should also get your employer (if you work as a programmer) or your school, if any, to sign a "copyright disclaimer" for the program, if necessary. Here a sample; alter the names:

Yoyodyne, Inc., hereby disclaims all copyright interest in the program `Gnomovision' (a program to direct compilers to make passes at assemblers) written by James Hacker.

<signature of Ty Coon>, 1 April 1989 Ty Coon, President of Vice

That's all there is to it!

The preceding information was all taken directly from the file **COPYING**; only the formatting was changed. You should find this file in the **etc** directory of your Emacs distribution. Of course, some details may be different, depending on the date of your Emacs distribution.

General Public License, Version 2

GNU GENERAL PUBLIC LICENSE
Version 2, June 1991

Copyright (C) 1989, 1991 Free Software Foundation, Inc.
675 Mass Ave, Cambridge, MA 02139, USA

Everyone is permitted to copy and distribute verbatim copies of this license document, but changing it is not allowed.

Preamble

The licenses for most software are designed to take away your freedom to share and change it. By contrast, the GNU General Public License is intended to guarantee your freedom to share and change free software—to make sure the software is free for all its users. This General Public License applies to most of the Free Software Foundation's software and to any other program whose authors commit to using it. (Some other Free Software Foundation software is covered by the GNU Library General Public License instead.) You can apply it to your programs, too.

When we speak of free software, we are referring to freedom, not price. Our General Public Licenses are designed to make sure that you have the freedom to distribute copies of free software (and charge for this service if you wish), that you receive source code or can get it if you want it, that you can change the software or use pieces of it in new free programs; and that you know you can do these things.

To protect your rights, we need to make restrictions that forbid anyone to deny you these rights or to ask you to surrender the rights. These restrictions translate to certain responsibilities for you if you distribute copies of the software, or if you modify it.

For example, if you distribute copies of such a program, whether gratis or for a fee, you must give the recipients all the rights that you have. You must make sure that they, too, receive or can get the source code. And you must show them these terms so they know their rights.

We protect your rights with two steps: (1) copyright the software, and (2) offer you this license which gives you legal permission to copy, distribute and/or modify the software.

Also, for each author's protection and ours, we want to make certain that everyone understands that there is no warranty for this free software. If the software is modified by someone else and passed on, we want its recipients to know that what they have is not the original, so that any problems introduced by others will not reflect on the original authors' reputations.

Finally, any free program is threatened constantly by software patents. We wish to avoid the danger that redistributors of a free program will individually obtain patent licenses, in effect making the program proprietary. To prevent this, we have made it clear that any patent must be licensed for everyone's free use or not licensed at all.

The precise terms and conditions for copying, distribution and modification follow.

GNU GENERAL PUBLIC LICENSE
TERMS AND CONDITIONS FOR COPYING, DISTRIBUTION AND MODIFICATION

0. This License applies to any program or other work which contains a notice placed by the copyright holder saying it may be distributed under the terms of this General Public License. The "Program", below, refers to any such program or work, and a "work based on the Program" means either the Program or any derivative work under copyright law: that is to say, a work containing the Program or a portion of it, either verbatim or with modifications and/or translated into another language. (Hereinafter, translation is included without limitation in the term "modification".) Each licensee is addressed as "you".

Activities other than copying, distribution and modification are not covered by this License; they are outside its scope. The act of running the Program is not restricted, and the output from the Program is covered only if its contents constitute a work based on the Program (independent of having been made by running the Program). Whether that is true depends on what the Program does.

1. You may copy and distribute verbatim copies of the Program's source code as you receive it, in any medium, provided that you conspicuously and appropriately publish on each copy an appropriate copyright notice and disclaimer of warranty; keep intact all the notices that refer to this License and to the absence of any warranty; and give any other recipients of the Program a copy of this License along with the Program.

You may charge a fee for the physical act of transferring a copy, and you may at your option offer warranty protection in exchange for a fee.

2. You may modify your copy or copies of the Program or any portion of it, thus forming a work based on the Program, and copy and distribute such modifications or work under the terms of Section 1 above, provided that you also meet all of these conditions:

   a) You must cause the modified files to carry prominent notices stating that you changed the files and the date of any change.

b) You must cause any work that you distribute or publish, that in whole or in part contains or is derived from the Program or any part thereof, to be licensed as a whole at no charge to all third parties under the terms of this License.

c) If the modified program normally reads commands interactively when run, you must cause it, when started running for such interactive use in the most ordinary way, to print or display an announcement including an appropriate copyright notice and a notice that there is no warranty (or else, saying that you provide a warranty) and that users may redistribute the program under these conditions, and telling the user how to view a copy of this License. (Exception: if the Program itself is interactive but does not normally print such an announcement, your work based on the Program is not required to print an announcement.)

These requirements apply to the modified work as a whole. If identifiable sections of that work are not derived from the Program, and can be reasonably considered independent and separate works in themselves, then this License, and its terms, do not apply to those sections when you distribute them as separate works. But when you distribute the same sections as part of a whole which is a work based on the Program, the distribution of the whole must be on the terms of this License, whose permissions for other licensees extend to the entire whole, and thus to each and every part regardless of who wrote it.

Thus, it is not the intent of this section to claim rights or contest your rights to work written entirely by you; rather, the intent is to exercise the right to control the distribution of derivative or collective works based on the Program.

In addition, mere aggregation of another work not based on the Program with the Program (or with a work based on the Program) on a volume of a storage or distribution medium does not bring the other work under the scope of this License.

3. You may copy and distribute the Program (or a work based on it, under Section 2) in object code or executable form under the terms of Sections 1 and 2 above provided that you also do one of the following:

a) Accompany it with the complete corresponding machine-readable source code, which must be distributed under the terms of Sections 1 and 2 above on a medium customarily used for software interchange; or,

b) Accompany it with a written offer, valid for at least three years, to give any third party, for a charge no more than your cost of physically performing source distribution, a complete machine-readable copy of the corresponding source code, to be distributed under the terms of Sections 1 and 2 above on a medium customarily used for software interchange; or,

c) Accompany it with the information you received as to the offer to distribute corresponding source code. (This alternative is allowed only for
noncommercial distribution and only if you received the program in object
code or executable form with such an offer, in accord with Subsection b
above.)

The source code for a work means the preferred form of the work for making
modifications to it. For an executable work, complete source code means all the
source code for all modules it contains, plus any associated interface definition
files, plus the scripts used to control compilation and installation of the executable. However, as a special exception, the source code distributed need not
include anything that is normally distributed (in either source or binary form)
with the major components (compiler, kernel, and so on) of the operating system
on which the executable runs, unless that component itself accompanies the executable.

If distribution of executable or object code is made by offering access to copy
from a designated place, then offering equivalent access to copy the source code
from the same place counts as distribution of the source code, even though third
parties are not compelled to copy the source along with the object code.

4. You may not copy, modify, sublicense, or distribute the Program except as
expressly provided under this License. Any attempt otherwise to copy, modify,
sublicense or distribute the Program is void, and will automatically terminate
your rights under this License. However, parties who have received copies, or
rights, from you under this License will not have their licenses terminated so long
as such parties remain in full compliance.

5. You are not required to accept this License, since you have not signed it. However, nothing else grants you permission to modify or distribute the Program or its
derivative works. These actions are prohibited by law if you do not accept this
License. Therefore, by modifying or distributing the Program (or any work based
on the Program), you indicate your acceptance of this License to do so, and all its
terms and conditions for copying, distributing or modifying the Program or works
based on it.

6. Each time you redistribute the Program (or any work based on the Program),
the recipient automatically receives a license from the original licensor to copy,
distribute or modify the Program subject to these terms and conditions. You may
not impose any further restrictions on the recipients' exercise of the rights
granted herein. You are not responsible for enforcing compliance by third parties
to this License.

7. If, as a consequence of a court judgment or allegation of patent infringement or
for any other reason (not limited to patent issues), conditions are imposed on you
(whether by court order, agreement or otherwise) that contradict the conditions of

this License, they do not excuse you from the conditions of this License. If you cannot distribute so as to satisfy simultaneously your obligations under this License and any other pertinent obligations, then as a consequence you may not distribute the Program at all. For example, if a patent license would not permit royalty-free redistribution of the Program by all those who receive copies directly or indirectly through you, then the only way you could satisfy both it and this License would be to refrain entirely from distribution of the Program.

If any portion of this section is held invalid or unenforceable under any particular circumstance, the balance of the section is intended to apply and the section as a whole is intended to apply in other circumstances.

It is not the purpose of this section to induce you to infringe any patents or other property right claims or to contest validity of any such claims; this section has the sole purpose of protecting the integrity of the free software distribution system, which is implemented by public license practices. Many people have made generous contributions to the wide range of software distributed through that system in reliance on consistent application of that system; it is up to the author/donor to decide if he or she is willing to distribute software through any other system and a licensee cannot impose that choice.

This section is intended to make thoroughly clear what is believed to be a consequence of the rest of this License.

8. If the distribution and/or use of the Program is restricted in certain countries either by patents or by copyrighted interfaces, the original copyright holder who places the Program under this License may add an explicit geographical distribution limitation excluding those countries, so that distribution is permitted only in or among countries not thus excluded. In such case, this License incorporates the limitation as if written in the body of this License.

9. The Free Software Foundation may publish revised and/or new versions of the General Public License from time to time. Such new versions will be similar in spirit to the present version, but may differ in detail to address new problems or concerns.

Each version is given a distinguishing version number. If the Program specifies a version number of this License which applies to it and "any later version", you have the option of following the terms and conditions either of that version or of any later version published by the Free Software Foundation. If the Program does not specify a version number of this License, you may choose any version ever published by the Free Software Foundation.

10. If you wish to incorporate parts of the Program into other free programs whose distribution conditions are different, write to the author to ask for permission. For software which is copyrighted by the Free Software Foundation, write

to the Free Software Foundation; we sometimes make exceptions for this. Our decision will be guided by the two goals of preserving the free status of all derivatives of our free software and of promoting the sharing and reuse of software generally.

NO WARRANTY

11. BECAUSE THE PROGRAM IS LICENSED FREE OF CHARGE, THERE IS NO WARRANTY FOR THE PROGRAM, TO THE EXTENT PERMITTED BY APPLICABLE LAW. EXCEPT WHEN OTHERWISE STATED IN WRITING THE COPYRIGHT HOLDERS AND/OR OTHER PARTIES PROVIDE THE PROGRAM "AS IS" WITHOUT WARRANTY OF ANY KIND, EITHER EXPRESSED OR IMPLIED, INCLUDING, BUT NOT LIMITED TO, THE IMPLIED WARRANTIES OF MERCHANTABILITY AND FITNESS FOR A PARTICULAR PURPOSE. THE ENTIRE RISK AS TO THE QUALITY AND PERFORMANCE OF THE PROGRAM IS WITH YOU. SHOULD THE PROGRAM PROVE DEFECTIVE, YOU ASSUME THE COST OF ALL NECESSARY SERVICING, REPAIR OR CORRECTION.

12. IN NO EVENT UNLESS REQUIRED BY APPLICABLE LAW OR AGREED TO IN WRITING WILL ANY COPYRIGHT HOLDER, OR ANY OTHER PARTY WHO MAY MODIFY AND/OR REDISTRIBUTE THE PROGRAM AS PERMITTED ABOVE, BE LIABLE TO YOU FOR DAMAGES, INCLUDING ANY GENERAL, SPECIAL, INCIDENTAL OR CONSEQUENTIAL DAMAGES ARISING OUT OF THE USE OR INABILITY TO USE THE PROGRAM (INCLUDING BUT NOT LIMITED TO LOSS OF DATA OR DATA BEING RENDERED INACCURATE OR LOSSES SUSTAINED BY YOU OR THIRD PARTIES OR A FAILURE OF THE PROGRAM TO OPERATE WITH ANY OTHER PROGRAMS), EVEN IF SUCH HOLDER OR OTHER PARTY HAS BEEN ADVISED OF THE POSSIBILITY OF SUCH DAMAGES.

END OF TERMS AND CONDITIONS

Appendix: How to Apply These Terms to Your New Programs

If you develop a new program, and you want it to be of the greatest possible use to the public, the best way to achieve this is to make it free software which everyone can redistribute and change under these terms.

To do so, attach the following notices to the program. It is safest to attach them to the start of each source file to most effectively convey the exclusion of warranty; and each file should have at least the "copyright" line and a pointer to where the full notice is found.

<one line to give the program's name and a brief idea of what it does.>
Copyright (C) 19yy <name of author>

This program is free software; you can redistribute it and/or modify it under the terms of the GNU General Public License as published by the Free

Software Foundation; either version 2 of the License, or (at your option) any later version.

This program is distributed in the hope that it will be useful, but WITHOUT ANY WARRANTY; without even the implied warranty of MERCHANTABIL-ITY or FITNESS FOR A PARTICULAR PURPOSE. See the GNU General Public License for more details.

You should have received a copy of the GNU General Public License along with this program; if not, write to the Free Software Foundation, Inc., 675 Mass Ave, Cambridge, MA 02139, USA.

Also add information on how to contact you by electronic and paper mail.

If the program is interactive, make it output a short notice like this when it starts in an interactive mode:

Gnomovision version 69, Copyright (C) 19yy name of author Gnomovision comes with ABSOLUTELY NO WARRANTY; for details type `show w'. This is free software, and you are welcome to redistribute it under certain conditions; type `show c' for details.

The hypothetical commands `show w' and `show c' should show the appropriate parts of the General Public License. Of course, the commands you use may be called something other than `show w' and `show c'; they could even be mouse-clicks or menu items—whatever suits your program.

You should also get your employer (if you work as a programmer) or your school, if any, to sign a "copyright disclaimer" for the program, if necessary. Here is a sample; alter the names:

Yoyodyne, Inc., hereby disclaims all copyright interest in the program `Gnomovision' (which makes passes at compilers) written by James Hacker.

<signature of Ty Coon>, 1 April 1989 Ty Coon, President of Vice

This General Public License does not permit incorporating your program into proprietary programs. If your program is a subroutine library, you may consider it more useful to permit linking proprietary applications with the library. If this is what you want to do, use the GNU Library General Public License instead of this License.

GNU Manifesto

Another fundamental document of the Free Software Foundation is the "GNU Manifesto." The Manifesto describes why the Free Software Foundation exists and what it intends to do. Even more fundamentally, it describes the foundation's vision of the software community. You may not agree with it, but you ought to read it. It's significantly longer than the license (though not terribly long), so we won't reprint it here. If you have kept the GNU Emacs source files on the system, you will find the manifesto in the file *emacs-source*/**etc**/**GNU**, where *emacs-source* represents the directory in which you placed the Emacs source distribution. It's also in the *GNU Emacs Manual*.

The League for Programming Freedom

If you are interested in free software, you should also be aware of the League for Programming Freedom. The League is not concerned specifically with free software, but with practices that threaten the continued development of all software. The League for Programming Freedom opposes the recent proliferation of software patents and copyrighted command languages. As the league states in one of its position papers, it "is not opposed to the legal system that Congress intended—copyright on individual programs. Our aim is to reverse the recent changes made by judges in response to special interests, often explicitly rejecting the public interest principles of the Constitution."

The LPF claims patents of designs and techniques rather than specific products turn everyday software design into a legally hazardous proposition and threaten the programmer's freedom to develop software. Patenting techniques and methods, rather than specific inventions, creates extremely large and broad-reaching monopolies. Imagine, for example, what programming would be like if someone had patented linked lists back in the 1950's. It is expensive, difficult and time-consuming for software developers to determine whether their designs and techniques have already been patented. No matter how innovative you are, it is impossible to write new software without relying on older techniques, any of which could potentially be patented.

While software patents and command language copyrights threaten all software development, their impact on free software could be devastating. The terms of a patent license are completely incompatible with the ways in which free software is distributed; for example, if software is circulating freely, it is impossible to keep track of the number of copies in circulation and calculate royalties. You could not give a program like GNU Emacs to someone else without reporting the transaction to the owners of *all* copyrights and patents involved. Furthermore, many developers of free may not be able to risk legal expenses or the imposition of licensing fees for programs which they are developing as a public service.

The LPF achieved some national notoriety in May 1989 and August 1990, when it picketed the headquarters of Lotus Development Corporation in Cambridge, MA, in protest of Lotus' interface copyright lawsuit against Paperback Software, Inc. (regarding Lotus' popular 1-2-3 spreadsheet program). This kind of lawsuit, popularly known as "look and feel" lawsuit, alleges that a mere similarity in user interface is sufficient grounds for copyright violation. Lotus won its lawsuit, engendering several other such suits in its wake, some of which have been successful. The LPF feels that such lawsuits create monopolies and stifle creativity in the software industry: companies are forced into making software gratuitously incompatible with existing software and are discouraged from making incremental improvements to existing products.

The following excerpts from the LPF's corporate charter state its aims:

1. To determine the existence of, and warn the public about restrictions and monopolies on classes of computer programs where such monopolies prevent or restrict the right to develop certain types of computer programs.

2. To develop countermeasures and initiatives, in the public interest, effective to block or otherwise prevent or restrain such monopolistic activities including education, research, publications, public assembly, legislative testimony, and intervention in court proceedings involving public interest issues (as a friend of the court).

3. To engage in any business or other activity in service of and related to the foregoing paragraphs that lawfully may be carried on by a corporation organized under Chapter 180 of the Massachusetts General Laws.

The LPF asks for your financial support and invites your membership. As of this writing, membership dues are $42 per year for programmers, managers, and professionals; $10.50 for students; $21 for others. Donations and dues are used for "filing briefs; for printing handouts, buttons, and signs; whatever will persuade the courts, the legislators, and the people." The LPF also publishes several mailings per year to its members. They have written two position papers that go into detail about the current state of affairs and what should be done to correct it. They are too long to reprint here, but you can obtain them in Texinfo format by sending mail to league@prep.ai.mit.edu. You can also call (617) 243-4091 for further information.

If you would like to join, you can use the following form, which is excerpted from one of the League's position papers:

To join, please send a check and the following information to:

> League for Programming Freedom
> 1 Kendall Square #143
> P.O.Box 9171
> Cambridge, Massachusetts 02139

(Outside the US, please send a check in US dollars on a bank having a US correspondant bank, to save us check cashing fees.)

Your name:

The address for League mailings (a few each year):

The company you work for, and your position:

Your phone numbers (home, work or both):

Your email address, so we can contact you for demonstrations or for writing letters. (If you don't want us to contact you for these things, please say so, but please give us your email address anyway.)

Is there anything about you which would enable your endorsement of the LPF to impress the public? For example, if you are or have been a professor or an executive, or have written software that has a good reputation, please tell us.

Would you like to help with LPF activities?

G

Give and It Shall Be Given

Developing and maintaining software is expensive, even with volunteer labor. It is only fair that we make it clear that the Free Software Foundation's work doesn't take place in a vacuum. Their publications always ask for contributions of:

- Computer hardware

- Labor (i.e., your time)

- Money

We won't presume to tell you what kinds of hardware or labor the foundation will find useful at any given time. If you'd like to donate your talent or equipment, contact them. However, as an abstract means of exchange, the FSF will always be able to put money to use. Should you wish to contribute, their address is:

> Free Software Foundation
> 675 Massachusetts Avenue
> Cambridge, MA 02139

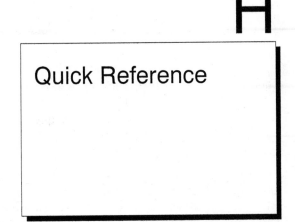

Quick Reference

This quick reference is arranged topically, in roughly the same order as the commands were treated in the text. Unfortunately, is impossible to be both "quick" and thorough, particularly with an editor as large and comprehensive as GNU Emacs. We've tried to take a middle ground between "completeness" and "quickness"—though we'll confess that, if we've erred, we've erred on the side of quickness.

Table H-1. Moving the Cursor (Chapter 2)

Keystrokes	Command Name	Action
C-f	forward-char	Move **forward** character (right).
C-b	backward-char	Move **backward** character (left).
C-p	previous-line	Move to **previous** line (up).
C-n	next-line	Move to **next** line (down).
ESC-f	forward-word	Move word **forward**.
ESC-b	backward-word	Move word **backward**.
C-a	beginning-of-line	Move to beginning of line.
C-e	end-of-line	Move to **end** of line.

Table H-1. Moving the Cursor (Chapter 2) (continued)

Keystrokes	Command Name	Action
C-v	scroll-up	Move forward one screen.
ESC-v	scroll-down	Move backward one screen.
ESC->	end-of-buffer	Move to end of file.
ESC-<	beginning-of-buffer	Move to beginning of file.
C-l	recenter	Redraw screen with current line in the center.

Table H-2. Deleting Text, Yanking Text, Regions (Chapter 2)

Keystrokes	Command Name	Action
DEL	delete-backward-char	Delete previous character.
C-d	delete-char	Delete character under cursor.
ESC-DEL	backward-kill-word	Delete previous word.
ESC-d	kill-word	Delete the word the cursor is on.
C-k	kill-line	Delete from cursor to end of line.
C-w	kill-region	Delete region (area between mark and cursor).
ESC-w	copy-region-as-kill	Copy region into kill ring.
C-y	yank	Restore what you've deleted.
ESC-y	yank-pop	Insert previous deletion (only useful after C-y).
C-@ or C-SPC	set-mark-command	Mark the beginning (or end) of a region.
C-x C-x	exchange-point-and-mark	Exchange point (cursor) and mark.

Table H-3. Stopping Commands and Undoing Edits (Chapter 2)

Keystrokes	Command Name	Action
C-g	keyboard-quit	Abort current command.
C-x u	advertised-undo	Undo last edit (can be done repeatedly).
(none)	revert-buffer	Restore buffer to the state it was in when the file was last saved (or auto-saved).

Table H-4. Transposing and Capitalizing Text (Chapter 2)

Keystrokes	Command Name	Action
C-t	transpose-chars	Transpose two letters.
ESC-t	transpose-words	Transpose two words.
C-x C-t	transpose-lines	Transpose two lines.
ESC-c	capitalize-word	Capitalize current letter.
ESC-u	upcase-word	Uppercase word.
ESC-l	downcase-word	Lowercase word.

Table H-5. Search and Replace (Chapter 3)

Keystrokes	Command Name	Action
C-s	isearch-forward	Start incremental search forward.
C-r	isearch-backward	Start incremental search backward.
ESC	(none)	Exit a successful search.
C-g	(none)	Cancel incremental search, and return to starting point.
DEL	(none)	Delete incorrect character of search string.
C-s ESC	(none)	Start nonincremental search forward.
C-r ESC	(none)	Start nonincremental search backwards.
ESC-%	query-replace	Enter query-replace.

Table H-6. Commands Used Within Query-replace (Chapter 3)

Keystrokes	Action
SPACE	Replace and go on to the next instance.
Y	Replace and go on to the next instance.
DEL or N	Don't replace; move on to next instance.
!	Replace all the rest and don't ask.
^	Back up to the previous instance.
ESC	Exit query-replace.

Table H-7. Spelling and Abbreviations (Chapter 3)

Keystrokes	Command Name	Action
ESC-$	spell-word	Spell check word under (or before) the cursor.
(none)	spell-buffer	Spell check buffer.
(none)	abbrev-mode	Enter (or exit) word abbreviation mode.
C-x -	inverse-add-global-abbrev	Define a global abbreviation
C-x C-h	inverse-add-mode-abbrev	Define a local (to the mode) abbreviation
(none)	write-abbrev-file	Write the word abbreviation file.
(none)	list-abbrevs	View the word abbreviations.

Table H-8. Working with Files and Buffers (Chapters 1, 4)

Keystrokes	Command Name	Action
C-x C-f	find-file	Find file and read it.
C-x C-v	find-alternate-file	Read and alternate file, replacing the one just read with C-x C-f.
C-x i	insert-file	Insert file at cursor position.
C-x C-s	save-buffer	Save file.
C-x C-w	write-file	Write buffer contents to file.
C-x C-c	save-buffers-kill-emacs	Exit Emacs.
C-z	suspend-emacs	Suspend Emacs (use **exit** or **fg** to restart).
C-x b	switch-to-buffer	Moves to the buffer specified.
C-x C-b	list-buffers	Displays the buffer list.

Table H-9. Windows (Chapter 4)

Keystrokes	Command Name	Action
C-x 2	split-window-vertically	Divides the current window horizontally into two.
C-x o	other-window	Moves to the other window; if there are several, moves to the next window in clockwise order.
C-x 0	delete-window	Deletes the current window.
C-x 1	delete-other-windows	Deletes all windows but this one.
C-x ^	enlarge-window	Makes window taller.
(none)	shrink-window	Makes window shorter.
C-x 4 f	find-file-other-window	Finds a file in the other window.

Table H-10. Sending Mail (Chapter 5)

Keystrokes	Command Name	Action
C-x m	mail	Open the *Mail* buffer, complete with template.
C-x 4 m	mail-other-window	Open the *Mail* buffer in a window.
C-c C-f C-t	mail-to	Move to the To: field.
C-c C-f C-c	mail-cc	Move to the CC: field (create one if there is none).
C-c C-f C-s	mail-subject	Move to the subject field.
C-c C-w	mail-signature	Insert the contents of the .signature file.
C-c C-c	mail-send-and-exit	Send the mail message and exit the *Mail* buffer.
(none)	define-mail-alias	Define an abbreviation for a name or a mailing list.

Table H-11. Reading Mail (Chapter 5)

Keystrokes	Function
ESC-x rmail	Starts rmail and reads your mail.
SPC	Scrolls to the next screen of this message.
DEL	Scrolls to the previous screen of this message.
.	Moves to the beginning of this message.
n	Moves to the next message.
p	Moves to the previous message.
>	Moves to the last message.
j	Jumps to the first message in the file.
d	Marks this message for deletion and moves forward.
C-d	Marks this message for deletion and moves backwards.
u	Undeletes a message that has been marked for deletion.
x or c	Deletes all messages slated for deletion.
o *filename*	Save message in RMAIL file format.
i *filename*	Read messages from saved file

Table H-12. Working with the RMAIL Summary List (Chapter 5)

Keystrokes	Action
h	From rmail, displays a window that lists all messages.
d	Mark the message for deletion (d appears next to the message number).
u	Undelete the current message.
n	Move to the next message and display it in the RMAIL window.
p	Move to the previous message and display it in the RMAIL window.
x	Exit the summary window and delete it.
q	Exit rmail.

Table H-13. Shell Mode (Chapter 5)

Shell Character	Emacs Keystrokes	Command Name	Function
(none)	(none)	shell-mode	Start a UNIX shell in a window.
C-c	C-c C-c	interrupt-shell-subjob	Terminate the current job.
C-d	C-c C-d	shell-send-eof	End of file character.
C-u	C-c C-u	kill-shell-input	Erase current line.
C-w	C-c C-w	backward-kill-word	Erase the previous word.
C-z	C-c C-z	stop-shell-subjob	Suspend the current job.

Table H-14. Working with Dired (Chapter 5)

Keystrokes	Action	Similiar to UNIX Command
r	Rename file.	mv
e	Edit file.	emacs
c	Copy file.	cp
d	Mark for deletion.	rm
#	Mark all auto-save files for deletion.	rm #*#
u	Undelete.	(none)
x	Delete files that are marked.	rm and rmdir
SPACE	Move forward by filename.	(none)
DEL	Move backward by filename.	(none)
n	Move forward by filename.	(none)
p	Move backward by filename.	(none)

Table H-15. nroff Mode (Chapter 7)

Keystrokes	Command Name	Action
(none)	nroff-mode	Enters nroff mode.
ESC-n	forward-text-line	Moves the cursor to the next text line.
ESC-p	backward-text-line	Moves the cursor to the previous text line.
ESC-?	count-text-lines	Counts the text lines in a region.
(none)	electric-nroff-mode	Adds additional features to nroff mode.
C-j	electric-nroff-newline	Complete common macro pairs.

Table H-16. TeX Mode (Chapter 7)

Keystrokes	Command Name	Action
(none)	tex-mode	Enters TeX or LaTeX mode according to file's contents.
(none)	plain-tex-mode	Enters TeX mode.
(none)	latex-mode	Enters LaTeX mode.
C-j	TeX-terminate-paragraph	Inserts two hard returns (standard end of paragraph) and checks syntax of paragraph.
ESC-{	TeX-insert-braces	Inserts two braces and puts cursor between them.
ESC-}	up-list	If you are within braces, puts the cursor following the closing brace.
(none)	validate-TeX-buffer	Checks buffer for syntax errors.
C-c C-b	TeX-buffer	Process buffer in TeX or LaTeX.
C-c C-l	TeX-recenter-output-buffer	Put the message shell on the screen, showing (at least) the last error message.
C-c C-r	TeX-region	Process region in TeX or LaTeX.
C-c C-k	TeX-kill-job	Kill TeX or LaTeX processing.
C-c C-p	TeX-print	Print TeX or LaTeX output.
C-c C-q	TeX-show-print-queue	Show print queue.

Table H-17. Macros (Chapter 8)

Keystrokes	Command Name	Action
C-x (	start-kbd-macro	Starts macro definition.
C-x)	end-kbd-macro	Ends macro definition.
C-x e	call-last-kbd-macro	Executes last macro defined.

Table H-17. Macros (Chapter 8) (continued)

Keystrokes	Command Name	Action
C-u C-x (	start-kbd-macro	Executes the last macro defined, then lets you add keystrokes to it.
C-u C-x q	(none)	Inserts a recursive edit in a macro definition.
C-ESC-c	exit-recursive-edit	Exits a recursive edit.
C-x q	kbd-macro-query	Inserts a query in a macro definition.

Table H-18. C Mode (Chapter 10)

Keystrokes	Command Name	Action
ESC C-a	beginning-of-defun	Move to beginning of function body.
ESC C-e	end-of-defun	Move to end of function.
ESC C-h	mark-c-function	Put cursor at beginning of funtion, mark at end.

Table H-19. LISP Mode (Chapter 10)

Keystrokes	Command Name	Action
ESC C-b	backward-sexp	Move backward by one S-expression.
ESC C-f	forward-sexp	Move forward by one S-expression.
ESC C-t	transpose-sexps	Transpose the two S-expressions around the cursor.
ESC C-@	mark-sexp	Set mark to the end of the current S-expression, cursor to the beginning.
ESC C-k	kill-sexp	Delete the S-expression following the cursor.
	backward-kill-sexp	Delete the S-expression preceding the cursor.
ESC C-n	forward-list	Move forward by one list.
ESC C-p	backward-list	Move backward by one list.
ESC C-d	down-list	Move forward and down one parenthesis level.
(none)	up-list	Move forward out of one parenthesis level.
ESC C-u	backward-up-list	Move backward out of one parenthesis level.
ESC C-a	beginning-of-defun	Move to the beginning of the current function.
ESC C-e	end-of-defun	Move the the end of the current function.
ESC C-h	mark-defun	Put cursor at beginning of function, mark at end.

Table H-20. FORTRAN Mode (Chapter 10)

Keystrokes	Command Name	Action
C-c C-n	fortran-next-statement	Move forward one statement.
C-c C-p	fortran-previous-statement	Move backward one statement.
ESC C-a	beginning-of-fortran-subprogram	Move to the beginning of the current subprogram.
ESC C-e	end-of-fortran-subprogram	Move to the end of the current subprogram.
ESC C-h	mark-fortran-subprogram	Put the cursor at beginning of subprogram, mark at end.

Table H-21. Using a Mouse with Emacs (Chapter 12)

Mouse Press	Command Name	Standard Emacs Equivalent
left	x-mouse-set-point	(move cursor to where arrow is)
middle	x-paste-text	yank (**C-y**)
right	x-cut-text	copy-region-as-kill (**ESC-w**)
C-middle	x-cut-and-wipe-text	kill-region (**C-w**)
C-right	x-mouse-select-and-split	split-window-vertically (**C-x 2**)
S-middle	x-cut-text	copy-region-as-kill (**ESC-w**)
S-right	x-paste-text	yank (**C-y**)
C-S-right	x-mouse-keep-one-window	delete-other-windows (**C-x 1**)

Table H-22. The Help System (Chapter 13)

Keystrokes	Command Name	Question Answered
C-h c	describe-key-briefly	What command does this keystroke sequence run?
C-h k	describe-key	What command does this keystroke sequence run, and what does it do?
C-h l	view-lossage	What are the last 100 characters I typed?
C-h w	where-is	What is the key binding for this command?
C-h f	describe-function	What does this function do?
C-h v	describe-variable	What does this variable mean, and what is its value?
C-h m	describe-mode	Tell me about the mode the current buffer is in.
C-h b	describe-bindings	What are all the key bindings for this buffer?

Table H-22. The Help System (Chapter 13) (continued)

Keystrokes	Command Name	Question Answered
C-h a	command-apropos	What commands involve this concept?
C-h t	help-with-tutorial	Run the Emacs tutorial.
C-h i	info	Start the **info** documentation reader.

Table H-23. Important Modes

Command Name	Function
fundamental-mode	Default mode, no special features.
text-mode	Major mode for editing plain text.
dired-mode	Major mode for editing directory contents.
nroff-mode	Major mode for editing **troff** documents.
tex-mode	Major mode for editing TeX documents.
latex-mode	Major mode for editing LaTeX documents.
scribe-mode	Major mode for editing Scribe documents.
fortran-mode	Major mode for editing FORTRAN programs.
c-mode	Major mode for editing C programs.
lisp-mode	Major mode for editing LISP programs.
indented-text-mode	Major mode for working with indentation.
picture-mode	Major mode for drawing simple pictures.
outline-mode	Major mode for editing outlines.
abbrev-mode	Minor mode for using abbreviations.
auto-fill-mode	Minor mode for breaking lines automatically.
overwrite-mode	Minor mode in which new characters overwrite existing text.

Index

H

hanoi program, 351
head, list, 289
header fields, mail, 103
help, accessing accidentally, 20
  apropos commands, 325
  commands, 17, 322
  for complex commands, 328
  online, 17, 318-329
  searching for key bindings, 285
  tutorial, 17, 327
Help buffer, 323
help-command command (C-h), 17, 19
help-for-help command (C-h C-h), 322
helpr-command command, 19
help-with-tutorial command (C-h t), 327
hidden text, deleting accidentally, 173
  editing, 173
  limitations of, 173
hide-body command, 170, 172
hide-entry command, 172
hide-leaves command, 172
hide-subtree command, 171-172
hiding text in outlines, 170
  (see also hidden text.)
history of Emacs, viii
home directory, abbreviation for, 12
horizontal windows, 86
.h suffix, 237
hung terminal, 13, 20, 42, 51, 218, 265

I

-ib option, 305
icon program, 349
iconifying a window, 304
icon-mode program, 349
if statement, 271
  FORTRAN mode, 254
incremental search, 50-51
  regular expression, 50
  remapping, 51
indentation, C mode, 238
  commands, 147, 234

FORTRAN mode, 252
  in code, 234
  LISP modes, 247
  paragraphs, 138
  regions, 146
  text, 137, 144
  variables for, 342
indented text mode, 4, 144
  tabs in, 145
indented-text-mode command, 144
indent-for-comment command,
  (ESC-;), 235
indent-new-comment-line command
  (ESC-j), 236, 242, 249
indent-region command (C-\), 146, 234
indent-tabs-mode variable, 141, 342
infinite loops, 265
info command (C-h i), 327
insert function, 274
insert-default-directory variable, 341
insert-file command (C-x i), 12, 19
inserting files, 12
insert-kbd-macro command, 206
insert-last-keyboard-macro command,
  212
integers, LISP, 261
interactive function, 267
  argument codes for, 267
Internet, getting Emacs from, 331
interrupt-shell-subjob command,
  (C-c C-c), 123
int-to-string function, 274
inverse video, 341
inverse-add-global command, 73
inverse-add-local command, 73
inverse-video variable, 341
invoking, Emacs, 6, 303
  etags, 243
-i option, 304
isearch-backward command (C-r), 54
isearch-backward-regexp command, 62,
  284
isearch-forward command (C-s), 51, 54
isearch-forward-regexp command, 62,
  284
italics, Scribe, 193

T

About the Authors

Debra Cameron is a freelance writer who has written books on communications protocols, midrange computer systems, CASE, PC software, and current UNIX standards. She received an award from the Society for Technical Communications for a quick reference guide she wrote for Adelie Corporation. Of all the writing tools she's used (including seven word processors), Emacs is Deb's all-time favorite. She's particularly obsessed with word abbreviation mode. Deb collects antique clothes and lives in a Victorian house in Franklin, PA. Her favorite authors include Charles Dickens, Victor Hugo, George MacDonald, and Dorothy Sayers.

Bill Rosenblatt is a native of Philadelphia who currently develops music software for The Rustin Group, Ltd., a small company in New York City. He is also a graduate student in the Computer Science Department at the University of Massachusetts at Amherst. Before starting grad school, he worked as a UNIX programmer in the Boston area, during which time he contributed software to GNU Emacs. He has worked extensively with Emacs LISP—in fact, it is the only LISP he really knows. Bill currently lives on the upper west side of Manhattan. He amuses himself by moonlighting as a radio disc jockey and as a jazz critic. He wishes his landlord allowed pets so that he could truthfully claim to have a dog and a cat with suitably droll names like "Coltrane" and "Hildegard."

Colophon

Our look is the result of reader comments, our own experimentation, and distribution channels.

Distinctive covers complement our distinctive approach to technical topics, breathing personality and life into potentially dry subjects. UNIX and its attendant programs can be unruly beasts. Nutshell Handbooks help you tame them.

The animal featured on the cover of *Learning GNU Emacs* is a gnu or wildebeest. Gnus are African antelopes which inhabit the Serengeti Plains. Male gnus are no more than 52 inches in height and 500 pounds in weight, but have the most lethal horns of any of the antelopes. Bulls are very territorial and tend to remain alone. The females and young generally live in small herds. However, they may congregate in the tens of thousands during migration. Gnus are the favorite prey of lions.

Edie Freedman designed this cover and the entire UNIX bestiary that appears on other Nutshell Handbooks. The beasts themselves are adapted from 19th-century engravings from the Dover Pictorial Archive.

The text of this book is set in Times Roman; headings are Helvetica; examples are Courier. Text was prepared using SortQuad's sqtroff text formatter. Figures are produced with a Macintosh. Printing is done on a Tegra Varityper 5000.

USING

UNIX AND X

Books from O'Reilly & Associates, Inc.

FALL/WINTER 1994-95

Basics

Our UNIX in a Nutshell *guides are the most comprehensive quick reference on the market—a must for every* UNIX *user. No matter what system you use, we've got a version to cover your needs.*

UNIX in a Nutshell: System V Edition

By Daniel Gilly & the staff of O'Reilly & Associates
2nd Edition June 1992
444 pages, ISBN 1-56592-001-5

You may have seen UNIX quick-reference guides, but you've never seen anything like *UNIX in a Nutshell*. Not a scaled-down quick reference of common commands, *UNIX in a Nutshell* is a complete reference containing all commands and options, along with generous descriptions and examples that put the commands in context. For all but the thorniest UNIX problems, this one reference should be all the documentation you need. Covers System V, Releases 3 and 4, and Solaris 2.0.

"This book is the perfect desktop reference... The authors have presented a clear and concisely written book which would make an excellent addition to any UNIX user's library."
—*SysAdmin*

SCO UNIX in a Nutshell

By Ellie Cutler & the staff of O'Reilly & Associates
1st Edition February 1994
590 pages, ISBN 1-56592-037-6

The desktop reference to SCO UNIX and Open Desktop®, this version of *UNIX in a Nutshell* shows you what's under the hood of your SCO system. It isn't a scaled-down quick reference of common commands, but a complete reference containing all user, programming, administration, and networking commands.

Contents include:

- All commands and options
- Shell syntax for the Bourne, Korn, C, and SCO shells
- Pattern matching, with *vi, ex, sed*, and *aw*k commands
- Compiler and debugging commands for software development
- Networking with email, TCP/IP, NFS, and UUCP
- System administration commands and the SCO sysadmsh shell

This edition of *UNIX in a Nutshell* is the most comprehensive SCO quick reference on the market, a must for any SCO user. You'll want to keep *SCO UNIX in a Nutshell* close by as you use your computer: it'll become a handy, indispensible reference for working with your SCO system.

Learning the UNIX Operating System

By Grace Todino, John Strang & Jerry Peek
3rd Edition August 1993
108 pages, ISBN 1-56592-060-0

If you are new to UNIX, this concise introduction will tell you just what you need to get started and no more. Why wade through a 600 page book when you can begin working productively in a matter of minutes? It's an ideal primer for Mac and PC users of the Internet who need to know a little bit about UNIX on the systems they visit.

Topics covered include:

- Logging in and logging out
- Window systems (especially X/Motif)
- Managing UNIX files and directories
- Sending and receiving mail
- Redirecting input/output
- Pipes and filters
- Background processing
- Basic network commandsThis book is the most effective introduction to UNIX in print.

This book is the most effective introduction to UNIX in print. The third edition has been updated and expanded to provide increased coverage of window systems and networking. It's a handy book for someone just starting with UNIX, as well as someone who encounters a UNIX system as a visitor via remote login over the Internet.

"Once you've established a connection with the network, there's often a secondary obstacle to surmount.... *Learning the UNIX Operating System* helps you figure out what to do next by presenting in a nutshell the basics of how to deal with the 'U-word.' Obviously a 92-page book isn't going to make you an instant UNIX guru, but it does an excellent job of introducing basic operations in a concise nontechnical way, including how to navigate through the file system, send and receive E-mail and—most importantly—get to the online help...."
—Michael L. Porter, Associate Editor,
Personal Engineering & Instrumentation News

Learning the vi Editor

By Linda Lamb
5th Edition October 1990
192 pages, ISBN 0-937175-67-6

A complete guide to text editing with *vi*, the editor available on nearly every UNIX system. Early chapters cover the basics; later chapters explain more advanced editing tools, such as *ex* commands and global search and replacement.

"For those who are looking for an introductory book to give to new staff members who have no acquaintance with either screen editing or with UNIX screen editing, this is it: a book on *vi* that is neither designed for the UNIX in-crowd, nor so imbecilic that one is ashamed to use it."
—*;login*

Learning the Korn Shell

By Bill Rosenblatt
1st Edition June 1993
363 pages, ISBN 1-56592-054-6

A thorough introduction to the Korn shell, both as a user interface and as a programming language. This book provides a clear explanation of the Korn shell's features, including *ksh* string operations, co-processes, signals and signal handling, and command-line interpretation. *Learning the Korn Shell* also includes real-life programming examples and a Korn shell debugger (*kshdb*).

"Readers still bending back the pages of Korn-shell manuals will find relief in...*Learning the Korn Shell*...a gentle introduction to the shell. Rather than focusing on syntax issues, the book quickly takes on the task of solving day-to-day problems with Korn-shell scripts. Application scripts are also shown and explained in detail. In fact, the book even presents a script debugger written for *ksh*. This is a good book for improving your knowledge of the shell."
—*Unix Review*

MH & xmh: Email for Users & Programmers

By Jerry Peek
3rd Edition Winter 1994-95 (est.)
800 pages (est), ISBN 1-56592-093-7

MH & xmh: Email for Users & Programmers is the most complete description of the MH mail program freely available on most UNIX systems. It covers all the MH commands as well as the new interfaces to MH: *xmh* (for the X environment), *exmh* (a tcl/tk X interface), and *mh-e* (for emacs users). It contains everything from an introductory tour to all these programs to reference pages for each of them as well. It features configuration tips and customization and programming examples. New for the third edition are the complete descriptions of exmh and mh-e, as well as a description of the Multipurpose Internet Mail Extensions (MIME) and how to use MIME with MH.

"The MH bible is irrefutably Jerry Peek's *MH & xmh: Email for Users & Programmers*. This book covers just about everything that is known about MH and *xmh* (the X Windows front end to MH), presented in a clear and easy-to-read format. I strongly recommend that anybody serious about MH get a copy." —James Hamilton, *UnixWorld*

Learning the GNU Emacs

By Debra Cameron & Bill Rosenblatt
1st Edition October 1991
442 pages, ISBN 0-937175-84-6

An introduction to the GNU Emacs editor, one of the most widely used and powerful editors available under UNIX. Provides a solid introduction to basic editing, a look at several important editing modes (special Emacs features for editing specific types of documents), and a brief introduction to customization and Emacs LISP programming. The book is aimed at new Emacs users, whether or not they are programmers.

"Authors Debra Cameron and Bill Rosenblatt do a particularly admirable job presenting the extensive functionality of GNU Emacs in well-organized, easily digested chapters.... Despite its title, *Learning GNU Emacs* could easily serve as a reference for the experienced Emacs user."
—Linda Branagan, Convex Computer Corporation

The USENET Handbook

By Mark Harrison
1st Edition Winter 1994-95 (est.)
250 pages (est.), ISBN 1-56592-101-1

The USENET Handbook describes how to get the most out of the USENET news network, a worldwide network of cooperating computer sites that exchange public user messages known as "articles" or "postings." These postings are an electric mix of questions, commentary, hints, and ideas of all kinds, expressing the views of the thousands of participants at these sites.

Tutorials show you how to read news using the most popular newsreaders—*tin* and Trumpet for Windows and *nn*, *emacs* and *gnus* for UNIX. It also explains how to post articles to the Net.

The book discusses things you can do to increase your productivity by using the resources mentioned on USENET, such as anonymous FTP (file transfer protocol), mail servers, FAQs, and mailing lists. It covers network etiquette, processing encoded and compressed files (i.e., software, pictures, etc.), and lots of historical information.

Using UUCP and Usenet

By Grace Todino & Dale Dougherty
1st Edition February 1986 (latest update October 1991)
210 pages, ISBN 0-937175-10-2

Shows users how to communicate with both UNIX and non-UNIX systems using UUCP and *cu* or *tip* and how to read news and post articles. This handbook assumes that UUCP is already running at your site.

"Are you having trouble with UUCP? Have you torn out your hair trying to set the Dialers file? *Managing UUCP and Usenet* and *Using UUCP and Usenet* will give you the information you need to become an accomplished Net user. The companion book is *!%@:: A Directory of Electronic Mail Addressing & Networks*, a compendium of world networks and how to address and read them. All of these books are well written, and I urge you to take a look at them."
—*Root Journal*

X User Tools

By Linda Mui & Valerie Quercia
1st Edition November 1994
856 pages (CD-ROM included)
ISBN 1-56592-019-8

 X User Tools provides for X users what *UNIX Power Tools* provides for UNIX users: hundreds of tips, tricks, scripts, techniques, and programs—plus a CD-ROM—to make the X Windowing System more enjoyable, more powerful, and easier to use.

This browser's book emphasizes useful programs, culled from the network and contributed by X programmers worldwide. Programs range from fun (games, screensavers, and a variety of online clocks) to business tools (calendar, memo, and mailer programs) to graphics (programs for drawing, displaying, and converting images). You'll also find a number of tips and techniques for configuring both individual and systemwide environments, as well as a glossary of common X and UNIX terms.

The browser style of organization—pioneered by *UNIX Power Tools*—encourages readers to leaf through the book at will, focusing on what appeals at the time. Each article stands on its own, many containing cross-references to related articles. Before you know it, you'll have covered the entire book, simply by scanning what's of interest and following cross-references to more detailed information.

The enclosed CD-ROM contains source files for all and binary files for some of the programs—for a number of platforms, including Sun 4, Solaris, HP 700, Alpha/OSF, and AIX. Note that the CD-ROM contains software for both emacs and tcl/tk.

Volume 3: X Window System User's Guide

Standard Edition
By Valerie Quercia & Tim O'Reilly
4th Edition May 1993
836 pages, ISBN 1-56592-014-7

 The *X Window System User's Guide* orients the new user to window system concepts and provides detailed tutorials for many client programs, including the *xterm* terminal emulator and window managers. Building on this basic knowledge, later chapters explain how to customize the X environment and provide sample configurations. The *Standard Edition* uses the *twm* manager in most examples and illustrations. Revised for X11 Release 5. This popular manual is available in two editions, one for users of the MIT software, and one for users of Motif. (see below).

"For the novice, this is the best introduction to X available. It will also be a convenient reference for experienced users and X applications developers."—*Computing Reviews*

Volume 3M: X Window System User's Guide

Motif Edition
By Valerie Quercia & Tim O'Reilly
2nd Edition January 1993
956 pages, ISBN 1-56592-015-5

This alternative edition of the *User's Guide* highlights the Motif window manager for users of the Motif graphical user interface. Revised for Motif 1.2 and X11 Release 5.

Material covered in this second edition includes:

- Overview of the X Color Management System (Xcms)
- Creating your own Xcms color database
- Tutorials for two "color editors": *xcoloredit* and *xtici*
- Using the X font server
- Tutorial for *editres*, a resource editor
- Extensive coverage of the new implementations of *bitmap* and *xmag*
- Overview of internationalization features
- Features common to Motif 1.2 applications: tear-off menus and drag-and-drop

Advanced

UNIX Power Tools

By Jerry Peek, Mike Loukides, Tim O'Reilly, et al.
1st Edition March 1993
1162 pages (includes CD-ROM)
Random House ISBN 0-679-79073-X

Ideal for UNIX users who hunger for technical—yet accessible—information, *UNIX Power Tools* consists of tips, tricks, concepts, and freeware (CD-ROM included). It also covers add-on utilities and how to take advantage of clever features in the most popular UNIX utilities.

This is a browser's book... like a magazine that you don't read from start to finish, but leaf through repeatedly until you realize that you've read it all. You'll find articles abstracted from O'Reilly Nutshell Handbooks®, new information that highlights program "tricks" and "gotchas," tips posted to the Net over the years, and other accumulated wisdom. The goal of *UNIX Power Tools* is to help you think creatively about UNIX and get you to the point where you can analyze your own problems. Your own solutions won't be far behind.

The CD-ROM includes all of the scripts and aliases from the book, plus *perl*, GNU *emacs*, *pbmplus* (manipulation utilities), *ispell*, screen, the *scs*spreadsheet, and about 60 other freeware programs. In addition to the source code, all the software is precompiled for Sun3, Sun4, DECstation, IBM RS/6000, HP 9000 (700 series), SCO Xenix, and SCO UNIX. (SCO UNIX binaries will likely also run on other Intel UNIX platforms, including Univel's new UNIXware.)

"Chockful of ideas on how to get the most from UNIX, this book is aimed at those who want to improve their proficiency with this versatile operating system. Best of all, you don't have to be a computer scientist to understand it. If you use UNIX, this book belongs on your desk."
—Book Reviews, *Compuserve Magazine*

"*Unix Power Tools* is an encyclopedic work that belongs next to every serious UNIX user's terminal. If you're already a UNIX wizard, keep this book tucked under your desk for late-night reference when solving those difficult problems."
—Raymond GA Côté, *Byte*

Making TₑX Work

By Norman Walsh
1st Edition April 1994
522 pages, ISBN 1-56592-051-1

TeX is a powerful tool for creating professional-quality typeset text and is unsurpassed at typesetting mathematical equations, scientific text, and multiple languages. Many books describe how you use TeX to construct sentences, paragraphs, and chapters. Until now, no book has described all the software that actually lets you build, run, and use TeX to best advantage on your platform. Because creating a TeX document requires the use of many tools, this lack of information is a serious problem for TeX users.

Making TₑX Work guides you through the maze of tools available in the TeX system. Beyond the core TeX program there are myriad drivers, macro packages, previewers, printing programs, online documentation facilities, graphics programs, and much more. This book describes them all.

The Frame Handbook

By Linda Branagan & Mike Sierra
1st Edition November 1994
542 pages, ISBN 1-56592-009-0

A thorough, single-volume guide to using the UNIX version of FrameMaker 4.0, a sophisticated document production system. This book is for everyone who creates technical manuals and reports, from technical writers and editors who will become power users to administrative assistants and engineers. The book contains a thorough introduction to Frame and covers creating document templates, assembling books, and Frame tips and tricks. It begins by discussing the basic features of any text-formatting system: how it handles text and text-based tools (like spell-checking). It quickly gets into areas that benefit from a sophisticated tool like Frame: cross-references and footnotes; styles, master pages, and templates; tables and graphics; tables of contents and indexes; and, for those interested in online access, hypertext. Once you've finished this book, you'll be able to use Frame to create and produce a book or even a series of books.

Exploring Expect

By Don Libes
1st Edition Winter 1994-95 (est.)
602 pages, ISBN 1-56592-090-2

Written by the author of Expect, this is the first book to explain how this new part of the UNIX toolbox can be used to automate *telnet*, *ftp*, *passwd*, *rlogin*, and hundreds of other interactive applications. Based on *Tcl* (Tool Control Language), Expect lets you automate interactive applications that have previously been extremely difficult to handle with any scripting language.

The book briefly describes *Tcl* and how Expect relates to it. It then describes the *Tcl* language, using a combination of reference material and specific, useful examples of its features. It shows how to use Expect in background, in multiple processes, and with standard languages and tools like C, C++, and *Tk*, the X-based extension to *Tcl*. The strength in the book is in its scripts, conveniently listed in a separate index.

sed & awk

By Dale Dougherty
1st Edition November 1990
414 pages, ISBN 0-937175-59-5

For people who create and modify text files, *sed* and *awk* are power tools for editing. Most of the things that you can do with these programs can be done interactively with a text editor; however, using *sed* and *awk* can save many hours of repetitive work in achieving the same result.

"*sed & awk* is a must for UNIX system programmers and administrators, and even general UNIX readers will benefit. I have over a hundred UNIX and C books in my personal library at home, but only a dozen are duplicated on the shelf where I work. This one just became number twelve."
—*Root Journal*

Learning Perl

By Randal L. Schwartz, Foreword by Larry Wall
1st Edition November 1993
274 pages, ISBN 1-56592-042-2

Learning Perl is ideal for system administrators, programmers, and anyone else wanting a down-to-earth introduction to this useful language. Written by a Perl trainer, its aim is to make a competent, hands-on Perl programmer out of the reader as quickly as possible. The book takes a tutorial approach and includes hundreds of short code examples, along with some lengthy ones. The relatively inexperienced programmer will find *Learning Perl* easily accessible. Each chapter of the book includes practical programming exercises. Solutions are presented for all exercises.

For a comprehensive and detailed guide to advanced programming with Perl, read O'Reilly's companion book, *Programming perl*.

"All-in-all, *Learning Perl* is a fine introductory text that can dramatically ease moving into the world of *perl*. It fills a niche previously filled only by tutorials taught by a small number of *perl* experts.... The UNIX community too often lacks the kind of tutorial that this book offers."
—Rob Kolstad, *;login:*

Programming perl

By Larry Wall & Randal L. Schwartz
1st Edition January 1991
482 pages, ISBN 0-937175-64-1

This is the authoritative guide to the hottest new UNIX utility in years, co-authored by its creator, Larry Wall. Perl is a language for easily manipulating text, files, and processes. Perl provides a more concise and readable way to do many jobs that were formerly accomplished (with difficulty) by programming in the C language or one of the shells. *Programming perl* covers Perl syntax, functions, debugging, efficiency, the Perl library, and more, including real-world Perl programs dealing with such issues as system administration and text manipulation. Also includes a pull-out quick-reference card (designed and created by Johan Vromans).

O'Reilly & Associates—
GLOBAL NETWORK NAVIGATOR™

The Global Network Navigator (GNN)™ is a unique kind of information service that makes the Internet easy and enjoyable to use. We organize access to the vast information resources of the Internet so that you can find what you want. We also help you understand the Internet and the many ways you can explore it.

In GNN you'll find:

Navigating the Net with GNN

The *Whole Internet Catalog* contains a descriptive listing of the most useful Net resources and services with live links to those resources.

The *GNN Business Pages* are where you'll learn about companies who have established a presence on the Internet and use its worldwide reach to help educate consumers.

The *Internet Help Desk* helps folks who are new to the Net orient themselves and gets them started on the road to Internet exploration.

News

NetNews is a weekly publication that reports on the news of the Internet, with weekly feature articles that focus on Internet trends and special events. The Sports, Weather, and Comix Pages round out the news.

Special Interest Publications

Whether you're planning a trip or are just interested in reading about the journeys of others, you'll find that the *Travelers' Center* contains a rich collection of feature articles and ongoing columns about travel. In the *Travelers' Center*, you can link to many helpful and informative travel-related Internet resources.

The *Personal Finance Center* is the place to go for information about money management and investment on the Internet. Whether you're an old pro at playing the market or are thinking about investing for the first time, you'll read articles and discover Internet resources that will help you to think of the Internet as a personal finance information tool.

All in all, GNN helps you get more value for the time you spend on the Internet.

 The Best of the Web

GNN received "Honorable Mention" for **"Best Overall Site," "Best Entertainment Service,"** and **"Most Important Service Concept."**

The *GNN NetNews* received "Honorable Mention" for **"Best Document Design."**

Subscribe Today

GNN is available over the Internet as a subscription service. To get complete information about subscribing to GNN, send email to **info@gnn.com**. If you have access to a World Wide Web browser such as Mosaic or Lynx, you can use the following URL to register online: http://gnn.com/

If you use a browser that does not support online forms, you can retrieve an email version of the registration form automatically by sending email to **form@gnn.com**. Fill this form out and send it back to us by email, and we will confirm your registration.

O'Reilly on the Net—
ONLINE PROGRAM GUIDE

O'Reilly & Associates offers extensive information through our online resources. If you've got Internet access, we invite you to come and explore our little neck-of-the-woods.

Online Resource Center

Most comprehensive among our online offerings is the O'Reilly Resource Center. Here, you'll find detailed information and descriptions on all O'Reilly products: titles, prices, tables of contents, indexes, author bios, software contents, reviews...you can even view images of the products themselves. We also supply helpful ordering information: how to contact us, how to order online, distributors and bookstores world wide, discounts, upgrades, etc. In addition, we provide informative literature in the field: articles, interviews, and bibliographies that help you stay informed and abreast.

The Best of the Web

The *O'Reilly Resource Center* was voted "**Best Commercial Site**" by users participating in "Best of the Web '94."

To access ORA's Online Resource Center:

Point your Web browser (e.g., `mosaic` or `lynx`) to:
`http://gnn.com/ora/`

For the plaintext version, `telnet` or `gopher` to:
`gopher.ora.com`
(telnet login: `gopher`)

FTP

The example files and programs in many of our books are available electronically via FTP.

To obtain example files and programs from O'Reilly texts:

`ftp` to:

`ftp.ora.com`
or
`ftp.uu.net`
`cd published/oreilly`

Ora-news

An easy way to stay informed of the latest projects and products from O'Reilly & Associates is to subscribe to "ora-news," our electronic news service. Subscribers receive email as soon as the information breaks.

To subscribe to "ora-news":

Send email to:
listproc@online.ora.com

and put the following information on the first line of your message (not in "Subject"):
subscribe ora-news "your name" **of** "your company"

For example:
subscribe ora-news Jim Dandy of Mighty Fine Enterprises

Email

Many customer services are provided via email. Here's a few of the most popular and useful.

nuts@ora.com
> For general questions and information.

bookquestions@ora.com
> For technical questions, or corrections, concerning book contents.

order@ora.com
> To order books online and for ordering questions.

catalog@ora.com
> To receive a free copy of our magazine/catalog, "ora.com" (please include a postal address).

Snailmail and phones

O'Reilly & Associates, Inc.
103A Morris Street, Sebastopol, CA 95472
Inquiries: **707-829-0515, 800-998-9938**
Credit card orders: **800-889-8969**
> (Weekdays 6a.m.- 6p.m. PST)
FAX: **707-829-0104**

O'Reilly & Associates—
LISTING OF TITLES

INTERNET

!%@:: A Directory of Electronic Mail
    Addressing & Networks
Connecting to the Internet:
    An O'Reilly Buyer's Guide
Internet In A Box
The Mosaic Handbook for Microsoft Windows
The Mosaic Handbook for the Macintosh
The Mosaic Handbook for the
    X Window System
Smileys
The Whole Internet User's Guide & Catalog

SYSTEM ADMINISTRATION

Computer Security Basics
DNS and BIND
Essential System Administration
Linux Network Administrator's Guide
    (Winter '94-95 est.)
Managing Internet Information Services
Managing NFS and NIS
Managing UUCP and Usenet
sendmail
Practical UNIX Security
PGP: Pretty Good Privacy (Winter '94-95 est.)
System Performance Tuning
TCP/IP Network Administration
termcap & terminfo
X Window System Administrator's Guide:
    Volume 8
X Window System, R6, Companion CD
    (Winter '94-95 est.)

USING UNIX AND X

BASICS

Learning GNU Emacs
Learning the Korn Shell
Learning the UNIX Operating System
Learning the vi Editor
MH & xmh: E-mail for Users & Programmers
SCO UNIX in a Nutshell
The USENET Handbook (Winter '94-95 est.)
Using UUCP and Usenet
UNIX in a Nutshell: System V Edition
The X Window System in a Nutshell
X Window System User's Guide: Volume 3
X Window System User's Guide, Motif Ed.:
    Volume 3M
X User Tools

ADVANCED

Exploring Expect (Winter '94-95 est.)
The Frame Handbook
Learning Perl
Making TeX Work
Programming perl
sed & awk
UNIX Power Tools (with CD-ROM)

PROGRAMMING UNIX, C, AND MULTI-PLATFORM

FORTRAN/SCIENTIFIC COMPUTING

High Performance Computing
Migrating to Fortran 90
UNIX for FORTRAN Programmers

C PROGRAMMING LIBRARIES

Practical C Programming
POSIX Programmer's Guide
POSIX.4: Programming for the Real World
    (Winter '94-95 est.)
Programming with curses
Understanding and Using COFF
Using C on the UNIX System

C PROGRAMMING TOOLS

Checking C Programs with lint
lex & yacc
Managing Projects with make
Power Programming with RPC
Software Portability with imake

MULTI-PLATFORM PROGRAMMING

Encyclopedia of Graphics File Formats
Distributing Applications Across DCE and
    Windows NT
Guide to Writing DCE Applications
ORACLE Performance Tuning
Multi-Platform Code Management
Understanding DCE
Understanding Japanese Information
    Processing

BERKELEY 4.4 SOFTWARE DISTRIBUTION

4.4BSD System Manager's Manual
4.4BSD User's Reference Manual
4.4BSD User's Supplementary Documents
4.4BSD Programmer's Reference Manual
4.4BSD Programmer's Supplementary
    Documents
4.4BSD-Lite CD Companion
4.4BSD-Lite CD Companion:
    International Version

X PROGRAMMING

Motif Programming Manual: Volume 6A
Motif Reference Manual: Volume 6B
Motif Tools
PEXlib Programming Manual
PEXlib Reference Manual
PHIGS Programming Manual
    (soft or hard cover)
PHIGS Reference Manual
Programmer's Supplement for Release 6
    (Winter '94-95 est.)
Xlib Programming Manual: Volume 1
Xlib Reference Manual: Volume 2
X Protocol Reference Manual, R5: Vol. 0
X Protocol Reference Manual, R6: Vol. 0
    (Winter '94-95 est.)
X Toolkit Intrinsics Programming Manual:
    Volume 4
X Toolkit Intrinsics Programming Manual,
    Motif Edition: Volume 4M
X Toolkit Intrinsics Reference Manual: Vol.5
XView Programming Manual: Volume 7A
XView Reference Manual: Volume 7B

THE X RESOURCE

A QUARTERLY WORKING JOURNAL FOR X PROGRAMMERS

The X Resource: Issues 0 through 13
    (Issue 13 available 1/95)

BUSINESS/CAREER

Building a Successful Software Business
Love Your Job!

TRAVEL

Travelers' Tales Thailand
Travelers' Tales Mexico
Travelers' Tales India (Winter '94-95 est.)

AUDIOTAPES

INTERNET TALK RADIO'S "GEEK OF THE WEEK" INTERVIEWS

The Future of the Internet Protocol, 4 hrs.
Global Network Operations, 2 hours
Mobile IP Networking, 1 hour
Networked Information and
    Online Libraries, 1 hour
Security and Networks, 1 hour
European Networking, 1 hour

NOTABLE SPEECHES OF THE INFORMATION AGE

John Perry Barlow, 1.5 hours

O'Reilly & Associates—
INTERNATIONAL DISTRIBUTORS

Customers outside North America can now order O'Reilly & Associates books through the following distributors.

They offer our international customers faster order processing, more bookstores, increased representation at tradeshows worldwide, and the high-quality, responsive service our customers have come to expect.

EUROPE, MIDDLE EAST, AND AFRICA
(except Germany, Switzerland, and Austria)

INQUIRIES

International Thomson Publishing Europe
Berkshire House
168-173 High Holborn
London WC1V 7AA
United Kingdom
Telephone: 44-71-497-1422
Fax: 44-71-497-1426
Email: ora.orders@itpuk.co.uk

ORDERS

International Thomson Publishing Services, Ltd.
Cheriton House, North Way
Andover, Hampshire SP10 5BE
United Kingdom
Telephone: 44-264-342-832 (UK orders)
Telephone: 44-264-342-806 (outside UK)
Fax: 44-264-364418 (UK orders)
Fax: 44-264-342761 (outside UK)

GERMANY, SWITZERLAND, AND AUSTRIA

International Thomson Publishing GmbH
O'Reilly-International Thomson Verlag
Attn: Mr. G. Miske
Königswinterer Strasse 418
53227 Bonn
Germany
Telephone: 49-228-970240
Fax: 49-228-441342
Email: anfragen@orade.ora.com

ASIA
(except Japan)

INQUIRIES

International Thomson Publishing Asia
221 Henderson Road
#05 10 Henderson Building
Singapore 0315
Telephone: 65-272-6496
Fax: 65-272-6498

ORDERS

Telephone: 65-268-7867
Fax: 65-268-6727

AUSTRALIA

WoodsLane Pty. Ltd.
Unit 8, 101 Darley Street (P.O. Box 935)
Mona Vale NSW 2103
Australia
Telephone: 61-2-979-5944
Fax: 61-2-997-3348
Email: woods@tmx.mhs.oz.au

NEW ZEALAND

WoodsLane New Zealand Ltd.
21 Cooks Street (P.O. Box 575)
Wanganui, New Zealand
Telephone: 64-6-347-6543
Fax: 64-6-345-4840
Email: woods@tmx.mhs.oz.au

THE AMERICAS, JAPAN, AND OCEANIA

O'Reilly & Associates, Inc.
103A Morris Street
Sebastopol, CA 95472 U.S.A.
Telephone: 707-829-0515
Telephone: 800-998-9938 (U.S. & Canada)
Fax: 707-829-0104
Email: order@ora.com